the visual afterlife of
ABDELKADER BENNAHAR

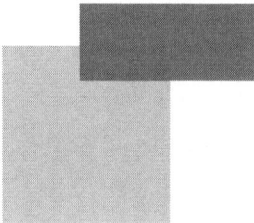

THEORY IN FORMS Series Editors
Nancy Rose Hunt,
Achille Mbembe, and
Todd Meyers

the visual afterlife of
ABDELKADER BENNAHAR

ROBERT DESJARLAIS

Duke University Press
Durham and London   2025

Project Editor: Livia Tenzer
Designed by Courtney Leigh Richardson
Typeset in Garamond Premier Pro and Poplar Std
by Westchester Publishing Services

Library of Congress Cataloging-in-Publication Data
Names: Desjarlais, Robert R., author.
Title: The visual afterlife of Abdelkader Bennahar / Robert
Desjarlais.
Other titles: Theory in forms.
Description: Durham : Duke University Press, 2025. |
Series: Theory in forms | Includes bibliographical
references and index.
Identifiers: LCCN 2025006502 (print)
LCCN 2025006503 (ebook)
ISBN 9781478032427 (paperback)
ISBN 9781478029069 (hardcover)
ISBN 9781478061274 (ebook)
Subjects: LCSH: Bennahar, Abdelkader. | Jabhat al-Taḥrīr
al-Qawmī—History. | Algerians—France—Paris—
History—20th century. | Riots—France—Paris—
History—20th century. | Algerians—Crimes against—
France. | Police misconduct—France—Paris. | Police
brutality—France—Paris. | Racism—France—Paris. | Paris
(France)—Ethnic relations. | Algeria—History—Revolution,
1954–1962—Atrocities.
Classification: LCC DC718.A4 D47 2025 (print) |
LCC DC718.A4 (ebook) | DDC 965/.0461—dc23/eng/20250528
LC record available at https://lccn.loc.gov/2025006502
LC ebook record available at https://lccn.loc.gov/2025006503

Cover art: Éric Manigaud, *Elie Kagan #1*, 2017, pencils and
graphite powder on paper, 163 × 163 cm. Palais de la Porte
Dorée/Musée National de l'Histoire de l'Immigration, inv.
2018.142.1. © EPPPD-MNHI, Éric Manigaud. Courtesy of
the artist and Galerie Sator.

publication supported by a grant from
The Community Foundation for Greater New Haven
as part of the URBAN HAVEN PROJECT

No one dies so poor that he leaves nothing behind.

—Blaise Pascal

Contents

Traces of his life are in my life now. He is close to me and terrifically far away. I craft aspects of a life and death through scarce images and remnant shards, what lives on of a body, a face, name, memory, later, in time.

Most lives leave traces, at least a few. Memories kept alive within a family, pictures in a photo album, words inscribed in a journal, the lasting lessons of a teacher, the legacy of a name, and anything from the transfer of genetic traits to the ruins of a lost civilization—aspects of a life can remain, still remain, as flint marks and trace particles in the world. Within the modern age there is also the trail of singular existences left in the annals of bureaucratic records, archives, or any number of online forums or digital databases. Obscurity and enigma can likewise follow the end of a life; features of a life, its sensate forms and reasons, can be lost forever. A life leaves traces, along with an absence of traces and poorness in knowing and understanding. I note this intricate tracework at a time when, all around me, lives and deaths, tenuous and uncertain, have come under question; one quick viral infection or a violent act can bring it all to an end. I write these words aware that there is a good chance they could prove to be bit traces left in the current of my own life, once the vital arc of that life, diminishing faintly, slowly, with irrevocable force, is rubbed out and what remains is a residuum of trace and absence.

The Beast's Skeleton

This book touches on traces and the absence of vital traces within the flow of life and death. It attends to a few select images and lines of writing, as well as the physical remains of a deceased body, left in the wake of a man who apparently was born around 1919 in northwestern Algeria and who died on the outskirts of Paris in October 1961. This man's name was Abdelkader Bennahar. The circumstances of his life are relatively obscure to me and, it appears, most others, as are the circumstances of his death. There are just a few traces to go by, a few nick marks left of a life in its final hours, and vestiges of his death. Aspects of the historical record are fragmentary in nature, often contradictory, sometimes absent. From scant remnant traces I have been trying to grasp certain features of Bennahar's life and death as well as the social and political terrains that informed this life death, alongside others.

Abdelkader Bennahar lived and died within a harsh climate of French colonial control of North Africa and military and governmental domination of the peoples who lived there or came to reside and work in France proper. He is known most, if he is known at all, for being the subject, often unnamed, of a series of photographs taken by Jewish-French photographer Élie Kagan the night of 17 October 1961 in Nanterre, a commune on the western outskirts of Paris. The photos show Bennahar as he lay on the ground, bleeding, probably after being attacked by officers of the Paris police, and then he is shown standing, wincing in pain, and then being brought to a hospital. By the next night Bennahar was dead, apparently in relation to actions undertaken by members of the Paris police force. The circumstances of his death and its causes remain vague and unclear. And so this book is also about the ways in which forms of political struggle and state violence shape the tenor of particular lives and deaths in situations of colonialism and political domination. It considers politically charged situations of life, death, burial, and uncertain mourning in situations of state and police violence against Algerians in France in the late 1950s and early 1960s, during the Algerian war of liberation.

I write of life and death, those most intense and sobering of topics, in colonial and postcolonial times. Achille Mbembe (2006, 119) speaks of how "postcolonial thinking aims to take the beast's skeleton apart to flush out its favorite places of habitation. More radically, it seeks to know what it is to live under the beast's regime, what kind of life it offers, and what sort of death people die from."[1] The current work follows the spirit of such postcolonial thought in trying to grasp what kinds of lives and deaths occurred under the French colonial regime in North Africa and elsewhere in the twentieth century. In focusing on a few specific lives and situations from that colonial era—and their reverberations, years later—one might gain a better understanding of the forces that shaped many lives and deaths at that time and in times since then.

A key locus of this inquiry is Paris, France, in 1961, particularly October of that year. On Tuesday, the seventeenth of October, between twenty and forty thousand North Africans who lived in various shantytown bidonvilles and urban suburbs set along the outskirts of Paris approached the center of the city, by foot, bus, or Métro train, to demonstrate peacefully against illegal curfews imposed upon North Africans by the Paris police force. This collective *manifestation* was supported and organized by the leadership of the FLN in France (Fédera-tion de France du Front de Libération Nationale, or FF-FLN), which compelled all able-bodied adult Algerians residing in the Paris region to participate in a unified, peaceful show of defiance and resistance; members of the FF-FLN leadership tried to make sure that no demonstrators carried weapons of any sort. Police officers and auxiliary police officers based in Paris learned about the plans for the demonstration sometime that day. Armed with guns and long clubs, they were waiting at bridges, Métro stations, and other strategic points when dem-onstrators arrived and tried to move more fully into the city center. Many of these police officers were enraged by the deaths of a number of their colleagues, some of whom in recent months had been assassinated by members of the FF-FLN. Their commanding officers, including Maurice Papon, prefect of the Paris police, apparently conveyed that there would be no repercussions against them if they acted aggressively toward any Algerians they encountered. Earlier that month, Papon set the tone and scale for violent retribution. "For every blow we receive, we will give them ten in return," he said at the funeral of an assassinated police officer (Cole 2003, 24).

During the course of the police's violent repression of the protests, through rainy hours that night, approximately thirty to two hundred men and women were killed, apparently by French police forces, chiefly through beatings, shootings, or drownings in the Seine.[2] Many of those killed went unidentified; corpses were buried in unmarked graves in cemeteries outside of Paris. Other bodies were reportedly buried in woods near the city. That same night the po-lice rounded up thousands of Algerian men and transported them to tempo-rary detention centers set up in stadiums and amphitheaters in Paris, where they remained in harrowing conditions for several days. Over five hundred of those detained were then sent by plane from Orly Airport to Algeria, banished from life and employment in France.[3] Others remained in prison until the war ended in March 1962 (Cole 2003, 24). Jim House and Neil MacMaster (2006, 6) observe that the "wave of murderous attacks" unleashed by security forces signify "the bloodiest act of state repression of street protest in Western Europe in modern history."

One person's account of what he went through the night of 17 October 1961 speaks to select forms of violence enacted by the Paris police. The account is drawn from a set of records and testimonies collected by the FLN in the aftermath of the violent events of October 1961. Jean-Luc Einaudi later received a copy of these materials in writing his book *La bataille de Paris: 17 Octobre 1961*, which, once published in 1991, alerted many readers in France and elsewhere to the violence wielded by Paris police officers that night. Ahmed Djoughlal's account of that fearful night is recounted in Einaudi's book, and now is retold here—this time in English translation.[4]

When Ahmed Djoughlal finished with work that Tuesday (17 October), he went to the train station of Villiers-le-Bel, a commune to the north of Paris where he lived. There he met with some forty other Algerian men, each dressed in their best clothes for meetings. The group had planned to take a train to Gare du Nord, to join in on the demonstrations in Paris, but when they arrived at the station in Villiers-le-Bel they found that the trains weren't running that day due to a strike. The group therefore decided to take buses to Porte de la Chapelle. From there, they intended to go to the rallying point of Place de la Concorde. When they arrived at Porte de la Chapelle, they were met by police forces concentrated in Place de la Chapelle and in the Métro stations nearby.

"We didn't have the possibility to avoid them and, by mutual agreement, our whole group, supervised by a leader, went toward the Métro station, head high and silently," Djoughlal related in a testimony recorded by members of the FLN, dated 22 October 1961.

> The forces of repression [the police] came to meet us, surrounded us and pushed us toward the police buses parked in the square. We walked in single file between two rows of police officers armed with clubs, some of them holding their submachine guns by the barrel and hitting us on all parts of the body. This went on all the way to the buses, approximately one hundred and fifty meters. Some brothers bent their knees under the blows, others fainted and got up a few seconds later under the insistence of the blows. This was also the case throughout the entire journey to a police station nearby. There, we found Harki auxiliaries who took over from the police. They beat us even more savagely than the police themselves. After identity and status checks, all the brothers present were taken away by bus to an unknown destination. Of all our group, only one unfortunate

Algerian whom I did not know and myself were left. We were both seriously injured.

The police told us they were taking us to a doctor. We both got into the car. There was the driver and an officer with a machine gun. When the car started, I don't know if the policeman was seized by an attack of madness or if he acted out of repressive spirit, in any case, he had drool in his mouth, his eyes were crazy. He raised his club to the height of his head and hit us with all his strength on all the limbs of our bodies. The brother who was with me fell unconscious under the blows. When the car stopped, the driver got out and told us to get out. Still under the threat of the machine gun, we got out and what we saw made us realize that our death was near. We started to say prayers, we understood. The cold water of the Seine was two meters away. This is the doctor to end our suffering.

We could not move, we had two hallucinating visions: the barrel of the machine gun and the implacable cold water.

One of the policemen raised his white baton and began his abuse. He was bludgeoning us in the hope of making us lose consciousness in order to sink us faster and have a certain death. In a supreme impulse of conservation, the Algerian brother and I embraced each other and we invoked our mothers and God to help us. The policeman, mad with hatred and seeing that we were united even in the face of death, struck a blow with his truncheon so terrible, yes, so terrible that the brain of my poor companion splattered on my face. I could only hear an agonized groan, the martyred brother died in my arm. Seeing this, the policeman gave me a final blow on the back of the neck. Before I fell unconscious I heard the policeman say, "They're dead, throw them away!"

When I came to my senses I thought it was raining, I was simply in the water. I was floating at the water's edge and it's providence that I did not sink. There were bloodstains on the water, my poor companion sank. The police car had disappeared. I was able to get back to the shore and, with superhuman efforts, I returned to the dock and fell back into unconsciousness. I had no sense of time, I don't know how long I was unconscious. In any case, I took my courage in both hands and, despite the damage which blinded me, I returned in the night to a home in Stains where the few surviving brothers took care of me, dressed me in clean linen and offered me a bed. I spent the rest of the night in the home, and in the morning I was able to return to my home in Villiers-le-Bel.

My brothers, I bring to your attention that the repression [the police] took my wallet and my identity papers. They also took my money. For the moment, I can hardly move about since I have no proof of my identity.

I have only two regrets, that of having lost my companion in suffering and of not having seen the demonstration.[5]

On 17 October 1961 police officers anticipated the arrival of Algerians in the center of Paris. They corralled off groups of men, preventing them from demonstrating peacefully, forced men to walk past rows of police officers, and beat those who walked past. They rounded up scores of men and confined them in demeaning conditions in detention centers. Police officers beat many of those taken into custody with guns and truncheons. Some officers threw men into the Seine, leaving their bodies to sink or drift away in its waters. These harsh methods and their damaging effects recurred throughout that night of state violence and other nights in Paris that October. Days after his ordeal, Ahmed Djoughlal recalled the crazed frenzy of the police, the hallucinatory waters of the Seine, the death of another man unknown to him clasped together in a dying embrace. Through the dark of that night emerged a twinning of life and death: one man perished, killed by the police; the other survived, having regained consciousness on the river's edge. Djoughlal's regret tied into two absences: not having participated directly in the demonstrations that night, and the loss of his "companion in suffering."

To my knowledge, the name of this second man has gone unknown and uninscribed in archival records.

In the days following the demonstration and violence of 17 October 1961, French police and national and city governments worked to prevent and censor any journalist accounts of the state violence and terror, and they denied claims by eyewitnesses to the amount and intensity of violent acts by police officers against unarmed participants. Partly as a result of these forms of state censorship and silence, and complicated processes of forgetting and effacement, many of those living in France and elsewhere did not learn of the violent attacks against Algerians in October 1961 until years later, if at all. As Joshua Cole (2003, 29) remarks, "In so far as one can measure the collective memory of an event by tracing its presence in public discussion, it is safe to say that many French people and many Algerians largely 'forgot' about 17 October almost immediately after it occurred. The reasons for this are simple and complex." Since the 1990s, there has been sustained interest in some circles to document and bring to public recognition the violence of that time. Until recently, however, details on the circumstances of the state-sanctioned violence have not been well known. In conversations with residents of Paris in recent years, I have found that most of these friends and acquaintances have heard of the events involved, and they understand that, at most, some thirty or fifty persons died the night of 17 October 1961; many did not know that it's likely that up to two hundred men and women were killed. I learned of the violence only a few years ago. Many of the Algerian participants in the demonstrations have tended not to talk much about those painful times and memories, including with their children or grandchildren, for complicated reasons. Those who were involved in the war of liberation or were troubled by the hardships and violence of those days have tended not to relate their experiences to younger family members, and often they have not passed on memories of those events to later generations in direct ways. "Li fat met," goes a Kabyle expression: "The past is dead."[6] "One doesn't speak of painful things."[7] With more recent generations, however, there has been an interest in learning about the events of the colonial era and the Algerian war of independence.

In general, there has been a kind of collective "amnesia" or "aphasia" around the events of Paris in 1961.[8] For many, it has been difficult to bring to mind or talk about what took place in those days, as well as about France's colonial conquest and domination of Algeria and the Algerian war of liberation. It was only in the late 1980s, and continuing in the 1990s, that the events of 17 October 1961 "entered history," as Joshua Cole (2003, 42; 2006, 127) puts it. Only from the late 1990s on have there been concerted efforts to delineate a clear historical record of what took place in October 1961 and to establish forms of collective memory around the state violence involved and resulting deaths, injuries, and traumatic legacies. Still, the events of that time present exceedingly difficult complexities and political positionings in the interpretation of the events involved. Cole (2003, 43) reflects on some of these challenges in historiographic understanding:

> No matter how one decides to tell this story, it seems impossible to render it on its own terms. What would these terms be? When one relates the events of 17 October 1961 can one really discern if the protestors were Algerians demanding independence, or French people demanding their rights to public space in the city, or simply frightened laborers and their families with few options, caught between the fear of punishment by the FLN for not participating and fear of certain violence from a police force that had been unhinged by attacks on its members? All of these possibilities are both more or less true, and more or less inadequate to address the complexities of a situation that cannot be entirely mastered by any particular historical account—or any particular act of commemoration.

Cole (2003, 43) ends his article with this cautionary statement: "The work of history, like the work of citizenship, requires an ability to hear the multiplicity of voices that constitute the social realm, and to be self-conscious about the ways in which the necessary institutions of public life—governments, political parties, universities, archives—determine which voices are more easily discerned, and which are forgotten."

Anyone trying to gain a clear and comprehensive understanding of 17 October 1961 needs to engage with multiple interpretive modalities, scales of history, and the politics of representation to make approximate sense of what happened and the complicated aftereffects and histories involved. Casting the events and eventualities of 17 October in broad strokes, one might speak of several temporal periods at work, several intersecting and partially overlapping domains of knowing and nonknowing, memory, forgetting, erasure, and inscription that have emerged through time: (a) the events themselves, and efforts soon after to document, publicize, or censor and silence communication about those events, circa Paris 1961; (b) years of relative silence and oblivion, unknowing and noninscription, for many, from 1961 to the early 1980s; (c) waves of historical research accounts and collective memory work and historical-societal reckoning, from the late 1980s into the 1990s; and (d) subsequent historiographic research, literary and artistic representations, and works of collective and personal remembrance, from the late 1990s on.[9] The current work proceeds within the throes of the contemporary moment, in all its complex histories and political positionings and entangled strands of painful recollection, while retracing tracts of inscription and erasure, absence, forgetting, memory, and political strivings that gird understandings of French colonialism in Algeria and elsewhere.

The events of the late 1950s and early 1960s in Paris, and 17 October 1961 specifically—that October date lingers as a *cicatrice* (scar) in time and memory—now stand as lasting wounds in the collective memory and political landscapes of France and North Africa, particularly among Algerians living in or around Paris, in Algeria, and elsewhere. With this, new abrasions repeatedly incise past and present harms in bodies, minds, and spaces of memory.

What wounds, theirs or others, did the police officers that night carry with them as they left desperate scenes and returned to their homes? Did they find themselves justified in any terror inflicted, with blows and killings retribution for fallen colleagues? Did they take themselves to be criminals—or righteous defenders of colonial rule, defiantly proud of their pasts? Did those who refused to take part in the massacres remain disturbed by the cruelty of their fellow officers? Were others haunted by dreams of those autumnal nights, pursued by frenzied anger and man-hunts? Or perhaps it would be too simplistic to cast the police officers who violated that night as solely bad or good, as if someone is either one or the other, without complex granulations in life death. Can it be said that members of the French police forces were themselves victims of colonial violence?

While in Denmark one summer I met a man from France who told me that, in the 1950s and 1960s, his father had served in the French gendarmerie, a military force with law enforcement duties among the civilian population. This man said that he had tried to get his father to talk about what it was like for him when he worked as a gendarme in Algeria during the Algerian war, in the late 1950s and early 1960s, but the former soldier always declined to speak about what he did or saw while in Algeria. Tears would come into his eyes when asked about it. "You don't need to know this. It's too painful," L's mother told him. The mother had heard at the time about the father's experiences, as she was the only one he would talk to about them. "He doesn't talk about it," said L. "It's like that for many of those who were in Algeria during the war, or for police officers who worked in Paris. They don't want to talk about it. It's too painful to recall."

This man spoke of an obscure memory of his father watching as others around him were killed and injured, Algerians and French alike.

Biothanatography

Writing often comes from disturbance. I first learned of Abdelkader Benna-har's existence through the photographs that Kagan took in Nanterre the night of 17 October 1961. Affected by their imaginal force and valences in wound-ing, I became interested in knowing more about the person portrayed in the photographs. This awareness came into play while I was writing a coauthored book that explores histories of political violence in contemporary Paris, par-ticularly those that have emerged out of state forms of governance and sover-eignty, which often have an oppressive cast.[10] As Khalil Habrih and I delved into traces of violence and lingering wounds embedded within the palimpses-tic histories of Paris, Kagan's photographs of the man wounded the night of 17 October 1961 held a singular hold on me. The more I learned (and did not learn) about the life and death of the man photographed, the more I wrote, the more I wanted to write, in a shifting desire to grasp the trace lines of another, with all this taking place within shoals of partial knowing.

The motives for such writing are manifold. In reading into what took place in France in 1961, I felt anger and indignation toward the Paris police for their murderous violence and the governmental regime that made that possible, and the collective erasures that ensued. That anger seeped into words. These words now strive to document what happened, in what might be called acts of secondary, or tertiary, prosthetic witnessing—the phantom of a witness, bearing witness. It could be that I have also been seeking to secure and sustain a trace of Bennahar's existence on earth. A single unique life compels me. There is also the intellectual and affective challenge in trying to know the life of another person, removed in time and place from one's own existence. I have become deeply concerned with the onetime actuality of a life and trace elements of that life in the years since its end.

The visceral force of the photographic images has led to rounds of intensive writing. This writing proceeds through words and images that are at once historiographic (the writing of a history), biographic (the writing of a life), and thanatographic (the writing of a death) in form and content. To consider the singular existence of a life is to consider the life and death of that (once) living being. Death is an integral element of any life, as life is a component of death. The death of a person is an intensive part of the life, and thus the biography, of that person, even if the person is not yet dead. This biographic orientation implies a *biothanatography*, a writing of life death, which entails an overlapping mix of the biographical and the thanatographical. Herein lies a *bios/thanatos/graphē*. A number of biothanatographies appear through this work, in fact. I write of how certain lives and deaths are related in time, in association, and in intensive significance through discontinuous flows of time.

Singularities are subject and method here. It's a matter of a few fragments, a few images and lines in life and death, as though an excavator-palynologist was tending to the remnant shards and dispersed pollen particles of an archaeological site from which certain patterns of life and death can be discerned. There are now a number of empirically sound and important historical accounts and political analyses of the violent events of Paris 1961 and of the role that French police and governmental apparatuses played in the violence.[11] Historians and other scholars have written of the violence of that night and its aftermaths in comprehensive and knowing terms, and of the terrain of "the colonial field" more broadly, chronicling the histories and politics involved and developing astute theories of colonial forms and forces and postcolonial political formations.[12] The current work is indebted to these studies at almost every turn, while advancing a different kind of inquiry. I return again and again to the words and images of others, to deepen understandings of the events and histories involved. My approach in writing is rather singular and precise—rather "micro," if you will: I write of a life and death or two, set within the broader context of such histories. I draw from a range of published accounts and archived texts and images to trace out a few singular pathways in life and death. In engaging with passages found in existing historiographies and archival texts, grafting onto the grafts of others, the current inquiry traces out lines of thought and significance in the histories involved for the purpose of telling an idiosyncratic story. (Motifs of *grafts* and *grafting* recur here in the sense of taking elements from one domain of life and grafting them onto another field of life, as with the grafts of plants or trees, or living tissue, or texts and writing. "To write means to graft. It's the same word," Derrida [1981, 355] observes). At hand is a certain "technique of nearness" (Benjamin), and a reading of archives that "brings the state *near*, to make it perceptive through reading sounds, images, persons, and moods," as Nancy Rose Hunt (2016, 9) proposes.[13] With these brief elements and archived lives there are entire worlds.

The focus on a single life reflects an analytic spirit akin to that conveyed through the autobiographical examples developed by Christina Sharpe and Saidiya Hartman in their writings on Black precarity and the afterlife of slavery.[14] Hartman explains that such an autobiographical example "is not a personal story that folds onto itself; it's not about navel gazing; it's really about trying to look at historical and social process and one's own formation as a window onto social and historical processes, as an example of them."[15] For Hartman (2008, 7), such an approach can help "to tell a story capable of engaging and countering the violence of abstraction." I strive for a like-minded biographical example in these pages.

The tenor of this writing compares to many biographical accounts, as well as the time-tested genre of life history research in anthropology, in which features of someone's life are portrayed in efforts to say something incisive about that person's existence and the cultural and sociopolitical forces that shape that life and others like it. Here, the most minimal of life histories is pressed into these pages. Inscribed are the reported date and place of birth of Bennahar, a reported residence on the outskirts of Paris, the remote absence-presence of a family, a handful of photographs, and a few obscure findings. Despite these few remaining vestiges of a past life, there is much that can be said about the circumstances of this singular life and death. The research and writing are multisited and multitimed, with many places and institutions, histories and temporalities involved. I follow the story of a particular life and death—as it makes its way through a number of domains, from Parisian streets and Métro stations to morgue examination rooms to a city's archives—and of images recurrent through photographs.[16] These excursions imply a "willful exposure to archive fever," as Ariella Aïsha Azoulay writes of similar kinds of researches.[17] They lead to a microhistory and counterhistory of a certain kind, one with an anthropological sensibility to it.

I explore certain events and situations within a revamped mode of "thick description," tracing out what's at stake, much like an anthropologist might delve into the intricacies of a ritual or violent event or a cultural historian might render the cosmos of a miller in sixteenth-century Friuli or the social world of a clog maker in nineteenth-century France.[18]

This is "history in the ethnographic grain," and ethnography as historiography (Darnton 1985, 1).[19] Rather than offering a straightforward historical account of the events involved (as if any such account could, in fact, be straightforward), I try, like an ethnographer striving to make sense of the nuances of a field site, to grasp the significance of particular moments, images, and strands of meaning, along with the seemingly incidental details that speak to the powers of a colonial state. The stress here is on the plural. There are not any unified social or intellectual-cultural worlds to speak of, but rather complex arrays of competing political positionings, assemblages of governmental techniques and police regimes, forms of knowledge and techniques of observation, and varying uses of photographs and archival records, with all of this churning through time.

One way to think about a life is to consider the many traces it generates during a long or relatively brief tract of existence, elements that spread out in different directions, disperse into various domains of life, or get cut short, dissipate; traces erased or disappeared, or re-marked; marks and remnants of a life that linger in the wake of a death, in how that person is remembered, recalled, or forgotten. The name and remnant memory and materialia and life death of a person might be regrafted, or obliterated, become nearly forgotten or last for centuries, millennia even.

There is something spore-like in all of this. Much as the spores of non-seed-bearing plants (such as liverworts, hornworts, mosses, and ferns) or eukaryotic organisms (fungi such as yeasts, molds, and mushrooms) or endospore-forming bacteria disperse throughout the world—where these reproductive cells might scatter explosively into the wind, shed into water, settle into sediment, or land on leaves, trees, or soil, and through such trajectories land or burrow elsewhere and sprout forth new life, with some spores germinating after years of dormancy—so trace elements of a life or a death disperse into myriad domains and environments, sprout forth in forms of life and inscription and materialia, graft onto new surfaces and recombinant possibilities, and germinate in hours or days or after years of dormancy. In life as in death, spore-like particles proceed like microscopic grains from a life, disperse freely and travel long distances, like so many waves of "viral shedding"—a kind of "self-shedding" (a language of emergence, contagion, contact, host, immunity, and diffusion is not, by analogy, unfounded here)—and then come to germinate or regerminate, are grafted into new situations and new sprouted forms of life; or they remain attached to other forms of life, living or inert, like burrs that stick to a patch of clothing. And once the spore lives and spore paths of other beings and species are thrown into this fecund mix—as with the pollen storms of a rain-bright spring day— what becomes evident is an expansive field of ever-shifting vitalities, survival and cessation, inheritance and errancy.[20]

Life Death, Survivance, Cessance

The terrain is one of *life death*. I use that term much as Jacques Derrida did in speaking of what he called *la vie la mort*, "life death." This phrasing does not include the usual coordinating conjunctures *and* or *or*, as with the phrases *life and death*, *life or death*, while also not saying that life *is* death, that life and death are the same thing, with no difference between them (Derrida 1987; 2011; 2020, 1–6).[21] There is neither opposition nor identification. The concept of life death is geared toward avoiding the static reproduction of a life/death positional or oppositional logic, while emphasizing the close relationship of life and death— the intricate play of life death, even—in forms of existence, reproduction, and inheritance, within heterogeneous fields of shifting valences, deferrals, difference, displacements, repetition, traces, survival, revenants, and ghostly hauntings.[22] It's not a matter of either life *or* death, or life *and* death, or of any kind of steadfast binary division between the two, but rather a complicated multiplicity of connections, possibilities, and intershadings shifting between different forms of existence, inexistence, and spectrality, "a multiplicity of organizations of relations between living and dead," with all of this intertwined with myriad events, processes, technologies, imaginings, and temporalities in life death (Derrida 2008, 31). As Derrida (1985, 6) couches the matter in *The Ear of the Other*, "What one calls life—the thing or object of biology and biography—does not stand face to face with something that would be its opposable ob-ject: death, the thanatological or thanatographical. This is the first complication." This complication is of signal importance to considerations of biology, survival, and extinction and the serious play of life and death in the Anthropocene, to reflections on the blurred margins between animate and inanimate forms of existence, and in efforts to grasp patterns of life death in singular and collective forms of existence.

It's important to mark out life death as a complex terrain and to plunge into this complicated terrain when writing about someone's life or a number of interrelated lives. In these pages, I write within the methods and sense and terrain of "life death." I work within its folds and contours and shifting multiplicities while wanting to strike down any presumed steadfast partitions between what is often called "life" and "death." With this, we move back and forth between a more general, philosophical sense of life death and considerations of specific instances of singular life deaths. I apply this way of thinking to the work of biography, of writing not just of a life—as the word "bio-graphy" might strictly imply (such as the Byzantine Greek βιογραφία, "writing of lives," etymologically suggests)—but of writing of the life death of a particular person or the life deaths of any number of persons or subjects. While elsewhere one tends to write biographically of "the life of ___," here I gravitate toward the phrasing "the life death of ___." Admittedly uncommon and slightly awkward, the phrasing gets at something crucial: that a life is more extensively, more accurately, considered a life death. To think of a life as a life only, as a positive value, without the death named or included in its realm of play, is to cut short the processes and graphic dimensions involved, including the complex play of survival and cessation that can run on for years past the biological endpoint of a life. Let's think of life death, then, as an open-ended, expansive field of relations rather than as a fixed entity or a finite state or process.

Life is grafted onto death, and death entangled with life. There is variably life-in-death and death-in-life; there can be moribund flesh or subjectivity, the living dead, or a negative, cancelling out social death in life, or bare life; while death can entail a sporadic or continuous emergence beyond the vital terms and biological terminus of a singular life, an excess of life beyond life itself.[23] There is also the matter of technology involved in any given field of life, a necessary substrate of technicity or materiality, inert and vibrant matter, which makes any given lives constituted and sustained by complex fields of vitality and technicity. Such biotechnological assemblances in themselves blur distinctions between vital forms and inert matter, living and nonliving. "Neither life nor death," writes Derrida (2001, 41), "but the haunting of the one by the other."

The subject is particular life deaths, singular or in association, linked in human striving or in annihilating violence, as well as the afterlives of a life; with this subject matter comes an array of forces and forms at work in these life deaths. And *survivance*—to relay another term of Derrida's, one invoked in his writings, especially in the later years of his life, to get at the kinds of "survival" and "sur-viving" or "living on" (*sur-vivre*) that are crucial dimensions of life death. "Survivance in a sense of survival that is neither life nor death pure and simple, a sense that is not thinkable on the basis of the opposition between life and death" (Derrida 2011, 130–31).[24] As a "movement of survival," *survivance* speaks to the ways that elements or vestiges of life, or life death, "live on" in life, continue on, even past the vital arc of a life, be they the lasting traces of something written or the physical remains of a once-living body (Derrida 1984, 28).

In tracing out pathways of survivance in any given life or death, one can consider the many intricate ways in which a life "lives on" in life death, even after the most direct and tangible biological forms of the life have expired. Vestiges of a life remain in writing or in material remainders, in forms of an afterlife as memory of trace remnants in the lives of others; memories recur and evolve through time; residual traces of a life often appear well past the actual living of that life. A kind of "survivance effect" kicks in with so much of life death; it's as if elements of a life (or a death) can break off, disperse in space and time, get rerouted or regrafted or appear in new forms, new graphic traces, or vanish altogether (Wills 2016, 99, 100).

Life death is characterized by forms of both trace and absence, recollection and forgetting, survival and cessation, and this in intricate, interfolding ways. I therefore find that, along with the concept of survivance, a concept of *cessance* is needed.[25] In writing within the terrain of life death or a singular life death, one needs to consider forces and forms of cessance as much as those of survivance. Aspects of a life cease to exist; traces are severed; there is annihilation, stoppage, oblivion, dissolution. Certain traces and dimensions of a life do not continue on. Survivance can be denied. The stilled end of a heartbeat, the end of speech, the disappearance of a body. Not everything lives on.

Life death involves an intricate weave of survivance and cessance in which the two processes fold into one another, pattern one another, such that life and death cannot be grasped as polar opposites. A cessance effect goes along with any kind of survivance effect. In many circumstances, there is a complicated play between movements of survival and cessation, including instances where there occurs an erasure of traces, or there recur trace effects of cessation or the ghostly inkling of a former presence. Often this implies complicated situations in which survival is not quite survival and death not quite death; "a survival that is not a survival, and a death that does not end anything," as Maurice Blanchot (1995, 340) puts it. There is a vast politics to both kinds of effects in life death, far beyond the interests or agency of any given lives at hand, be it the history of a singular life, or within a family or household or colonized peoples, or in the holdings of an archive or a field of collective memory or oblivion. This, in effect, is the subject of this book: the politics of trace and absence within the meshwork of life death. The work moves along a trajectory reflecting charged gradations in life and death. Intensities in life death emerge and dissolve within the opaque histories of a troubled existence.

Biophantasmatics

The processes and effects of life death and survivance include not just what is biographically actual—what actually happened in a life and what is recalled of it—but also the imagined and fantasized, the conjectured, the dreamed of, the possible and impossible. For the imagined, conjectured, and fantasized are integral aspects of life death. If "phantasm" can be considered in the variable sense of "an apparition or illusion; a ghost or phantom; an imaginary construct; a fantastical image or vision; a haunting memory; a fanciful idea; or a cohering fantasy, momentary or lifelong, conscious or unconscious"—as the phantom of a scholar once proposed—then such phantasmal aspects can be said to course through myriad thoughts, perceptions and encounters and imaginings in and of a life (Desjarlais 2018, ix).[26]

A *biophantasmatics* is in play with any given field of life death. Biophantasmatics, the phantasmal flows and currents of life, can be taken as a counterpart to biopolitics, the field of biopower, politics of life. The phantasmal is as much a part of life and death as are power and the phantasmal reach of power. In what ways do the politics of life death intersect with phantasms and imaginings of life death? These biophantasmatic considerations point to the phantasmal imaginings of and in life; of what a life is, or is not; of what a life could be or should be. Such phantasms and phantasmatics of life are at work at both an individual and a collective level, from a singular life to the life deaths of a population. This implies phantasms of death as well, imaginings and phantasms of the death of a person or of a colonized people. If necropolitics refers to "who matters and who does not, who is disposable and who is not," as Achille Mbembe (2003, 26; 2019) avers, then necrophantasmatics, the phantasmal phantasmatics of death and nonlife, lights on powerful imaginings of who matters and who does not, of who dies, how, and why, along with phantasms of burial, the treatment and disposal of corpses, and any phantasmal inklings of trace afterpresences.

We also have to consider the idea that life is phantasmal in its makings and operations, at least to a degree; that large portions of life operate through processes of a fantastical, imaginal sort, including the phantasmatics of memory, forgetting, denial, obsolescence. Much of a life—or *bios*, life, more generally—is built out of conjecture, revery and fantasy, crafted memories, fictions of selves and scurrying interpretations, illusions and allusions propelled by personal and collective desires, fears, hopes, anxieties. A biography is a phantasm as much as it is anything else—the phantasms of the thread of a life, its winding course, events, and significance, biophantasmally inscribed within the "exact fantasy" of a bounded script.[27] I go beyond the actual, the strictly historical, because the imaginal and virtual are implicit in the actual. What if we thought of a human life not as the locus of a finite series of actions, tethered to a distinct body, but as the ground of an open-ended, indeterminate, multidimensional field of events, potentialities, and imaginings?

And so I write of phantasms and spectrality. "One must stop believing that the dead are just the departed and that the departed do nothing. One must stop pretending to know what is meant by 'to die' and especially by 'dying.' One has, then, to talk about spectrality" (Derrida 1995, 30). With events, effects, phantasms, revenants, and remnants of a life living on, surviving, remaining in some ways or not, life and death become altogether intertwined and interimplicated and, in a certain sense, indissociable.[28] A biothanatography does not separate life and death as such but rather keeps in mind vast interchanges and blurred boundaries.

Once completely unknown to me, he appeared in a sequence of images, a series of flashes and marks of wounding. His life and death have since tied into my own. I render him so, search through the dust. Track the spores, mark pollen residue of remaindered life.

A Shifting Series of Exergues

The prose exceeds the typical structures and textual conventions and psychology of most biographic accounts (many of which I find to be rather conventional, bound at the seams). In tracing the course of a particular life death, mapping the lands that surround and shape that riverine flow, the writing overflows its banks. With this biographical canvas come different overflows, displacements, blurred borders between one life and others, a crossing of limits and thresholds, intersecting relations among various forms of life death. Life is always in excess of itself. Death, too, for that matter. A life involves much more than the life itself; life is never lived on its own. There is life beyond life, after life, before life, alongside life, against life, life death transformed. I write of overflowing excesses in life death in a spirit of affirmative transgression.

These excursions go beyond the directly biographic. Each supplemental graft-text proceeds as an *exergue* on biographic and historiographic writing so-called proper. An exergue, as the *Oxford English Dictionary* defines the word, is "a small space usually on the reverse of a coin or medal, below the principal device, for any minor inscription, the date, engraver's initials, etc. Also, the inscription there inserted."[29] As Akira Mizuta Lippit (2012, 1) contends in his book *Ex-Cinema*, which considers the ways in which experimental films and videos operate on the outside of more standard forms of filmmaking, "An *exergue*, from the Greek *ex* (outside) and *ergon* (work), refers to a space outside the work, outside the essential body of the work, and yet part of it, even essentially—a part and apart. An exergue locates an outside space that is included in the work as its outside."

In literature and philosophy, an exergue usually appears at the interstitial beginning of a work. Here, the exergues are multiple. They appear throughout the text as moments of conjectural, exploratory writing, like spectral marginalia, separated and marked in italics, and interspersed within the more direct historiographic and biographic writing (as with the passage in italics above). These passages relate in chiasmatic ways to the writing found in the main text, with each line of writing implicitly crossing into and informing the other. Occasionally the words inscribed are addressed to potential interlocutors or within the imaginal intimacy of a possible, spectral readership. Quiet voices whisper to the side, sotto voce, not necessarily in my name. The more imaginal of these passages stem from recent phantasmal inquiries of mine.[30] They also bear an affinity with the "critical fabulation" explored by Saidiya Hartman in her recent writings, such as "Venus in Two Acts" (2008) and *Wayward Lives, Beautiful Experiments* (2019), in which this historian essays a creative semifictional style of writing that recalls the lives and suppressed voices of the past through a critical engagement with the histories and silences involved. "Lack and absence made poesis necessary," Hartman remarks in reflecting on the literary approaches to the histories of Black life that have inspired her, in which novelists create "fictions of the archive."[31] Yet the poetics of the current approach refract in ways different from Hartman's critical fabulation, for I do not imagine the intimate richness of lives through vivid, historically informed narratives so much as I ruminate, partially and tentatively, on a few possibilities in life and death. A marginal method is made of these shifting intensities, which can be read as being outside the essential body of the work, yet also integral parts of it, to the point where inside and outside, corpus and ex-corpus, text and margin become blurred and nearly interchangeable.[32] I ask readers to give thought not only to historical events and interpretive assessments but also the many imaginings and conjectures that swirl about a life death—and thus consider the ways that the actual and the phantasmal are imbricated within one another.

Beyond the specifics of any writing with exergues, several notable dimensions are involved in the blurred borderlands of these pages. One pertains to the interpolations between life and death. Death informs a life, and life, death. Each life told is implicitly biothanatographic, a writing of life death, anticipatory or after the fact. Along with the intergraftings of life death come relations, affinities, and interconnections among different lives and deaths. Lives are related to other lives, deaths to other deaths, and certain lives to specific deaths.

To write biothanatographically is to write of the historical and the genealogical. Specific tracts of life death in colonial and postcolonial times are considered here within the complex historical formations in which certain lives took form and fell away. The delivery of a corpse to a forensic morgue in Paris in October 1961, for instance, prompts considerations of the history of that morgue and the various practices of recordkeeping, inscription, and visuality in place during that time, practices that emerged out of long-standing political and cultural sensibilities related to the postmortem care, tracking, and burial of the dead in France and elsewhere. The riverine flow of a life death is grasped within the terrains that shape that flow.

Throughout this work I adopt a first-person narrative voice in reflecting on my engagements with the subject matter at hand and how these research inquiries have affected me through the course of the research. I also explore questions tied to the ethical and epistemological challenges involved in trying to understand and portray the lives and deaths of persons outside of my own circumstances in life. This self-reflexive approach, interlaced with the more direct inquiries found in the text, is in line with forms of reflexivity in contemporary ethnographic writing, in which moral quandaries and complex relations with one's interlocutors are crucial aspects of the inquiries at hand (such as with Anthony Stavrianakis's *Leaving* [2019], Todd Meyers's *All That Was Not Her* [2022], and Alexa Hagerty's *Still Life with Bones* [2023]).[33] In engaging with self-reflexive modes of anthropological thought and writing—or with reflexive historiographic writing, for that matter—readers of such works might in effect experience something of what a researcher has encountered and, ideally, learn by traveling alongside the author for a while. This is far from narcissistic self-indulgence or subjective "navel-gazing"—labels that can make any memorist wince. Such writings can delve into the cauldron heat of relating to others. Accordingly, around the edges of the more direct historiographic and analytic writing I write of the pressing thoughts, unsettled anxieties and concerns, tentative knowings, and shape-shifting imaginaries that have come my way in trying to comprehend the lives of others. If anything is particularly distinctive with the reflexivity found in these pages, it might relate to the stress on the imaginal—phantasm as subject and method.[34]

Inscribed is the busy interchange between biography and biographer, between the life death of a biographical subject and the life (and yet to come, but anticipated, known of, shadowed by) death of the biographer. With any biography, two lives are implicitly involved, to begin with: the life death of the person written about, and the scribe of another's life death. These two lives can become linked in all sorts of ways: scriptive, imaginative, political, psychodynamic, ethical, hauntological, or nearly obsessional. When one writes of another's life death, a certain biographical immersion can be in effect, in which the histories and imaginaries involved in the life death of another affect one's own life, and certain thoughts and imaginings flow into the subject matter at hand. One life death grafts onto another.

There is an intricate play between the biographical and the phantasmal, the actual and the imagined. All biographies and autobiographies carry a strong measure of spectrality and imaginative rendering. Portraying a life, conjuring its forms and features, speculating on its rhythms and reasons—such interpretive endeavors bring forth all sorts of phantasmal depictions and imaginings of life events. These phantasmal lines of thought and speculative renderings run alongside apparently more empirical observations on so-called historical actualities. In this writing near the margins, one finds spectral echoes and phantasmal musings and inscriptions, for the phantasmal and the spectral are integral parts of a life death. A condition of spectrality informs terrains of life death, like a coefficient or a governing law—the allusive, wavering law of spectrality. Anyone meandering though these pages might encounter myriad fantasies germinating in mind and body and tracks of writing—cryptic fantasies, say, of a family's uncertain mourning or ghostly images in an archive, in which a biographer reconstructs violence and repair in a number of lives. With this comes a speculative thanatography; a speculative writing of the features and possibilities of a man's death and its aftermath proceeds uncertainly, in unproven ways.

Running through these pages are thus several threads of thought and imagery, each interwoven with the others. One thread speaks to the shifting intensities of life and death emergent in the historical and biographical grounds of the existence and afterlives of Abdelkader Bennahar, in relation to other, intersecting life deaths. A second, related thread traces the visceral engagements and movements of Bennahar's body, from the visual record of that body on the night of 17 October 1961 through the days that followed, as a body-in-life death moved from the obscure moments of a death to the institutional structures of a governmental morgue in Paris to the subsequent burial of the corpse in a cemetery outside the city. Yet another thread relates to the histories of the photographs taken by Kagan in Paris and Nanterre in October 1961, potent images that have circulated in recurrent ways since that time and taken on various significances and affective intensities. And then, roaming about this tissue of connected threads, like ghostly apparitions, are reflections on the phantasmal and spectral dimensions of these histories. Held in your hands, then, is a knotted interweave of life death, body, image, and phantasm.

It's a simple idea, at first glance: retrace remnants of a life and death. This becomes infinitely more complex the more one gets into it. Such an endeavor opens into vast recesses of life death and, along the way, touches on the forces that shape and embody a life death in relation to other lives and deaths. A winding path is set, for once an author or reader gets going with this, they soon delve into a vertiginous shadow play of living and dying.

I came upon the trace of a life and followed that trace into the graph of a death.

The more I shadow one person's life death, soaking up the remnants involved, the more an unghosted nonpresence specters my own.

Lest anyone think that the histories involved here are a matter of the distant past, far removed from present-day concerns, we need only consider the fact that police violence has been a recurrent theme for many years now in the Paris metropole and in France more generally. Time and again, young men of African and Arab descent have suffered from the violence enacted by French police officers. On 19 July 2016, Adam Traoré, a twenty-four-year-old Black man, died while in custody after being apprehended and detained by the police. On 14 June 2023, Alhousssein Camara, a nineteen-year-old whose family hailed from Guinea, was killed during a road check in Angoulême, a city in southwestern France.

On 27 June 2023, Nahel Merzouk, a French seventeen-year-old of Moroccan and Algerian descent, was shot at point-blank range and killed by Florian Menesplier, a French police officer. The shooting took place at Place Nelson Mandela in Nanterre, on lands that once provided homes for migrants from Algerians in the bidonvilles there. The site of the death is about two kilometers from where Abdelkader Bennahar was beaten and left for dead the night of 17 October 1961. The morning of 27 June 2023, police officers spotted Nahel Merzouk driving a Mercedes-Benz, reportedly at high speed. A police patrol stopped the car that he and two other youths were occupying. Two officers approached the car and spoke with Nahel Merzouk through the window area on the driver's side, while pointing a gun at him. When the car began to move away, Menesplier fired one round from his handgun. The bullet struck Merzouk as the car lurched forward and came to a stop. Merzouk died soon after. The incident led to widespread protests in the days that followed, including the destruction of many civil institutions and symbols of the state—town halls, schools, police stations. It also brought rounds of condemnation from various persons and institutions, including Emmanuel Macron, the president of France, who called the killing "inexplicable" and "inexcusable" (Le Monde 2023). Menesplier was placed in custody with the charge of voluntary manslaughter. Others pointed out that Merzouk's death was one of many instances of police violence against people of African and Arab descent in France and called for assessments of the systemic racism in its police forces.

A video recording of the incident, taken by a bystander, served to document the criminal actions of the police officer who shot Nahel Merzouk, contradicting the claim that the officer acted in self-defense. At a memorial site at Place Nelson Mandela a sign read, "Combien de Nahel n'ont été filmés?" (How many Nahels have not been filmed?)

WOUND IMAGES

On Photography and Wounding

There is, at first glance, the grain of the fabric within the grain of the photograph. He was wearing a corduroy jacket and a tie that night—dressed up for the event, like many of his compatriots, for a respectful, dignified demonstration in the center of Paris. The ridges of the jacket's surface material were evident in the photographs taken that night, a granular texture of light and dark. The tie at that moment was loosened, as if the day's work was done and formalities were no longer required. That tie was stained with blood, as were the jacket and shirt. In the black-and-white photographs taken that night, those stains appear as dark patches on the surface of the man's clothes and skin as well as the surface of the film. The dark patches parallel the stains of the photographs. The stains in the photographs correspond to the stain of photography. The stain of wounding has continued, like a blot of ink seeping into fine cloth, spreading irreversibly.

We might begin with a single photograph, to consider the implications of that politically charged image and its possible tonalities through time. And then, stepping back some, we can move on to other photographs. Readers might sense a delay in the opening pages of this book, with words prefacing but not immediately showing any overt visual images. With this deferred action, the photographic images appear gradually, in the bath of their development. It's true we're proceeding cautiously, as though preparing for the treatment of a wound. And wounds there are, in the content and force of Kagan's photographs from the night of 17 October 1961. It's not easy to engage with such images. But we need to give thought to representations of colonial violence. We need to hold onto the "right to look" (Mirzoeff) at the forces and consequences of political violence and so enact forms of countervisuality that knock against modes of visuality and silence so often promoted by state and police powers.[1]

"But the war goes on," wrote Frantz Fanon of the Algerian war of liberation, in *Les damnés de la terre* (*The Wretched of the Earth*), published in 1961. "And for many years to come we shall be bandaging the countless and sometimes indelible wounds (*blessures*) inflicted on our people by the colonialist onslaught" (Fanon [1961] 2005, 181). Histories of wounding trail in the wake of colonial regimes. A historical genealogy of a colonial system marks acts of wounding among families, communities, or peoples, wounds seared into bodies and persons, injurious, ruinous. A singular genealogy of wounding might consider how such wounds recur or linger in time, get incised in collective or personal memories, appear in formations of language and image as well as becoming effaced or denied in time. One might also take note of efforts in mourning and repair and acts of creative renewal and memorialization in the afterlives of violent wounding.

Time is crucial to such considerations, from the ways that photographic images work in and through time to the complex temporalities involved in particular lives and deaths, to the historicity of archival materials and the multiple, shifting temporalities of place and materiality. Time is one of the interpretative elements of this inquiry. Readers are invited to consider the temporal processes involved in the perception and changing nature of a few select photographs as well as the life deaths of certain persons who have come to be associated with those images. Yet any occurrence of time here is not of a continuous singular flow. The temporalities involved are multiple, at once polyphonic and polysemic. Perhaps we might identify a particular *time signature* in the events and materials involved: time here is fractured, choppy, porous, multiply interrelational, with moments of dispersal and frayed partial recurrence. *Time is wounded*, afflicted by bruising effects of colonial harm, fractured within histories of violence, marked by scattered images of rupture. To press the metaphor—yet don't we have only metaphors when speaking of time?—(post)colonial time groans and winces, hobbles along, as do the subjects and images that range through its complex enfoldments.[2]

Concepts of wounding are of pressing significance here, particularly as they take form in particular social worlds and collective histories. In his 2015 essay "When Wounds Travel," Omar Dewachi (2015, 64–65) reflects on the semantic and discursive terrain of wounding in the Arabic language:

> In the Arabic language, "wound" (*Jurh*) is a loaded term. In addition to its literal use in naming a physical injury, it is often used as a metaphor to highlight constellations of personal and social injuries, losses, and grievances. To be "wounded" (*majrouh*) is to carry on lingering memories, pain, or history of wounding processes, that might range from a personal insult to the loss of one's land or beloved ones. While referring to actual and literal wounds . . . the notion of the "social wound" also traces histories and geographies of violence that are entrenched in the ambivalences of everyday social experiences of war and displacement.

We can draw from these connotations of wound and being wounded in considering the interrelated physical, personal, and collective wounds entrenched in histories of colonialism, warfare, and state-sanctioned violence.

Many physical or psychological wounds resulting from political violence are also social wounds and reflective of "historical wounds" (Chakrabarty 2007). They often carry potent political force and significance. Certain social and psychic wounds can last for generations, taking on different social forms and psychic valences for the members of distinct generations. This has been the case, for one, with the families of the "Harkis" who sided with the French military and police forces and served as auxiliaries (*supplétifs*) in the French army during the Algerian war of independence. A number of men who served as auxiliary soldiers and survived the war ended up residing in settlement camps in remote areas of France, living in deadening atmospheres of disgrace and silence. Their children have lived in the aftermath of this traumatic wounding. As Vincent Crapanzano (2011, 13) observes of this painful history, the children of the Harkis have lived with "a double trauma," namely, "the silence of the father—the dead but alive, the live but dead father" and "the wounds one has experienced oneself." These wounds cannot readily be healed or resolved. For the children of the Harkis, there is a "wound that never heals."[3]

With these thoughts and histories in mind, we return to a scene of wounding. Bennahar probably attended the collective demonstrations on 17 October 1961, joining others who resided on the western outskirts of Paris in a mass procession toward the center of Paris, only to be stopped at a bridge crossing the Seine by police officers wielding guns and clubs. Later that night, he and others probably clashed with police officers in Petit-Nanterre, a neighborhood in the commune of Nanterre; the specifics of this are uncertain. As Bennahar lay wounded and bleeding along the side of Rue des Pâquerettes, Kagan arrived on the scene. He took a series of photographs of Bennahar as he lay on the ground and then tried to stand upright. Kagan and an American journalist then brought Bennahar to a hospital in Nanterre that night for treatment of his wounds. After that, it's unclear what happened. Police reports and brief newspaper accounts suggest Bennahar died the next night, 18 October 1961, in Colombes, a commune neighboring Nanterre, while participating in a demonstration against the French colonial regime. The demonstrators clashed with French police forces. Around the same time, Kagan developed the negatives of the photographs he took in Nanterre and then made positive images of them. Soon after, several of the images appeared in newspapers published in Paris.

The photograph shown here is one of several that Kagan took in Petit-Nanterre the night of 17 October 1961 (figure 1.1). The man photographed has subsequently been identified as Abdelkader Bennahar. For many, that identification came years later, if at all. Kagan did not learn the name of the man he photographed in Nanterre that night, then or later on. The man's name went unknown to most people for several decades. (There will be more on the history of this identification and its deferrals and displacements through time later in this text.)

I show this photographic image cautiously, hesitantly, with intent seared with ambivalence. The potential effects of the photograph make me anxious.

What do you see and sense in Kagan's photograph of Bennahar, lying wounded on the ground? Does the image strike you with visceral force, does the image wound? This was the case for me when I first saw this photograph and others in a series on wounding. This has also been the case for others to whom I have shown the photographs. These viewers have been affected, slightly or markedly. "It stays in your mind," said one person on seeing the photograph. In viewing the image one plunges into an unsettling scene. The photograph hurts. "It's difficult to look at," said A. in seeing the photograph for a second or third time. Difficult to look at, hard to take in, the photographs from that night have come to work in evidentiary and affective ways through torn strands of history.

"We want such images . . . and yet they knock the air out of us," writes Lisa Stevenson.[4] *We need such images, yet they work through a medium of pain.*

FIGURE 1.1. Rue des Pâquerettes, Nanterre, 17 October 1961 [Abdelkader Benna-
har]. Photo by Élie Kagan. LC_KAG_00004N_B04 © Élie Kagan "Collection La
Contemporaine."

*A few others, in contrast, have told me that these and related photographic im-
ages do not wound them. It's a photograph of a wounded person, they say, not
necessarily an image that wounds them. Any engagements with the photographs
are entangled within this variable tension between representation and affect,
wounded and wounding.*

The photographs taken of Bennahar the night of 17 October 1961 circulated in important ways in the days and weeks after that night, and for years

later. The images became known as testimonial evidence of the brutal violence. One person's physical pain indexed the wounding and deaths of others. The original prints and negatives of Kagan's photographs from that night, as well as his photographic work as a whole, are now kept in the Fonds Élie Kagan (Élie Kagan collection) in the archives of La Contemporaine: Bibliothèque, Archives, Musée des Mondes Contemporains, now housed on the campus of Paris Nanterre University. By the early 2020s, La Contemporaine had composed a comprehensive digital archive of Kagan's photographs, which can be found online.[5] Reproductions of the photograph shown here can be seen in any number of publications and on websites and various postings online, in varying dimensions and resolutions. These days, the image circulates widely, wanders far afield of the first enactments—while seemingly, imaginally, the man portrayed continues to lie supine, in pain.

One aspect of the present work is an attempt to trace out the ways in which Kagan's photographs from the night of 17 October 1961 have circulated in time and in space, through various texts and films and creative efforts, in archival holdings, and through recurrent mentions of the pictures and their connotations, with many texts and readings involved, including the current text and any reflections that might follow. Through this tracking of the photographic images and their varied, shifting meanings through a *longue durée* of colonial histories, from the heated days of French coloniality to the age of the internet and social media, I want to explore how the affective intensities of the images and their political, moral, and evidentiary significances have emerged and changed through time. This is a story, in part, of the social life and political history of a few select images and a specific photographic event, first enacted on the outskirts of Paris in October 1961, recurrent since then.

My approach to Kagan's photographs from October 1961 and the circumstances of their creation and myriad uses and circulations through time resonates with the research and writings of anthropologists and other scholars who consider closely specific photographic images and practices within the contexts of both local histories and "world-system photography."[6] Works by Deborah Poole, Christopher Pinney, Elizabeth Edwards, Karen Strassler, Christopher Wright, Georges Didi-Huberman, and Kaja Silverman, for instance, go beyond considerations of cultural discourses and political ideologies about photography to examine specific photographic practices and people's uses and understandings of photographic images within particular times and places.[7] This orientation to photographs and their uses can entail detailed ethnographic and phenomenological analyses of specific photographic images and people's perceptions of and engagements with them. It can also strive to trace the political histories and "social life" of certain photographic images through years of their recurrence in the world.[8]

These select kinds of analysis—the ethnographic, the phenomenological, and the historiographic—are in play here, in interwoven ways. In effect, we are to consider the *development* of Kagan's photographs through time, to draw from a concept central to the art of photographic processing. In considering the polymorphous development of photographs through time, I take inspiration from Kaja Silverman, who, in her 2015 book *The Miracle of Analogy*, points out that in photography's early years the development of images was often a slow, gradual, and unfixed process. The first generation of photographers and developers often found it difficult to keep a photographic image from vanishing or darkening too much. Some early photographers encountered the phenomenon of "unstoppable development," in which a light-sensitive image would continue to take on further light, further altering and darkening the image, after the initial act of photographic creation.[9] William Henry Fox Talbot, author of *The Pencil of Nature* (1844–46), found that his photographs were not only drawn from natural forces of light and darkness but were "self-developing" whenever exposed to further conditions of light.[10] "One day last September," Talbot wrote in a letter to the editor of the *Literary Gazette* in February 1841, "I had been trying pieces of sensitized paper . . . in the camera obscura, allowing them to remain there for only a short time. One of these papers was taken out and examined by candlelight. There was little or nothing to be seen upon it and I left it lying on a table in a dark room. Returning sometimes after, I took up the paper and was very much surprised to see upon it a distant picture. . . . The only conclusion that could be drawn was that the picture unexpectedly *developed itself* by a spontaneous action."[11]

Photographs ceased to spontaneously develop in such unexpected and dramatic ways only after the emerging technology of photographic "fixing" became more fully realized in the decades after Talbot's and Louis Daguerre's early photographic endeavors, with the use of photographic processing techniques that worked to fix analog photographic images in more stable, lasting forms. And yet photographic images continue to develop further, beyond the efforts of any specific photographic agents or subjects. Silverman takes the phenomenon of "unstoppable development" of photographic images as foundational to photography, past and present. "Photography is still a dynamic medium," she remarked in an interview in 2010. "Photographs are constantly developing into other things: paintings, novels, computational images" (Silverman and Baker 2010).

This has been the case with Kagan's photographs. The first act of photographic development took place when Kagan processed the rolls of monochrome film used during the night of 17 October 1961. Through the use of darkroom chemistry, he turned the latent images, chemically graphed on the unprocessed film rolls, into negative images—into so many filmic strips of "negatives" set on transparent plastic film. He then used these negatives to make "positive images" in the form of prints and contact sheets. Yet this transformative process proved to be only the initial development of the images. A multiform development of the photographs has continued to this day. From Kagan's initial photographic negatives and prints have come numerous reproductions through time, as well as recurrent perceptions, interpretations, and imaginative renderings of the photographs and their implications. In recent years, the photographs have further developed into images located in archival holdings, digital technologies, certain kinds of artwork, and the rampant circulation of images on the internet and in social media. The development of the more imaginal and phantasmal, subjective and intersubjective dimensions of Kagan's photographs—beyond any actual prints or digital reproductions—also needs to be considered here. This is because, as Silverman (2015, 65) observes, "the human psyche is another of the places where the photographic image develops."

I trace out the multidimensional developments of Kagan's photographs from October 1961 in part to chronicle a long history of photographic wounding. The violence and pain implied in the photographs make this interpretative inquiry an especially delicate one, fraught with ethical and political concerns. It's a tricky thing to invoke and to analyze photographic images of pain and wounding and visceral representations of violence. There might be an important historical and pedagogical value to Kagan's photograph—and yet this is a picture of a once living man, with family in Algeria, who was harshly subject to the powers of French colonialism, the violent force of which contributed to his death one night later. Bennahar's death and those of others then became memorialized through the images. Should we circulate and comment on such photographs of violent pain, or try to steer clear of posting them in public forums? What challenges and responsibilities come with such scholarly slideshows? Is it possible for us to understand what's involved with this and related images of colonial violence without causing further violence? Should we keep the wounds open or try to forget them? How might we establish forms of looking that might promote "humane insight" (Baker 2015) into the pain and suffering of other beings in the world and the political circumstances of such hardship and the looking, rather than prurient fascination or indifferent regard?[12] Can looking, or looking away, ever be neutral acts? Such questions unsettle any seemingly straightforward invocations and assessments of the photographs.[13]

In writing this book, I cannot say that I have come up with any conclusive answers to the questions above or have devised clear-cut statements on the exceedingly complex ethics and politics of representation involved. Rather, I have been trying to find my way, image by image, through the intricate challenges of such concerns.

A sustained and delicate scrutiny is engaged through these pages, a close analysis of photographic traces and remnant materialia of a life. (The word *scrutiny*, it's worth noting, comes from Latin *scrutari*, "to examine, investigate, search," with the original notion of the Latin word perhaps being "to search among rubbish," via the plural *scruta*, "trash, rags, rubbish"; or the original sense might be "to cut into, scratch."[14]) Beyond forensic probing for its own sake, I would like to think that a close attention to visual nuances and afterlife echoes might offer constructive ways of thinking about the vicissitudes of photography, images, texts, fantasy, and life death through time.

The sustained looking here involves a *pensive looking*. The idea of pensive looking draws from Laura Mulvey's concept of "the pensive spectator" as it relates to the ability of viewers of film in the age of video recordings and digital technologies, which open up "new perceptual possibilities, new ways of looking, not at the world, but at the internal world of cinema," as Mulvey (2006, 181) conveys the gist of film viewing in this new century. With the use of digital technologies in particular, films and filmic sequences can be slowed, delayed, fragmented, copied, and reedited. Viewers can pause, delay, and slow films down, leading to the "oscillation between temporalities" (185). Films can be viewed and reviewed closely and pensively, thereby opening up to "new kinds of relations and revelations," proceeding in ways different from modalities of viewing premised on the figure of a possessive, "fetishistic spectator" (179).

Mulvey takes the concept of "the pensive spectator" directly from Raymond Bellour's 1987 essay by that title, while modifying the concept in considering the intricacies of pensive spectatorship in an age of video and digital technologies. In his essay, Bellour writes of films in which photographs play an important role in the unfolding narrative of the film, such as Max Ophüls's 1948 film *Letter from an Unknown Woman*:

> What happens when the spectator of film is confronted with a photograph? The photograph becomes first one object among many; like all other elements in the film, the photograph is caught up in the film's *défilement* [unfolding]. Yet the presence of the photograph on the screen gives rise to a very particular trouble. Without ceasing to advance its

own rhythm, the film seems to freeze, to suspend itself, inspiring in the spectator a recoil from the image that goes hand in hand with a growing fascination. . . . Creating another distance, another time, the photo permits me to reflect on the cinema. (Bellour 2012, 88–89)

Bellour then reflects on the presence of film stills:

As soon as you stop the film, you begin to find time to add to the image. You start to reflect differently on film, on cinema. You are led towards the film still—which is itself a step further in the direction of the photograph. In the frozen film (or still frame), the presence of the photograph bursts forth, while other means exploited by *mise-en-scène* to work against time tend to vanish. The photo thus becomes a stop within a stop, a freeze-frame within a freeze-frame; between it and the film from which it emerges, two kinds of time blend together, always inextricable but without becoming confused. In this the photograph enjoys a privilege over all other effects that make the spectator, this hurried spectator, a pensive one as well. (92–93)

In her 2006 book *Death 24× a Second*, Mulvey argues that the dynamics of a pensive spectatorship prompted by the use of photography within film, which Bellour analyzed in 1987, has taken a more general form with the advent of video and digital technologies of film viewership. Since the time of Mulvey's writing on this topic, the potential for pensive spectatorship has only increased further, given the ubiquitous use of digital technologies and social media interfaces.

A similar kind of pensiveness can take form *through writing*, specifically through processes of writing in depth about photographs as well as the myriad texts and inscriptions found in archives and other tracts of history. A movement toward patient, phenomenologically attuned writing can promote certain perceptual sensibilities in which photographic images and textual passages can be closely regarded, images and words reconsidered time and again and looked at from different angles and through shifting focal intensities. In my own engagements along these lines, I have found that writing about photographic images also tends to involve rounds of writing and rewriting, in which a pensive writer traces, retraces, and sometimes reworks perceptions as time images on. A close, recurrent regard of photographic images goes hand in hand with a close, recurrent attunement to any words and perceptions inscribed. Time and again, the writer can "zoom in" on the images, in ways both actual and figurative. Photography plus writing opens to a wide range of perceptual thoughts and imaginings. It's important to take our time with photographs.[15] The complicated temporal dimensions of any given photograph, the many forces of time at work in an image, can be thought about through an unfolding process of writing. In reflexively thinking through images, one can trace out different histories of power, time, representation, and imagining involved in images and the kinds of affective perceptions they tend to promote, while grasping some of the imaginaries that swirl about scenes of imaginal conveyance.

This pensive looking-through-writing can perhaps lead to novel and generative forms of perception in the world, which might offer the potential to think through and rework certain habits of perception. Such generative looking brings to mind the "productive look" that Kaja Silverman identifies in certain films, such as Chris Marker's 1983 film *Sans Soleil* (*Sunless*), Isaac Julien's 1989 film *Looking for Langston*, and Harun Farocki's 1988 film *Bilder der Welt und Inschrift des Krieges* (*Images of the World and the Inscription of War*). In *The Threshold of the Visible World*, Silverman (1996, 193) reflects on what she calls a "cinema of the productive look":

> *Sans Soleil* and *Bilder der Welt* indicate that, although the camera "sees" what the eye cannot, the images it produces through this fictive act of "seeing" can be retroactively worked upon in all kinds of transformative and destabilizing ways, and thereby stripped of their ostensible objectivity and authority. And *Sans Soleil* and *Looking for Langston* indicate that the look can also interfere with the camera's normative operations at the very moment of photographic "capture," leading to the production of films which, in addition to challenging the complacencies of the self and the limitations of the given-to-be-seen, speak more about desire, memory and fantasy than about epistemological mastery.

Perhaps one day we will speak of a related anthropology of the productive look. Generative looking is the aspiration here, at least. There's no guarantee it's realized.

For the moment, I would like to offer some hypotheses on photography and wounding. These modest, tentative hypotheses—reflections that range from the phenomenology of images of wounding to the politics of their circulation—are of direct relevance to any consideration of Kagan's photographs from the night of 17 October 1961, as well as to photographic images of violence and wounding more generally. The idea is not to try to prove these hypotheses or to document them in any direct or comprehensive way, but rather to let them linger in thought and image within the reflections grafted in these pages.

- Photographs of wounded persons carry distinct qualities. Theorists of photography have often likened photographs to the steady-state stillness of death, as if a photograph is like a death mask, embodying a surceased moment in time.[16] But photographs of wounded persons (or any living wounded animals and sentient life-forms more generally) work differently than the valency of stillness and death often ascribed to photography. A wound involves a tender, liminal process that emerges in between any causes of the wound and its possible healing or other consequences. Any photographic image of a wound is *in medias res* (Latin, "in the midst of things"). "Wound implies *en media res* [*sic*]: the cause of injury is in the past but the healing isn't done; we are seeing this situation in the present tense of its immediate aftermath" (Jamison 2014, 118). A photograph of a wounded person suggests something ongoing, unended; not a corpse-like matter, not quite like something "preserved in amber," but a body in pain (Bazin 1960).[17] Time is not frozen or embalmed in photographs of wounding so much as it is wounded. The temporality of an image of wounding is open-ended. There is no clear terminus to an image of someone wounded. The wounded subject might appear as interminably alive, unceasingly wounded—marking a laceration in time and subject, flesh and feeling. In a sense, the apparent wound never fully heals, never scars over, never becomes mere stillness or unharmed flesh of the world. The wound, disembodied, can last longer than the photograph that once bore it.[18]
- There is an inherent affinity between images and wounding, in that images carry the capacity to wound. In *Camera Lucida*, Roland Barthes (1981) shaped his intuition on the potential of photographic images to wound into a singular method; "I wanted to explore photography not as a question (a theme) but as a wound," he wrote (21).[19] Certain photographic images prick, sting, puncture. Some images deeply affect their viewers, as if the content and force of a particular, wounding image were like the pointed edge of a dagger. Other images, bland and ineffective, resound for some like the dull side of a butter knife. ("But in it, for you, no wound" [73].) Photographic images carry the potential to wound and rewound. This is particularly the case within situations and histories of political violence and oppression.
- There is an acute singularity to photographic images of wounded persons. This is a single person in pain, just then, just now, within a particular instance of body, sensation, time. A photograph of someone

in pain is not simply a general representation of pain or collective suffering. A photograph of a wounded person compares to the intensive singularities of pain. At the same time, that singularity of pain can point to the pain of others. A single wound can become a fulcrum of collective sensation and signify collective and historical wounding. At once interior and exterior to the subject of wounding, the pain extends inward and outward for subjects and perceivers of the wounds.

- A photograph of someone wounded is a sensate trace of that wound. It's like a mark, index, scar, or vestige of an earlier wound. Each return to an image of wounding can entail a perceptual-phenomenal-political act that tears open the wound anew, as when one tears at a scab, which has the effect of keeping a healing wound freshly open, painfully tender.

- A photograph of a wounded person, someone in pain, can be considered a "wound-image," an image of a wound and image as, possibly, wound. Within the intensive, multiple temporalities of photography, a photograph of wounding can be both scar and wound of past and or present harm. Any viewer of such a wound-image might possibly be affected, wounded, in perceiving an image of wounding. Any such effects and affects can vary between different viewers or through different encounters with images through time. For some, there is wounding. For others, this might simply be a photograph of a wound or wounded person. The personal and political histories of any potential viewers count for a lot.

- Images of wounding can prompt affective relations between the subject of the wound and any viewers of it. A viewer can identify with the subject and the wounds involved, in both conscious and nonconscious ways. Pain can serve as a "conduit of identification" (Hartman 1997, 26) between perceivers and subjects of suffering. That identification, which can last for fleeting moments or for long durations, comes with political significance. That identification can also be largely imaginary in scope.

- In regarding a photographic image of a wounded subject, one might relate to the experience of pain inferred, and this at times in intensively recursive ways. Yet one cannot feel the same pain that the subject feels or felt. You might imagine, intuit, or empathize with the pain of the wounded, but the pain sensed is not the same pain. All sorts of psychological, imaginal, discursive, political, and ethical processes are involved in how people relate to the pain of others.

- A photograph of a wounded person can imply both intimacy and exposure. Images often carry a sense of intimacy, for one is drawn into a singular scene of intimate, intensive force. Jean-Luc Nancy (2005, 4) remarks that "the image throws in my face an intimacy that reaches me in the midst of intimacy." Photographs of wounding can accentuate such intimacy. One might readily sense the intimate pain of a moment, or a duration of wounding, while that personal hurt is cast upon a lasting visual canvas that can be observed, analyzed, and circulated in a general public realm—intimacy, exposed.
- Images of wounding tend to have propulsive, affective force. They can duplicate and disseminate quickly, suddenly go viral. They make people look. They can seize the imagination, root themselves in a perceiving body and not let go. They often carry a strong performative and rhetorical efficacy. Used in particular ways, they can work to show, document, or prove something. The technological reproduction of photographic images makes any wounds conveyed in a photographic image highly iterable, reproducible. Partly because of this, photographic images of wounding often circulate far and wide. Generative and dispersive, they lend themselves to media dispatches and interpretative readings and moral judgments. Images of wounding relate in various ways to what anthropologists have come to call "wound culture" (Solomon 2022b); they tie into understandings of wounding and injury, breach and repair in the lives of human beings and other forms of life, and resonate with the interests of scholars, artists, and journalists into the causes and consequences of injury and suffering in the world.[20] (Significantly, "wound culture" is also a medical term, denoting a test that looks for bacteria or other organisms in a wound.) With this, wounds and their imageries are often grasped and perceived as being part of broader, interconnected fields of semiotic significance and affective force, alongside related phenomena of pain, injury, assault, violence, disability, violence, trauma, breach, repair, and healing.
- In the contemporary world, the swift and fluid vehicles of photographs, video, and other visual media enable wounds to "travel" (Dewachi 2015) across different social worlds in quick and extensive ways.[21] These imagistic journeys often occur beyond the awareness and specific life circumstances of the immediate subjects and agents of those wounds. Wounds marked on an individual body are both distinct from, and related to, any visual representations of such wounds. Marks of wounding can transfer quickly from singular bodies to photographic images and

then jump from specific lifeworlds to a global public scene. During times of war and conflict, images of wounding, trauma, and death appear frequently and repetitively through the visuals of the news, like the sudden force of flashback memories. Quite often there appears to be an uncommon hunger and call for such images. An observation made by Susan Sontag in the early 2000s, during a keening time of war and ethnic conflicts, holds true decades later: "It seems that the appetite for pictures showing bodies in pain is as keen, almost, as the desire for ones that show bodies naked" (Sontag 2003, 40). The algorithmic computations of certain social media devices and "news feeds" now have the capacity to transmit specific imageries of wounding to select audiences, with the images that interest them most (such as injured children) appearing at the top of their media feeds. With this algorithmic amplification of wounding, interested viewers get more of what they have been looking for, with delicate images held in the palms of their hands. The acute recurrence of such images can get to be too much, calling at times for the need to look away.

- Images of wounding involve an ever-shifting number of effects and purposes: possibly, here or there, distress, sympathetic regard, witnessing, spectacular displays of suffering, curiosity or voyeuristic intrigue, political mobilization and resistance, scholarly analysis and creative insight, imaginative wandering, connection, denial, contestation, erasure. Images of wounding can constitute a political strategy. They can vividly show the wounds inflicted on a person or a collective of people, calling for a response. Images of wounding also carry the potential to rewound.

- The nature and affective force of wound images can change through time. A photographic image that is, at one time, quite raw and painful can gradually turn into something less acute, less directly painful, as with photographs of violence that eventually become historical documents of past warfare and political terror. Yet these same smoothed-over images can suddenly become painful and wounding once again if they are considered closely and the earlier wounding interrogated anew. To draw from biological motifs, it's as if a scab or a scar covering over a former wound is ripped open, exposing the flesh to a newly rendered wound. While some persons and collectives might want the wounds to heal fully, others might strive to keep the wounds freshly exposed.

- Photographs of wounding unsettle. They disrupt form, make thoughts flinch. They seed their way into dreams and imaginings and hold the potential to upend political orders. Some uses of wounds and images cause further pain. Some acts of writing respond to images of wounding as though they are trying to suture a wound. Certain hypotheses on photography and wounding might appear like so many stiches tying together a deep cut—writing wounds and writing sutures in crisscrossing lines of inscription.

- Such considerations call for an abiding, open-ended responsibility in the use and regard of images of wounding. One needs to take care when it comes to circulating, showing, or analyzing such images. Recurrent is the question of how this call might be listened to, answered, heeded, if at all.

Let's keep these hypotheses unresolved for now. Let's let their affective and imaginal intensities linger in the air, unsettled, as is the case with many images of wounding, as we turn to the photographs produced by Kagan from the night of 17 October 1961.

What is involved when one thinks and feels and writes within a modality of wounding, of witnessing and analyzing the wounds of others, falling wounded and potentially wounding others through acts of writing, imaging—to know life through wounding?

In giving thought to the wounds of that night and the damages of colonialism in France, Algeria, and elsewhere, I cannot but feel that I am pressing into the sore of a wound, causing hurt there or elsewhere. I write from within and upon such wounds. I do not wish to wound further, yet I show through wounding.

Encounters in Paris

A lifelong resident of Paris, Élie Kagan was known for his tempestuous nature and political outbursts: "In 1948 he achieved a certain fame when he threw contraceptives at the Communist leader Maurice Thoren. . . . But he already had the reputation of being difficult, insulting German tourists, picking quarrels, disagreeing violently with editors who published articles that he disliked. He had a formidable presence, with red hair and a bristly beard and it is not surprising that some of his colleagues were frightened of him" (Johnson 1999). Kagan was also known for his varied photographic work, most notably the photographs he took the night of 17 October 1961. In many respects, this one night's work came to define his career as a photographer.

Early that evening, Kagan took a set of photographs in Métro stations lodged in the center of Paris. He then moved on to the western edge of Paris, where he took a number of photographs near Pont de Neuilly, a bridge that spans the Seine. He then took another set of photographs in Nanterre, a commune just west of Paris. In the years since then, Kagan told the story of his travails that night, and this on several occasions, through the media of speech, text, and film.[22]

I would like to trace out the details of Kagan's photographic work that night, for the efforts and encounters involved speak in important ways to the moral, affective, and epistemic dimensions of the photographic images that came from that night and, relatedly, to the significance and history of the photographs since then. In regrafting Kagan's efforts, I draw primarily from the account that appears in a book coauthored by Kagan and Jean-Luc Einaudi, with Einaudi as first author. Titled *17 Octobre 1961*, this slim volume vested with Einaudi's prose and Kagan's photographs was published in 2001, two years after Kagan died. There is a posthumous tone to the published work, at least in terms of Kagan's role and authorship and with Einaudi surviving Kagan: a twinned act of coauthorship and homage, with the surviving first author signing in place of the second. In considering this book, I work with the texts and photographs involved nearly as though they were archival materials, in which understandings might be gleaned from certain nuances and telling details.

When it comes to Kagan's narration of his engagements through the night of 17 October 1961, his appearances in language, thought, and perception are cast in the third-person ("Élie Kagan monte sur son scooter Vespa " [Élie Kagan gets on his Vespa scooter]), while Einaudi writes in the first person ("J'ai connu Élie en 1980" [I met Élie in 1980]). One gets the sense that Kagan spoke directly with Einaudi about his photographic work that night, and the photographer might have read through a draft version of the manuscript, while his words, as inscribed in the book, take on a testimonial, third-person voice beyond the immediate consciousness of the narrator. The once-voiced "I" of the speaker and photographer was there until the grammar of that particular life death shifted over into the necessity of a third-person voice, the "he" of the published narrative. This has the effect of positioning Einaudi as scribe and medium for the postlife survivance of Kagan's words and images.

It's important to note that Kagan's narrative recollections of that night have been promoted as an eyewitness testimonial account of the state-sanctioned violence that took place then. Einaudi, for one, contributed to the understanding that Kagan was a principal witness of the events. "Élie Kagan, le témoin," runs the title of the first section of the coauthored book, *17 Octobre 1961*: "Élie Kagan, the witness" (Einaudi and Kagan 2001, 7). A significant performative-rhetorical dimension underwrites the book and Kagan's photographs and narratives combined, the import being that what Kagan encountered, saw, and photographed—and recounted, years later—was accurate, true, and politically and morally significant, and held lasting significance in later reckonings of the events of 17 October 1961. This potent rhetoric of perception and testimony runs through Kagan's narratives and many representations of his photographs. We need to engage with Kagan's words and images with the slant of this rhetoric in mind. We need to stay aware of its potential effects and implications.

In reading Kagan's account, we are soon brought into a rhetorically designed immediacy of perception. Our perceptions come to be grafted onto the photographer's perceptions, as grasped through the prism of a co-inscribed text. We begin, as Kagan himself began that night, close to his home in the 10th arrondissement, then largely composed of ethnically diverse working-class neighborhoods. In translation: "In the early evening, on Boulevard Bonne-Nouvelle, Élie Kagan first notices that people are starting to look alike; 'A population brown, unusual,' he says to himself. He immediately understands that the demonstration of the Algerians is being prepared."[23]

The grammar of the narration, set in the present tense—"Kagan first notices ... he says to himself ... he immediately understands"—contributes to what might be called the "immediacy effect" of the words and perceptions conveyed through this narrative. The effect of this apparent immediacy is similar to the ways in which a photograph can convey the sense of an immediate, one-time, now-past presence, as pictured in a photographed moment. And yet, like Kagan's narratives, the impression of photographic immediacy is a deeply constructed one. The narration by Kagan/Einaudi entails a discourse of immediate, first-person presence through the prismatic lens of conjoined, embodied eyewitnessing and photographic visuality.

By some accounts, Kagan and "other leftists" were tipped off by the FF-FLN leadership about the planned demonstrations, with the idea that they could help record what was to take place.[24] Whether or not he knew of the plans for the demonstrations ahead of time, Kagan saw that something was taking form in the city that Tuesday evening. The appearance of people who looked different from most residents of central Paris was, for Kagan, noticeable. Women and men from Algeria had apparently entered the social and political space of central Paris and were preparing to demonstrate en masse, to make known their presence and concerns. While the sentences quoted here are not really a beginning, these words mark the start of a seemingly smooth but jolted narrative, one founded on a patchwork of images, memories, discourses and counter-discourses, intersecting strands of life deaths—shards of perception, rife with charged intensities.

> But just then, the police start to bludgeon [*matraquer*] on the boulevard. He [Kagan] sees some Algerian men seeking refuge inside a small arcade of slot machines and pinball machines: Police chase them and club them. Algerian women try to protect themselves in the entrance to the communist daily newspaper *L'Humanité*, whose iron curtain is immediately lowered before them to stop them. His disgust will remain indelible in the face of this hostile gesture toward men in danger and he will never miss an opportunity to remember this in the future. (Einaudi and Kagan 2001, 12)

Kagan had clear, "indelible" memories of how people acted, or did not act, in response to the violence and dangers perceived. He was marked by this.

The Einaudi-Kagan narrative continues:

> Elsewhere, right now, in Paris and in the suburbs, the same violence is becoming widespread. Many police officers have promised to take the opportunity to "settle their scores," "*bouffer du bougnoule*" [fight some Blacks/Arabs]. They know that their bosses will protect them. They will be able to indulge in a great bloody release that will allow them to vent their dissatisfaction, as has so often been the case in Algeria in the last few years. The manhunt is open, with racial hatred as motivation. As will be said a few days later, when Deputy Eugene Claudius-Petit addresses Minister of the Interior Roger Frey: "Happy are the blond Kabyle who could escape from the police networks!" The hatred is made all the greater by the fact that fake news circulates on the police radio waves, according to which Algerians have killed police officers. Nothing will be done to contradict this. (Einaudi and Kagan 2001, 12–13)

There is more than Kagan's voice here. Einaudi is adding on to the photographer's perceptions with layered optics and observations of his own, as well as those of others. A single testimony contains many voices, points toward many listeners. The "manhunt" (*la chasse à l'homme*) had started, the signal given for police violence in hatred. Revenge beatings and killings. Bloody release, as with the war in Algeria, long scar line of colonial violence. Violence recurs in time, repeats its motifs, circles back, scars. Those in Paris that day were distinguished by physical characteristics. Violent perceptions and actions worked through visual, racial codes. Those perceived as bearing darker skin tones risked being beaten or killed. False reports rippled through the police radio communiqués, with unfounded dispatches of Algerians assaulting police officers, damning the demonstrators to a violent end. Someone in the police force could have tried to put a stop to the rumors and transmissions, but no one did.

> Élie Kagan rides his Vespa scooter and goes to Place de la Concorde. The Ministère de la Marine [Ministry of the Navy] is then under repair, and while he is circulating the *place*, he sees Algerians who are tackled, hands on the wall, against the fences of the building site: the police are clubbing, clubbing, clubbing. . . . He stops his Vespa to take the Métro. There he sees police everywhere, armed with machine guns. He is afraid to take photos and hides his camera because he is aware that if he is caught he will be beaten and his film taken. . . . The prefecture of the police does not want images. (Einaudi and Kagan 2001, 13)

With the use of his Vespa, Kagan was physically and visually mobile—darting from place to place, glimpsing aspects of the state-sanctioned violence. He and others sought to render visible that violence through a lasting visual technology. The police, in turn, demanded invisibility. They did not want any trace-images circulating of the violence inflicted on Algerian protestors. To take photographs of the violent actions or their effects was to risk rendering violence onto one-self. From this ensued a severe game of visibility and invisibility, image and dissimulation.

Kagan entered the Concorde Métro station and descended the stairs to a platform where trains pass and stop. Standing on the quay were a number of Algerian men, penned in by police officers holding machine guns. Place de la Concorde, arguably in the symbolic center of Paris, is named in reference to peace and harmony. Kagan perceived the irony of people getting beaten, arrested, and harassed at gunpoint at this site of peace and accord. Then again, during the French Revolution, the *place*, known then as Place de la Révolution, was the site of many notable public executions, including the executions by guillotine of King Louis XVI and Marie Antoinette, in 1795. Within these palimpsestic tracts of history and violence, Kagan moved about like a documentary photographer, picturing scenes, images, signs, and portents.

> He then decides to take his first photo. To do this, he climbs aboard the Métro train, which passes, goes to the next station, changes, and returns to Concorde. His camera is under his jacket. When the Métro train stops, he is right in front of the rounded-up Algerians while hurried travelers jostle past him. He has time to take two or three photos and leaves

FIGURE 1.2. Concorde Métro station, Paris, 17 October 1961. Photo by Élie Kagan. LC_KAG_00001N_A01 © Élie Kagan "Collection La Contemporaine."

without being spotted by the police. He will not see the outburst of police violence in the corridors of the Concorde Métro. (Einaudi and Kagan 2001, 13–14)

One of the pictures Kagan took at that moment, while photographing from the open door of the Métro car—the doors functioning like a camera shutter, opening and closing—shows a number of men standing with their hands held against the wall, confined and surveilled by the police (figure 1.2). These men were probably taken to detention centers set up in Paris and kept there for several days, with many of those detained then sent by plane to Algeria. A sign with the name of the Métro station is inscribed in fixed tiles above them. Beneath that sign is an advertisement for the dish soap Rex, which, as Hannah Feldman (2014, 197) contends in her 2014 work *From a Nation Torn*, "seems almost deliberately placed to allude both to the whitewashing vision that needs (still) to keep the Algerians out of the public view and—with the advantage of hindsight—to the disastrous events taking place almost simultaneously underneath the marquis of the Rex theatre [cinema]." Subterranean signs and perceptions were laden with moral and political significance, deep histories of conflict.

Another reading of this photograph, along with other photos taken that night, points to the possibility of a political, spectacular presence of Algerians in the heart of Paris—and thus a signal of a postcolonial turn in the histories of Europe and North Africa. Feldman writes of this image, "While it is usually reproduced as a stand-alone image, if we view it in the durational context of its production, and so endow the still photograph with something of the sustained visibility of film, we put ourselves in the position of beginning to witness these subjects' investments in the tactics of a simultaneously spatial and spectacular demonstration" (H. Feldman 2014, 196). This image and others like it depict not just suffering; they evidence political agency, "agential Algerians" (193). As Feldman interprets the significance of this event, "the Kagan photographs stand as proof of a subaltern appropriation of the reins of representation through the mechanical prosthesis of the camera. This, I propose, is true of all of the photographs of the demonstration of 17 October 1961, and part of why we must attend to the emphasis that the French term *manifestation* places on the aspects of producing and making manifest, real, and concrete, even when such realities can only be witnessed in the temporal duration provided by the image they produce" (193). Feldman argues that these collective political efforts worked to introduce a postcolonial sensibility and politics in the French nation and beyond.

> Conforming with the nature of the mandate inherent in Fanon's urging colonial subjects to overturn and so decolonize these lamentable urban conditions, the Algerians' eruption into Paris marked the true arrival of the French nation to the conditions of postcoloniality, insofar as this is generally demarcated by the struggle between a re-emerging, formerly colonized culture and the legacy of the colonial authority, developed in and through the vestigial apparatuses of colonial power such as, in this instance, urban form. This was precisely the struggle in which the demonstrating Algerians participated, inscribing their refusal of the colony across the very heart of the colonial empire and thus imaging for history and the métropole the colonial dynamics that de Gaulle's administration had obliterated, both from memory and from public view. (193)

The photographs taken by Kagan in the Concorde Métro station signaled both suffering under political oppression and the advent of political contestation and transformation within germinative conditions of postcoloniality, of a time, history, and collective political consciousness beyond the harsh conditions of colonialism proper.

Einaudi and Kagan (2001, 14):

He [Kagan] goes to the Solférino Métro. The police are charging. He sees a young man—who remains anonymous, though he will know that he is a PSU [Parti Socialiste Unifié] activist—who has bought a booklet of Métro tickets, and distributes them as the Algerians arrive, fleeing the police. It will be one of the few rare gestures of solidarity he will witness. He photographs the young man. Arriving at the platform, he sees a man on a bench, who had been shot in the shoulder. He photographs him.

Kagan took a Métro train two stops south, to the Solférino station. While in the corridors there he saw a man, who went unnamed, going out of his way to distribute Métro tickets to several persons trying to flee the police. Presumably these men and women, afraid and fatigued, some of them wounded, would try to return to their home neighborhoods, most of which were located in the banlieues outside of Paris. The young man's sympathetic gesture stood out, for it was one of the few kind and supportive acts that Kagan saw residents of Paris undertake that night. Marking the distinction, Kagan photographed this man as he was talking with a man seated on a bench, with blood streaming down his head (figure 1.3). Kagan also photographed men helping this man leave the Métro station (figure 1.4). He photographed another man as well, who reportedly had been shot in the shoulder. The resulting photograph shows the man leaning against a bench, grimacing in pain, his right hand held to the shoulder (figure 1.5).

Kagan was moving like a camera then, with body, eye, and lens combining to focus on images of pain and violence.

When he [Kagan] comes back out of the Métro, the police charge up Rue de Lille. They hit, hit, hit. He is very afraid. He enters a urinal to hide. He sees helmeted police officers passing by. He fears that one of them will in turn enter the urinal and discover him. He is so afraid that, to cool off, he puts his head in the water that runs down the wall. Once they've all passed, he hears one shouting, "No, not by there, by there!" And they go past again. (Einaudi and Kagan 2001, 14–15)

Kagan feared being seen, singled out. There was a recursive biopolitical backdrop to his fear and his nervous actions in hiding, beyond reach of the police. During the German occupation of France during World War II, Kagan and his family had to hide their Jewish heritages and identities from the Nazi regime. In 1942, when he was fourteen, Kagan's parents secretly sent him to a small town in France, to escape detection and wait out the war there—as was the case with other *enfants cachés*, "hidden children," in France at the time. For Kagan and others, that October night in 1961 held nervous reverberations

FIGURE 1.3. Solférino Métro station, Paris, 17 October 1961. Photo by Élie Kagan. LC_KAG_00002_N_A01 © Élie Kagan "Collection La Contemporaine."

of interconnected histories of violence, racial discrimination, and powerful arrangements in life death. One fearful memory graphed upon another. One tract of violence recalled another.

Kagan rode his Vespa scooter to the Pont de Neuilly, which crosses the Seine on the far western side of Paris.

At the Pont de Neuilly, Élie Kagan sees buses, driven by RATP [Régie Autonome des Transports Parisiens] employees. As the police vans no longer sufficed for roundups, the prefect of police requisitioned RATP buses

FIGURE 1.4. Solférino Métro station, Paris, 17 October 1961. Photo by Élie Kagan.
LC_KAG_00002_N_A04 © Élie Kagan "Collection La Contemporaine."

with their drivers. None of the drivers refused to obey this requisition. As the police bring back Algerians, they are brought up there, hands on their heads. He photographs. He sees police officers who signal to him from afar. "That's it," he said to himself, "I'm done. They're going to search me." Discreetly, he gets rid of his film by throwing it on the *quai* [platform by the river] below. The police search him, look for the film, but do not find it. He recovers it from the *quai*. He hears that there were gunshots in Nanterre, gets on his Vespa, and heads that way. (Einaudi and Kagan 2001, 17)

FIGURE 1.5. Solférino Métro station, Paris, 17 October 1961. Photo by Élie Kagan. LC_FDKAG_1688T_000095 © Élie Kagan "Collection La Contemporaine."

The Pont de Neuilly, which crosses the Seine on the western edge of Paris, was one of the main sites of clashes between the demonstrators and Paris police officers that night. The demonstrators, numbering in the thousands, who had gathered in Nanterre, Colombes, and other communes to the west of the Seine, had walked toward the bridge, with the idea of proceeding toward the center of Paris. Just near the bridge they were stopped by police officers, who shot at the approaching crowds of men, women, and children. A number of people were reportedly killed; others were thrown into the Seine. Hundreds of men were detained and taken by bus to makeshift detention centers set up in sports and public arenas in the city. Many of the buses were used by the RATP for regular transport in the city. They were requisitioned that night by the prefecture of the police for transporting the arrested demonstrators. As Kagan tells it, no drivers refused to obey this requisition. While observing that scene Kagan took more photographs. He then hid his film by tossing it onto the platform below the bridge. He was able to recover it after getting away from the police officers who searched him. The photographic film, later developed, contained faint images of men waiting on the buses, their hands held to the backs of their heads.

Yet Kagan's first set of photographs from that night—from the first rolls of film loaded into the camera and then hid from the police—are not our only or primary concern here. The graph-traces of other life deaths soon came into focus. As for the photographs he took later that evening, we cross the Seine and travel to Nanterre, as Kagan did the night of 17 October, after recovering the film stashed below Pont de Neuilly.

In the jaws of the wolf. "Dans la gueule du loup," a poem by Algerian poet, writer, and playwright Kateb Yacine, first published in June 1962, speaks directly to the people of France:

People of France, you [*tu*] saw it all
Saw it all with your own eyes
You saw our blood flow
You saw the police
Beat the protestors
And throw them into the Seine.
The reddening Seine

. . . . . .

And now will you speak?
And now will you be silent?[25]

In this searing critical voice of a poem Yacine states with uncommon clarity that the people of France witnessed and knew about the massacre of 17 October 1961. He asks if the French people—addressed as "tu," the informal "you"—will now speak of these violent events or remain silent. Many kept silent.

Years later, Yacine authored a reflection on the ways in which the poem took form for him. He wrote that, in the days after 17 October 1961, the newspapers were full of "ces images insoutenables," unbearable images that led to the formation of the poem. One subsequent reading of the poem is that the FLN threw its rank-and-file members "into the jaws of the wolf," the carnivorous powers of the French state and police force (Yacine 1990).[26]

The Photographs from Nanterre

The ten photographs that Kagan took in Nanterre the night of 17 October 1961 suggest a filmic sequence (figures 1.6–1.15). The images lead to a photo series that tells an elliptical story of suffering and care, wounding and exposure. In choppy seriation the photographs move from injury to potential repair, and (in hindsight) from life toward imminent death. Within a shifting balance between forces of life and death, the potential damage from the assault intensifies or diminishes with each image-moment. Each of the photographs has a charge to it, a visceral thrust that jostles perception. The voltage charge is different with each photograph. Shifts in consciousness, perception, and relationality are obliquely apparent. Each image fills one's sight with pain. This is a series in intensive wounding, a stark tableau of colonial struggle.

Gaps and displacements mark the syncopated flow of Kagan's photographs. "The photographic take is immediate and definitive," writes Christian Metz (1985, 84). "Photography is a cut inside the referent, it cuts off a piece of it, a fragment, a part object, for a long immobile travel of no return." Kagan's photographs of Bennahar, which have traveled far, are cut from particular moments in time. Silences and unphotographed moments are absent in the intervals in between the photographs. Any words exchanged during the movement implied are lost; much goes unheard, unseen. The approach of the men with their vulnerable charge toward the entrance of the hospital is evident, but not what happened once Bennahar was inside the hospital or what, if any, medical treatment was provided for him. It's unclear what took place in the time and space between the photographic images or before or after them. The photographs do not show beyond their apparent showing.

The persistently worrying complication: that the photographs make violence inescapably visible, but they use a wounded person to do so. There is always the danger, the risk, of aestheticizing images of violence, at any moment.

"These are devastating," said an interlocutor upon seeing the images for the first time. "Yes, they are," I said in response. I'm ambivalent about using them. I don't want them to cause further wounding. "How could they not?" A piercing ambivalence jags this work, troubles each sentence. Don't shy away from the ambivalence. Sear into its fissures.

While working on this book I gave thought to not including the photographs and instead only describing key aspects of the images when need be. If any readers wanted to see the photos, I reasoned, they could find them online. But this would make for an awkward way to refer to the pictures. And even if I refrained from placing the photographs in the text in a direct way, the images are still there, in the world at large; they recur in unsettled, apparitional ways. In the end, I decided to include prints of the photographs in this book. The visual details and visceral force of the images are important to grasp directly in relation to the violence preceding and following the photographs taken by Kagan that night.

The Wounded Man

From the opening act of Kateb Yacine's 1954 play, Le cadavre encerclé, which establishes an intense scene: "Casbah, beyond the Roman ruins. At the end of the street, a merchant crouched in front of his empty cart. A cul-de-sac leading to the street in a right angle. Heap of cadavers overflowing the wall. Arms and heads desperately move about. Some injured people come to die in the street. At the corner of the cul-de-sac and the street, a light is projected on the cadavers which express themselves first of all by a plaintive murmur which is personified little by little and becomes voice, the voice of wounded Lakhdar" (Yacine 1959, 17).

It's likely that Yacine, in writing such a phantasmagoria of heaped cadavers and dying forms and the voice of a wounded man emerging from a dense aftermath of violence, was drawing from scenes he had observed within the actualities of life and phantasmatics of violence that marked the French colonial occupation of Algeria, during the 1945 massacre at Sétif and other towns as well as before and after that terrible violence.

Here, too, one senses a plaintive murmur, diffuse and spectral, the voice of a wounded man emerging from a street-side scene of death and injury, beneath an overflowing wall.

Years later, Kagan related that when he arrived in Nanterre around 10 p.m. that night he heard bursts of gunfire. He rode his Vespa to Rue des Pâquerettes, near the bidonvilles of Petit-Nanterre and La Folie, and then hid the scooter off to the side of the road. He encountered no demonstrators but

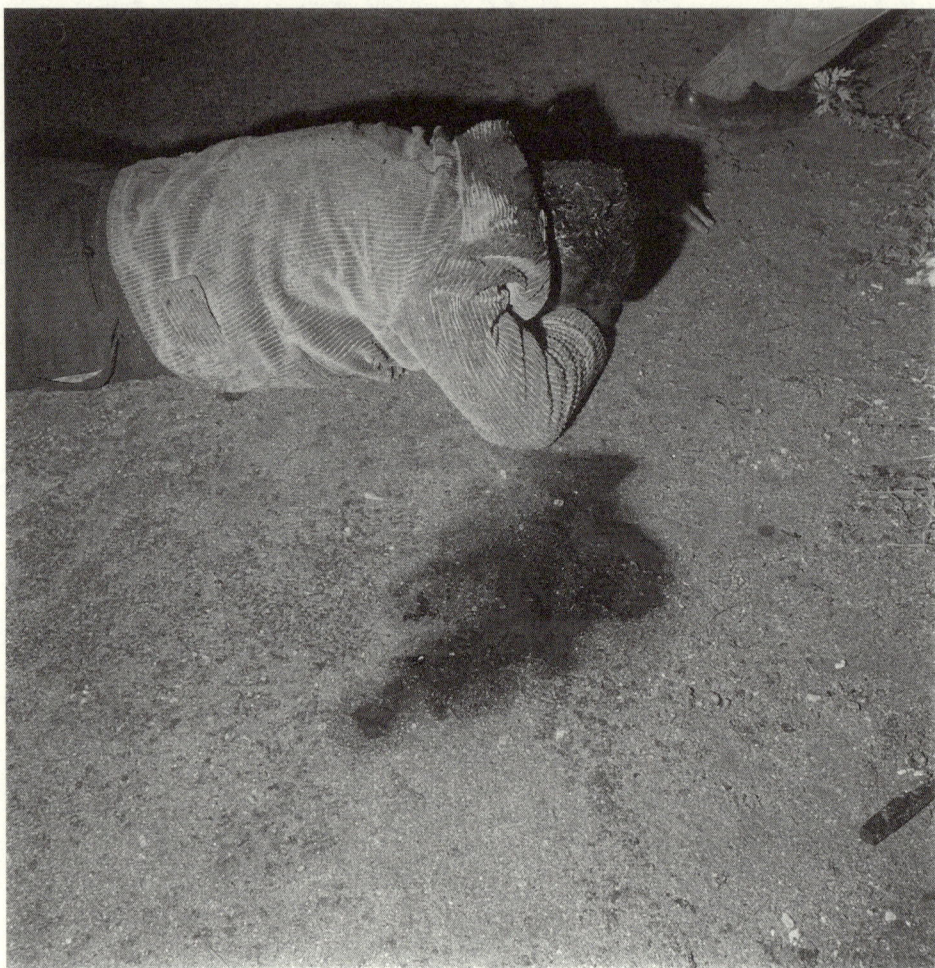

FIGURE 1.6. Rue des Pâquerettes, Nanterre, 17 October 1961 [Abdelkader Bennahar]. Photo by Élie Kagan. LC_KAG_00004N_B01 © Élie Kagan "Collection La Contemporaine."

rather wounded men. He heard moaning. He saw a man draped over a low wall made of stone and mortar, as if he had been trying to cross over this obstacle to escape his pursuers. He was dead. Just before this man lay another who was badly wounded, his face toward the ground. Others were apparently dead, further away.[27]

Kagan used his Semflex 6 × 6 camera and an electronic flash to photograph the closest two men. He went on to take another six or seven photographs of the man who was wounded, and then later (perhaps that night, or the next day)

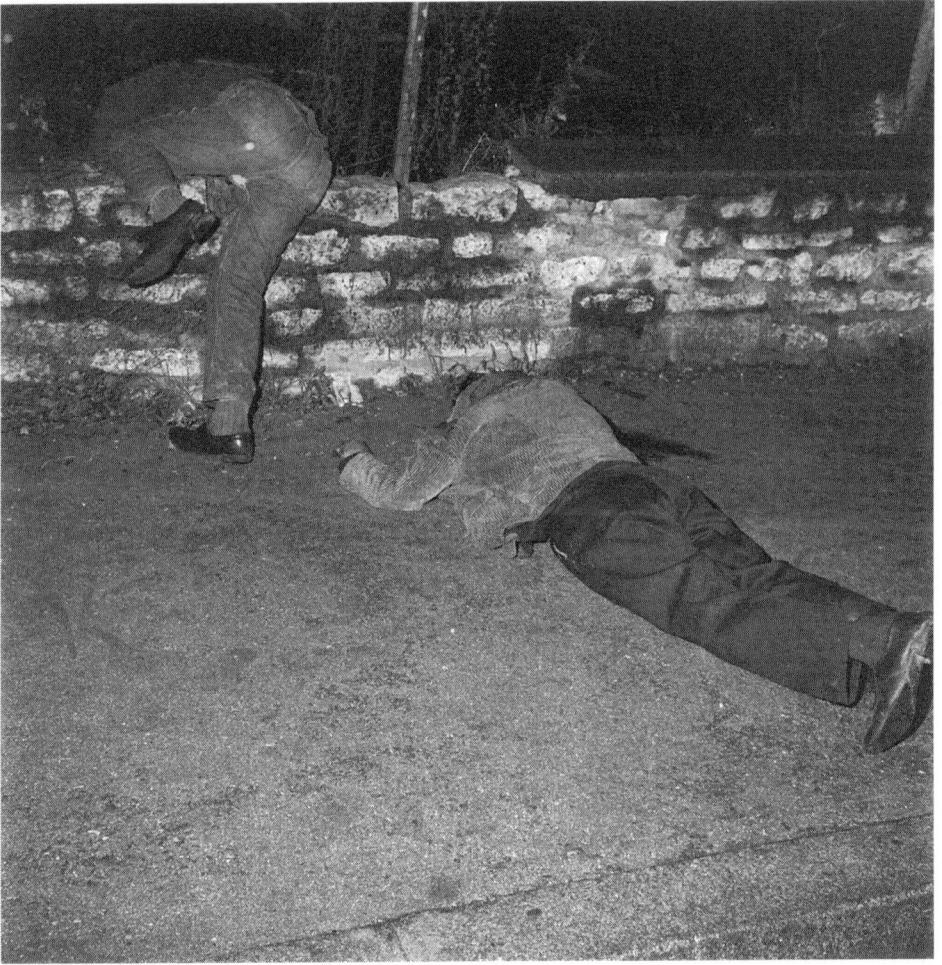

FIGURE 1.7. Rue des Pâquerettes, Nanterre, 17 October 1961 [Abdelkader Benna-har]. Photo by Élie Kagan. LC_KAG_00004N_B02 © Élie Kagan "Collection La Contemporaine."

developed the photographic negatives. This photographic sequence, twelve or thirteen pictures in all, entails a "suite of images" (H. Feldman 2014, 193) that speak of violence, wounding, possible life and death, care and racism, and the politics of visibility and erasure.[28]

It's significant that this is a sequence of photographs, rather than just one or two distinct photographs. "The movement-sequence must be elliptical, in-termittent," writes Raymond Bellour (2012, 114–15) of the art of photographic sequences, "in other words marking phrases that generate massive spaces into

FIGURE 1.8. Rue des Pâquerettes, Nanterre, 17 October 1961 [Abdelkader Benna-har]. Photo by Élie Kagan. LC_KAG_00004N_B03 © Élie Kagan "Collection La Contemporaine."

which the imagination may penetrate and start functioning, in relation to both a before and an after." The sequence of ten photographs that emerged from Kagan's efforts in Nanterre carries much the same qualities, even if the movement-sequence at hand is more the product of documentary journalism than a crafted work of art. This sequence, which tells a minimal but potent story, phantasmally charged, rich with connotations and aftereffects, is inde-terminate and ambiguous. It has unclear beginnings and endings. Throughout the sequence much remains uncertain; much goes unseen and unknown, while

FIGURE 1.9. Rue des Pâquerettes, Nanterre, 17 October 1961 [Abdelkader Benna-har]. Photo by Élie Kagan. LC_KAG_00004N_B04 © Élie Kagan "Collection La Contemporaine."

some elements can be perceived, especially when the photographic images are combined with Kagan's narrative accounts of that night—apparently, he is the only one whose narration of the scene of his photographs on Rue des Pâque-rettes has been recorded. Through a close engagement with the photographs, sifting through words and images, retracing the grains of that night while draw-ing from historiographic and archival impressions, we can piece together a récit of the events and "life in the folds of the images" (Didi-Huberman) through an interpretative montage.[29]

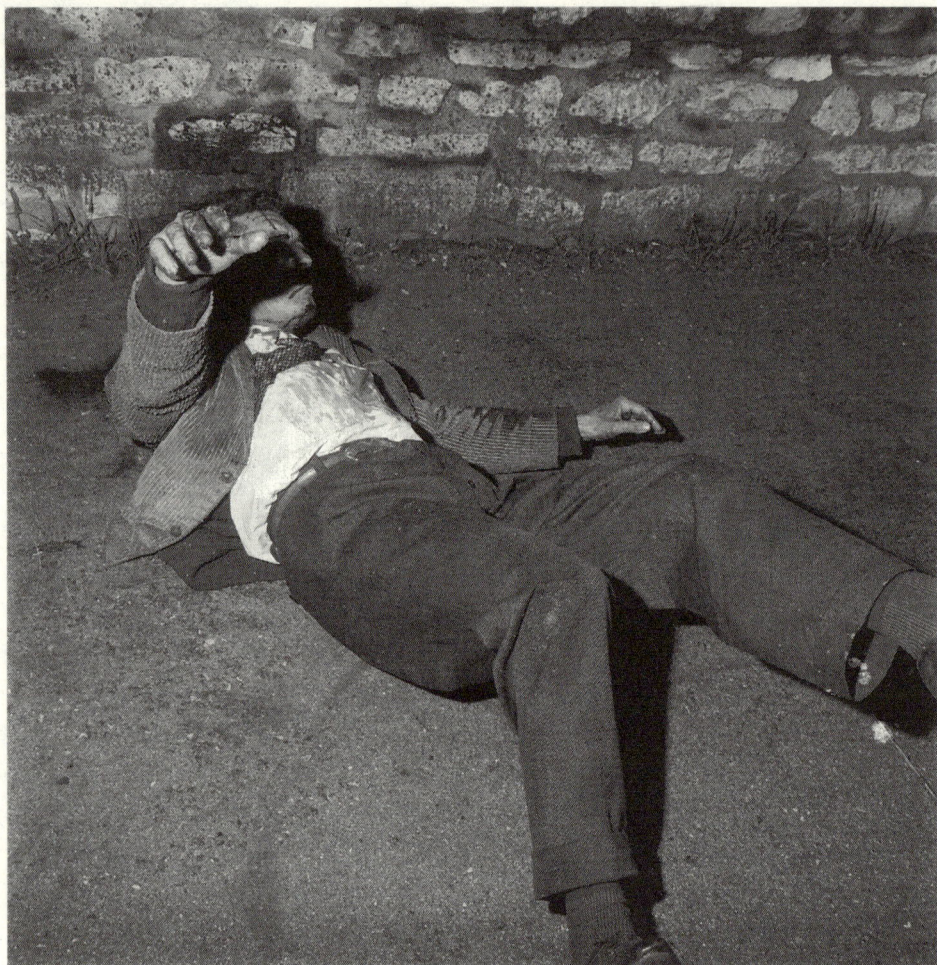

FIGURE 1.10. Rue des Pâquerettes, Nanterre, 17 October 1961 [Abdelkader Benna-har]. Photo by Élie Kagan. LC_KAG_00004N_B05 © Élie Kagan "Collection La Contemporaine."

One of the first photographs that Kagan took in Petit-Nanterre shows a man lying on the ground, close to a dark spot on the ground to his right (figure 1.6).[30] Most likely this was a stain of blood, which possibly came from the man lying nearby. This man has subsequently been identified as Abdelkader Bennahar. The blunt force of a *matraque*, the short heavy stick wielded with deadly effect by Paris police officers, could have caused Bennahar's scalp and skull to crack and spill blood. The blood could have poured from a wound in his head and seeped into the ground, and the man had since turned his body

FIGURE 1.11. Rue des Pâquerettes, Nanterre, 17 October 1961 [Abdelkader Benna-har]. Photo by Élie Kagan. LC_KAG_00004N_B06 © Élie Kagan "Collection La Contemporaine."

away from that patch of ground. The light from the flash of the camera high-lights that dark blood spot in ways that can give a feel of the sinister and a life severely at risk of annihilation.

Two other photographs that Kagan took soon after arriving at Rue des Pâ-querettes show Bennahar lying close to another body (figures 1.7 and 1.8). The man whose body is sloped over the wall had died before Kagan arrived on the scene. It's possible that those who attacked Bennahar presumed that he was also dead and then moved on, for lack of living "opposition."

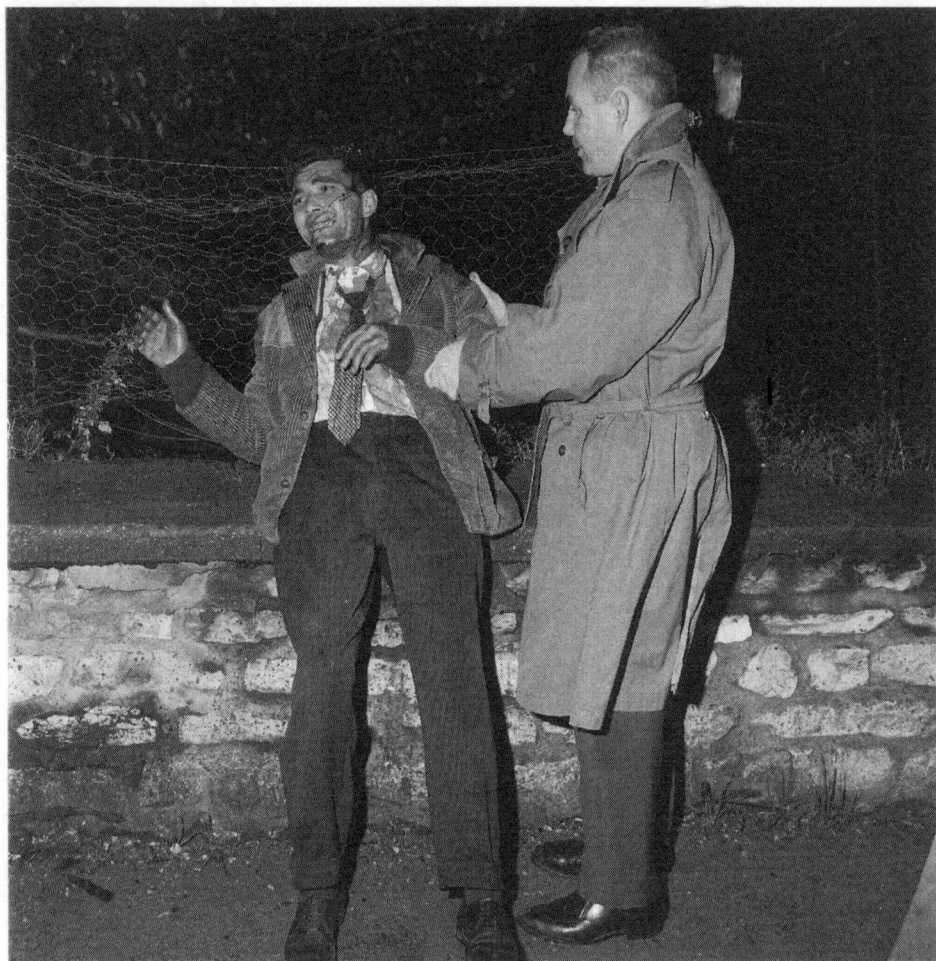

FIGURE I.I2. Rue des Pâquerettes, Nanterre, 17 October 1961 [Abdelkader Bennahar]. Photo by Élie Kagan. LC_KAG_00004N_B07 © Élie Kagan "Collection La Contemporaine."

When I look at the images of the man lying across the wall, I see a body spanning a threshold between life and death, suspended within a movement into death. The man's left leg is raised toward the wall, caught in the act of climbing. The right leg lies tautly still against the ground, as though supporting the body.

If one looks closely at the photograph, one can make out, faintly, what looks like wire-mesh netting, just past the stone wall. The netting might have impeded the man's further movement. Later, it held him gently in death, as

FIGURE 1.13. Hospital of Nanterre, 17 October 1961 [Abdelkader Bennahar]. Photo by Élie Kagan. LC_KAG_00004N_B09 © Élie Kagan "Collection La Contemporaine."

did the photograph, in an altogether different way. (Is a photograph a kind of net?)

It's unclear what lay beyond the netting and the wall in those days. The façade of a building is faintly seen. Beyond that the terrain could have been marked by woods or a field or pasture or guarded property.

The two men apparent in the photograph, lying prone, are cast in a visual field of relationality and doubling, as though giving imaginal form to certain possibilities in life death. Their bodies are set within relations at once sensorial, historical, imaginal.

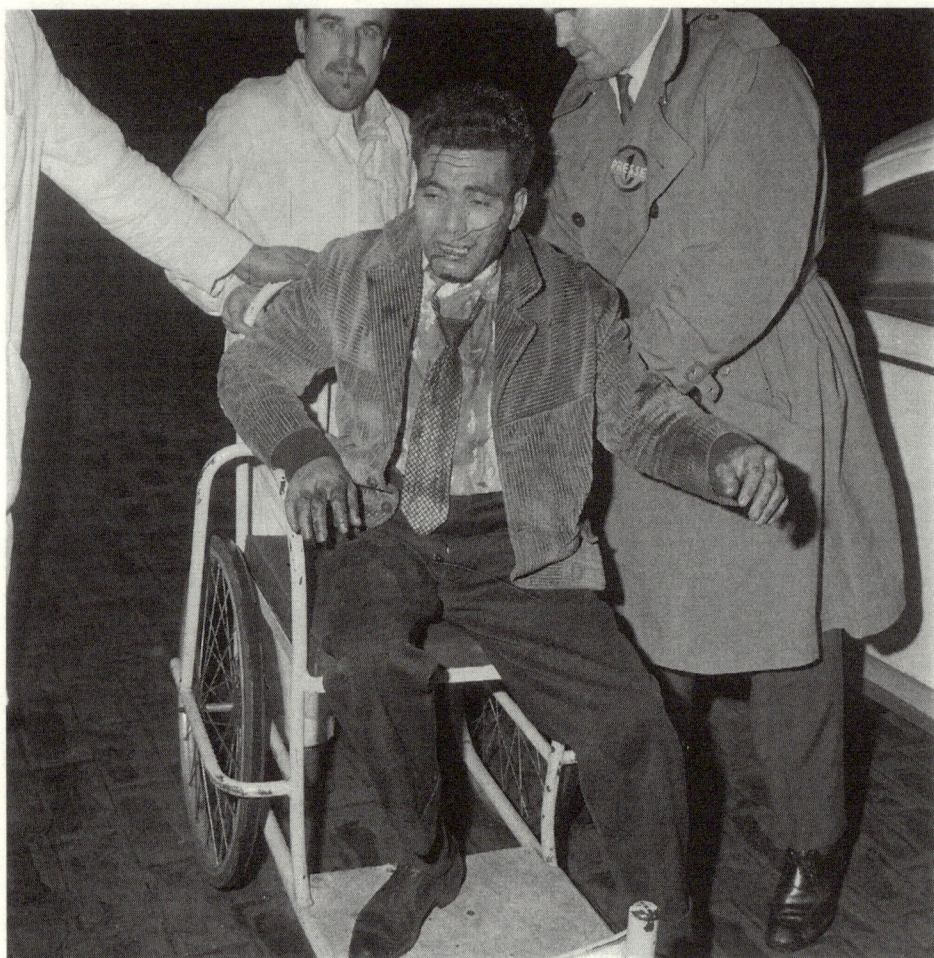

FIGURE 1.14. Hospital of Nanterre, 17 October 1961 [Abdelkader Bennahar]. Photo by Élie Kagan. LC_KAG_00004N_BIO © Élie Kagan "Collection La Contemporaine."

The two men were companions in suffering (to draw from Ahmed Djoughlal's words [Einaudi 1991]). Each man is the double of the other, with the double slightly different from its other, within gradations in life death. One of the men was dead, the other still alive. Their plights could easily have been reversed if the circumstances of violence were slightly different. The body other to Benna-har's sadly foreshadowed his own death. By the next night, Bennahar's body had become like the deceased body of the other man visible in this night scene. The twinned coupling of bodily forms reflects the twinned coupling evident in life

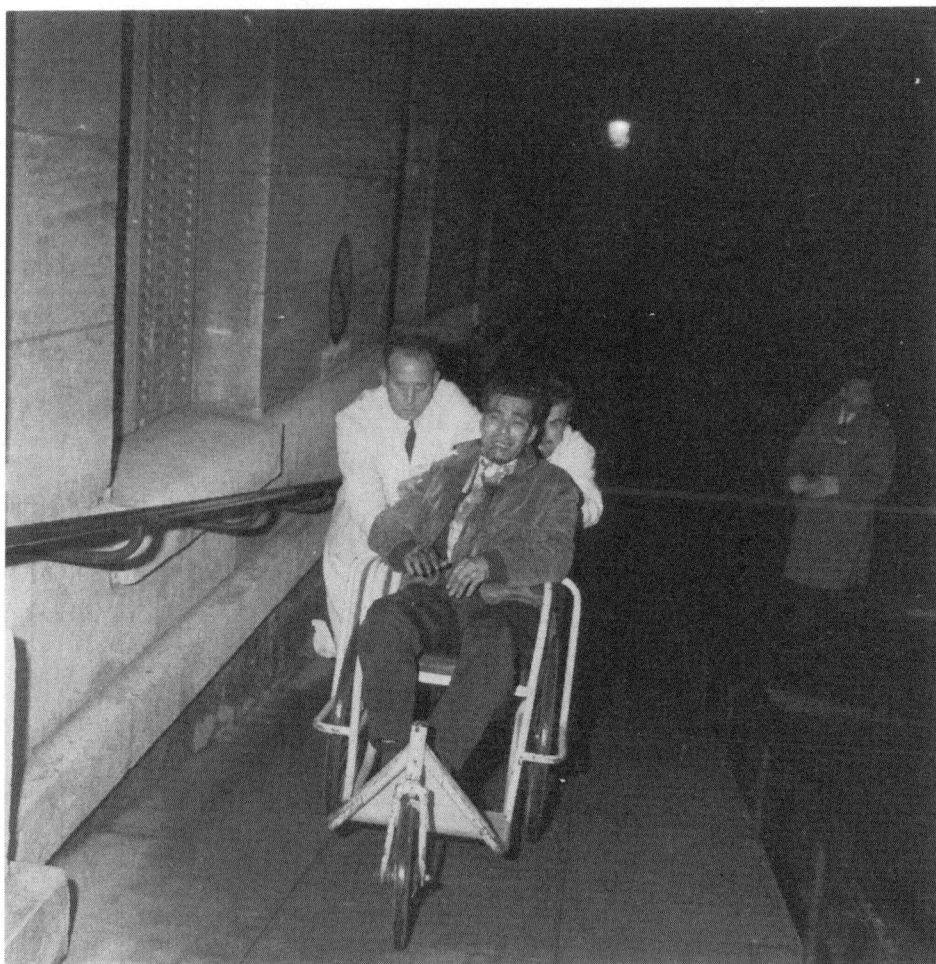

FIGURE 1.15. Hospital of Nanterre, 17 October 1961 [Abdelkader Bennahar]. Photo by Élie Kagan. LC_KAG_00004N_B11 © Élie Kagan "Collection La Contemporaine."

death, in which forces of life and death tie into one another in intricate relations of coupling, doubling, displacements, and supplemental grafting, an intermeshing of light and shadow.

The two bodies suggest a ruptured continuum from life and wounding onto death and beyond. Following this line of wounded life death, I have envisaged another body, a third, phantom body, further past the wall, within a forested space of death. It's difficult to step imaginatively into that stratum of death. There are no distinct images, only obscure potentialities, further elsewhere.

Upon photographing with light flashes, Kagan heard someone say, "Laisse, laisse! Il fait des photos, laisse-le faire!" (Leave him alone, leave him! He's taking photos, let him do it!)

Kagan found that the voice came from a group of Algerians, hidden nearby. These men, unseen by Kagan, were apparently waiting for him to finish his photographic work so that they could help the wounded and recover the dead. They could have stopped the photographer from taking pictures if they had wanted to. Perhaps even then these men, hiding from the rough violence of the police, waiting to recover their dead and wounded, understood the value of photographic evidence of that night's disasters. They let the photographer do his work, anticipating visual traces of violence that would document the police brutality in Nanterre. From the first flashes, then, the photographs emerged out of a complex field of political and perceptual-sensorial relations, with different agents and distributed agencies involved. In effect, the men who were hiding, in giving their tacit consent to the photographs, were coauthors of the subsequent published images.[31]

Kagan later said that he saw three or four dead men in that part of Rue des Pâquerettes. It's unclear why he did not photograph them as well. He was rushed for time. The conditions weren't right, the other corpses did not lend themselves to good photographs. Or he found it in bad taste or an act of religious-moral transgression to photograph their battered corpses. Or he feared the police would soon arrive. The lack of photographs of the other deceased men makes their deaths less tangible, more abstract and anonymous. Vague and spectral, these deaths are less traceable. A photograph of a dead man concretizes that death in powerful ways. It gives a visual and concrete imaginal form to that death. A photograph assigns a vivid corpus to the death, a corpse-image, while unleashing a swirl of fantasies.

Einaudi and Kagan's book *17 Octobre 1961* notes that "the dead that Élie Kagan saw in Nanterre, the one [dead man] he photographed, do not officially exist, nor do dozens of others. But his photo is like a breach [*brèche*], from which the truth can make its way" (Einaudi and Kagan 2001, 19).

The identity of the deceased man went unknown to those who photographed or wrote about the events of 17 October 1961. Others must have recovered his body. Protectors of the dead, they probably would have known his name and his family. Perhaps it was better for the dead man's body to be claimed that way than for it to be shipped off to a police-controlled forensic morgue and then buried in a cemetery managed by the city of Paris.

Within the black-and-white photographs, the petite wall, *le muret*, carries the appearance of staining; emergent mold and fecund growth marked the white-gray facades of stone and mortar.

Kagan took several more photographs of the man lying on the ground, focusing the lens of the camera on him alone. One photograph shows Bennahar lying on his back, his right hand raised slightly, his face now away from ground, facing upward (figure 1.9). Streaks of blood are visible along his forehead. The tie lies across his chest. The light-colored shirt is stained and soiled. There are stains on the ground, below the man's hand, and a dark shadow-stain beneath his head.

Glanced at quickly, perceived out of context, the picture of Bennahar lying on the ground, his arms spread out, could be taken for a crime scene photo. (In some respects, it is.) The hand raised stiffly carries a semblance of rigor mortis. There is a still-life immobility to the photograph, which is nonetheless charged with forces of time and that quality of arrested, seizure-like trembling characteristic of many photographs, as Jean-Christophe Bailly (2020, 27) remarks in reflecting on photographs of instants and their shadows in the aftermath of the atomic bomb dropped on the city of Hiroshima: "Strangely—and just as, without thickness, it still has (can still have) a depth—the image, without duration and fully complete in the instant, still has a tempo, a kind of length or integrated duration, which is condensed. This could be summed up in a formula: immobility is a vibration, an absolute vibration, and it is this trembling in time, this trembling of things in time, that photography enables one to see." The photographs from that October night, like those from that August morning in 1945, emit a trembling of bodies in time.

The photograph in figure 1.9 is the first to show Bennahar's face. With this comes a singularity, the vital life of a single person, on his own. The visual impression of that singularity is enhanced through Kagan's photographic method. In several of the photographs taken at Rue des Pâquerettes, Bennahar is presented lying or standing alone, at a remove from other possible bodies or persons, distinct from other elements of that potential scene. The photographs carry a vivid sense of "the distinct," which Jean-Luc Nancy argues is a crucial feature of an image—something set aside, removed, cut off, much like the sacred is set apart from the mundane world. "The distinct, according to its etymology, is what is separated by marks (the word refers back to *stigma*, a branding mark, a pinprick or puncture, an incision, a tattoo): what is withdrawn and set apart by a line or trait, by being marked also as withdrawn [*retrait*]." As with the sacred, an image distinguishes itself from the world at large because of "the force—the energy, pressure, or intensity" at hand, "the very force of its distinction" (Nancy 2005, 2).

The wincing figure of Bennahar is distinguished through the photographic imagery, much as portraits delineate and draw (out) their subjects. The idea of "drawing (out)" here relates to the fact that the second part of the word *portrait*, in both French and English, stems from the Latin verb *trahere*, "to drag, draw." Nancy (2005, 4) refers to this association in writing that "every image is in some way a 'portrait,' not in that it would reproduce the traits of a person, but that it pulls and *draws* (this is the semantic and etymological sense of the word), in that it *extracts* something, an intimacy, a force. And, to extract it, it subtracts or removes it from homogeneity, it distracts it from it, distinguishes it, detaches it and casts it forth. It throws it in front of us, and this throwing [*jet*], this projection, makes its mark, its very trait and its *stigma*: its tracing, its line, its style, its incision, its scar, its signature, all of this at once."

The photographs of a distressed Bennahar extract the intimate force of those painful moments, the trace drawing of wounds, leading to distinct images that became a signature wounding. The incision of painful wounding is thrown in front of any perceivers of the photographs. These are portraits in pain.

In one photograph, plausibly next in Kagan's sequence, Bennahar is shown having raised his back and shoulders slightly from the ground, with his right arm and hand lifted up from the ground (figure 1.10). That hand obscured his face—incidentally or intentionally—from the sensate visual shock of the camera flash. In a series of body blows the fierce flash succeeds the shock of violence.[32] It's possible the sudden bright flashes from Kagan's camera strobe-shocked Bennahar's body and provoked him to regain a certain vital form and get up from the ground, shifting away from the serious possibility of death.

Those same photographs have kept the image of Bennahar alive for some time. Paradoxically, it's the photographed wounding that keeps the image of him alive. The wound image prevents closure. It disturbs the surcease of the person photographed.

A lifetime later, this photo's imagery of occlusion reflects recurrent aspects of the photographic sequence and its modalities of perception and knowing. We see a man in distress, hand reaching out, yet we can't see his face clearly, we cannot know him well.

An uncommon visceral quality animates these photographs. A sheer corporeality, a pain that sears, transmits into any viewing of the images. In regarding this man's body in pain, I feel the distress, his brutal exhaustion; a body soaks up the bruising in visceral transfer—at least to an extent. I'm not sure I can know well what he felt, what he and others went through on that night and other nights. The pain of others is analogous to and elsewhere to my own.

In moments I imagine that Bennahar is about to say something while he is beginning to leave the interior of the Volkswagen, his look toward the camera caught by the photographer. I imagine such an instance of almost speaking, though I do not know if this imagining ties into any actuality in that long-ago moment. A photograph invites all sorts of conjectures.

I note the name of the man shown in these photographs, Abdelkader Bennahar, and yet there are temporal displacements and linguistic multiplicities crevassed within the fault lines of that naming. One might write, within the same breath of language, "the photograph of an unknown Algerian man" or "the photograph of Abdelkader Bennahar," for the proper name came only later on, if at all, for many. Most of those who have produced and written about these images have not mentioned Bennahar's name. Chances are they did not know it. A proper name for the subject of the photographs is often not noted in contemporary representations of them. In its place stands a phrase like "Kagan's photographs of an Algerian man." The name appeared belatedly, the name, deferred, was inscribed and associated in print with the reproduced photographs much later on, and then only in limited circumstances. Evident is a lacuna between the photographic images as circulating and the identity of the person depicted in those images. Only in certain situations is the image matched with a proper name.

It's unclear who harmed Bennahar that night and killed the other men near where he lay wounded. One distinct possibility is that those involved were members of a police unit that reportedly had moved about the communes just west of Paris the night of 17 October, with the intent of inflicting lethal violence on any Algerians they encountered. Such a unit was part of two *compagnies d'intervention* (also known as *sections spéciales*), which were run by commanders of the six police districts into which Paris was divided. House and MacMaster (2006, 171–72) note of these "companies of intervention":

> The compagnies, similar in kind to the CRS [Compagnies Républicaines de Sécurité] were essentially riot squads held on standby to intervene quickly and, inevitably, their main function was to carry out street operations against Algerians. The units were made up of young, physically tough volunteers who enjoyed "combat duty," and by 1961 the backbone was provided by ex-paratroopers, "a lumpen class, often veterans of Indochina and Korea." . . . The companies became hot-beds of "ultra" activism and of a cult of anti-Algerian violence, and commanders called on these units, armed with riot sticks (*bidules*), whenever they wished to "teach a lesson" to demonstrators, as on 17 October [1961]. . . . It seems likely that officers of compagnies d'intervention, located in police stations in which a culture of violence was entrenched, did take a leading role in inflicting lethal force on Algerians.[33]

Raoul Letard, then a young police officer who operated with a company in the third district during 1960–61, spoke of his experiences with this company in an interview recorded in May 1993. He described the ambience of the unit as "extremely energetic, muscular and particularly restless," and engaged in constant operations "of extreme violence."[34]

Letard recollected that on the night of 17 October 1961, he and the other members of his company went to Colombes, a commune just northeast of Nanterre (close to Petit-Nanterre), and attacked a number of Algerian men they encountered. Letard spoke of a frenzied atmosphere of killing, in which numerous Algerians died at the hands of this company of police officers:

> We were off. . . . We threw ourselves into what we called "a bit of hunting," which took us into an area of house blocks in Colombes. It was already eleven o'clock. . . . The residents who were afraid called out to us. . . . We went up to their apartments to see better, and we shot at everything that moved. . . . It was horrible, horrible. . . . For two hours, it was a real manhunt, terrible, terrible, terrible! . . . Finally, we had to leave, lacking opposition. There was a van that followed us, a police van that was responsible for collecting the demonstrators. In that van there were quite a few dead bodies. But that caused a ruckus because the commander was unhappy that we brought back the corpses. We should have left them there. . . . We were so out of our minds that we had become uncontrollable. The atmosphere was such that if an officer, or the commander, had tried to take us in hand, he would have been mistreated in turn.[35]

Letard was likely recounting the so-called *ratonnades* that reportedly took place in western suburbs the night of 17 October 1961, into the early hours of 18 October, with mobile police units pursuing and killing individuals or small and isolated groups of Algerians.[36]

It's possible that members of Letard's company, or one like it, passed through Petit-Nanterre, killed several men by Rue des Pâquerettes, and beat Bennahar close to the point of death.[37] Perhaps the police officers thought they had killed Bennahar as well, and then moved on. Perhaps these bodies were "left on the spot," to use Letard's phrasing, as the company's police van had already taken in a number of dead bodies and the police commanders did not want to deal with the recovery and reporting of the dead, which ideally would have entailed a set of formal legal and forensic procedures—although it's just as likely that the police would have disposed of any bodies recovered in informal, unrecorded ways (burying bodies in wooded areas, placing them in the Seine, and so on).

Kagan later said that, while taking these photographs, he realized that the police were a few hundred meters away. When he triggered the flash, he heard them shout, "Y a des flashs! Y a des flashs!" ("There are flashes! There are flashes!")

The violence itself remained a nonphotographed moment. The photos that Kagan took near Rue des Pâquerettes present afterimages of violence, trace effects of blows and resulting trauma. As an index of violence, the photographs are like open wounds or lasting scars that point to unseen, off-scene violence. The occurrence of a wound-sign within multiplicities of time brings forth trace histories and phantasmal imaginings. Through time, the wounding recurs, the wounds are multiple. Wounding variably intensifies or diminishes.

"Scar adds something," writes Hélène Cixous (2005, xii) in Stigmata, *"a visible or invisible fibrous tissue that really or allegorically replaces a loss of substance which is therefore not lost but added to, augmentation of memory by a small mnesic growth."[38] Some photographs linger like scars, they add something to an instance in life, the image augments memory or marks a surface like a fibrous tissue. Trace left on skin by a healed wound, burn, puncture—a scar marks the earlier wound that it replaced.*

All photography is scarry.[39] A photograph is the crystallized mark of a photographed instance. In situating photography within a domain of wounding, within the corporeal logic and phantasmatics of wounds, one can say that every analog photograph works on a principle of scarification: particles of light strike a sensitive surface and the impact of that exposure to light and resulting photochemical effects get fixed into lasting marks through a process of photographic development and printing, much as a scar might form where a burn once occurred through a process of cicatrization. A photograph carries the trace-structure of a scar. Suture, skin graft. Scar tissue. Disfiguration or necrosis even. The filmic skin of photography carries the mark of such phenomena, as do many bodies—the enfoldments and graftings of skin and filmic surfaces, doublings and supplements; engraving, re-marking, and graft writing.

Perhaps we can think of a photograph as often involving, like a wound, a transformational process through time, from wound to scab to healing and possible scarring or the eventual diminishment of any trace of an earlier wound. I would wager that certain photographs carry through time a temporality and metamorphic potential similar to the biology of wounding and healing.

The next set of photographs show Bennahar trying to stand, close to the low wall and the netting (figure 1.11). He is hunched over, in pain. Within a complex

vector of intimacy and exposure the sensation of pain radiates as though in-
sular to the man, crumpled within a searing bodyworld of pain, just while his
body and his pain are cast within the exposure of a photograph. An insularity
of pain has extended out into the world. The radiance of this pain reaches us,
years later.

The photograph suggests that Kagan was standing a few feet away from
Bennahar, photographing him in this moment while not aiding or comforting
him in any direct way. He was photographing only, framing his subject well.
Perhaps in these moments Kagan was following a documentary photographer's
creed of pure and untainted documentation, with no alterations of a photographed scene permitted or accepted. Kagan's photographs in these moments
entail acts that involve a tone of optical violence—harsh photographs of a
wounded subject—and a tone of testimonial care, documenting the violence
enacted upon this man.

While Kagan was taking photographs, a Volkswagen automobile arrived
and stopped close to him. A man got out of the car. He wore a press badge on
the front of his raincoat. Kagan later related that this man was an American
journalist. The journalist berated the photographer, saying, "How can you take
photographs of the wounded and the dead while they are suffering?!"

Vexed by this, Kagan shot back, "Tu m'emmerdes. Je fais mon métier."
(You're shitting on me. I'm doing my job.) He then added, "If you're so chari-
table, let's take this one and bring him to the hospital in Nanterre."

The American agreed to this.

The journalist has gone unnamed and unknown. I have since wondered if
he wrote any articles on the police violence that October night, for, say, the
International Tribune or the *New York Times*.

In one photograph, the journalist, tall and sturdy, a postwar physique
garbed in a raincoat free of blemishes, is trying to help the man stand upright
(figure 1.12). Bennahar is leaning back, toward the wall and the netting. The
photograph reflects the two bodies that night, in physical contrast, in mortal, moral linkage. The image also conveys the implicit fact that, in aiding the
wounded man, the journalist acted in ways that Kagan did not.

*I have tried to locate the identity of this man, the one in the overcoat, searching
through any of the journalistic bylines and photographic images of American journalists based in Paris at the time. To date, my searches have been inconclusive,
and he remains an unnamed figure. What did this man recall of that night? Did
he ever write about it? Did he tell the story to friends and family and speak with
intimate others of Kagan's photographs, that night he drove the wounded man to*

the hospital in Nanterre? Did he pass stories of that violent night on to his grand-children while retiring on a green-grass estate sloping into the Long Island Sound?

While those hiding nearby presumably watched, quietly, the American journalist helped Bennahar to sit in the Volkswagen. I gather that Kagan followed the two men on his Vespa as they made their way to the hospital, though that detail has gone unstated. Kagan later recalled that, as the Volkswagen moved away, several Algerian men came to recover the dead.

The bodies were probably buried elsewhere. House and MacMaster (2006, 164) note, "Numerous dead or fatally wounded Algerians were removed from the streets by fellow Algerians, or managed to drag themselves away. . . . Algerians were keen to wrest control of the bodies of loved ones from the much feared and detested French authorities, and ensure burial with full nationalist honours and following Islamic ritual." These authors quote the journalist Camile Gilles, who during a nocturnal visit to a shantytown in Nanterre was taken to a hut by an FLN cadre, "[who] showed me, underneath a blanket, the naked corpse of a North African who had been killed by several bullets to the body. 'You see,' Amar said to me, 'we took our dead as well as our wounded with us. They will be buried with all the honors they deserve.'"[40]

The three men arrived at the grounds of the hospital. Kagan photographed Bennahar while he was seated in the automobile, the right door open, framed by the sleek modern curves of the Volkswagen (figure 1.13). Bennahar's hand is raised toward the face. The reporter, seen by the side of the car, appears to be helping Bennahar step out of the car. Another man, whose identity I do not know, stands to Bennahar's left.

In this instant of the photograph, Bennahar is looking toward the camera. But a close regard of the image suggests he is not looking directly at the camera or at Kagan as he held the camera. Bennahar is apparently looking just to the left and below the sight line of the camera. His gaze appears a bit away, lost in itself, marking displacements in sense and consciousness, as though perhaps he has not fully registered where he is or what is happening, or how he should relate to those standing close to him.

In viewing the photographs taken by Bennahar that night, we never directly exchange looks with him, however virtual and temporally delayed that exchange might be. We are always one glance removed from a fabulation of visual copresence.

I get a bit lost in this elsewhere look of his. The threshold of relation in the photo-graphs of Bennahar, in which vertiginous life takes place in the span between looking elsewhere and looking directly, between absence and near presence, imagination and actuality, marks this book's space of engagement.

Kagan's optics and narrative accounts of that night's events have tended to hold sway over any direct reflections on the photographic images. Yet Bennahar's non-verbal appearance in the photographic images carries an affective, political charge of its own, within streams of image and silence. At no point in Kagan's recollections of that night is Bennahar said to have spoken to Kagan or the journalist. It's unclear whether Bennahar spoke with these two men while they were at Rue des Pâquerettes or while they were on their way to the hospital or when they arrived there. There is no direct or apparent voice of Bennahar in these moments, beyond his visual-imaginal recurrence in the photographs and the consciousness implied. Yet how much of a voice might come through the images alone? Bennahar's bodily bearing, and the look in his eyes, resounds like a tremulous voice, a cry in and of life. Perhaps Bennahar did not speak French well, which would have limited any verbal exchanges. Or he was in too much pain and distress to be able to communicate effectively with words just then. Any potential speech on Bennahar's part has been displaced, is now forever elsewhere. Yet the spectral potentiality of such speech carries through to this day.

If it can be said that Bennahar was an eyewitness to the violence encountered in Petit-Nanterre that night, then it's also the case that this witnessing never took the form of a direct spoken testimony. Any possible acts of witnessing soon transferred from Bennahar to Kagan, from Bennahar's possible oral testimony and embodied wounds to Kagan's photographic prints and Kagan's own testimony, voiced repeatedly later on. Kagan's perceptions of that night came to be grafted onto the imagistic afterlife of Bennahar's life and body, while the photographic visions of a wounded body are subsequently graphed within these pages. A testimonial of pain circuits from body to photograph to text, while it remains to be seen how Bennahar might speak, indirectly, or at all, through these pages. As for any secondary, supplemental witnessing, a question voiced by Saidiya Hartman (1997, 31) in Scenes of Subjection continuously unsettles: "Is the act of 'witnessing' a kind of looking no less entangled with the wielding of power and the extraction of enjoyment?"

I am looking for indications, impressions, in an uneven patchwork effort to gain at least a partial, tentative understanding of this life death through the dizzying prismatics of photographic time. In the photographs, Bennahar looks younger than me, as I might appear now. He would be much older now, older than me, if his life had continued, though now I am further in years than he ever reached.

If one considers anew the expression of Bennahar as he sits along the edge of the vehicle and prepares to stand, it's difficult to grasp for certain what this look entails, for there is much to perceive or imagine through it. So much goes into a single look, so much that runs multiply, uncertainly, phantasmally. This is the countenance of a man in bodily pain and distress, in untrusting reliance on others. It's the look of someone searching for and in need of help, the look of someone who is not sure whom to trust that night. The look is one of confusion and uncertainty in the rush of the moment; perhaps the man is stunned that someone is photographing him in these critical moments. Bennahar's look relates as a plea, a cry for help among strangers. Or does his look also convey hatred?

Bennahar's look surges well beyond the instant of the camera, reaches any number of potential perceivers of the photograph. This look establishes a relation between subject and viewers. Strange to say, in looking at the image I find that the man is looking toward me, the viewer of this body in pain, even though that looking is terrifically displaced—my own act of looking comes sixty years after the instant of photographic arrest, and the man died thirteen months before I was born.

Pain is at odds with direct meaning and stable imagery. One recurrent conceptual model of photography holds that a photograph is composed of visual representations and tonalities that have the capacity to affect viewers. Yet this semiotic, "affect theory" arrangement does not go far enough. Instead, we might consider a photograph as part of an extensive nervous system radiating through and from a photograph or array of visual and acoustic media. Image, perception, and sensation combine in transmitting and receiving neural messages. Introduce pain into a network of photographic nervosity and the system further intensifies. Pain radiates within and beyond the photographic template, transmits through space and time; nerve impulses reach the bodies of others. This can be a wild searing pain, at once acute and chronic, in which physical pain combines with psychic distress.

Medical researchers have identified the physiology of pain in the bodies of human beings as consisting primarily of acts of "transduction, transmission, modulation and perception."[41] *Similar modalities of sensation, modulation, and perception occur within the phenomenality of photographs. With a series of photographs of wounding, the pain might be mercurial, shooting from image to image, body to body, like a shooting pain dancing through the length of a limb. Or there is liquid, molten pain.*[42] *As with physical pain, photographic pain courses, pulses. At times, such pain exudes into a lifeworld, extending into a viewer's body and field of awareness. The pain can cut too close to home, seep into a body.*

Analgesic networks can also be in force, potentially diminishing intensities of pain. Move away, look elsewhere. Replace the pain realm with another scene. Obscure and efface, soften the blow. Strive to numb innervated perceptions on heightened alert. Patch over the wound with words. Various forms of anesthesia might be used to diminish intensities of pain and harm at either the personal or collective level.[43] *And yet pain still radiates through strained ligaments.*

In the next photograph in the sequence, Bennahar is shown accepting a seat in a wheelchair (figure 1.14). He is seriously injured, yet still alive. The photograph is apparent, visual proof of that. That image proved to be significant in the years that followed, as it's the last direct sign and visual trace of Bennahar, while alive.

In this photograph, two men wearing white shirts—nurses or orderlies working for the hospital—are standing by the wheelchair, along with the journalist, his *presse* badge fixed to his raincoat. One of the men in white holds in his mouth a lit cigarette butt, *un mégot*—a *blanc gris* punctum of burning tobacco.

Kagan later recalled that this hospital employee said, while pushing the wounded man, "Et un raton, un de plus!" (And a *raton*, one more!)

Raton, as in a "young rat"; as in the demeaning racist term applied to North Africans in France. As built into the word *ratonnade*, a racist "rat hunt" attack on North African Arabs. It's as though the man was announcing a new admission to the hospital, an unwanted, tainted creature brought into the medical facilities, but just "one," a single wounded person lumped into a damaging racist category. The utterance "Et un raton, un de plus!" was a jarring, demeaning racial slur, voiced within earshot of the man for whom the orderlies were ostensibly caring. It left a mark.

It could be that the orderlies returned to their homes that night, exhausted after their shifts ended at midnight. One of them went back to his wife and young son in a small apartment in Bois-Colombes, or so I imagine. He had a glass of wine, some bread, smoked one last cigarette, crawled into bed, woke his sleeping wife. She found he reeked of blood and cleaner fluids, the snuff odor of mégot tabac. A mark of disdain lay between them. While unconscious he forgot about his work for a while, the petty hierarchies and constant demands. He slept lousy, woke late, groaned toward his next shift, one more day at the hospital. That night, other injured persons arrived at the hospital, fearful of police incursions.

A final photograph, not often printed in publications—perhaps because it's darker in dimly lit tones and thereby difficult to reproduce in a printed text—shows the two orderlies pushing the wheelchair that holds Bennahar, past the side of a stone wall, presumably up a ramp leading to the entrance of the hospital (figure 1.15). The men assisted in the care of the wounded man, who is leaning toward one side of the chair, his face in apparent pain (Einaudi and Kagan 2001, 55). The rampway leading up to the hospital implies a vanishing point in space and time. This is the last photograph that Kagan took of Bennahar. Kagan was probably prevented from taking any photographs inside the hospital itself. In the book *17 Octobre 1961*, the narrative relates that "Élie Kagan took a last photo of the unknown man and then left, leaving him in the care of the doctors. He will be unaware of his fate" (Einaudi and Kagan 2001, 18).

At that time, the hospital of Nanterre (on Rue Rigault, a few kilometers to the south of Rue des Pâquerettes) was a service of the Maison Départementale, which came under the authority of the prefecture of the police. It's possible police officers gained entrance to the hospital later that night and were able to interrogate and further harass, detain, and harm some of the patients in this intersecting matrix of medical, penal, and juridical apparatuses. At the time, the French colonial state ranged from the Sahara to the shores of Normandy, onto the Caribbean and the South Pacific, from "relocation centers" in Algeria to torture centers and hospital rooms outside of Paris. The hospital was part of the "disciplinary archipelago" radiating through France and its territories at the time, to use a Foucauldian term.[44] Is it surprising that hospitals in France then resembled detention centers, morgues, barracks, and colonies, which all resembled prisons?

Many Algerians knew well the dangers of seeking medical care in the hospitals in and around Paris at that time. The hospital of Nanterre was known as a place where police officers sought out injured Algerians, to beat them further, seize and arrest them, or worse.[45] It's conceivable that Kagan and the American journalist knew that bringing the wounded man to this hospital could potentially lead to further violence at the hands of the police. While possibly aware of the expansive, potentially violent reach of the police, they might have concluded that the man needed direct and immediate medical care.

An awareness of the dangers the hospitals in and around Paris posed for people from Algeria fractures any perceptions of Bennahar being brought to safety and care at the hospital in Nanterre. Along with any pain and distress he felt in those moments, Bennahar might have been terribly ambivalent about being brought to that institution. In viewing the images, I trace the consternation in his face and in the gesture of his hand as he begins to move out of the confines of the Volkswagen. While seated in the wheelchair, he's worried about where he is being taken, knowing that his life could soon face a violent end.

In Listening to Images, *Tina M. Campt advocates a research practice with archival photographs that homes in on "listening to images," rather than looking primarily or solely at the visual features involved. "Listening to images," writes Campt (2017, 9), "is constituted as a practice of looking beyond what we see and attuning our senses to the other affective frequencies through which photographs register. It is a haptic encounter that foregrounds the frequencies of images and how they move, touch, and connect us to the event of the photograph."[46]*

If we listen in this way to the photographs that Kagan took at the hospital that night, what do we sense and hear and touch in the moments conveyed? A frantic energy pulses through the scramble of that night, electric frequencies of weariness and hurried care. Agonized vocalizations that remain silent. The clank of car doors and photographic clicks, rushed voices, the warped cadence of a rickety wheelchair. Atmospheric frictions, anything but quiet. A fugue of pain throughout, and then the buzz cuts off with the last photograph. What sounds follow an image?[47]

In Einaudi's book *Octobre 1961*, it's noted that Kagan returned to the hospital of Nanterre the next day, the eighteenth of October. This would have been after he made it home the previous night and, conceivably, developed the negatives of the photographs he took in Paris and Nanterre. Perhaps Kagan sought to locate the man that he had photographed the night before, to learn if he was recovering well and, possibly, to learn his name and who he was in life. Perhaps he had in mind continuing the photographic sequence of violence, death, and wounding established hours before, which would have made for a good photojournalistic story. Motivations were multiple. While there, writes Einaudi, Kagan "saw some doctors prevent the police from re-entering the hospital to interrogate or seize the wounded" (Einaudi and Kagan 2001, 21).

There is no mention of Kagan re-encountering the man he had photographed the night before. Chances are the two did not meet again. Bennahar was probably no longer there.

The man who lay dead upon the wall at Rue des Pâquerettes has gone unidentified, for many. There is so little I can write about him, who he was in life, what became of his body in death. No records to build an archive around. Others might have known more of his existence, tended to his body in death. The body might have been buried nearby, in a grave site for Algerians, with full honors and following

Muslim burial rites and customs. Perhaps others knew his name and carried that name further.

Is there a violence in Kagan's photographs from that night? Was Bennahar an "overphotographed subject," with image upon image gleaned from his troubled circumstances? Is Bennahar becoming an overanalyzed, overinterpreted subject in my own renderings of him? Has a minor "hypervisibility" been ascribed to the visual form of him, in which a damaged, negated body is repeatedly on display while the actual ethical, embodied substance of his life remains invisible?[48]

A SPORADIC HISTORY OF IMAGES

A Biography of These Images

He would have had no sense that his visual likeness was circulating after that night, or that the pictures of him would still be around, years later. The images survived his life.

The flash of an image arrives one evening in New York, and with it come entangled intricacies of time, image making, and semblant truth. On the seventeenth of October 2019, after a long Thursday of teaching, while I was scrolling through a series of recent posts made on Facebook, I came across an instantly recognizable image: the photograph that Élie Kagan took of Abdelkader Bennahar as he was being set in the wheelchair at the hospital of Nanterre, three men standing behind him. Fifty-eight years to the day of that photograph's first enactment, a gender and ethnic studies scholar based at an elite university in California, politically engaged and exceptionally aware of political injustices throughout the world, had posted a JPG version of the photograph, along with the statement, "Remembering October 17, 1961, the date of French police assassinations of Algerians demonstrating in Paris for national liberation." Below the posted image was a link to an article from that day's edition of *Le Monde*, titled "17 Octobre 1961: 'Ce massacre a été occulté de la mémoire collective'" (This massacre has been obscured from collective memory).

In contemplating this apparition of the photograph within the *longue durée* of Kagan's photographic images, I found myself tracing out minute displacements and deferrals in time, history, and identity. Given the pairing of text and image, I wondered if any contemporary viewers of the man shown in the photograph would infer that he was one of those killed that night. His visual likeness, an icon of colonial erasure, stood in for others—the image of a beaten man signified the wounding and death of others—while his own death was deferred by one night.

In considering the photographs taken by Kagan, we might ask, what comes of images of violence? What work do images of violence do in the world? How do violent images circulate through various media of print, film, language, thought, and sensation, and how do they sear through bodies or fuse within the reaches of collective and personal imaginings or get snuffed out by forces of power? An exploration of Kagan's photographs from October 1961 can help us to address such questions, especially if we consider the many uses and iterations of these select images through various media and discursive formations in the past sixty years and counting. We can in fact undertake something like the biography of these images, tracing out histories and forms of photographic life through time, noting transformations of significance and affective force, imagistic survivance and cessance—giving thought to the life death and afterlife of images.[1]

Delving into the life histories of a linked sequence of photographic images, we might turn anew to considerations of the spore-like qualities of traces in life death: to the ways in which images can get cut from the grounds of a subject or a situation and, unmoored and dispersed, spiral through space and time, where they might land in some new situation or graft themselves onto the pages of a text, germinating there, or lie dormant in a barren land. Image elements latch onto bodies and enter the recesses of minds, archives, and databases through dispersive trajectories beyond the reach and consciousness of any initial subjects or singular ground of the images.

There is always a politics to what proceeds from a subject or an event or situation in life, and what happens to a trace or vestige that is left behind, including whether a trace (or nontrace) lives on in other forms and possibilities in life, or ceases to do so. A broad number of subjectless processes can work with, on, or against any such traces. A piece of writing, for instance, can get copied by hand or photocopied. It can be rewritten by others, or reproduced in recurrent texts or multiple editions, or housed in libraries or archives. Or it can fall straight into a trash bin. The words written can be read, coded, decoded, reiterated, reinterpreted, with writing on the margins. Those same and different words can also generate fantasies, fears, anxieties, countless imaginings, and fantastical worlds while spawning new rounds of writing and imagining. The textual artifacts can also get destroyed or ruined, damaged, cut to pieces. The work of inscription can be censored or prohibited. Distorted, misconceived. A trace of writing can live on, or cease altogether, in effects of survivance, cessance, and *errance.*

Much the same holds for a photographic trace of a moment or a situation or person—such as Kagan's photographs from October 1961. A photographic negative or digital record can be duplicated, cropped and edited, distorted, canceled out. Reworked and refashioned. Printed in newspapers, reprinted in books, preserved in historical archives, or repurposed in museum retrospectives. Materialia, phantasms, or graph-traces can be cast about, dispersed, recirculated, obliterated.

Many processes can be involved in what continues of a life and what does not. This includes the apparatuses of the state (*dispositifs* concerned with policing, governing, and securitization and juridico-administrative machineries); apparatuses of surveillance, documentation, recordkeeping, and archiving; and families, communities, or any number of forces. There can also be collective efforts and state apparatuses that work to deny or destroy traces, in line with actions to annihilate perceived enemies of the state and any traces of the means of that annihilation. These efforts can sever remnants of a life from other relations in life death.

This was often the case during the years of the Algerian war of independence. In Algeria and in France, French military and police forces often worked to hide the bodies of persons they had killed. In Paris in the fall of 1961, a number of men were drowned in the Seine, or their bodies placed in the river's currents after death, so as to obscure or destroy any marks on the bodies that indicated the manner of death and wipe out the possibility of forensic traces. In a way, these were acts of countersurvivance, for they worked to deny the living of physical traces. A body was cut off from the contexts and indications of its endlife. The bodies of those killed would then often be found, days or weeks later, recovered from the river's waters. They were then often sent to the forensic morgue in the city, where the corpses would be chronicled and autopsied, their features and identifying marks and indications of the causes of death inscribed in forensic reports and morgue record books. Lost, disappeared bodies might be searched for, imagined, mourned, and later memorialized in absence by members of a family or community. The cadavers received and processed by the forensic morgue were usually sent to city-owned cemeteries, where they were buried in graves identified by markers, with all this inscribed in the record books kept by the cemeteries. Some of those records can now be found online in digital databases managed by the archives of Paris—with some archived documents kept off-limits to the general public, due to their legally and politically "sensitive" nature. Others might then come along years later, locate the archived records, photograph the log entries, jot notes, and then go on to write pages of prose that tell of what's involved through these histories of trace and effacement.

All this is to say that a significant number of processes, efforts, technical devices and procedures, state and governmental apparatuses, and politically charged economies of survivance and cessance weigh into the production, circulation, and continuation or annihilation of traces within terrains of life death. One needs to consider the politics, technics, and poetics of traces shorn from a life or from any number of collective actions—which range far beyond the interests, intentions, awareness, or agency of any given subjects. What forces of relation, power, domination, erasure, and subversion go into what "survives" a body, a life, an event, or a situation? What political semiologies, phantasmatics, and spectral reverberations might be at work here?

Such considerations apply directly to Kagan's photographs from the night of 17 October 1961. Cut from the time and circumstances of their first enactment, a number of these images have circulated widely in print and other media. The photos have appeared in numerous newspapers, journals, books, scholarly texts, and films, for six decades and counting now.[2] Several of the images presently appear and reappear on website pages and social media posts. Other pictures taken that night have never made the cut, so to speak, and lie fallow in light-proof boxes kept in archival holdings. Still other images are not frequently shown or seen.

The photographs that recur invoke much the same visual themes through the repetition of the images, while at the same time there can be differences in their appearance, whether in terms of framing and shaping (through cropping, contrast, the clarity or opacity of an image) or the contexts in which photographic images appear. This speaks to the ways in which photographs in general engage a "complex intersection of visual continuity and transformation (a certain tenacity of iconicity mixed with mutability)," to quote Christopher Pinney (2023, 38) on the subject. Kagan's photographs carry a strong measure of *iterability*, this being Jacques Derrida's word for the ways in which forms of writing can be reiterated—they are necessarily iterable, in fact—while always implying a degree of difference and variation in those repetitions. In his essay "Signature Event Context," Derrida (1988, 7) remarks that the "iter" in the word *iterability* "probably comes from *itara*, *other* in Sanskrit." The logical force of the "iter" "ties repetition to alterity." As Barry Stock (2006, 170) explains the concept, "Iterability is the possibility of repetition that necessarily contains the possibility of difference and the possibility of sameness, because every repetition creates something different but something that is the same."

Photography, like writing, is highly iterable. Every repetition of one of Kagan's photographs from October 1961 establishes something similar to other appearances of that photographic image as well as something different. Along with holding a quality of iterability, the photographs hold a measure of *alterability*, I would say. The photographic images are alterable. They can be altered, reframed, edited, refashioned, and they can appear in visual media distinct from the medium of analog photography (such as with films, book covers, artwork, digital libraries, and blog postings, for instance). The history of Kagan's photographs speaks to their iterable, alterable qualities, with variations on the visual motifs taking form in distinct ways through time. These variations include interpretations of what the photographs might mean and signify.

The trace visuals from the violent encounters of that night come with complicated affective resonances and epistemic entanglements. Kagan's photographs are often understood to signify direct evidence of police violence of that night. Yet it can also be said that the photos have, in time, come to tell a particularly shaped story of the violence of that night, of the suffering of victims damaged by colonial violence. A few distinct yet interrelated interpretative registers have been at work in engagements and perceptions of the photographs. There is, for one, *the mode of the evidential*, in which the photographs are said to be indications of the real—in this case, the actuality of violence.[3] There is also *the mode of the constructive*, in which the photographs are taken as constructions of the real, and of the histories involved, with these apparent constructs shaping understandings of what took place in Paris in October 1961. Streaming through all this is *the mode of the affective*, wherein the potentially affective and rhetorical-political force of the photographic images is crucially in play. In tracing out the complex and multiply rendered social histories involved with Kagan's photographs, I write with all the ambiguities and tensions that such perspectives bring.

With this, we move away—in part, but not entirely—from a close consideration of the circumstances of life, death, and photographic conveyance on Rue des Pâquerettes the night of 17 October 1961 to the myriad histories of a few distinct images culled from that night and sporadically reapparent since then.

The first public appearance of Kagan's photographs from the night of 17 October was apparently on 19 October 1961, when his photograph of a young man helping another man leave the Solferino Métro station appeared on the cover of *L'Express* with the accompanying title "Le F.L.N. à Paris."[4] Two of Kagan's photographs, including one of Bennahar, appeared in print on 26 October 1961—nine days after the pictures were taken—to illustrate an article in *France Observateur*, with the title "Aucun français ne peut plus ignorer ça" (No Frenchman can ignore this any longer).[5] On this publication Hannah Feldman (2014, 194–95) remarks, "The byline was by 'A. Delcroix,' the pseudonym that [French historian] François Furet used after 8 May 1958. No information was given about the subject of the photograph. It is unlikely that any was available, either to the author or the editor. The article presented a direct appeal to the French left, especially the former Resistance, to organize in condemnation of the events of 17 Octobre 1961." Another photograph included in this investigative report—not taken by Kagan—depicted a large crowd of men in a detention center, accompanied by the caption "Cela ne vous rappelle rien?" (Does this remind you of something?)[6] The implied reference, which would have been clear to many readers in France at the time, was to the rounding up and detention of Jews at the Vélodrome d'Hiver in Paris in July 1942.

Kagan's photos appeared in other newspapers in 1961, including *L'Express*, *L'Humanité*, and *Témoinage Chrétien*. The last of these, whose title might be translated as "Christian Testimony," ran a special issue of eight pages on Friday, 27 October 1961. The cover held an image of the Bennahar standing in pain at Rue des Pâquerettes, being supported by the American journalist—an image-arrangement that perhaps subliminally conveyed the idea of the good Christian Samaritan helping someone in need (figure 2.1). Six other Kagan photographs were reproduced inside the special issue, including three from the night of 17 October 1961—and two of Bennahar, as photographed at Rue des Pâquerettes.

Six of Kagan's photographs were included in Paulette Péju's *Ratonnades à Paris*, published in November 1961 by François Maspero. This small, pamphlet-like book included testimonies of the demonstrations and police violence on 17 October 1961. The paper cover of the book showed an image of the man Kagan photographed at Métro Solférino, grimacing in pain (figure 2.2).

This is a wound-image, I would say. The unnamed man, his body clearly in pain—the figure cut in relief from the Métro scene of the broader photograph taken by Kagan—appears as if moving across the canvas of the booklet cover, along a blank-white tableau, slanting downward. The bludgeoning blow of a

FIGURE 2.1. Cover, *Témoignage Chrétien*, no. 903, 27 October 1961, with image of Abdelkader Bennahar. Cover photo by Élie Kagan; see figure 1.12.

ratonnades
à paris

cahiers
libres
n° 29

FRANÇOIS
MASPERO

FIGURE 2.2. Cover, first edition of Paulette Péju's *Ratonnades à Paris* (Éditions Maspero, 1961). Cover photo by Élie Kagan; see figure 1.5.

police officer's hardwood baton goes unseen but powerfully sensed. The wound is *in medias res*. The pain evinced is alarming, concerning, a call to awareness to cruelties taking place in the Republic. An image of violence potentially sparks further action.

The first printing of *Ratonnades à Paris* was seized by the police at the binder's office.

In December 1961, the FLN produced a booklet, titled *Les manifestations Algériennes d'Octobre 1961 et la répression colonialiste en France*, that included a number of photographs, including several of Kagan's from the night of 17 October 1961 (Ministère de l'Information, FLN, 1961). Audrey Leblanc (2022, 20) writes of this publication, "In December 1961, the FLN Ministry of Information appropriated these images [Kagan's photographs]; they show bodies and, in the face of state censorship, they have been used in very strategic ways by militant circles who work for the political recognition of the massacre and brandish them as evidence for the prosecution."

Kagan's photographs also appeared in Jacques Panijel's *Octobre à Paris*, a clandestinely made film completed and released in early 1962 by this immunologist turned filmmaker—with copies of the film then seized by the French police and banned by the French government for a number of years.[7] Kagan's photographs recur in one sequence of the film, in which film clips and photographs are combined in a montage of images cued to discordant music (figures 2.3–2.18). The sequence moves from films and photographs of the demonstrators leaving the bidonvilles of Nanterre and then gathering en masse in the streets of Paris, where they join spirited demonstrations. The filmic camera pans across the still images and sometimes zooms in suddenly on a single person in the gathering crowd. The streaming images convey a rush of excitement and uncertainty in the encroaching night. Bands of armed police officers soon appear in this filmic sequence; they are shown chasing, holding, and detaining a number of persons, who try to flee. Several of Kagan's photographs then appear, including images of the two wounded men that Kagan photographed in Métro Solférino and six photographs of Bennahar at Rue des Pâquerettes. The camera abruptly zooms in on some of these photographic images, intensifying the pain displayed through Bennahar's body. Several film clips follow, which show groups of armed police officers wielding what look like long *bidule* clubs against demonstrations. The film then shifts to a new series of images, which includes clips of several men showing the scars of wounds received the night of 17 October 1961, and then scenes of women, men, and children talking about what they experienced then.

FIGURES 2.3–2.18. Stills from Jacques Panijel's film *Octobre à Paris* (1962), including photographs by Élie Kagan.

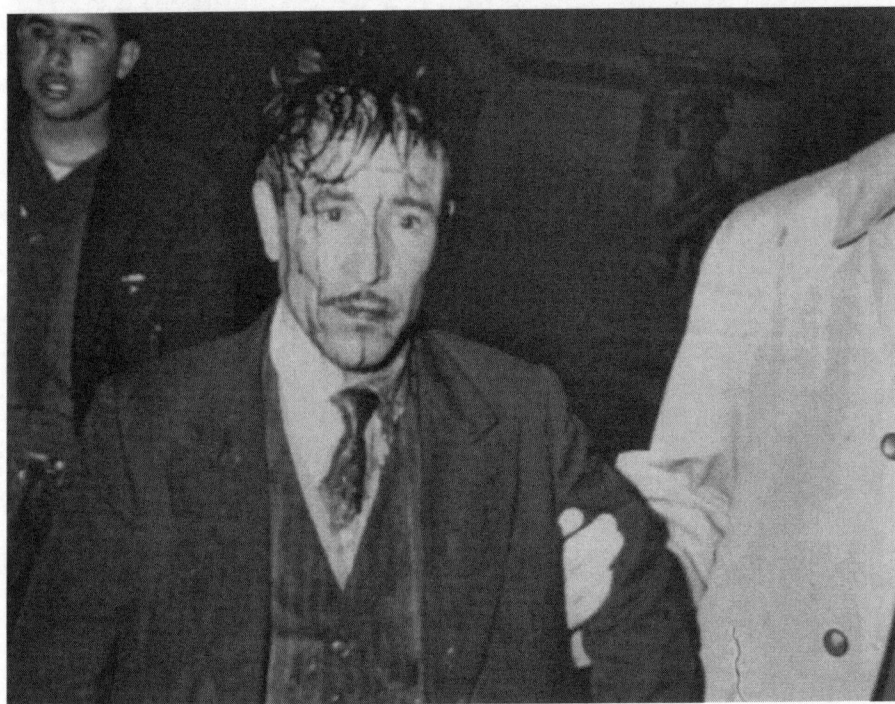

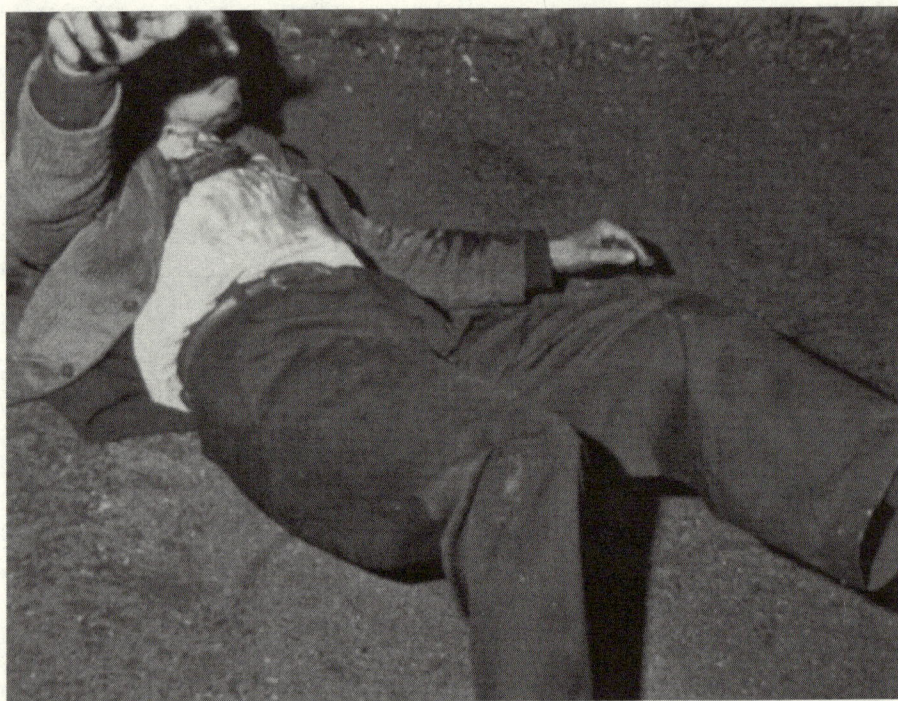

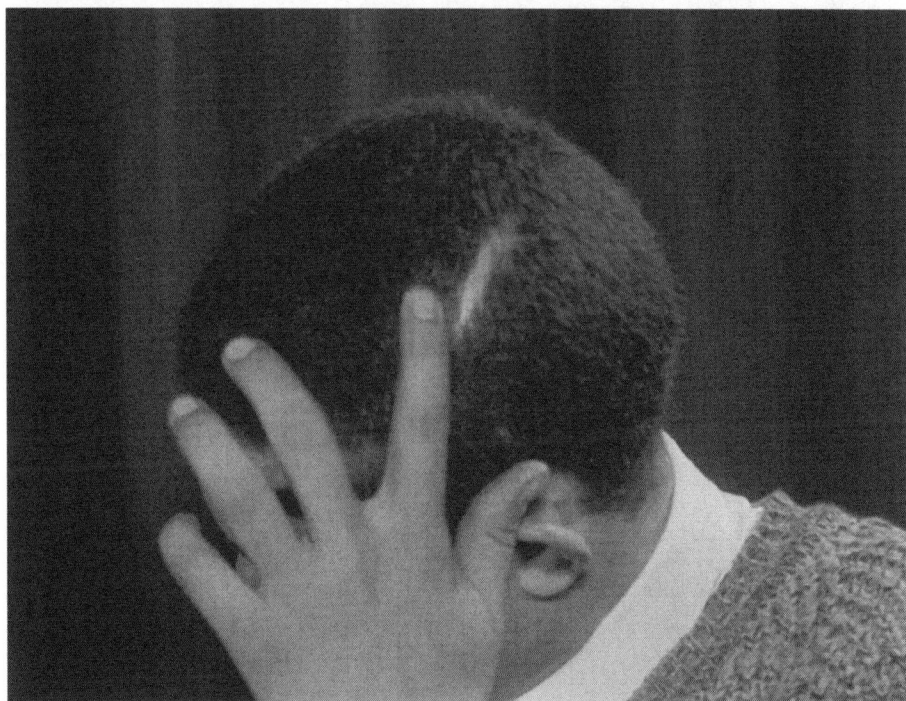

Through this implicitly narrative sequence, from the collective arrival of the demonstrators in Paris to the violent police responses to their presence, to the wounding and deaths that resulted, the sequence of film footage and photographic images documents the violence of that night. With this filmic interweaving of images, Kagan's photographs are situated within a broader expanse of collective demonstrations, state-sanctioned violence, and wounding and death. Bennahar's unnamed body is linked to the bodies of others and comes to signify the pain and suffering that many faced at the time.

In viewing this segment of Panijel's film, years after its construction, I am struck by the filmic sequences from that night. Many of the film clips I have not seen elsewhere. These filmic sequences do not circulate so often these day—Kagan's photographs get around much more. The clips of the many demonstrators gathering in Paris serve as an important counterpoint to Kagan's pictures of singularly wounded persons.

The mix of film footage and still photographs enacts a taut flow of images through cinematic time. The filmed sequences of the police officers, wielding clubs and glistening coats and helmets in the Parisian night, are especially dark; there's not much light about them. Many of the film sequences and still photographs are rather poor in quality. Some of the persons shown appear rather ghostly, as off-tone grays and bleached-out whites fade into obscure filmic haunts. I consider the faces portrayed, distinct and singular, as if caught in the time of the film. In glimpsing aspects of the lives shown in these vital, fearful moments, I am aware that many of the persons preserved in the film are no longer around.[8] Years past the promise and hardships of that October night, the cinematic apparitions of these human figures reverberate like ghosts, haunting the found footage of colonial history.

Reproductions of Kagan's photos that appeared in various media and formats soon after the events of October 1961 fit with efforts to make an "emergency claim," to use the words of Ariella Aïsha Azoulay, a scholar of photography and visual culture. In her book *The Civil Contract of Photography*, Azoulay (2008, 197) defines an emergency as "a situation involving calamity or mortal peril that demands immediate attention." An emergency, writes Azoulay, "is produced from a situation entangled in disaster, war, terrorist attacks, massacres, catastrophes, or accidents, but it also emerges from ongoing situations of poverty, misery, abuse, or humiliation." The state violence enacted by the police against Algerians in Paris in 1961 provoked one such emergency, and a few left-leaning writers, journalists, editors, publishers, and filmmakers sought to claim an emergency—to shout it out, as it were—in the hopes that

French citizens and others would be alerted to the brutal beatings and killings undertaken by the French police.

In time, several of Kagan's photographs have circulated far and wide and have been invoked and reimaged on countless occasions. Along with other photographs and film clips from that time, the images have worked to show the effects of violence on wounded subjected persons in visually dramatic ways. The police, in turn, tried to diminish the force of such claims or censor them outright. They wanted to cancel out the images and obscure the violence they indexed—to render their actions and its consequences "invisible," as Jacques Rancière (1998, 28) writes in his essay "The Cause of the Other" of the "savage repression and news blackout" that came of 17 October 1961: "From the French State's point of view, the demonstration meant that Algerians in struggle had emerged within the French public space as political participants and, in a certain sense, French subjects. The result of that intolerable event is well known: savage beatings and drownings. In a word, the police cleared the public space and, thanks to a news blackout, made its own operations invisible."

In striving for an invisibility of the demonstrators, their collective protests, and the state's violent repression of such actions, agents of the police wanted to render invisible any wounds suffered, the bodies of those killed, persons detained, and any testimonies offered, as well as to obliterate the discourses and images that began to gather about that violence. They sought to destroy any and all traces that might survive the violent events.

Others in turn fought for visibility. In effect, they strove for a certain kind of "countervisuality," as Nicholas Mirzoeff, a theorist of visual culture, finds is often the case for peoples resisting the "colonial visuality" enforced by colonial and imperial powers, including the strident efforts of police and military regimes to establish certain ways of seeing and thinking about the world and to negate other forms of looking. "At stake is the possibility of a movement toward the right to look, the counter to visuality, against the police and their assertion that there is nothing to see here," Mirzoeff (2011, 241) writes on the "cultural work" of the Battle of Algiers in Algeria and elsewhere, from 1954 on. Similar concerns were at stake with representations of 17 October 1961. A number of groups and persons struggled for the "right to look" at the violent actions of the police and their damaging effects and to put into circulation a counterhistory and countervisuality of the state violence, much at odds with the scopic regime of the Paris police and French government. Kagan's photographs existed and circulated—or not—within these competing forces of invisibility and visibility, visuality and countervisuality.

In the years that followed, Kagan's images recurred in various texts and films, especially from the 1980s on, when there emerged renewed interest and debate on the state and police violence of 1961. One significant publication that included the images was an article authored by Jean-Louis Penino, a French anticolonial activist and journalist, which appeared in *Libération* on 17 October 1980. Joshua Cole (2003, 32) observes of its context and significance,

> The reassessment of the history of 17 October that began in France in the 1980s thus did not come because of a push emanating from official sources in Algeria. Instead, it emerged from within discussions on the French left about how to confront the legacy of French colonialism. Before 1980 only a few anti-racist organizations, such as the Maoist Mouvement des Travailleurs Arabes and the publishers of a small alternative journal called *Sans Frontière*, explicitly commemorated the events of 17 October. On 17 October 1980, however, Jean-Louis Penino took advantage of the nineteenth anniversary of the demonstration to publish a commemorative article in *Libération*, a left-wing Parisian paper with wide readership. Penino noted that the French Left's ability to mobilize effectively around acts of anti-Semitic violence by right-wing extremists contrasted sharply with their silence about the history of colonial atrocities. Penino's article was accompanied by a multi-page spread about 17 October and photographs taken in 1961 by Élie Kagan were reproduced for the first time in a daily newspaper.

Penino's article reintroduced Kagan's photographs to a wide readership in France. Since then, the images have circulated often. A number of them have appeared in significant publications, including the 1991 volume *Le silence du fleuve*, collectively produced by the organization Au Nom de la Mémoire. The book's publication coincided with the release of a film made by the same group and with the same title (Tristan 1991; Denis and Lallaoui 1991). A number of Kagan's photographs are shown in the film, including at around the eighteen-minute mark, when the camera pans across the image of the two bodies near Rue des Pâquerettes and the narrator says—his words moving across the image— "The man on the wall is dead. He would not be counted in the official count [of those who died then]" (Denis and Lallaoui 1991). In the accompanying book version, a set of Kagan's images is presented in a spread of several pages, with each image carrying a caption telling the story of Kagan's efforts that night.

Several of Kagan's photographs also appeared in Jean-Luc Einaudi's book *La bataille de Paris: 17 Octobre 1961*, published by Éditions du Seuil in October 1991. Along with other documentary and creative works published around the same time, this controversial, politically explosive book was of signal importance in bringing an awareness of the events of 17 October 1961 to the public in France and elsewhere. Based largely on oral testimonies and documents from the FF-FLN, as well as morgue and cemetery records—the police archives in France were not then available to the public, and Einaudi was repeatedly denied access to them—*La bataille de Paris* told in crucial detail of the violent events in Paris in October 1961.[9] Three of Kagan's photos printed in the book were taken at Rue des Pâquerettes: the two men at the wall and Bennahar being seated in the wheelchair upon arriving at the hospital. Following that set of images are the portrait-like photographs of thirteen Algerian men, under the caption "Des disparus," of the departed, deceased—literally, the disappeared. The book's cover features a close-up image of Bennahar as he was standing in pain by the wall, blood streaking his face.

State television in France, meanwhile, made use of Kagan's photographs to illustrate reports broadcast in 1991 (on Antenne 2) and 1997 (on France 2) (Welch and McGonagle 2013, 87).

One powerful person who had no use for Kagan's photographs, and tried to negate their existence, was Maurice Papon, the prefect of the Paris police from 1958 to 1965. The photographs strongly suggested that the police officers under his supervision acted in criminally violent ways against the protestors the night of 17 October 1961. When brought to trial in 1997 for his role in the arrest and deportation of 1,560 Jews from France to Germany from 1942 to 1944, Papon was asked about Kagan's photographs from that night. "Je n'y crois pas, c'est du montage," he reportedly responded.[10] His statement can be translated as "I don't believe in them, it's a montage," with the word *montage* implying something edited, altered, pasted together, doctored, artificially constructed— "photoshopped," to use a recent phrase. As Papon conveyed it, the photographs were not true, evidential traces of the real but rather concocted by someone who sympathized with the Algerian, anticolonial cause; they were constructed to the point that there was no truth or actuality in them. Others similarly argued that Kagan was complicit in the planning and structure of the demonstration and worked with the FLN to produce photographic images that "mediatized" the event.[11]

In a text published in *Le Monde* in February 1999, titled "Les mensonges grossiers de M. Papon" (The gross lies of Monsieur Papon), writer and publisher François Maspero ([1999] 2000, 200) spoke to this accusation. "It's not true that, as he [Papon] dared to pretend, the photos of Élie Kagan could have been a montage. I saw him work; I saw the contact sheets in the days that followed and these, like the negatives, exist."

That the contact prints and negatives exist is significant, as they imply the lasting reality of direct photochemical impressions before any actual prints were made. Eyewitness accounts were especially important in those days, in the "era of the witness" (Wieviorka 2006) that took form in Europe in the wake of the Holocaust. Maspero testified to Kagan's authentic photographic efforts, the visual imprints of which tainted Papon's life and public reputation.

By and large, Kagan's photographs have been taken as important indexical, documentary traces of the violence that October night. Some of just a few photographs that documented the blows and aftereffects of the state-sanctioned violence that night, they are important material reminders and remainders of that violence. As a 1999 essay titled "Photopsie d'un massacre" couched it, "But, if one can deny, burn, stifle the traces of the past, memory survives. Testimonies exist—among which are the photographs of Élie Kagan! . . . These snapshots, burning with truth, are an imprint, an indelible trace of events and must be a legitimate source for the historian" (Benayoun 1999, 65, 67).

Benjamin Stora invoked a similar language in writing on Kagan's photographs for an essay in the 2004 coauthored book *Photographier la guerre d'Algérie*: "So strong and so significant was the vision of Élie Kagan (his candid and direct pictures have been published in the many books dedicated to this event) that it has permanently invested our own memory of this cruel event. His photography, published on the front page on 19 October 1961, where Algerians were seen crammed into a RATP bus, with their hands raised, left a lasting impression" (Stora 2004, 105). In such readings of the photographs, a double imprinting has been at work. As indelible traces, "burning with truth," the photos are at once imprints of the force of violence and a force of imprinting. The photographic images have impressed themselves on memories of the event.

These images of wounding and death have marked bodies and consciousnesses and have been seared into life in France and elsewhere. Within the ways of knowing found in the conceptual framing of Kagan's photographs as traces of evidence of the real, it could be said that each photo is a "tear-image" (*image-déchirure*) from which "a fragment of the real escapes," to invoke Didi-Huberman's (2008) phrasing in writing of four surviving photographs made by Jewish prisoners at Auschwitz in the summer of 1942. Taken clandestinely and in rushed, fearful circumstances by members of the *Sonderkommando*, the photos show a group of naked women being herded into the gas chambers.[12] While not the same horrific, "terrifying image" of the death camps of Auschwitz—and from a history of violence altogether distinct from that of the Shoah—Kagan's photographs similarly involve processes of "rupture, displacement" and "pushing to the limit"; the images are "the exception rather than the rule"; they cause "an upheaval of territories and thus of limits" (Didi-Huberman 2008, 80–81). These tear-images work in contrast to the "veil-images" (*images-voile*) proposed by the Paris police and the French state in regard to the state-sanctioned violence that night, which served to mask and obscure what took place.[13]

Such interpretative uses and regard of the photographs tie into the evidential mode of the photographic images, when invoked and perceived that way. Kagan's photographs from the night of 17 October 1961 have often been taken to be indexical traces of the actuality of violence, and they reflect in important, evidentiary ways to the historical fact of state-police brutality and colonial violence in France at the time.

Yet a distinctly different mode of assessment and perception of Kagan's photographs needs to be considered, one that underscores the ways in which the images have contributed to certain historical understandings and political imaginaries of state violence in France circa October 1961. An exemplary reflection on this constructive mode of perception and assessment can be found in Edward Welch and Joseph McGonagle's book, *Contesting Views: The Visual Economy of France and Algeria*. In this coauthored work, published in 2013, these two scholars of French cultural history examine the ways in which photography has tied into the histories and discourses of Franco-Algerian relations in colonial and postcolonial times. In a chapter devoted to "the visual career of 17 October 1961," Welch and McGonagle argue that photographs—Kagan's included—have worked in important ways to shape collective and personal understandings of the events of 17 October 1961, as well as understandings and recollections of the kinds of violence and its damaging effects that occurred then.[14] As they note, "From the immediate aftermath of the events to their resurrection in the 1990s and 2000s, the photographic image has had a key role in the representation of 17 October" (Welch and McGonagle 2013, 67). This analytic perspective is in line with the authors' interest in theorizing that photographs do not simply reflect historical events. They also contribute in important ways to how such events are understood and recalled and related through time.

Much the same could be said of existing photographs of the collective demonstrations and state violence that took place on 17 October 1961, for uses of and references to specific photographic images have contributed to how people have made sense of and recalled those events. Welch and McGonagle (2013, 68) make the case that "visual representation—and photographic representation, especially—is key to the historical fortunes of 17 October over time, by which is meant both its place or visibility within the historiography of the Algerian war and the ways in which the events of 17 October have come to be understood." As for such photographic historicities, Welch and McGonagle find that "what emerges in particular is the pivotal role played throughout by the body, and the male, Algerian body, specifically, in the visual portrayal of the events" (68). In many respects, the bodies of Algerian men and women were fundamental to the forms of collective protest undertaken on 17 October 1961. As Welch and McGonagle note, "It can be said that 17 October was an event in which the body was overtly put to work for symbolic ends, as massed bodily presence on the streets of the capital was used to express resistance by a population which had finally been granted French citizenship in 1958, and yet had found itself singled out for repressive measures by the authorities" (76).

Agencies of the French press represented in divergent ways the collective, embodied demonstration in and around Paris on 17 October 1961 and the forceful state and police responses to it. Visual media coverage in France at the time tended to depict Algerian demonstrations in two distinct ways. One form of visual representation, largely taken up by conservative and progovernment media outlets, including television and print media such as *France-Soir* and *Paris Match*, a weekly photo-reportage news magazine, portrayed crowds of male demonstrators as a threat to residents of Paris and the French Republic, with this threat successfully contained and neutralized in a few days through arrests and deportations to Algeria. Welch and McGonagle (2013, 78–79) observe that such representations entailed a "classic narrative structure of threat, disruption and ultimate return to order, confirmed by images not just of containment (arrest and removal to detention centers) but of expulsion, as the foreign bodies which caused the disturbance were dispatched definitively from metropolitan territory." Much reporting of the demonstrations "staged Algerian masculinity as disruptive, destabilizing and dangerous, a power in need of containment and castration" (83).

A second form of visual representation, advanced by the progressive press in France, denounced the events of 17 October 1961 "in terms of a narrative of repression by the French state" (Welch and McGonagle 2013, 77). Newsweeklies such as *France-Observateur* and *L'Express*, critical of the Gaullist regime, featured articles in October and November 1961, "with coverage of the aftermath of the repression, the containment of the demonstrators, and analysis of the government's handling of the Algerian question. Visually, it highlighted the physical violence done to protestors, drawing in particular on the images taken in and around Paris by Élie Kagan" (81–82). These included the photographs Kagan took of wounded men at Métro Solférino and of the man wounded in Petit-Nanterre (Abdelkader Bennahar). "In each of these cases," Welch and McGonagle contend, "photographs are being used in a way which is now axiomatic of the rhetorical strategies of human rights discourses. Visual evidence of physical violence and repression by the state is mobilized in order to stimulate a range of responses—indignation, guilt or shame—and, in so doing, to reinforce a call to action" (82). In stark contrast to pro-government publications, which asserted the innocence of those in metropolitan France, in need of rescuing by the state, "the mainstream progressive press confronted its readers with images of wounded and broken bodies and displays of corporeal vulnerability, in order to make manifest the inherent violence of the colonial dynamic being acted out on the streets of Paris. Here, Algerian men appear not as a redoubtable threat to the public and political order, but as tragic victims of that order" (83).

Photographic images also played a central role when the events of October 1961 were reinscribed in French public sphere in the 1990s. Here, too, Welch and McGonagle (2013, 83) contend, the male Algerian body became "the key site for understanding, negotiating and revalorizing the meanings of 17 October." As the events of Paris 1961 have become less a scene of current political and cultural debate in France and more a matter of historical analysis and collective memory, "certain images begin to serve as a visual shorthand for an episode of narrative complexity and temporal duration, occluding certain threads and foregrounding others" (87). While some photographs from October 1961 portray Algerian men and women undertaking the collective demonstrations in and around Paris and show the political agency of the state in suppressing these demonstrations (with truncheon-wielding police officers detaining groups of Algerian men on the streets of Paris, for instance), other photographs show singular, wounded bodies. Of these latter representations Welch and McGonagle remark:

> In other images, the moment of violence itself is often absent, and we see only its aftermath. The viewer is confronted by broken male bodies displaying pain and anguish, physical contortion and streaming blood. Dazed expressions and trickling blood on beaten men imply the existence of an omniscient power beyond the frame of the image. Figures are often seen in isolation, thereby accentuating a sense of their vulnerability and abandonment. There is a marked emphasis on facial expressions, as well as looks directed at the camera. . . . In short, the visual enactment of 17 October in the contemporary period is defined by a rhetoric of affect, in which photographs are mobilized to produce ethical responses through provoking emotional or affective reactions to corporeal vulnerability. Moreover, the viewer's exposure to such vulnerability is reinforced by subjection to the look of the repressed and the victimized. (87)

Through time, a rhetoric of affect and effect has become grafted into the photographs.

From the 1990s on, Kagan's photographs have taken on a privileged, iconic status as visual documents of the police violence of 17 October 1961. As Welch and McGonagle (2013, 75–76) write, "Not only does the photographic act privilege certain moments over others, but it also institutes a privileged way of seeing, and therefore of understanding those moments. This is most obvious in the case of those images which acquire 'iconic' status: that is to say which are seen to concentrate or encapsulate an event and its meanings, and which do so through repeated circulation and reproduction. Nick Ut's 'Accidental Napalm' would be one such example. Élie Kagan's images of 17 October 1961 are another." Welch and McGonagle continue their assessment of Kagan's photographs:

> If an iconography of victimhood takes center stage in the contemporary period, it is thanks in particular to the increasing prominence afforded to the work of Élie Kagan. Not only are Kagan's images often selected to accompany retrospective accounts of 17 October in the print and televisual media, but he is also promoted as the principal eyewitness to the events. . . . If Kagan's images are privileged, in other words, it is because they enable and reinforce a narrative of suffering and victimhood, and if the visual display of corporeal vulnerability is perceived as the key to grievability, it is because the historical conditions of representation which frame the circulation of those images increasingly allow them to be read as images of victimhood and injustice. (87, 88)

Welch and McGonagle (2013, 88) further contend that the performative aspects and the rhetorical effect of focusing so much on photographs of wounded, vulnerable individuals are that the images render the persons portrayed primarily as victims, with little agency as political subjects. "Positioning these people as victims," they argue, "almost inevitably implies neutralizing or denying their agency as subjects." Kagan's photographs have been produced, perceived, and circulated within the terms of such an "iconography of victimhood," Welch and McGonagle find, and this is largely due to the efforts of memory activists and historians in the 1990s (such as Einaudi and the authors of Le silence du fleuve) to relate the histories of violence involved to a general public. "The focus of memory activists and historians in 1990s and subsequently is precisely on asserting the status of the victims of police brutality at the time *as* victims" (85). Such a framing of the histories involved, which are in accord with contemporary discourses on human rights, works to provoke strong affective responses among viewers of the images, which might stimulate a range of responses, from indignation and shame to calls for action.

It's not convincingly clear that Kagan's photographs depict subjects solely as passive victims of state and colonial violence, as there is a lot implicitly within and around the photographic images that indicates the strong agentive and political action that these persons undertook in contesting French colonial rule. Still, the points made by Welch and McGonagle are well taken. Kagan's photographs from 17 October 1961 have gained an uncommon currency. They have circulated widely and been invoked time and again, in large part because of their visual-visceral portraitures of Algerian men, with singularly framed bodies and faces grimacing in pain. Through the past thirty years and count-ing, the images have entailed strong rhetorical effects and carried a robust per-formative efficacy.

A certain "reality effect" (Barthes 1989, 141–48) has become engrained within Kagan's photographs from that night. The presumed reality of violence is fash-ioned here, shaped and tempered through the anvil of photographic capture, production, reception, and media representation. Kagan's photographs have be-come "formative fictions," as Zeynep Devrim Gürsel uses this term in her study of journalistic news images in the age of digital circulation. As Gürsel (2016, 11) understands the intricate processes involved, based on long-term ethnographic fieldwork with journalists and news media outlets, photographs—"news im-ages" in particular—are "formative fictions, constructed representations that reflect current events yet simultaneously shape ways of imagining the world and possibilities within it." Kagan's photographs have similarly come to reflect key historical events in ways that shape ways of imagining a particular world of state violence and terror and the many happenings and possibilities apparent there.

The evidential mode and the constructive mode of perceiving and assessing Kagan's photographs have thus emerged in intricate, crosscutting arrangements through time. No doubt these two modes are in tension with each other. But this doesn't necessarily mean they are completely opposed, or that, by definition, the terms and procedures of one negate those of the other. A dizzyingly compli-cated imbrication of ideas and percepts is often involved, with the evidential wrapped up in the constructed. The evidential is continuously constructed through thought, imagining, language, discourse. The constructive shapes ideas of what the evidential implies. The evidential takes on performative and affective force, while all along, politically charged affective intensities course through reflections on the photographic images as those images recur in flashes through time.

Here is a story on the differential reception of images, varying coefficients of hurt. A few months ago, I asked M. if they would be willing to read the manuscript of this ever-emergent text once it was sufficiently completed. They said they would be willing to do so and offer their thoughts on the ideas and materials involved. Given their knowledge of French and Algerian histories and their family's intimate engagements with such histories, their reflections could add a lot to the work. I gave M. a printed copy of the text when we next saw each other in person. Several months have gone by now, and I have not heard from them again on this, while we have continued to converse on other topics. When I have mentioned further progress on my part in writing the book, they have kept silent. Perhaps they have been too busy to find the time to read into the manuscript, or they find it all rather drab and ineffective and they hesitate to tell me this. But I sense something more. I recall M. saying, when I mentioned my ongoing analysis of Kagan's photographs of Abdelkader Bennahar, that their regard of these images would be different than my own. "I relate to them differently," they said, or words to that effect. For M., I gather, there is an intimate connection, a history to be traced, for viewed in Kagan's photographs taken in Petit-Nanterre is a man in pain, suffering, who comes from much the same kind of political and sociocultural history as M. and their family, Algerian kin who have settled in France. I take it that M. relates to the life and body of the man wounded and other Algerians injured or killed in that dark October of 1961 in deeply affective ways. A raw wound is there, and it might be that M. is wounded simply in touching upon the photographs and the lives and afterlives involved—while for me the images and histories of wounding are primarily the subject of anthropological inquiry. The terms and qualia of relation are distinct for each of us. Perhaps as well M. identifies with the body and appearance of Abdelkader Bennahar as glimpsed in the photographs—it's someone like them, could be—and they readily envision themselves in a similar position, beaten down by police officers in France. All this must be unnerving for M., making for a painful read. I can understand why they might not want to delve too deeply into the pages of this manuscript and trace out its wounds and fissures. Perhaps they are wary of stepping into its many sharp edges. Perhaps we'll keep silent on this.

Image Drift

The images have drifted. Kagan's photographs from 17 October 1961 have at times wandered far afield of their initial enactments, becoming free-floating signifiers of police violence. All this speaks to the meandering, unstable qualities of images in historical time. In the 1970s and 1980s, in particular, the referential significances of Kagan's photographic images drifted unmoored from the specific historical circumstances of the photographs' production—the specific events of 17 October 1961—and came to stand, instead, for police violence in France more generally. Mogniss Abdallah, a journalist and activist based in Paris, finds that this was the case in the 1970s and 1980s in certain circles in France, when left-leaning political organizations invoked the photographic images as potent signifiers of state violence. Abdallah writes of the uses of Kagan's photographs during the 1970s in his article "Le 17 Octobre et les médias: De la couverture de l'histoire immediate au 'travail de mémoire,'" published in 2000. In speaking of the revolutionary movements born in 1968, Abdallah observes that these movements often tended to conflate and interchange specific histories and imageries of violence, particularly those of October 1961 and February 1962 (the latter date marks the time of the Charonne Massacre on 8 February 1962, in which officers of the Paris police beat up or crushed to death French antiwar protestors by and in the Charonne Métro station in the 11th arrondissement of Paris). Abdallah writes,

The beginning of the seventies will confirm and accentuate this tendency to confusion. After May 1968, the Maoists of the Gauche Prolétarienne (GP) took up the theme of "fascization." They denounced the racist terror that reigned in the factories and the racist crimes that multiplied. On 25 February 1972, Pierre Overney, a young specialized worker, was killed at the gates of Renault-Billancourt by a security guard while distributing a leaflet entitled "On assassine à Paris" [We kill in Paris], calling for a demonstration that evening at the Charonne Métro station. Ten years later, intellectuals, including Michel Foucault, also went to the scene. Alongside them, the leader of the GP, Alain Geismar, mixed evocations of February 1962 with the police charges of that 25 February 1972. He also interspersed his speech with more or less implicit references to the "ratonnades" of October 1961. . . .

Numerous militant films of the 1970s will bear the stigma of this confusion. These films circulated in multiple parallel networks, especially among young high school and university students who had not directly experienced the situation of the 1960s but who remained fascinated by the revolutionary and separatist mythology of May 1968. However, the militant imagery of the time generally without shame instrumentalizes images to illustrate ideological discourses. The photos taken on 17 October 1961 by Élie Kagan are thus used to illustrate . . . the "ratonnades" of the seventies. The consequences of this more or less conscious manipulation of images that have become almost timeless will prove devastating. They predispose the new generations, already marked by the primacy of the image on the written word, to a catch-all memory that mixes historical references and genres. (Abdallah 2000, 128–29)

In such situations, the specific temporal and historical circumstances of Kagan's photographs from 17 October 1961 were glossed over, knowingly or not, or confusingly related to other historical events. The photographic images became part of a "catch-all memory" that came to document varying histories of police violence in France.

Clotilde Lebas traces out similar shifts in the referentiality of Kagan's photographs, in her 2007 article "Au fil de nos souvenirs: Le 17 Octobre 1961, emblème des violences policières."[15] Lebas finds that, in the 2000s, Kagan's photographs from 17 October were put to varied political and discursive uses, given the social and political concerns at hand. She draws from two ethnographic vignettes to detail this; each reflects intensive imagery from Kagan's photographs. The first account tells of a commemorative gathering in October 2005 at the Pont Saint-Michel, where a number of Algerian demonstrators were reportedly beaten by Paris police officers the night of 17 October 1961. Some of these men were killed, their bodies tossed into the Seine.

17 October 2005: at the end of the day, a compact crowd surrounds the memorial plaque (by Pont St. Michel). The first to speak is one of the founding members of Au Nom de la Mémoire. Representatives of the Mouvement contre le Racisme et pour l'Amitié entre les Peuples and the Ligue des Droits de l'Homme follow. All three pointed out the importance of this symbolic date, of its commemoration and asked for official recognition of the crimes committed by the police force. On placards held at arm's length, yesterday's commemorations are mixed with today's denunciations: "17 October 1961: Night Assassin / 17 October 2005: the repression continues; Algerians yesterday / undocumented migrants (*sans papier*) today / Racist crimes continue; Yesterday's gunshots, today's raids." The collectives of support for undocumented migrants took place on the Pont Saint-Michel. The trained eye can recognize a photograph by Kagan that has slipped between the lines of these claims. It's of a man, looking haggard, being helped out of a car. The blood flowing from his face has left its prints on his clothes, on his hands. After a minute of silence, flowers are thrown into the Seine, where the bodies of Algerian demonstrators were thrown. For a while, the crowd occupies the roadway. The discussions are lively. Some recall the debates provoked by the law of 23 February 2005.[16] Others evoked the resumption of raids—an announcement of future bills on

immigration—and police violence against undocumented migrants. This gathering was more than a simple commemoration. The reminder of yesterday's atrocities sounds like an echo of contemporary forms of violence. (Lebas 2007, n.p.)

Here the events of 17 October 1961—and Kagan's photographic images of violence from that night—are interrelated with other histories of political struggle in the Republic.

Lebas's second vignette reflects the ways in which Kagan's photographs at times came to stand for representations of police violence more generally rather than as representations specifically of the events of 17 October 1961. This second account is from December 2005, in the worrisome days after "riots" took place in the suburbs of Paris and other French cities in October and November 2005, following the death of two youths on 27 October 2005 in Clichy-sous-Bois. The two were electrocuted while hiding in an electrical substation in an attempt to elude police officers, who were trying to interrogate them and other youths in the aftermath of a reported break-in at a building site.

6 December 2005, in the corridors of the University of Paris X-Nanterre. My gaze stops on a large sign denouncing police violence. A poem by Kateb Yacine, an Algerian author, questions the indifference of the French people toward the demonstrators of October 1961:

People of France, you saw it all,
You saw our blood flow,
You saw the police
Beat the protestors
And throw them into the Seine.
. . . .
And now will you speak?
And now will you be silent?

Two photographs by Kagan surround the text. The scene of one takes place in the Solferino Métro. The other brings us to Nanterre. Kagan took a series of photographs there. . . . From this series of pictures, the members of the student union chose the one where the man is on the ground. A student explains to me that the posters were made a few years ago. It is now two years since they have been doing any "consciousness raising" about 17 October. If they have chosen to bring them out in these first days of December 2005, it is to better question the current situation. For more than a month, the media have not stopped reporting on the "urban riots." A state of emergency and a curfew are some of the measures decreed by the government to put an end to these outbursts of violence. The images presented on the poster are there, according to the unionized student, to remind us that police violence is not new. It is, in her eyes, important to remember this. On the images themselves, she knows nothing, and can't tell me much: "They speak for themselves. You can see . . . the violence . . . the suffering. And these are the fathers, the grandfathers of those who, today, are victims of this same violence." (Lebas 2007, n.p.)

Kagan's photographs thus came to "speak for themselves" on the problem of police violence in France. More generally, Lebas (2007) finds that the visual content and composition of Kagan's photographs lend themselves to new appropriations and reinterpretations of the images. "In Kagan's images one can read the pain of the people, not the police violence. They bear no inscriptions. New commentary is therefore necessary for new appropriations. The anonymity of the immortalized demonstrators also seems conducive to reinterpretation. From one reappropriation to another, from one memory entrepreneur to another, these anonymous Algerians become symbols of police repression."

These narrative accounts support Lebas's analysis of the ways in which the histories and imageries stemming from the events of 17 October 1961 have come to be appropriated and reinterpreted according to different circumstances and social and political concerns in France. As the abstract to the article explains, Lebas's (2007) reflection shows how "a traumatic event can constitute a memorial landmark which generates substitutions and successive transformations. Then, the reference to a unique event becomes less visible and scatters in various directions. From an evocation to another, from one *entrepeneur de mémoire* [memory entrepreneur] to another, the memory of 17 October 1961, supported by photographs left by Kagan, becomes the symbol of police violence. This example illustrates the complexity of memory dynamics by revealing how an event can return, by the detour of photography, as a fact or a trace, and be reinvested in a present time where it still makes sense."

Since the time of Abdallah's and Lebas's writings on the histories of images associated with 17 October 1961—their articles were published in 2000 and 2007, respectively—it appears that Kagan's photographs have regained a certain historical specificity. This is what I gather from contemporary invocations and discussions of Kagan's photographs: they are usually linked to the events of 17 October 1961. The images do not often appear today as general, free-floating symbols of police violence, but rather as representations of specific events of police violence in and around Paris in October 1961. Perhaps the wave of detailed historiographic accounts of 17 October, starting in the late 1980s, has something to do with this, as well as the advent of the internet and social media: information spreads more extensively, more virally, with myriad hyperlinks and connections involved.

Within the polymorphous history of the images, there has been a plethora of possible ways to perceive and invoke and refer to the photographs. Through the years, Kagan's photographs have taken on distinct names and meanings, variable intensities, and situated interpretations—various uses in different times and contexts—through a range of media, print, film, text, and imaginal thought. There is no single meaning to the images, no one way to comprehend them, no single use put to them. Rather, the photographic images, each and in combination working as a kind of "crystal image" (Deleuze 1989), have generated diffuse significations and political intensities and affective-ethical resonances. Through time, the images have been put to varied uses in distinct fields of perception and interpretation. Time is central to such shifting appearances in the life deaths of photographic images. A volatile flow of time is a wavering force and processual element in the many uses and invocations of the photographs. It's not just what a photograph is, from the start. It's what a photographic image becomes, and becomes anew, discordantly through time.

Multiplicities, yes, in the readings and invocations of photographic images from that night. As though returning to the same set of pictures, placing them on a table, looking at them one way and then another, and through that multilayered looking complexities of images through time can be grasped. Metaphysics of time and image clash, combine, intersect. At work are multiple traces of power and violence and testimonies against such violence, processes of inscription, interpretation, assessment. These multiplicities of form and interpretation entail disparities and tensions within crosscutting fields of interest and signification.

The Rhetoric of the Face of the Other

A compelling framework with which to consider Kagan's photographs from the night of 17 October 1961 comes from Ariella Aïsha Azoulay's discussion of "the event of photography" in her 2015 book *Civil Imagination: A Political Ontology of Photography.*

In this work, Azoulay, a philosopher and visual studies scholar, gives thought to various "photographic events" in developing a conceptual take on the political ontology of photography. In asking "What, then, is photography?" Azoulay (2015, 26) provides an answer that is succinct and striking: "Photography is an event." In critiquing the customary tendency in scholarship and art history to focus primarily on the photographer and a photographic work, which tends to leave out other actions, effects, materialities, and traces at hand in a photographic act, Azoulay shifts attention away from "the event photographed"—photographs of refugees in a detention camp, say, or a victim of state violence. She does so to give sustained thought to the many other acts and processes involved in a photographic event. Azoulay rightly posits that neither the photographer nor any other single participant is "sovereign" over the features or meaning of the photographs (51–52). Along with the photographer and any apparent subjects in a photograph, there are also the many actual and potential viewers and "spectators" of the photograph as perceived and circulated—all those who might encounter or be affected by or comment on a photograph, this entailing a potentially "infinite series of encounters" (26). As Azoulay argues, "The photograph is a platform upon which traces from the encounter between those present in the situation of the photograph are inscribed, whether the participants are present by choice, through force, knowingly, indifferently, as a result of being overlooked or as a consequence of deceit." The photographic event continues to exist, potentially, far beyond the event photographed. There is an "always unfinished nature of this event"; "the notion of a closure is overthrown thanks to the agency of the spectator" (27).

Azoulay's main tangible interest in her work is the politics of the occupation of Palestinian territories by the Israeli state, and the ways in which a careful, archival-like study of photographs, past or present, by any number of spectators, can show traces of the politics of that occupation. Through this, a "civil imagination" can be gained. That kind of engaged attentiveness lends itself to other politically charged situations, where witnessing, testimony, and historical reckoning and reinterpretations count for a lot.

In considering Kagan's photographs from the night of 17 October 1961, one can similarly say that with this photographic event—or, more precisely, this rhizomatic, open-ended network of photographic events—the photographs are a platform or subjectile of sorts, an ever-shifting palimpsest upon which traces of an array of encounters and imagistic transfers can be perceived. The agentive grounds of the photographs are multiple and multiply dispersed. Kagan has never been sovereign over the meaning of his photographs. No one is.

Along with the photographer, there are those who tried to stop him from taking photographs or sought to take and destroy any film cartridges in his possession that night, and those who permitted him to take the photographs in Petit-Nanterre that night. Within the tracework of the event are the subjects depicted in the photographs, persons alive or deceased, as well as those outside the frames of the photographs, including all the possible or actual viewers and users of the images. Along with the various media publications that have played a role in the representation and circulation of the images, through the media of newspapers, film, books, archives, there are also the various technologies and materialities and nonhuman "actants" involved—camera, film, darkroom, technologies of editing, duplication, circulation—as well as the various domains in which the photographs have been published and commented on, and instances of censorship or occlusion or denial of the content of the images.[17] Part of the photographic event as well are Kagan's words, stories, memories, and testimonial accounts of his experiences that night, voiced by him or others, and how those narrations intersect with other accounts and images. In effect are the ways in which any possible prints of the photographs, or talk of the photographs, any phantasmal imaginings of them, have circulated in any number of communities or families, or among friends or enemies in France, Algeria, or elsewhere. All this is involved in the gradual exposure of the events photographed. They contribute to the photographic event, which is multiply configured, open-ended, and ongoing.

What is not shown, what is not seen or traced or noticed within the photographs, is also part of the photographic event. Photographs not taken, when a camera is presumably available but goes unused—what Azoulay calls the category of the "untaken photograph"—can also create a photographic event.[18] The same holds for photographs taken but then made inaccessible to certain persons or the public more generally. What untaken photographs or unprocessed, uncirculated images from October 1961 in Paris are we not aware of, years later?

The event of Kagan's photographs is unfinished. Sixty years and counting, this event, which we might also consider as an "image-event" (Strassler), is still ongoing, in a messy, "complexly mediated" public sphere.[19] Within the history of a syncopated sequence of image-events, slight shifts in connotations and reverberations occur with each new online posting of the images or with each new publication or interpretive reading of the images. New possibilities in imagery, perception, interpretation, ethical engagement, and photo-fantasy emerge. In the present text, the photographic event laces through the writing and potential viewing of the images; any possible readers and readings, actual

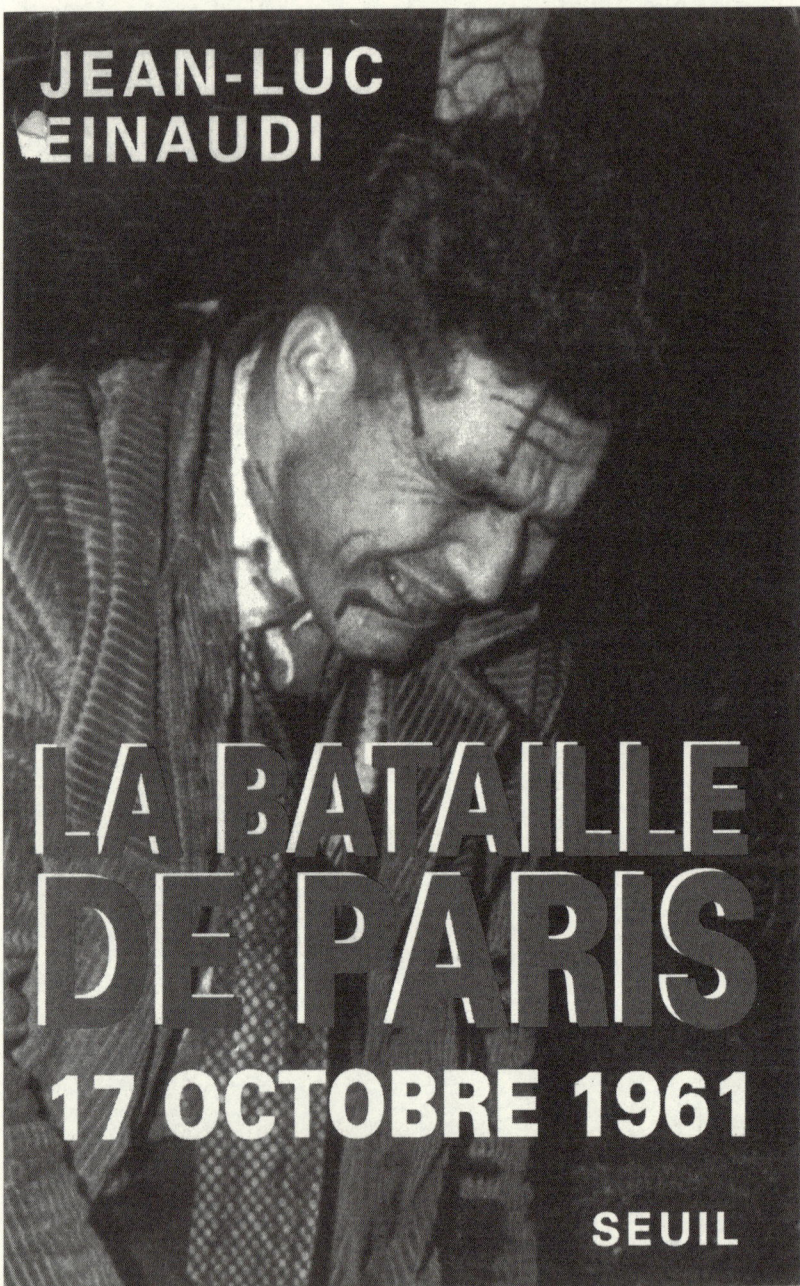

FIGURE 2.19. Cover, first edition of Jean-Luc Einaudi's *La bataille de Paris* (Éditions du Seuil, 1991), with image of Abdelkader Bennahar. Cover photo by Élie Kagan; see figure 1.11.

or imagined, contribute to the trace-effects of the photographs within a potentially infinite series of encounters.

Certain uses of the photographs have helped to constitute the event of them. This includes the cover image of Jean-Luc Einaudi's book *La bataille de Paris: 17 Octobre 1961*, published in October 1991—thirty years to the month of violence. The book's cover shows a close-up image of Bennahar as he was standing in pain by the wall along Rue des Pâquerettes (figure 2.19). Running across the lower portion of the cover—visually, virtually, upon the image-space of the stained coat, shirt, and tie—were the words, set in bright-red font, *La bataille de Paris*. The title, echoing the Battle of Paris of 1814, as well as the title of Gillo Pontecorvo's 1966 film, *The Battle of Algiers*, situates the war in the empire's capital. The overlaying of print onto image indicates the bloodstain of violence, fused into print.

This is a powerful, intensified image. It's continuously unsettling. The head of the person depicted is shown facing down, as though subjected to the force of the French state, "hit" and crushed by the police's blows. The pain and blood are within arm's reach. The image radiates wounding, loss of dignity, disaster of destruction. The cropping of the earlier photograph intensifies the scene of violence. We might consider this a *wound-image* in that the picture is an image of wounding, an image *as* wound. This is photography as wound. The image has remained a wound, in an open-ended, unhealed way, and capable of wounding. The wound-image has continued discordantly through time.

Why imprint the discrete image of this wounded, anguished man on the cover of this book? In 2007, Clotilde Lebas wrote about a moment in which she asked Jean-Luc Einaudi why he chose to use Kagan's photographs to illustrate his book—namely, with prints included in the text, and with the intense cover image. "Because Kagan is the only photographer who had this look, who got close," Einaudi responded. "The other few photos are from a distance. You see the crowd of protesters.... Kagan captured...the suffering...like this man who is on the cover [the one Kagan accompanied to the hospital]."[20]

The idea that Kagan captured the suffering through a direct and candid picture, in contrast to more general representations of the collective demonstrations and police violence, helps to explain the visceral force and potential power of this photographic image and other photographs produced by Kagan and why they are still in circulation years later.

Any direct intentions and perceptions aside, my sense is that the close-up photograph on the cover of Einaudi's book intensively conveys "the face of the other," to use Levinas's words for an ethical encounter with the presence and potential suffering and death of another sentient being in life.[21] For many readers in France, circa 1991—or 1962, or 2024—the countenance of the man photographed could directly signify or bring to mind the face of the other: that of a man apparently from North Africa, presumably Muslim, a migrant living in France, subject to the powers of the state; one of many persons who lived alongside other residents of the Republic, who tended to identify as white, Christian, French.

The face of the other is often expressed through the body of another, a morally salient, woundable body, *this body that hurts*.[22] This includes the body's capacity for pain and wounding, potentially unto death. The sensate ground of possible wounding can tear into another; it can wound and affect. With that regard of a woundable body can come a sense of an infinite "responsibility for the other," the ethics of which Levinas so powerfully wrote. Reading and looking here implies an ethics: to hold *La bataille de Paris* in one's hands is to engage with a responsibility for those fellow residents of France, harmed by the Paris police. To read its pages and take in its images is to respond to the faces and bodies of others and the histories of hardship experienced by the colonized.

Here it's important to note that the "face of the other," as rendered by Levinas and others, is not simply a philosophical concept, touching on an important phenomenon in life which many persons can relate to—namely, the presence or potential presence of suffering others in the world, to whom one feels a responsibility, an "infinite responsibility" (Levinas), an enduring call to respond to such suffering. Specific invocations of "the face of the other" can have significant perlocutionary force, holding the ability to persuade, which in turn can imply significant rhetorical and political effects. Kagan's photographs of Bennahar imply a *rhetoric of the face of the other*. In showing the face of this wounded man, the photographs carry the potential effect of provoking visceral, potentially ethical responses, or at least prompting the question of a response, in anyone who encounters the images.

For many residents of France, Kagan's photographs notably depicted the body and face of a wounded other, not those of a wounded person much like oneself. At the time, Algerians largely remained an "other" in French political consciousness. As French philosopher Jacques Rancière has conveyed them, the events of 17 October 1961 provoked several crucial realizations among residents and citizens of France, a political subject position that Rancière describes as "us." Born in Algiers in June 1940, Rancière would have been twenty-one in October 1961 and, presumably, a student living and studying in Paris. Like many others, he was appalled by the actions of the French state and the "police" aspect of the war between France and Algerians fighting for the liberation of Algeria. As he writes in his essay "The Cause of the Other,"

Now, it has to be remembered, that, officially, the Algerian war was not a war. It was a police operation on a large scale. The political response was therefore a response to the "police" aspect of the war, and that is not the same thing as a recognition of the *historical* validity of the war of liberation. From that point onwards, there becomes possible a political subjectivation that did not take the form of external support for the other's war, or an identification of the other's military cause with our cause. This political subjectivation was primarily the result of a disidentification with the French state that had done this in our name and removed it from our view. We could not identify with the Algerians who appeared as demonstrators within the French public space, and who then disappeared. We could, on the other hand, reject our identification with the State that had killed them and removed them from all the statistics. (Rancière 1998, 29)

Rancière goes on to note there was an "impossible identification" with the other—in this instance, Algerian, Maghrebian others in the mainstream of the French political-cultural imaginary—"an identification with an other with whom one cannot in normal circumstances identify: the 'wretched of the earth' or some other object. In the case of the Algerian war, there was no identification with those fighters, whose motives were not ours, or with those victims, whose very faces were invisible to us. But an identity that could be assumed was included in a political subjectivation—in a rejection of an identity" (Rancière 1998, 29).

Rancière's broader argument on political subjectivation, politics, and the police is an intricate and complicated one. It suffices to note here that, as Rancière contends, there remained an "impossible identification" for many French residents with Algerians fighting for their independence. Often the faces of those fighting for independence were rendered invisible by the French police; more generally, at the time, Algerianness was an abstract category of French political consciousness. There was an awareness of "the cause of the other" (*la cause de l'autre*), but this was largely another's cause, one with which many could not directly identify. This particular cause functioned in French politics as an impossible identification. These positionings would in themselves have complicated any potential viewings of images like the one that adorned the cover of Einaudi's 1991 book *La bataille de Paris*. The man depicted could have been perceived by many as a wounded other, an abject or heroic other—but the face of the other, nonetheless. What they saw was a person and imaginal figure for whom one might feel sympathy, but this was not necessarily a subject position, a wounded body, with which one could directly identify.

For many persons from Algeria, in contrast, and for others who identify as residing or coming from North Africa or other colonized and French "territories," the viewing of the image on the cover of *La bataille de Paris* could have been one of immediate identification. Many might have related directly to the wounding conveyed and the physical-political hardships involved. Many would have known intimately the state-sanctioned violence implied. Recognition of this violence would be quick and immediate. This recognition would not have been simply cognitive or semiotic in form; people would recognize the violence with and through their bodies. For the image of wounding was already there, in people's lives and histories, before it took this specific tangible form in the photographic image emblazoned on the cover of Einaudi's book. The image carries the trace of other images. Any perceptions of this image were already haunted by other perceptions of violence and wounding and their correlated images. The cover image spoke to the haunting recurrence of state-sanctioned violence, touching on past, present, and future acts of police violence, from the streets of the Goutte d'Or to the banlieues circling Paris. The breach of the violence elicits memories of wounds and breaches snared within other histories of violence. Still today, the pain and terror implied cut all too close to home.[23]

Yet another response to the cover image that conceivably has been in circulation—perhaps with greater force and currency in recent years— would tie into concerns that the book's surface imagery displayed an intensified image of a male body, damaged and nearly negated, within a spectacular scene of violence. Imageries of anti-Black violence, as found with photographs of lynchings in the United States and images of violence in Europe and North America, relate similar imaginaries of spectacular violence and Black and brown bodies in cultural visual discourses.[24] The close-up of the face shown in the cover image further spectacularizes the suffering of the subject portrayed. The book's intense scenography of wounding would have the generative capacity to draw the looks of many potential spectators while causing possible consternation among those who glanced at the cover image and winced from its troubling implications.

This single image, once launched into the world, carried distinct perspectives and tensions within the folds of its imaginal potential. I would like to suggest that this can be a matter of intensification: different engagements with the image imply distinct ways of looking at and rendering the image, which variably intensify motifs apparent or implicit in this scene of violence. We can think of a photograph as "a bloc of sensations, that is to say, a compound of percepts and affects"—as Deleuze and Guattari (1994, 164) find is the case with a work of art. The cover image carries a compound of sensations and perceptual and affective intensities that potentially reach perceivers of that image (164).

In theory, then, differently positioned people have encountered and perceived and imaginatively rendered Kagan's photographs in disparately charged ways. Perceptions of the photographic images have been "refracted" through myriad personal and collective memories and experiences. In speaking of the process of refraction here, I draw from Karen Strassler's (2010, 23) inquiry into the "refracted visions" apparent in engagements with photographic practices in Java, in which "everyday encounters with photographs entangle widely shared visions with affectively charged personal narratives and memories." With the photographs of Bennahar, conceivably, both the photographed event (the man lying on the ground, standing up, and then being brought to the hospital) and the photographic event (Kagan's photographs, imagery recurrent through time) could mean and affect and trouble differently. The events implied proceed in disparate ways, depending on shifting positions in relations of power, violence, and perception.

The cover image of Einaudi's *La bataille de Paris* carries a valency of assault, wounding, and scarring. The uncertain qualities of the image and the unknown name and identity (for many) and the post-assault status of the person harmed contributed to that tear and *blessure*. But the wound was not that of the person photographed alone. It might also signify—metonymically, part for whole—the wounding of a collective of peoples, namely, those dominated through French colonial rule in North Africa and elsewhere. That wound has not healed, not fully. The wound had never been properly sutured.

I can imagine, imagine only, how people perceived the cover of Einaudi's book when it first hit newsstands and appeared in bookstores and then was passed from hand to hand. Suddenly there is a glance at the man pictured on the book's surface and the sight of blood streaming down his face. There is sympathy or disgust or alarmed concern for the man pictured and for the violent histories scored through the pages of the text. Some viewers would have suffered similar wounds or knew of family or neighbors similarly beaten or killed by police or military forces of the French state.

Viewers of the book's cover—and the author himself—must have wondered who, precisely, this person photographed was, what happened to him, and what became of him. They might have wondered if the man, if still alive, had seen this image of himself, strangely cut from that night of violence. For years, the man photographed carried an uncertain, unrecognized history.

I own a copy of the first edition of Einaudi's *Bataille* book, unmarked, kept on a bookshelf. I purchased a later edition one afternoon at a bookstore on Rue des Écoles, near Boulevard Saint-Michel (where Algerian protestors were badly beaten that October night). This is a *livre de poche* paperback, first printed in 2007 by Éditions du Seuil, in a series called Points Histoires. The copy I have has been well read. Dog-eared pages are marked up with notes and asterisks; sentences underlined by me in one moment or another; dates and place-names highlighted; words circled and translated into English alongside statements scribbled on the margins. Imperfect, contested, the fiery work of a "militant historian," the book's pages have become a source text for me, an archive of chronicles, names, testimonies.

The cover image of the 2007 *livre de poche* edition of Einaudi's *La bataille de Paris* also features a photographic image of Bennahar, with blood streaming down his face (figure 2.20). More than a simple representation, the image is a force, a neuralgic intensity. It's a searing portrait of suffering in the harsh epoch of a colonial state, a puncturing wound in time. The man portrayed is exposed, seen and imagined constantly, this iterable face of another. He is unknowing of his fate, either in the realm of photographic traces or in the afterlife of a life death.

A. writes, "When you read the book's pages, your hands touch the bloodied face, even if you forget that visceral contact for a while. To read the book in public, you have to carry the image with you." The wounding stays close.

"The image touches me, and, thus touched and drawn by it and into it, I get involved, not to say mixed up in it," writes Jean-Luc Nancy (2005, 7). I am mixed up in the grain of Bennahar's image, entangled within his arms and hands, the pain felt in his body as though that body were close to my own. Repeated viewings of the image hold me in an embrace of body, thought, vision, pain. When I trace my fingers on the pictural image and then withdraw my hand I am half-surprised to find that the edges of my fingers are not marked by the ink of remnant staining.

While searching the internet for other occurrences of Kagan's photographs, I encountered another book cover image that carries a trace of the wounded body of Bennahar. This was the cover image for a *livre de poche* Folio edition of Didier Daeninckx's *Meurtres pour mémoire*, a murder mystery of a novel that begins with a stark portrait of the atrocities of 17 October 1961 while telling the story of the death of a middle-aged history teacher in a public school in Paris, killed the same night as the demonstrations. First published by Gallimard in 1984, and later translated into English as *Murder in Memoriam*,

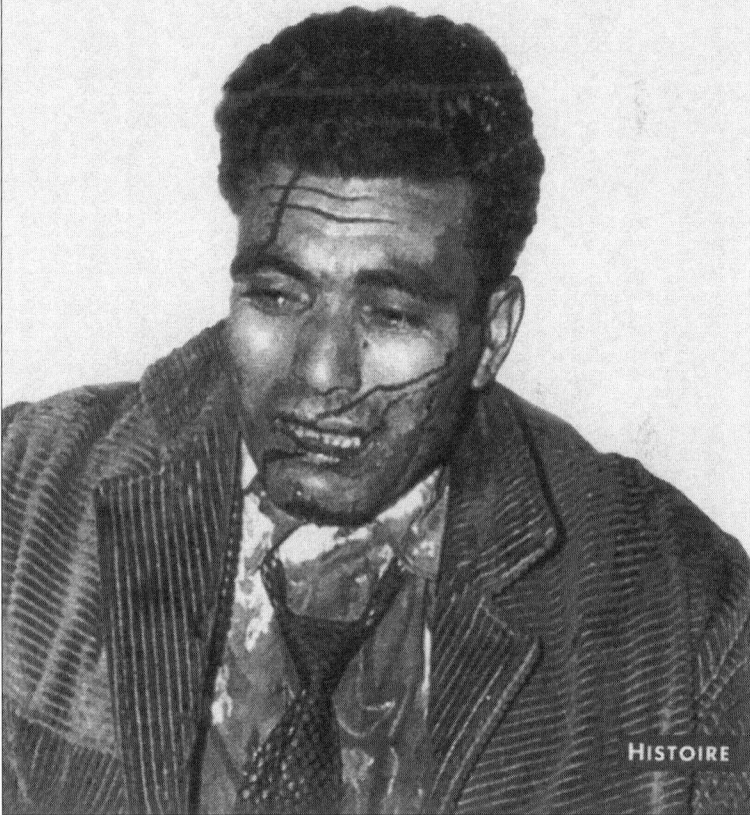

FIGURE 2.20. Cover, *livre de poche* edition of Jean-Luc Einaudi's *La bataille de Paris* (Éditions du Seuil, 2007), with image of Abdelkader Bennahar. Cover photo by Élie Kagan; see figure 1.14.

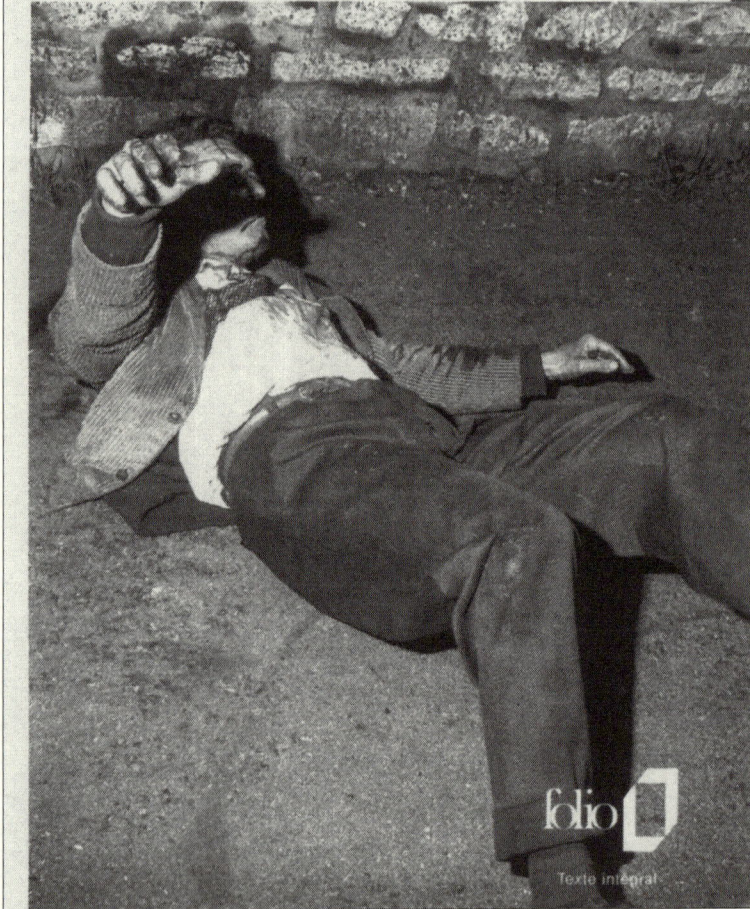

FIGURE 2.21. Cover, *livre de poche* edition of Didier Daeninckx's *Meurtres pour mémoire* (Gallimard, 1988), with image of Abdelkader Bennahar. Cover photo by Élie Kagan; see figure 1.10.

this *roman policier* brought public recognition to the police violence against Algerians in Paris in October 1961 (Daeninckx 1984, 2012). Gallimard published the *livre de poche* edition of the novel with their Folio series in 1988.

I held the pages of this book in my hands a few days later, after ordering a used copy online. I keep returning to the image imprinted on the cover (figure 2.21). While I had looked closely at representations of this same photograph by Kagan before, I had not previously encountered this particular framing and apparitional intensity of the image. This novel recurrence of the photographic image speaks to its iterability and alterability—the paperback's cover image is at once similar to and distinct from the images I had viewed before. Another spore-like issue, yes, and yet the specific tones and textures of the image have led me to perceive anew its appearance. A newly rendered image brings new perceptions—and a further development in Kagan's photographic work.

It's a harsh image. Disturbing, I find. The image on the cover of *Meurtres pour mémoire* shows a cropped, further intensified photograph of Bennahar lying on the ground at Rue des Pâquerettes, his hand raised toward the glare of the camera. This glare is refracted through the glossy sheen of the book's plasticky paper surface, on which indirect flares of shiny light are easily cast, adding to the optical complexities of any stable perception of the cover image. The man's identity and fate linger as a mystery, as befits the narrative suspense of Daeninckx's *Meurtres pour mémoire*. The dark wounding could intrigue potential readers of the novel, while phantasmally through time the man portrayed is exposed to the looks of others in any number of bookstores in Paris, Algiers, and elsewhere, even if his face cannot be clearly seen.

Looking closely at Bennahar's appearance in this incarnation of the photograph, my eyes are drawn to the area around his face. I see the blood streaming from a wound on his chin—apparently the result of being struck with a club or gun. A line of blood flows from the top of his scalp, as though the forehead bears a track of stitches. A few features of Bennahar's face can be seen slightly, opaquely, beyond the magmatic shadow that obscures any direct view. His eyes are closed in this photographic moment. The apparent distortions of the facial features in these moments of injury and exhaustion and photographic wounding reflect a state of corpse-like arrest. Perhaps this cadaverous hue relates to photographic effects and circumstances. Still, the contorted face brings to mind photographs of corpses I have come across in recent years, in unsettling moments. An intensification of the troubled aspects of a damaged, occluded face in the temporality of this image anticipates the imminent death of the living subject photographed. This is a face near death, while in the moments after the photo's taking Bennahar was still moving on in life.

What does it mean to become the subject of a formative fiction, either while alive or within the potentially unending duration of a life death, to have aspects of a life cast in an iconic image or two, couched in visuals that roam the world and root themselves in minds, newspapers, websites, ranging from social media feeds to scholarly discourses?

Multiplication and Proliferation

And now cut to the contemporary scene, with the ubiquitous use and circulation of images in the vast reaches of the internet and fast-paced currents of news feeds and social media channels, with all of these digital-virtual domains imbued with a "'frenzy' of image making," to quote Daniel Rubinstein and Katrina Sluis (2013, 30) from their essay "The Digital Image in Photographic Culture." "The image is everywhere all at once," these authors observe, "accessible from any point in the network, establishing a regime of intoxication and plenitude through its rapid multiplication and profusion." Rubinstein and Sluis continue, "The present tendency of the image to move through the network in several directions at once, decomposing and recombining, multiplying and aggregating into different contexts, further undermines the notion of the photograph as a singular cultural unit that operates as an archive of time" (30). These two authors contend that the qualities of photographic images in the contemporary digital, interconnected world are distinct from those apparent in photographs from an earlier, analog time. Digital photographic images in the contemporary moment are less tied to indexical reference and singular discrete images, and they proceed largely through multiple data streams, patterned by algorithmic computational programs. "When the photograph became digital information, it not only became malleable and non-indexical, it became *computational* and *programmable*" (29).

Digital reproductions of Kagan's photographs from October 1961 are presently cast among countless other images, dispersed like an explosion of stars in a galaxy. They recur in rhizomatic ways among an ever-emergent, ever-shifting multiplicity of blog postings, newspaper records, media feeds, archive profiles, and partial histories. The multiplication and proliferation of images is the abiding constant in this fractal regime of virtual intoxication. This exponential digital rendering of the images marks another significant development in Kagan's photographs through time: from a few analog photographs, culled from a finite set of negative film strips, has emerged a profusion of digital reproductions appearing in various digital formats (JPG, PNG, TIFF, PDF, etc.) and virtual interfaces and computation-based data streams. The images dwell and wander apparitionally within vast networks of data feeds that are programmed and cultivated by algorithmic calculations. The photographic images are not from any single source or archive or distinct set of photographic prints. There is no clear sovereignty over the images, no single author or agent who manages or controls these constantly disseminating pictures. A certain wildness animates the images, which are uncontrolled and uncontrollable. So goes the itinerant spore life of images.

These days, it's relatively easy to conjure up Kagan's photographs. All you need is a computer or cell phone and a live connection to the internet. Just type the words "Kagan 17 Octobre 1961" into a search bar, and a profusion of images will appear. I did just that one December morning, priming a Google search in the category for images. This prompted the search program to draw from its vast index, a large database compiled from countless automated acts of "crawling" by Google web crawlers—courtesy of a program called Googlebot—through billions of pages found on the internet, with the data gleaned from these crawls analyzed and stored on the Google index.[25] Within moments, a bevy of high-quality images that Google found relevant to my query had lined up in neat formation on the LCD screen of a laptop (figure 2.22).

Most of the images spawned from this search I had seen before, including a photograph of Élie Kagan in his later years. The top array of the digital search (as shown in figure 2.22) produced seventeen versions of Kagan's photographs from 17 October 1961, as well as two photos taken on 19 October 1961. Seven of the images gleaned from the tracts of October 17 show the body of Bennahar as photographed by Kagan that night. These thumbnail icons are so small that they do not convey directly the intensity of the violence and wounding signified through the images. But once someone clicks on a given icon, they arrive at a specific history and intensity.

Within this mosaic of violence and its reverberations, certain scenes recur, anguished movement onto political defiance and collective action, political imaginaries at work. "Ici on noie les Algériens" (Here we drown Algerians). While the array of thumbnail icons is largely pictural in form, what I sense most is pain circuiting from body to body, ache to wound. Raw sensation pulses through a fabula nervous system.

Threaded through the screenshot mosaic is the imaged body of Abdelkader Bennahar, bad dream fragments drifting through an oneiric expanse of digitalized histories. Often going without a name or specific identity, the fractured figure of Bennahar courses through the many-stranded histories of Kagan's

FIGURE 2.22. Screenshot of the results of a Google image search for "Kagan 17 Octobre 1961," December 2023. Courtesy of the author.

photographs from 17 October 1961. This visual graph of a person in pain has been dispersively printed and reprinted, copied and reduplicated; images of an unnamed man refract through a thousand media; there is no original image here, nor final image, no terminal end point—just different emanations of a wounding image. The eventualities of a subject have been edited and reproduced, posted and reposted, reconfigured time and again, taking on new valences with each new turn of the images.

Along with the diffusion and proliferation of the images, certain themes recur. From their first enactments, the history of these photographic images has been troubled by certain epistemological complexities and phenomenological quandaries. Accordingly, while tracing out the multiplicities evident in Kagan's photographs—haunted by multiplicity—I write in epistemic tension.

Like others, I find a sense of the real, and evidential traces of violence, in these photographic images. At the same time, I realize that evidential traces tie into certain discourses of the real and specific ways of thinking about life, history, traces, and images. I also comprehend that Kagan's photographs have occurred during a historical era and a cultural-political world where such "instants of truth" (Arendt 1966, xxix–xxx) have counted for a lot. I see something of the actual in these photos while knowing that the actual is a construct, a photograph is a formative fiction.

Yet another tension, more phenomenological in spirit: the photographs appear to convey at once, within the same spectrum of vision, something of the real and something of the apparitional. Precisely, trace elements of that man on the ground, wounded, stains of blood on his shirt and coat, getting to his feet, on his way to the hospital; spectrally, apparitions of a wounded man. Appearance and apparition. Medium of film and spectral medium. "Reality effect" intermeshed with "spectrality effect."[26] A photographic image is "an hallucination that is also a fact" (Bazin 1960, 9). "I would also say that one of the characteristics of what we call an image is its ability to cross borders, walls, and other obstacles—like a kind of ghost" (Didi-Huberman 2015, 99). Modern technologies of photography, media, and communication enable images of wounding to travel from place to place and leap from one local history to another. And now, with the internet and its constant phantasmagoria of images circulating in endless loops of links and associations, these ghostly images recur in virtual, apparitional forms with potentially infinite repetitions of wounding, including the iconic image that landed on the surface screen of a laptop one autumnal night in New York.

A similar tension holds for any writing on Kagan's photographs and the images, events, and life deaths drawn out of them. I am reaching for the actual while knowing that any words advanced involve a deeply imaginal history—a formulation, an extended phantasm. These doubts and tensions are caught up in the complexities of Kagan's photographic images. I cannot say I rightly know how to proceed within these conceptual and perceptual tensions—they imply aporias, in themselves—outside of living with paradox. I write with these tensions in mind, which vex any pensive regard of the images.

A wandersome biography of Kagan's photographs from 17 October 1961 thus suggests multiplicity, a life death of images fused by complicated epistemic and affective entanglements, with a few motifs recurrent. In some moments, the images burn with the real of violence.[27] They are powerful in their revenant returns.

On occasion, while talking with others about the histories of violence I have been trying to comprehend, I've opened the internet browser on my cell phone to locate online postings of the photographs. A quick search command brings up an array of stark monochrome images, including those of a wounded Bennahar (typically unnamed). I then show the images to my interlocutors, who look at them with an air of serious focus. In later reflection, I have felt crass in showing the images this way, as if they are not to be shown so casually, in such a quick and common manner without careful consideration—cheap, that way.

Lately, in similar circumstances I have refrained from showing any of the possible smartphone pics. The moment passes, an interval of silence without direct image.

INTERSECTING LIVES

Assailed by Memories

I would like to tell you, if possible, about the ways in which a life might be marked by images, graced or rattled by them. Or that images constitute a life death, in relation to others. A person might be haunted by an image or a wounding event. Scenes burrowed in the depths of memory reemerge in uneven moments.

It can be a matter of two lives intersecting, as if by chance through brief moments, and yet so much can be said of that intersection of two lines in life death, among others. So much is possibly graphed, marked, recalled, survived, lost, sedimented, buried in and through fleeting, lasting encounters. Much of our lives is composed of nicks, wounds, scuff marks, scars, incurable bruises, or gentle care and repair in crisscrossing clashes and connections with others.

"Une soirée qui aura marqué toute sa vie." It was "an evening that had marked all of his life," wrote French author and publisher François Maspero of the intensity of perceptions Kagan faced the night of 17 October 1961.[1] *Marqué*, as in marked, scarred, branded, impressed, notched, haunted. By all accounts, Kagan was deeply affected by what he encountered that night, in which he saw and photographed under duress the aftereffects of numerous Algerians beaten or killed by the Paris police, while evading potential violence against himself. These acts of state violence, racist brutality, and fearful escape brought to mind similar acts and terrors in his childhood, during World War II and the years of the Nazi occupation of France.

"October 1961 was an experience that Kagan never forgot," reads one obituary in the wake of Kagan's death. "It was, he said, the painful return to his childhood. He was born in 1928, the son of poor immigrant Jewish parents, the mother Polish and the father Russian. He spent the war in hiding, living in terror. He emerged with the Liberation ready to celebrate and to protest" (Johnson 1999).

Kagan's biography admits to painful returns in a life of marks and graphs. In 1941, his parents had their young son leave their home in Paris in fearful anticipation of the imminent roundups of Jews by the Nazis and the French police. In one written document, reproduced in the book *17 Octobre 1961*, Kagan related that his mother was arrested in Paris on 16 July 1942—a day of mass police roundups of Jews in Paris—and then escaped from the police station where she was taken (Einaudi and Kagan 2001, 70; House 2010, 32). Elijah Kagan traversed France at the age of fourteen and then spent the war in hiding until it was safe to return to his family's home in Paris. Once there, he was able to reunite with his mother, while learning that many of his neighbors and childhood friends were no longer alive, having been deported to Germany and killed in concentration camps.

Le reporter engagé relates aspects of a difficult, unsettling childhood for Kagan:

A Polish Jew born in France in 1928, Élie Kagan was eleven years old when the Vichy government imposed the wearing of the yellow star. His parents, foresighted, worried or lucid, placed him in a house near Le Mans [in northwestern France]. On the very day that the Germans invaded the southern zone and put an end to the fiction of a French Independent State, the young Elijah, fourteen years old, took the bus heading south. He did not know that the occupation army had the same idea a few hours before him.

The bus appeared on the demarcation line around Angoulême. The German soldiers made all the male members get off the bus, about thirty in all, and lined them up by the side of the road. At the first summons, the suspects lowered their pants and an officer passed the inspection. By chance, which has yet to be explained, Kagan was not circumcised. Besides the bitter feeling of humiliation of having one's pants down to one's ankles, Kagan will always keep with him the unspeakable certainty of having missed the irremediable. (Kagan and Rotman 1989, 10–11)

The possible arrest and annihilation of anyone branded an unwanted, tainted outsider; the detention and segregation of groups of people based on religious identities and racist prejudices; the need to flee the potent authority and organized violence of the governing powers; the terror of forced detainment and the bitter humiliation of bodily exposure and examination; the wounding and killing of perceived enemies of the state; hiding in fear of being caught, banished, killed, traumas of violence and loss—all of this seared Kagan's memories of the war and of the state violence of October 1961. This was a doubled, repetitive searing-scarring, crossing a span of twenty years, when he was aged fourteen, and then thirty-three. Others living in France also traced affinities between the state and police violence in Paris in the late 1950s and early 1960s and the collective violence of the German occupation and the Vichy regime during World War II. For Kagan, there were clear personal dimensions to such perceived parallels.

Certain telling marks on his person would have done him in. If Kagan was wearing the yellow star on his clothing the day he took the bus to the south of France, or if he had been circumcised—he lacked the distinguishing mark of a Jew, that "exemplary counterscar that we have to learn to read without seeing" (Derrida 1993, 24), that sign, variably, of a scapegoat, hostage, victim; of a sacred community or cultural heritage; of purity, or of assigned shame—if he had been "cut" and marked in that way, then he would have been seized by the German soldiers and, in a matter of days, banished to a concentration camp in Germany, where he probably would not have survived the harsh labor and living conditions nor the camps' industries of incineration. Inscribed in Kagan's biography was the certainty that he had missed "the irremediable" (*l'irrémédiable*)—the unrecoverable, incorrigible event of death (Kagan and Rotman 1989, 11). That was a marked line he did not cross then. Others were not so fortunate, including the playmates he knew as a child or the lifeless man he photographed at Rue des Pâquerettes, the body slung across the low stone wall. ("This was war: life for some, for others, the cruelty of assassination," wrote Maurice Blanchot in *The Instant of My Death*, which tells of the narrator's close brush with death in facing a firing squad. "I am alive. No, you are dead" [Blanchot and Derrida 2000, 6–7, 9].) *Le reporter engagé* tells it this way:

Stashed away until the end of the war, Kagan will find again his mother, who miraculously escapes the great roundup of Vel d'Hiv. To possess from the start of adolescence the clear and acute consciousness of being a survivor gives to things and to life a detached look which only attaches to the essential. Through persistent fidelity to an ever-present past, Kagan lives today in the small apartment where he was born and where the police force of the collaboration requisitioned one morning in July, 1942. As for the neighbors, and playmates in the paved courtyard, there are not many left. Regarding Drancy, one lost sight of them. (Kagan and Rotman 1989, 11–12)

The visible and its absence are recurrent motifs in Kagan's sensory biography, one that incorporates, in marked and hurting ways, the life deaths of others.[2] He and others "lost sight" (*on les a perdu de vue*) of those sent to Drancy, that infamous internment camp to the northeast of Paris that served as a way station for trains bound to Auschwitz, crammed with anxious, fearful people, many of whom never returned to France. With the clear and acute consciousness of a survivor who sees life and death clearly comes a "detached look" (*un regard détaché*) that fits well the optical modalities of a journalistic photographer. Each instantaneous photo conveys "un passé toujours présent," an always-present past (much as a trauma does). Kagan possessed a survivor's vision—if not survivor's guilt, though that is also possible. His photographs from the night of 17 October 1961 carried an acuity of violence, imprinted in clear photographic "*vues*" that have lasted for years, while he lost sight of those photographed that night.

Motifs of violence, vision, marking, and photographic and autobiographic fixing are recursive and interwoven here, as they were in Kagan's life and memories. An extract of a poetic text written by Kagan in the late 1960s, handwritten in a *petit livre gris* (a "small gray book"), made available to the public by his family after his death, touches on the intensity of memories of the night of 17 October 1961.[3] A few passages, in translation:

17 October 1961 . . .
Later we will call
this heated day
Ratonnade in Paris.
Of Arabs by the thousands,
Concorde, Solférino,
Rue de Lille, helmeted men.
My fear, which surprises me.

October 61
July 42
October 61
July 42
Métro, crowded cars
French, noses against windows,
indifferent,
We shoot, we kill,
and then we quickly erase.
And me Alone, all alone
with fear in my stomach
Who does his job as a man
And fixes forever [*fixe pour toujours*]
The crime, the murder
The death of innocents
In hoping, naively
That perhaps my images
will wake up others [*mes images réveilleront les autres*]
Amorphous, sleeping,
selfish . . . or rotten. . . .
On the Métro platform
I photograph an Arab
who is suffering
A bullet in the shoulder
He is there grimacing, crying
. . . .
Of the memories that assail me
16 July 42
The Vél d' Hiv full of Jews
French indifferent
And leave then
Die from afar
Innocents, innocents
And me I survived, I read
I studied
Success
Do what I want
do what I must.

Memories "assailed" or "attacked" Kagan that October night ("des souvenirs qui m'assaillent"), as though the flashbacks were violent forces capable of causing lasting harm. Among these were the visceral recollections of the *rafle* roundups of Jews in July 1942, with many of the detained locked up for several days in the Vélodrome d'Hiver (also known as the Vel d'Hiv) before being sent on to Drancy and then to labor and concentration camps in Germany; these innocents "left, died away." Kagan survived this genocide, as did his mother, but many, including friends and neighbors, were swept away by the collaborationist French police. That same Vel d'Hiv was used as a detention center for Algerians in the late 1950s. In October 1961, thousands of Algerians were detained in sports arenas and exhibition halls in Paris for several days after being arrested and transported in buses from the sites of the demonstrations. Several hundred of these men were then deported to Algeria on flights that left from Orly Airport. Kagan lived and perceived these two histories of violence, and he traced affinities between them.

Others in France also actively found and articulated connections between the events in Paris of October 1961 and those of July 1942. From the start of the Algerian war, a number of persons in France had established thematic connections between the Nazi occupation and the Vichy regime, on the one hand, and French colonialism and the political oppression of Algerians, on the other. As Jim House (2010, 23) concludes his analysis of the histories involved, from the post–World War II era on, "connections established between the Nazi Occupation and the repression of Algerians were therefore commonplace." A "similarity in difference" was discerned and established; this entailed "the emergence of a radical comparison" (15). The events of 17 October 1961 underscored these presumed parallels.

While historians have made it clear that these two historical formations are significantly, qualitatively different, some have pointed out that many left-leaning persons and activist groups in France nevertheless drew these connections, for various reasons, political motivations, and discursive and rhetorical strategies.[4] For one, activists found that the political techniques involved were often similar in the two histories of state violence and domination. As Jim House (2001, 364) observes, "The parallels established by activists highlight the police techniques involved, the singling out of a social group—very often racialized—for violent treatment, the impunity of those responsible and subsequent official reluctance to disclose information, and the messages this sends out to racialized groups (and their persecutors)." At the same time, certain persons and groups established more general affinities between memories and representations of the Holocaust—particularly the roundup of Jews in Paris in July 1942 and the state and police violence against and detentions of Algerians in October 1961. As Michael Rothberg posited in 2009, in exploring the then nearly half-century-long archive of memory and representation of 17 October 1961, "The October events have long functioned as a relay articulating anti-Semitic racialization during World War II, colonial and postcolonial racism, the violence of decolonization, and the problems of twentieth- and twenty-first-century multicultural societies faced with new forms of globalization and imperialism." In developing his thesis that collective memories of such events work in "multidirectional ways," with diverse connections and "rhetorical interchangability" involved, Rothberg observes that "the Holocaust and October 17 have served as vehicles of remembrance for each other: the racist repression of the early 1960s served as a means to continue the very incomplete coming to terms with Nazi genocide then in its early stages in France and elsewhere, while in the 1980s, 1990s, and early twenty-first century, a more established Holocaust memory archive has come to serve as a source for the articulation (the expression and cross-cultural linkage) of memory of the October events" (Rothberg 2009, 229).

Jim House develops a perspective similar to Rothberg's in his 2010 essay "Memory and the Creation of Solidarity During the Decolonization of Algeria."[5] Here, House (2010, 37) points out that, for some persons and groups, there were significant personal and generational dimensions involved in the associations traced between the Nazi genocide and French colonial oppression of Algerian peoples: "There was a small but determined group of people in France whose relationship to the Algerian War of Liberation, and decolonization more generally, was heavily influenced by their diverse experiences of World War II and, specifically, of anti-Jewish policies." House continues,

> The political "space" for an avowedly multidirectional memory may be larger, wider, and richer at some historical moments than at others, and the Holocaust may not always or explicitly be one of the vectors. It is clear, nonetheless, that during the Algerian war in France there developed a particularly strong repertoire of themes that drew analogies between the Occupation, the Holocaust, and the Resistance on the one hand, and, on the other, the Algerians' struggle for independence and the repression that this struggle met. Yet we have also seen that this rhetorical field did not emerge from a political and memorial void, just as generational factors were important in its elaboration and expression: they would also play a key role in its transmission. (37)

House finds that personal experience and transmitted memory often played a key role in the affinities that people drew between the two histories, and the "counter-knowledge" implied in such a perspective. "Given that the French people were socialized into hostility against Algerians," he writes, "and educated to believe that Algeria constituted an integral part of France, the counter-knowledge that preceded such a decision to help the FLN, or indeed to denounce torture and other abuses, had to come from somewhere" (House 2010, 31).

House considers Élie Kagan, among a few others, as someone whose experiences during World War II, especially in relation to anti-Jewish policies, influenced his relationship to the Algerian war of liberation.[6] The personal and political history of this photographer during the Nazi occupation of France, and the complicity of residents of France in the detention and deportation of Jews to Germany during World War II, sharply informed his understandings and embodied experience of the police violence against Algerians in 1961, the complicity of French residents in that violence, and the passive reactions to and occlusions of this state violence. Such considerations contributed to Kagan's positioning as a photographer and eyewitness to the violence of 17 October 1961, as well as to the rhetorical field in which his photographs and testimonial accounts subsequently took form. House (2010, 33) remarks, "Kagan's personal trajectory clearly—and understandably—figures July 1942 and October 17, 1961 together as key events."

This brings us back to Kagan's poem, inscribed in the late 1960s in the "small gray book" that he kept, a portion of which was published by Kagan's family after he died. This poem-text can be taken as an artifact of "multidirectional memory," as Michael Rothberg proposes in his 2009 book by that name, an interdisciplinary work that discusses how memories of the Holocaust are reiterated in the articulation of other histories of victimization in Europe, Africa, and elsewhere. Rothberg (2009, 301) finds that Kagan's text "reads Papon's brutality multidirectionally in the Vel' d'Hiv' roundup of Jews. . . . Writing in the late 1960s, Kagan simultaneously captures the mood of 1961, which already read the events in relation to the Vel' d'Hiv' roundup, and draws on the experiences of the aftermath of forgetting. But as his text demonstrates . . . multidirectional memory can emerge even out of the depths of oblivion."

Kagan's poem verbalizes an intergrafting of histories of disaster and painful memories. The verse reads like a photographic contact sheet, fixed into poeticized words, of flash memories, intensive marks, and perceptions. Kagan wrote that his fear "surprised him" (*ma peur, qui me surprend*). The fear, unexpected, surprisingly pervasive, might have surged through his body and unnerved his thoughts and perceptions. The events brought back the anxious phenomenon of Jews being caught, deported, and killed during the Nazi occupation of France, as his interleaving reiteration of infamous dates suggest: "Octobre 61,

Juillet 42, Octobre 61, Juillet 42." Two interhaunting dates; each a wound-scar signifying a singularly marked event, presumably unrepeatable, yet violence recurred.

October 1961 was for Kagan a time of violent return, incised by repetition and difference. The photography-of-disaster he undertook the night of 17 October implied visual echoes, trauma-images of other scenes of violence in Paris. Memories grafted onto memories; fear spliced into fear. Kagan was haunted by spectral apparitions of the police roundups of 1942, the violence of which returned to him like a revenant. It's understandable that Kagan felt fearful of the police, who in their rage were out to destroy anyone who got in their way and sought to cancel out any trace evidence of their violent actions that night. Fears of being "singled out"; of hiding from helmeted police officers searching the streets of Paris; of being "spotted" (*repéré*), "signaled," and signified by police officers; of being "discovered" by *les policiers* in a street-side urinal, site of bodily intimacy and vulnerability; of being stopped and searched for incriminating possessions, damning marks and signs, staining film; of hiding instruments of his trade and *métier* (the film canisters, the camera, the photographer's vision)—these and other anxious concerns and actions recalled the terror that Kagan and his family and others felt during the German occupation of France.

"On tire, on tue, et puis on efface vite," Kagan wrote in his poetic text from the late 1960s, as if paraphrasing the actions of the police and the nonactions of French residents of Paris: "We shoot, we kill, and then we quickly erase" (Burté and Leblanc 2022, 110). Effacement and invisibility reigned that night. The photographs worked to counter erasure. Visibility through photographic images and circulation was deemed an act of resistance. In contrast to the Paris police and the French government's complicity in denying and obscuring the massive scale of police violence throughout the fall of 1961, Kagan's photographic work had the effect of "fixing forever" trace-marks of the criminal murder of innocents. His "naive" hope was that these images of sudden violence might wake up others, in a shock-pedagogy of sorts. In his poem Kagan described the potential viewers of these images of wounding violence as "amorphous, sleeping, selfish . . . or rotten." Many French were "indifferent," looking but not acting or intervening. Passive before the troubled faces of others, they made no effort to stop the police or report on their criminal actions. Jim House (2010, 33) conveys the gist of Kagan's scathing critique: "Kagan thus denounces both the active agency involved in the repression and the complicity of many Parisians in this violence, and these for 1942 and 1961."

Numerous writings have positioned Kagan's life within a precarious field of life death: driven by an acute clarity of vision and a daring workman's ethic, he took photographs that night that engraved in film the faces of persons who might otherwise have gone untraced, forgotten. His subsequent words and narrations, prostheses of sight and image and moral acumen—words grafted onto images—later underscored that visual record.

Did Kagan seek out images of wounded individuals on their own, and identify with such scenes and subjects? Did he take photographs that were primed to his own ways of being in the world—apertured in accord with ways of sensing and seeing recurrent in his life? Isolated male figures, wounded, hurting, beaten down by police agents of the state, bodies and lives made precarious, killed or nearly killed—these are figurations in Kagan's life as well as a key tonality of images enacted the night of 17 October 1961. "Every photograph you take is a self-portrait," runs an adage in photography circles. Kagan's photographs could imply oblique self-portraiture. With subliminal awareness or without conscious awareness, he might have responded most to scenes of violence and hardship familiar to him in moments of photographic vision or in developing and circulating prints later on. On that October night he photographed wounding, his and that of others.

The Question of Trauma

What is involved when a person's life is marked, and known to others, by a troubling event or two—or when a life is marked by images while producing images that mark others? A life can be marked, continuously, by precise encounters, wounds, and openings into new forms of life death. For many, and apparently for the photographer himself, Kagan's life story took on the mark of his actions the night of 17 October 1961. This event, and the wound-images inscribed, became a select "biographeme" of Kagan's life death, to use Roland Barthes's term for those "few details, a few preferences, a few inflections" that indicate the biographic trace-life of a "dispersed subject."[7]

The biographemes of Kagan's efforts that night—the Vespa he rode; the intrepid photographic testimonialist searching for images of violence that might survive threats of annihilation and erasure; becoming doubly wounded; repetitive scenes of state-sanctioned violence—have dispersively recurred. Obituaries written in the days after Kagan's death speak of the night of 17 October 1961 as a defining moment of the life that had just passed. "Kagan became a victim of his own almost accidental success," begins one of these epitaphs. "He was the sole photographer to effectively cover the events of that night, when 25,000 North Africans responded to a call for a peaceful protest in defiance of the curfew imposed upon them via the hated chief of police Maurice Papon" (Hopkinson

1999). An obituary—*une nécrologie*, in French, an apt and haunting term, "a notice of death"—is usually a textual site ripe with biographemes on a recently expired life. Kagan's obituaries graph the biographical and political import of his photographic work that October night. A jolted sequence of violent wounding marked the life deaths of a photographer and his subjects.

Kagan's efforts that night eventually took on the elements of a biographical mark and narrative, a heroic fable and testimonial record, promoted by others as much as by Kagan himself. The figure of Kagan, riding on his moped through a dark Paris, risking his life and career to photograph police violence, has entered the collective imagination of more than a few persons. The now near-mythic tale of that photographic journey figures in at least one novel, Leïla Sebbar's 1999 "roman polyphonique" *La Seine était rouge* (*The Seine Was Red*), in which one of the narrators—identified as a "French student" whose Ukrainian mother tried to persuade him from attending the demonstration, out of fear of the violence that might result—relates:

> I was in the Solférino station that day, 17 October 1961.... Out of solidarity, certain people would be present. One of the orders for the [support] Network was to observe, to be a witness, not to participate directly. Photographer friends risked their lives, they took photos, Concorde, Solférino, Pont de Neuilly, Nanterre. One of them, especially, a friend of my parents, Élie Kagan, crossed Paris on his Vespa all the way to Nanterre where he knew that Algerians had been killed. I saw the photos of that tragic day. Overall, the journalists did not do their job. (Sebbar 2008, 81)[8]

The implication is that the student speaking here is the one whom Kagan photographed helping the man at the Solférino station. From *La Seine était rouge*: "When I arrived at Solférino, the station was deserted. A man was seated all alone on a bench. He had been wounded in the head. Blood was flowing from the wound. He was disoriented. I helped him. I took the métro with him. He didn't want to go to the hospital. He said it wasn't serious" (Sebbar 2008, 82).

With such recollections and reimaginings of Kagan's efforts that night come repetitions, retellings, reenactments. Kagan himself apparently told the story of 17 October 1961 on numerous occasions. Along with his recounting to Einaudi, as transcribed in the books previously mentioned, Kagan narrated events of that night in the coauthored, semiautobiographical work *Le reporter engagé* (Kagan and Rotman 1989). With each (re)telling, Kagan's words addressed much the same moments and events, but in slightly different ways, with a few words and images recurrent or refashioned. It's as though the narrator was drawing from the same contact sheet of memories, while editing, cropping, and reframing the distinct pictures apparent there. The story is told much the same way, on separate occasions, built out of so many distinct photographic "vues" and "clichés," snapshots, visual and acoustic in nature, with slight variations in the narrative retellings.

Filmic representations recur as well. In the 1992 documentary film *Drowning by Bullets*, directed by Philip Brooks and Alan Hayling, Kagan is shown speaking of the events in the film, in a matter-of-fact, "it happened like this" voice. And then, a few minutes further along in the film, we watch as Kagan rides a Vespa through the streets of Paris, onto Petit-Nanterre—retracing a route of memory-images. One scene shows Kagan seated on the Vespa, by a street sign that reads "Rue des Pâquerettes," while he speaks of what he encountered there.

With such repetitive returns comes the question of trauma. Would it be fair to say that Kagan was traumatized by both rounds of violence and fear? Kagan's biography speaks of his "persistent fidelity" to "un passé toujours present" (Kagan and Rotman 1989, 11–12). Could it be that memories of October 1961 and correlated memories of July 1942 carried for Kagan a similarly timed "always present past"—much as traumatic memories are said to have an always present quality in the lives of traumatized persons? Kagan apparently experienced two "scenes of trauma," with the second scenography, on 17 October 1961, possibly recalling and reworking elements of the first scene from July 1942, perhaps through a traumatic temporality of "afterwardness" (*Nachträglichkeit*, "deferred action"), to draw from psychoanalytic concepts.[9]

Nachträglichkeit is Sigmund Freud's term for the "deferred action" that he found often occurs with traumatic events and memories, in which the significance of a trauma experienced by someone earlier in life takes on a new psychodynamic significance at a later date. Jean Laplanche and Jean-Bertrand Pontalis (1988, 111) explain the psychoanalytic idea here: "Experiences, impressions and memory-traces may be revised at a later date to fit in with fresh experiences or with the attainment of a new stage of development. They may in that event be endowed not only with a new meaning but also with psychical effectiveness." As Freud himself wrote in a letter to Wilhelm Fliess in 1896, "I am working on the assumption that our psychical mechanism has come into being by a process of stratification: the material present in the form of memory-traces being subjected from time to time to a *re-arrangement* in accordance with fresh circumstances—to a *re-transcription*."[10] In writing about Freud's evolving theories of trauma, John Fletcher (2013) argues that Freud came to understand that specific traumas often take form in the memory of a subject through specific scenes of trauma. These scenes often spur later manifestations of traumatic effects through the process of *Nachträglichkeit,* or "deferred action/afterwardness."

Within the "structure of scenic repetition, by the relay from scene to scene," an earlier trauma is retranscribed into a later scene of trauma (6).

These reflections on trauma and memory might shed light on Kagan's memories of significantly fearful and painful events in his life, for his recollections tied into *scenes* of state violence rather than specific violent acts. One pervasive scene of violence became intergrafted, years later, with a citywide scenography of state oppression. It's possible that Kagan's encounters with state violence in 1961 brought to conscious memory, in newly significant, retranscribed ways, scenes of state violence that he encountered as a child in the early 1940s. Kagan's constant retelling of his experiences that October night might have reflected the ways in which those experiences kept marking him, kept him remembering and talking about wounding events that he was trying to make sense of, memories of violence and fear that "attacked" him—forces from outside the self harming the self.

Cathy Caruth (1996, 5), a leading theorist of trauma, suggests that "to be traumatized is precisely to be possessed by an image or event." Kagan appeared to be possessed by images and events from both disasters of violence, in 1942 and 1961, with the second complex of trauma an unnerving trace-echo of the first. Trauma has been described as a disorder of time and memory. Did Kagan know and live with a sense of disordered time and memory? I cannot say for sure; we are invoking a hypothesis of trauma only, siting traumatic recurrence in his life. But it could be that two overlapping, intergrafted traumas marked his life from the age of thirty-three on—doubly assailed, with the story retold. The constant retellings of the same wounding events bear the structure of a traumatic event that keeps repeating itself, whether in the mind and body of the person who most directly experienced that event or for those at large who have been trying repeatedly, unresolvedly, to make sense of it. The subsequent representations and imaginal reenactments of the violent events bear the impress of a wound-trauma at once personal and collective.

Kagan had lived through painful situations, with wounding memories trailing his days, yet still there was a joie de vivre apparent with him, a passion for work and images that might count for something. In the documentary *Drowning with Bullets*, Kagan appears almost serene, but not removed, as he speaks of the events of October 1961. In the short clips from the film *Les années Kagan* I have managed to see, the photographer appears quick-witted, alive with thought and action, conversing animatedly with interlocutors (Krief 1989). Kagan was not fixed in trauma and wounding only. Labyrinthine complexities of hurt and joy apparently shaped his life, lasting damage entangled with the capacity to live and create anew, as is the case with many lives.

If trauma was a recurrent pattern in Kagan's life, then this would be only one line of life within complex arrangements in life death. In reading various accounts and portraits of Kagan, I am struck by the irascible vitality portrayed, the multiplicities of the man, such that no interpretative assessment of his life and photographic work can be entirely singular or overriding in conclusion. Such accounts include the varied reflections of Kagan's first wife, Marguerite Langiert, as conveyed in an interview with Cyril Burté and Audrey Leblanc, conducted in December 2019 and July 2021:

Photography became his profession by chance. He did it with sincerity, imagining the power he gave to the photo not to change anything—he was a realist, in any case—but for his testimony. And what better witness than the photo, something that survives and gives a real image of a current event at a given moment. The capture of reality is more important than words. . . .

We got married and soon had a little girl, in 1961. Our life as a couple was a little altered because of the events [the Algerian war and the repression of the demonstration of 17 October 1961]. I finished my pregnancy alone because Kagan was on the battlefield. He had real physical courage. . . .

In 1961, I must admit that it was difficult. We lived on René Boulanger, near Place de la République, and when I crossed the *place* to go to Les Bleuets [the maternity ward at Hospital Pierre Rouquès], I would pass police buses that were parked all around. I don't know if it's my imagination, but we knew that they [the police officers] were drugged a bit at the time, we even talked about making them take ether to make them drunk, to make them lose consciousness of reality because it was violent. In fact, when I was a student, I was almost hit with a [police] baton. I was able to enter a delicatessen and it was the window that was smashed instead. . . .

We had a small lab at home [for developing photographs] and I helped him a lot. I saw wounded or killed Algerians emerge from the void to appear in the developer. I was like a witness. Kagan was what we call today a bipolar. In this intense period of activity and struggle—from October 1961 to Charonne [in Febuary 1962]—he was in a [manic] high. Afterwards it was the fall and I experienced this same situation seven times. . . .

Adrenalin, yes, because in times of high tension, indeed, it was his way of confronting events, of getting up on the street lamps [to take photographs] and doing things that others did not dare to do, and even of provoking. He was outgoing and, at times, in an extraordinary way! He would get the people, his audience, on their feet. In society, he was a good performer. He was a kind of force of nature, this man. . . . He was a special character, a complex personality like many.[11]

Langiert knew Kagan well, of course. Her words speak to the emotional tenor of the fall of 1961, for him, for them, the desire for testimonial images and the sincere belief in the value of photographic witnessing, the presumed "capture of reality" and the lasting significance of a "real image" that might survive through time; apparitions of wounded or killed Algerians emerging from the darkroom void; the threat and fear of police violence, phantasmal notions that the police were on drugs or should be drugged, to make them less prone to violence; the adrenaline rush of high tension events, the manic high that fueled Kagan's creativity, and then the depressive fall from those heights months later, in 1962 (the bipolarity a repetitive cycle, recalls his former wife). With such biographical and familial recollections, the apparitional and imaginal are enmeshed in the actual and the evidentiary—a fevered real.

From the vestiges of Kagan's photographic efforts on 17 October 1961 comes a complicated interfolding of photographic images and intensive perceptions, eyewitness testimony meshed within a rhetoric of testimony, political and moral critique, trace-marks of recurrent fear and wounding, thematic of trauma. The photographs themselves carry the valence of these different forces and energies. Glimpsed through certain refractions of time, each photograph from that October night appears as a palimpsest of wounded perception, imagining, and historical trace.

Apparent are a regrafting and commingling of wounds and memories within a field of doublings and redoublings and echoic reverberations, doubling assailments. The odd thing is that they did not know each other, these two men wounded by events of that night. A brief encounter, lasting less than an hour, and yet the life deaths of both men were forever marked by that encounter and surrounding events. One of them suffered the cruel blows of his enemies that night, which brought him to the ground. He happened to be photographed by the second man, who worked in fear and rushed circumstances. Just a few looks exchanged, a few images recurring in potentially infinite ways, and then through fractured time emerges a swirling vortex of images, histories, political positionings, and imaginaries in which the itinerant, nearly anonymous figure of Abdelkader Bennahar might be traced.

Time at the Archive

I can see him there, in his apartment on Rue René Boulanger. Bookcases line the walls of the living room and a small study, close to a few black-and-white photographs set in frames. Boxes of photos are piled on a desk. Prints, contact sheets, negatives stored in a cabinet. Drawings in vibrant colors. One window overlooks the leafy quiet of a courtyard. He's testy to the end, combative, multiple. Histories cling to him. He moves about hesitantly, unsure of his body. He's been losing weight. He knows his body is coming undone, it's just a matter of time, or so I imagine Kagan's last days. And then later on, from a cramped and cluttered apartment, filled with photographs, drawings, notebooks, receipts, the leavings of a life, come the materials for an archive.

Reflections on a past life tend to speak of the life within a larger frame of life death. In commenting on Kagan's photographic work from the 1960s to the 1990s, Thérèse Blondet-Bisch, artist, writer, and director of the photographic library (*la photothèque*) at the Bibliothèque de Documentation International Contemporaine (BDIC), now known as La Contemporaine, recalled:

> It is well-known that Élie Kagan became famous at the beginning of his career for the striking pictures he took openly, with a flash, at night, of the police beating up Algerians working in France who had come to Paris to take part in demonstrations. The only newspaper that dared to publish these pictures was *Témoignage Chrétien* [Christian witness], a publication he remained faithful to all his life. He got his press pass at the end of that year.
>
> From that moment on he photographed more indiscriminately than ever, haughtily ignoring conventional rules of composition and recording intensely and insatiably the world around him with an almost youthful enthusiasm, all the while turning his back on what fashion dictated. His sense of justice, or rather obsession, led him to take photos of life in the streets, especially social outcasts for whom he had particular affection. He was an activist who fought for an ideal society, a better world. Independent almost to the point of being an anarchist, he was the companion of Mouna Aguigui [anarchical political activist and eccentric Parisian "clochard-philosophe pacifiste"] and never really belonged to a press agency as such. He saw himself as a "politically engaged reporter." . . .
>
> After an accident in 1994, he had to stop working for a while and to leave Paris for Briançon. He was profoundly affected by this: it comes

out in the photos he took at that time and until the end of his life, which are imbued with a sort of lack of commitment which was probably unconscious. His spontaneity faded.[12]

Kagan died in Paris in January 1999, at the age of seventy. With the cessation of his life *il est disparu*, as one says in France, "he disappeared." Departed. An absence, then, of body, speech, and vision, while trace-effects remain. One obituary remarked:

> Traditional in his working practices, using only black and white film and a 35mm camera, the one-time protégé of Jean-Paul Sartre fell out into anonymity. He died alone in the same small apartment in the 10th arrondissement where he was born. The last story he covered was of a demonstration by a group of disenfranchised citizens, the *sans-papiers* [undocumented persons], at the church of St Bernard.
>
> To the end, Francois Maspero maintained that all he talked about was that unpublished book about the 1961 demonstration. "That night," said Maspero, "was a painful return to his childhood." Kagan left an archive of more than 40,000 largely uncatalogued images. (Hopkinson 1999)

In the logic of testimony evident at the time, Kagan's death implied the death of a witness, one less possible *témoin*, witness, who could speak about catastrophic events in 1942 and 1961 (Wieviorka 2006).

At the end of 1998, Einaudi had asked Kagan if he wanted to testify at the trial of Mauice Papon.[13] Kagan, gravely ill at the time, agreed right away. But he died a few days before the trial started.

"The witness is a survivor, the third party, the *terstis* as *testis* and *superstes*, the one who survives," writes Derrida. In death, a witness can no longer give or pass on "surviving speech" (Blanchot and Derrida 2000, 45). And yet in death the photographs have survived, lived on past the lead maker of those photographs. Within the logic and rhetoric of testimony that undergird Kagan's words and photography, the surviving images continued to exist as *témoinage*, evidence, in the absence of the living witness. This was repetitive testimony, fixed in wounding.

After his death, Kagan's body was buried in the cemetery of Bagneux, a town southeast of Paris. Afterward, his family donated his entire photographic work to the BDIC, then based in Nanterre. In November 1999, the agreement of the Fonds Élie Kagan at the BDIC stipulated that the institution had from then on exclusive rights to the use and diffusion of Kagan's photographs.

Blondet-Bisch, who worked to secure Kagan's photographic oeuvre for the photographic library at the BDIC, has written of her first encounter with the entirety of Kagan's photographic work.

I did not know what was in store when I was contacted in summer 1999 by Judith Kagan, daughter of the photographer Élie Kagan who had died in January of that year. Several times we left each other messages on answering machines, but finally we met. And early in the autumn I finally entered the mythical den, in Paris, of Élie Kagan, born in 1928. His eclectic world, shaped over the years, overwhelmed me. A blizzard of pictures pinned or stuck to the walls, political and religious posters, pamphlets, poems, postcards, press passes, drawings by friends such as Plantu or Tim, and photographs. On the other hand, his photo lab was completely bare: Kagan's world already tidied away. Along the corridor, bookcases still packed with political literature.

Then, in a large room bathed in sunlight that filtered through the closed venetian blinds, dozens of boxes on the floor all packed up for their final journey. Crammed full of prints, contact prints, slides, negatives, albums, newspaper cuttings, contracts for reportages, payment slips filed by year, pins, diaries with business appointments. The entire photographic life of Élie Kagan.[14]

Much of the imagery and materialia of Kagan's photographic life came to be stored in the multifaceted chambers of an archive. The Fonds Élie Kagan is composed of some 200,000 images, an estimated 200,000 negatives, and around 9,000 contact sheets—all aspects of Kagan's photographic work, including around forty photographs taken the night of 17 October 1961. Some originals from that night disappeared before 1988, but *contretypes*, duplicate reproductions, were made for *Le reporter engagé*, a book on Kagan's lifework of photography, published in 1989. Also preserved in the collection are some thirty 6×6 negatives, a 24×36 band of negatives, several prints and reprints, and several original argentic contact sheets.

La Contemporaine, which manages the Fonds Élie Kagan, is a library, museum, and archive center specializing in the history of the twentieth and twenty-first centuries. Its library is presently housed in a building at the University of Paris–Nanterre, while its museum stands at the Hôtel des Invalides in Paris. During the late 2010s, the materials of the Kagan collection, along with other archived materials, were lodged in a building at the Hôtel des Invalides.[15] Also known as Les Invalides, this famous complex of buildings in the 7th arrondissement of Paris, which for centuries has served as a hospital and retirement home for French soldiers, now also houses several museums, including the Musée de l'Armée, as well as the Dôme des Invalides, a large church with the tombs of some of France's war heroes, most notably the austere, majestic tomb of Napoleon Bonaparte. Les Invalides hosts a set of overlapping, entangled histories and institutions—the chambers of hospitals, military offices, museums, archives—assembled by and in the governmental-military-civil operations of the French state. It might seem odd to lodge a museum archive of visual artifacts in a den of military history, yet it's also the case that visual technologies, writing, and warfare share a long and intimate history.[16]

I visited Les Invalides one sultry summer afternoon in July 2018. That same day a military funeral was being held in the Cour d'Honneur (Courtyard of Honor) for a distinguished member of the French resistance, who had died that week. In trying to find my way to the building where Kagan's photographs were archived, I passed by a number of military personnel and police officers dressed in fine military uniforms, waiting for the funeral proceedings to begin. A soft-spoken man dressed in the white of a commander's uniform, with a sense of presence and respected authority about him, helped me to locate the winding route to "escalier M." I took those stairs and reached the third floor of that building and walked down a long and narrow hallway, along each side of which were office suites, museum workspaces, and storage rooms. All of this, I thought, could have once been the site of hospital rooms and medical facilities, with soldiers returning from the front lines and treated for war wounds. Affixed to the doors were signs for La Musée de l'Armée. Toward the end of this corridor was the archival office of La Contemporaine. I rang a buzzer by the door and was soon greeted by a man who was the curator of the Fonds Élie Kagan. He had arranged for my visit that day.

Soon I was sitting at a table toward the back of a long, narrow room, which might have served once as a ward of the hospital, the beds of bandaged soldiers arranged in neat rows. Visual images from these times had been preserved in the archive. Along one side of the room stood large storage bins that contained rare photographic prints and negatives from World War I. Along the other side ran a series of glass windows through which hazy sunlight shone.

I tried to explain to the curator and his assistant who I was and my reasons for wanting to see the original photographs that Kagan took that night. These two men nodded their heads in agreement, and the curator jotted down a few words on a sheet of paper. Apparently, I passed whatever test and criteria were required to gain access to the collection. The archivists showed me different sets of prints and contact sheets, which they had prepared in advance of my visit, namely, "the photographs of Élie Kagan relative to 17 Octobre 1961 (repression of the demonstration)," as the curator and I agreed upon in our email exchanges before the visit. This compendium was just a small portion of the entire Kagan collection, which ranges from photos of Jean-Marie Le Pen, François Mitterrand, Jean-Luc Godard, Marguerite Duras, Michel Foucault, and Catherine Deneuve; *flâneuresque* photos of clochards, graffiti, and street art in the streets of Paris; photographs that Kagan made while working as a photographic journalist in Algeria in 1962–63; and images of the attempted coup d'état of Charles de Gaulle's government in April 1961, student-led protests in May 1968, and many other political events, politicians, film stars, and celebrities in French life, as well as of a contemplative visit to Auschwitz in the 1970s, where Kagan photographed the extermination camp and its death-bringing crematoriums. All this came from a freelance photographer who lived much of his life in the same apartment in the 10th arrondissement in which he was born.

"Kagan is a flayed Jew [*ecorché juif*]. When as a smooth-faced young boy he hung the star on his schoolboy's apron, dropped his trousers in front of a German officer searching for a revealing circumcision, saw a part of his family wiped away and his mother narrowly escaping deportation, it would not be surprising to manifest an increased sensitivity to what is called the Jewish question" (131). These words are from *Le reporter engagé* by Élie Kagan and Patrick Rotman, published in 1989. Among the many photographs printed in the book is one of Kagan, dressed in dark clothes and standing somberly with Serge Klarsfeld, a Holocaust survivor who sought to hunt down former Nazis. Both men are wearing yellow stars fixed to the clothing at their chests. "Juif" is inscribed on both symbols. "The yellow star, he carries it on him," the accompanying text says of Kagan. "Like a past and incurable bruise [*Comme une meutrissure passée et inguérissable*]. Like a challenge [*défi*]" (132).

The first set of Kagan's photos from 17 October 1961, held in a large paper envelope, was placed on the surface of the table where I was stationed. With cautious, ceremonial gestures I donned a set of white cotton gloves provided to me—to keep any dirt or oils on my hands from soiling anything I touched. I opened the envelope and began to look closely at its contents, one item at a time, as the two curators returned to their work at nearby desks.

Contained within were a set of prints, *tirages* of varying sizes and quality. Here were some of the original prints from that night, I thought, even though I knew the concept of "original" had to be kept in abeyance.

Held in my hands was the photograph of the man wincing in pain while trying to escape the Métro Solférino. Supported with white-gloved fingers were the photographic prints of Abdelkader Bennahar at Rue des Pâquerettes, his dead companion lying across the low stone wall. In the stillness of the room I felt as if I was holding something precious and sacred, like the relics of a saint preserved in the inner sanctum of a church.

It's remarkable, I said at one point to the man seated at the desk across from where I sat and held and regarded the photographic prints. "Yes," he said in response. To hold the actual images in one's hands, and see them for oneself, that's really something.

When this man was not attending to my questions, or quietly overseeing my work with the materials from the Kagan collection, he appeared to be working, in a painstakingly careful way, with a scalpel and a kit of chemical processors to extract small photographs from an aged booklet.

Being in the museum archive that day brought to mind the writings of Arlette Farge, a historian who has devoted long hours to working in the judicial archives of Paris, in particular the Bibliothèque de l'Arsenal, where many police archives are kept, to find the "rough traces of lives that never asked to be told in the way they were, but were obliged one day to do so when confronted with the harsh reality of the police and repression" (Farge 2013, 6). Of the historian's reading of police interrogations and testimonies from centuries before, Farge finds that "it is a rare and precious feeling to suddenly come upon so many forgotten lives, haphazard and full, juxtaposing and entangling the close with the distant, the departed" (8). Through the painstaking work of combing through various compendiums of documents and reading police reports found in these archives, Farge has been able to piece together intricate histories of the poor, especially women, in prerevolutionary France. "The archive is an excess of meaning, where the reader experiences beauty, amazement, and certain affective tremor," Farge observes in her astute reflection on such archival efforts, in *The Allure of the Archives* (31). "The archives reject any ready-made tropes. . . . The archives bring forth details that disabuse, derail, and straightforwardly break any hope of linearity or positivism" (Farge 2013, 41–42; 1989, 55).

An unruly excess of meaning was in play during my encounter with Kagan's photographic archive, for this collection held not a single set of prints set up in a chronological fashion, but rather a loose-leaf compendium, a discontinuous assemblage of varying picture shapes, sizes, and material substances in no sustained or rigorous order. In working through a small portion of the photographer's collected work, I gained the sense that the museum-archive had received the full bulk of his oeuvre and its archivists had been working effectively to inventory and give order to this learned disorder.

The diverse array of Kagan's photographic oeuvre reflects the working conditions in which he produced and sold photographic images to various media outlets as well as his own personal sensibilities. Kagan was active from 1961 to 1996 as a *pigiste*, or freelance, photographer—as evident in a membership card he carried for an association of journalists that formed in the early 1960s (figure 3.1). As was the case for other freelance journalists and photojournalists at the time, he was paid for each *pige*, or item purchased by newspapers and journals—in Kagan's case, for each print of one of his photographic images. Kagan sold and resold photographic prints and images to various publications, ranging from daily newspapers to popular magazines, with some images—such as those from 17 October 1961—eliciting more interest than others and reprinted often. This workaday inventory of images includes any photographic negatives and prints from 17 October 1961, which have never existed in a complete and undisturbed state. "Manipulated many times," Leblanc (2022, 23–24) writes, "the negatives and contact sheets, damaged and disordered, of the shots of 17 October 1961 are preserved as they are; the originals have circulated, have been handled a lot: they are partly lost." Leblanc goes on to note that a number of Kagan's photographs were cleaned up and resized for inclusion in *17 Octobre 1961*, by Einaudi and Kagan: "For the layout of the book published in 2001, the images were printed from negatives, cleaned, cropped and straightened: the editing work gave them real legibility and conferred on them the authority of beautiful images [*belles images*], turning them from press *scoops* into the photographs of an *auteur*" (24).

In sorting through Kagan's photographs from October 1961, I stumbled upon irruptions of imaginal form and displacements in meaning. Faced with the complexity of what I previously thought visually clear and temporally linear, I encountered a billow of excess, multiplicity, fractal arrays of duplication and reiteration within an unbound corpus of images that appeared in forms at once clear and obscure, familiar and novel. In referring to the "gap-riddled puzzle of obscure events" known through judicial archives, Farge (2013, 94) writes, "It is like a kaleidoscope revolving before your eyes. Pausing for an instant, it fixes the precise shapes of imagined figures, which then burst into iridescent light before coming together in different configurations. These figures are ephemeral, and the smallest movement scatters them to produce others." I found the collection of Kagan's photographic work to be similarly kaleidoscopic, with a shifting array of patterns and reflections forming in a viewer's optical consciousness.

A life, too, might entail a kaleidoscopic array of myriad forms, possibilities, graphs and images. Within the ordered disorder of life death there can emerge patterns of fractal recursivity, in which small singular moments reflect much the same forms

FIGURE 3.1. Élie Kagan's membership card for the Association Nationale des Journalistes Reporters Photographes (ANJRP, founded in 1962). Fonds Élie Kagan, La Contemporaine.

found in larger arrangements. One definition of the word fractal *runs, "any of various extremely irregular curves or shapes for which any suitably chosen part is similar in shape to a given larger or smaller part when magnified or reduced to the same size."[17] As with a tree or a coastline, situations in a person's life or in life more generally tend to reflect recursive constructions. Would it be possible to calculate the fractal forms of a life death, with similar forms, lines, curves, patterns, and arrangements recurring time and again? There is often significant recursivity and seriality within the biopolitics and biophantasmatics of any given life death, and this within a single life or a series of lives, such as with the generations of a family.*

Fractals of silence, arrogance, and deception and dissimulation have recurred in French colonial systems, from brief moments in life death to grand schemes of political domination.

None of the prints from 17 October 1961 that I saw that day gave an overwhelming appearance of being the originals. There were no ur-photos of extraordinary auratic originality to speak of, but rather a differentially repeating array of images spun from that night and preserved in the archive. With this irruption of images, any one of the prints could have been made in the 1960s, 1970s, or 1980s and for different purposes, publications, and destinations. The spore-like issues of Kagan's photographic work were recursive, sporadically disarrayed, extending toward boundless relations in photographic imagery (Farge 2013, 30).

Written on the backs of some of the prints were brief notes, etched in ink or with a pencil. "Student—buying ticket . . . the only expression of solidarity," ran one phrase of words in French on the back of a photographic print of the young man buying a métro ticket for a wounded Algerian demonstrator.

My eyes took in the textures of the prints, and I looked with care at the white and black shadings. I had difficulty placing one photograph in space and time. This was of a darkly lit view of a bicycle strewn on the ground, shoes and objects scattered about (figure 3.2). The lower halves of three men stand in the background of the photograph, as they apparently look on the scene.[18]

Absence is present in this photograph. No figures of injured persons are shown, although one can readily imagine that several people fled a scene of actual or imminent violence. The possible violence appears in absentia, and that absent, errant violence reverberates long after the moment of its photographed aftermath.

Once I had looked slowly through the first envelope of photographs and written out some first impressions in a notebook, I was presented with another set of materialized images, kept and preserved in an envelope. I donned the white gloves anew in working gently through its contents. This second set held several contact sheets (*planches contact argentiques*) that Kagan had created from the negatives produced that night. With one of these contact sheets, distinct and separate negatives of photos had been placed to bring out the distinct "positive images" of each negative to give the photographer a sense of the visuals at hand. At some point, Kagan used a red marker (as photographers often do) to write on individual images on a contact sheet that contained photos taken the night of 17 October 1961, editorially thinking through how best to compose effective photographic prints (figures 3.3 and 3.4). With such annotations, his ideas were grafted onto film, *signalées en rouge en vue de publication*—marked in red for publication.[19]

Within the phantasm of a vision, I see the red marks on the contact sheets ("blood-like," writes A.) as diagrams that highlighted that night's graftwounds of violence. The photographer was apparently retracing, reframing and reprinting, anticipating images that could work well in published form. The red marks radiate like the ganglions of a febrile nervous system, linking body eye and pain.

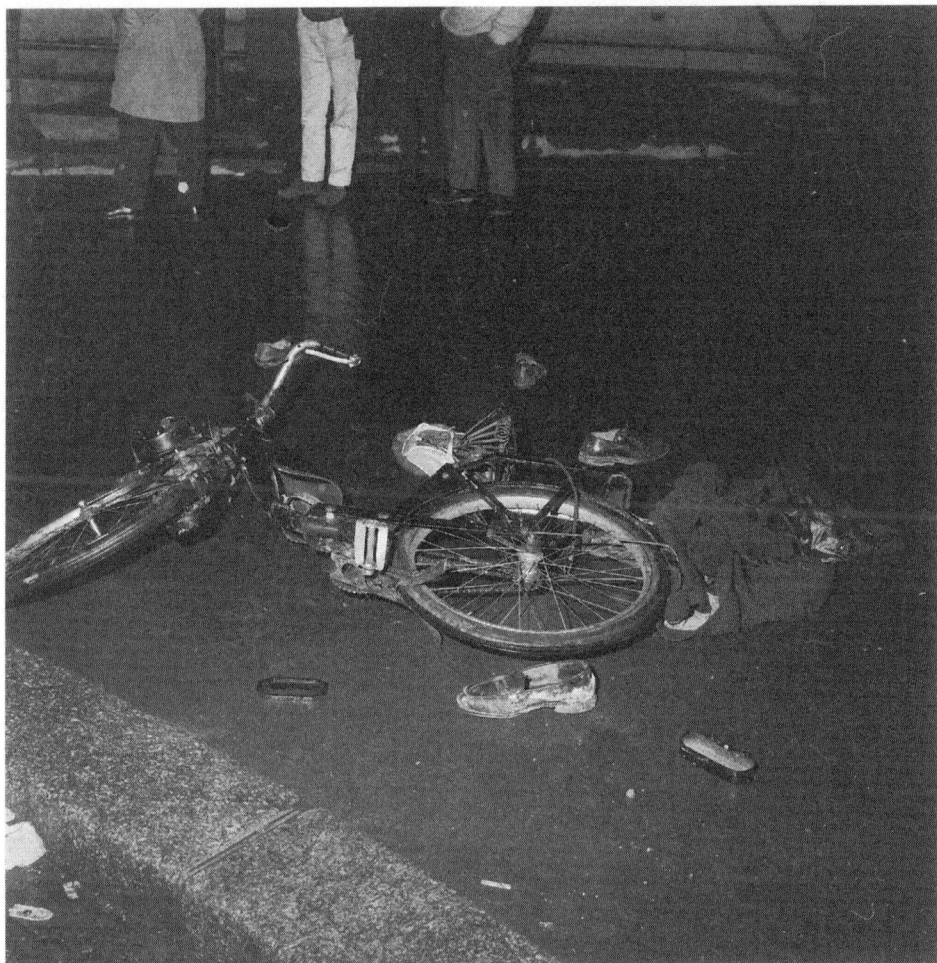

FIGURE 3.2. Abandoned bicycle, unknown location, 17 October 1961. Photo by Élie Kagan. LC_KAG_0004N_C01 © Élie Kagan "Collection La Contemporaine."

With the picture of the man leaning against a bench in the Métro Solférino, wincing in pain, Kagan drew strong red lines to the sides of the image, and then drew an X at the center of the man's chest (figure 3.4). It's unclear what the photographer/editor intended with this mark, though I take it that Kagan sensed the intensity of pain and sought to graph it so.

The photograph taken near the wall along Rue des Pâquerettes was also marked for cropping, to frame a vision of the shapes of Bennahar lying on the ground, the dark stain of blood on the ground beside him, and the man collapsed across the wall.

FIGURE 3.3 Contact sheet of photographs taken by Élie Kagan on 17 October 1961. LC_KAG_PL_52 © Élie Kagan "Collection La Contemporaine."

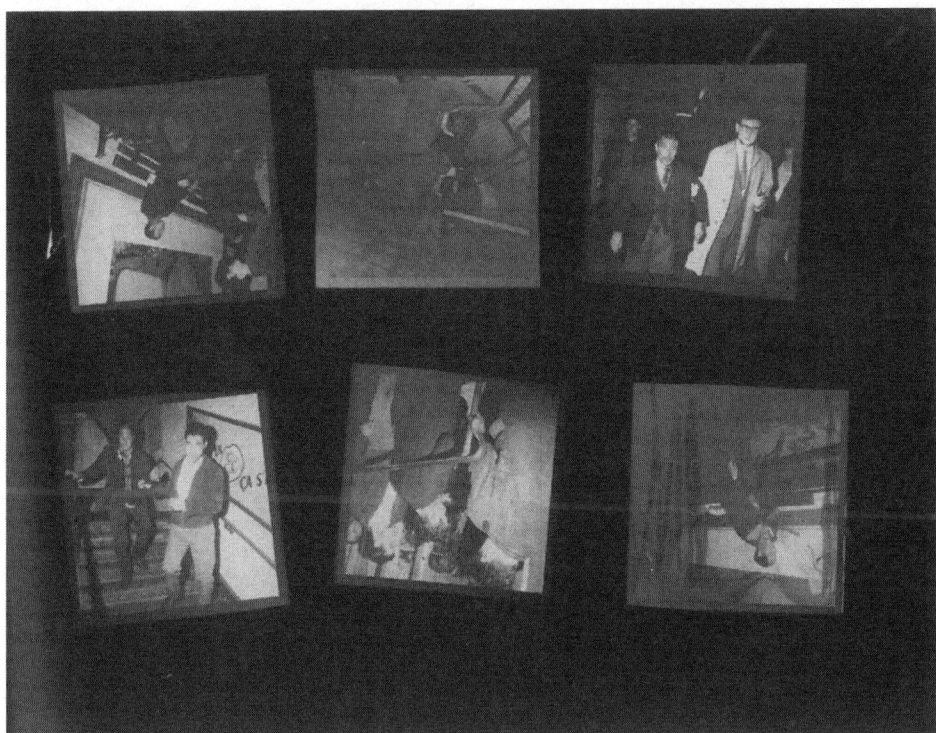

FIGURE 3.4. Contact sheet of photographs taken by Élie Kagan at the Métro Solférino, Paris, on 17 October 1961. © Élie Kagan "Collection La Contemporaine."

Other contact sheets did not carry any editorial marks; only the small photographic images appeared on the *planche contact*. Apparently, one use of these contact sheets was to give Kagan a ready template to draw from when it came to any potential sales or prospective buyers of his photographs.

With each printed photograph that came from that night, the first manifest image had been edited, worked on, reformed, and sized to produce effective photographic prints. There was no pure, original, unprocessed image, rather a mélange of the actual and the constructed. Technologies of reiteration, duplication, prosthetic supplementation, and ink and image transfer enabled the traces of those brief moments to continue dispersively in time.

Other images set on the contact sheets showed dim, blurred light most of all. This was especially the case with some of the photographs Kagan tried to take from a Métro car as it arrived at Métro Concorde, his vantage point a way to avoid detection from the police.[20] Dim tungsten light, lack of focus, no flash in a moving vehicle—gray hues of *Concorde* lettering and crowds of men corralled by the police. Within the frame of one vision, these blurred underground Métro "vues" attest to the violence and fear of that night.[21] While ostensibly "poor images" (Steyerl), they say so much.[22]

Another sequence of prints showed a number of Algerian men seated on a bus, with their hands held to the backs of their heads. These were photographs Kagan took while near the Pont de Neuilly before he traveled to Petit-Nanterre. The vehicle shown must have been one of the RATP buses requisitioned by the police, with the plan of carting the detained men off to a detention center such as the Palais des Sports. In one of these photos a man appears to be looking directly at the lens of the camera—the flash might have caught his eye, the photographer a stranger to the subject photographed (figure 3.5). The photograph reflects a charged moment of stasis and movement. A highway sign is reflected in the vehicle's window. Posted on the side of the bus is an advertisement for "Bonbons," with words that read, "Un mot sur toutes les lèvres" (A word on all the lips). The irony in that scene has caught the eye of cultural historians: What was said, and not said, of the violent events of that night?

In that incidental, photographed moment, the man's look is one of humiliation, exhaustion, as though tired despair encroached on this body exposed to the glare of police harassment and journalistic capture. The man's fate is unclear to us, as are the other persons held captive near him.

The man shown seated on the bus, looking toward the camera, his arms held behind his head, is caught in a specular history. The image spirals on through time while the man perhaps never knew about the actuality of this photographic reflection of him. His eyes look on us looking at him, past the vanishment. In this man's look I glimpse the stain of humiliation and colonial wounding, of a man being ground down into submission, his fate uncertain. This is the face of subjection to state power, damaged integrity within the colonial metropolis—the diminishment of a man who lived on into an uncertain future. "Those eyes, which are absolutely without protection, the most naked part of the human body, none the less offer an absolute resistance to possession," Emmanuel Levinas (1990, 8) wrote. The man looks defeated and exhausted, but still within his look toward the camera is a reluctance to being possessed.

In looking into the eyes of this man who appears to be looking at us, years past the initial moments of photographic capture, we might enter into a relation with him, one of possible care and respect and/or solidarity, or denial, forgetting, even though this embodied ethical relation implies a dizzying mix of the actual and imagined. The man looks at us, looking at our looking at him; we see ourselves

FIGURE 3.5. Arrest of Algerians at the Pont de Neuilly, Paris, 17 October 1961. Photo by Élie Kagan. LC_KAG_00003N_A16 © Élie Kagan "Collection La Contemporaine."

looking at this man. Delay and displacement shape this looking. The potential exchange of looks involved—even if terrifically delayed and virtual—adds a distinctive quality to the photograph, one that is different from a photograph that enables us to look at someone who is not directly looking at us. The dialogic space of mutual looking, between a you and an I (or a we), situates the phenomenality of looking within a space of potential intimacy, knowing, and vulnerability. We are opened up by this kind of mutual looking, rendered vulnerable by the reciprocal gaze upon us. The man's look disturbs and displaces. The look wounds.

If I were positioned differently in this intense space of looking—in terms of political and social and cultural identities, that is—how might the imagined exchange of looks be different? How might other, differently positioned viewers of this photographic image perceive and relate to the man glimpsed in the photo, who perhaps imaginally returns their gaze? If the photographer who took the picture looked as if he might be from the Maghreb, would the man photographed still look toward the camera in the same way? What do you see in the looks implied in this photographic image?

The multiple optics and visualities in play here are complicated by the temporal displacements involved in regarding a photograph of exchanged looks years after any earlier moments of looking. The displacements of looking situate the looking within a phantasmal space of looked-at looking and not-looking, marking a ground of visual engagement that is at once distant and intimate, direct and indirect, never immediate but through the illusion of immediacy.[23]

Chances are that this man ended up that night in the Palais des Sports, or one of the other "centers of identification" set up in Paris, where Algerian men were confined and kept in humiliating, dangerous conditions for several days. Either he survived that harrowing detention—and was perhaps deported to Algeria—or he was one of those who died in those days, or obscurely "disappeared" in the days and months after being banished from Paris.[24] This is another line of life death, difficult to trace. Perhaps, however, at some point someone looking at this photograph recognized the man portrayed and knew who he was in life and what became of him.

I doubt it would be possible now to recover a sense of who this man was, and of how he later fared in life. One might think of this as the *postcolonial dissolve*, the way in which the names and lives of certain persons struggling to make do in colonial times are mentioned in writers' accounts, archival records, historical accounts, or newspaper articles, or their figures appear in photographs or films, and then mention of them—any mention at all—disappears from tracts of inscription.

As I sat at the table at the museum archives that day and sifted quietly through photographic prints and contact sheets, trying to take in all that I was sensing, I became faintly aware of the music coursing through the air outside the building, a brass and drum pageantry of military-funerary music. I thought I heard the soaring, aggressive chords of "La Marseillaise," "Aux armes, citoyens / formez vos bataillons / Marchons, marchons!" but these sounds were unclear and uncertain. I thought of the scenes of violence and heroism recorded in the photographs from World War I, kept in large folders a few meters away. I came to wonder what Kagan would have thought of the fact that his life's work was preserved in an authorized depository dedicated to historic feats and artifacts of the French army, a visual codex of military conquests and painful defeats.

Filaments of time swirled about the archive that afternoon, in intersecting registers. Materialia of warfare and weaponry. Old and fading photographs kept in storage bins, marked with the faces of long-forgotten conscripts. Photographs of killed and wounded Algerians, a few traces preserved. The specter of maimed soldiers back from the front, lying on the white sheets of hospital cots.

Ghost soldiers in ghost daguerreotypes. Leaflets, posters, ledgers, decaying journals, visual artifacts of French life and history sustained in digital databases. The three men alive in the room just then, their life's work destined to survive in fragments. The apparent stillness of the room, no sound of a ticking clock to be heard. If I could take a photograph of time itself—an impossible, nearly imaginable feat—I would want to have done so at the archives that day and tried to convey its many dimensions of time and history. For this was an archive of time, a site for images and traces in time, intergrafted folds and recursive workings of time. The many forces and measures of time could be reflected in a single photograph, or so I impossibly imagine, and that many-timed image could be destined for an archive one day.

Resemblance and Its Absence

In the volatile days after 17 October 1961, Kagan continued his photographic work on the lives and struggles of Algerians living in France. While examining the archival holdings of Kagan's photography at La Contemporaine, I came upon a set of photographs that he had taken on 19 October 1961 outside La Santé Prison, in the 14th arrondissement of Paris. The photos show Algerian women gathered outside the prison, protesting the arrest and possible confinement of their husbands. One of Kagan's photographs shows them standing on a street and looking toward the camera with an air of forthright strength and dignity (figure 3.6). A contact sheet of photographs showed some of the women standing together while police officers try to escort them away from an area just near the prison.[25] These photographs serve to document the role that women played in the resistance to the Paris police's arrest and confinement of Algerian men at the time.

Kagan took another set of photographs on 21 October 1961, during a visit to the bidonvilles of Nanterre. The resulting contact sheets and photographic prints show aspects of life among the Algerian families who resided there.[26] I gather that Kagan had returned to Nanterre in search of a photojournalistic story, of vitality in hardship in the muddy lanes of La Folie. Crisp, sunlight-driven photographs show men and women on the streets of the bidonvilles. Several men stand outside a *coiffure* barbershop, looking toward the camera in unsmiling ways. They probably did not know Kagan and were perhaps suspicious of his motives and how any visual images of them might be used. In a few photographs, women shielded their eyes and faces from the camera's stare.

FIGURE 3.6. Demonstration of Algerian women in front of La Santé, Paris, 19 October 1961. Photo by Élie Kagan. LC_KAG_00049N_B04 © Élie Kagan "Collection La Contemporaine."

One set of photographs showed a man, a woman, and their young children, in various poses, in the interior of their modest home (figures 3.7 and 3.8).[27] With these photographs comes a sense of distance and unfamiliarity, a gap between the photographer and his subjects. The subjects appear wary and hesitant, willing to appear in the pictures yet perhaps not fully on board with Kagan's agenda.

The photographs taken by Kagan in the bidonvilles of Nanterre in the days after the violent clashes of 17 and 18 October 1961 show features of life, family,

FIGURE 3.7. Bidonvilles of Nanterre: An Algerian family, 21 October 1961. Photo by Élie Kagan. LC_KAG_00005N_A01 © Élie Kagan "Collection La Contemporaine."

and vital relations in the communities there. They also suggest the forms of structural violence and colonial racism on which life in the bidonvilles was predicated. And yet, could it also be that, when Kagan returned to Nanterre, he was also trying to locate and identify and meet anew the man he had photographed the night of 17 October 1961 on Rue des Pâquerettes? One can readily imagine Kagan bringing printed copies of those photographs with him while approaching the bidonvilles and showing them to anyone he could, asking the viewers of those prints if they recognized the person portrayed. I have not come across any mention of Kagan learning anything at all about the man he

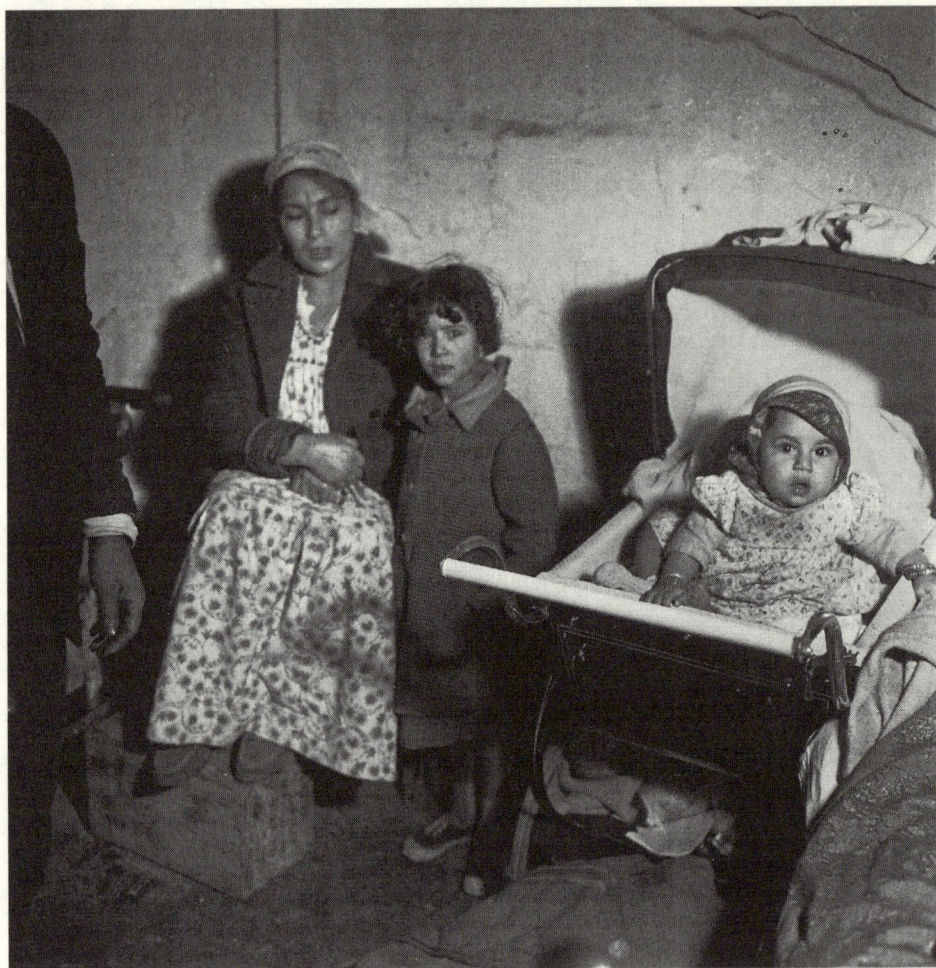

FIGURE 3.8. Bidonvilles of Nanterre: An Algerian family, 21 October 1961. Photo by Élie Kagan. LC_KAG_00005N_A02 © Élie Kagan "Collection La Contemporaine."

had photographed in Petit-Nanterre a few nights before, whose name he did not know.

One publication at the time, the journal *Témoignage Chrétien*, included prints of three photographs that Kagan took during his visit to Nanterre on 21 October 1961, along with some of his images from 17 October. Six of Kagan's photos appeared on pages 4–5 of the issue of *Témoignage Chrétien* printed on 27 October 1961, one of a man being led out of the Métro station, two of Bennahar lying on the ground at Rue des Pâquerettes, and three of scenes of life in a bidonville in Nanterre (figure 3.9). The title running above the photos reads,

QUAND NANTERRE MONTE AUX CHAMPS - ÉLYSÉES

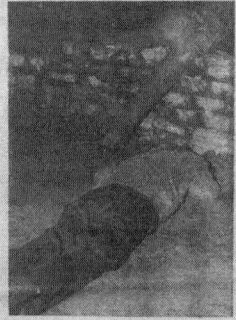

FIGURE 3.9. "Quand Nanterre Monte aux Champs-Élysées" (When Nanterre takes to the Champs-Élysées), *Témoignage Chrétien*, 27 October 1961, no. 903 bis, 4–5.

"Quand Nanterre monte aux Champs-Élysées" (When Nanterre takes to the Champs-Élysées).

This is a brief *photo-roman* of sorts, a novella told through six images. The three photos set along the top of the page indicate the police violence against Algerians in October 1961, while the next three images portray aspects of life in the bidonvilles of Nanterre: a muddy street running past makeshift houses, a man standing with a child held in his arm, a young woman seated next to a child.[28] The imagistic narrative moves from Paris to Nanterre, from violence enacted against men to women and children waiting for their husbands and fathers in their homes in the bidonvilles. The linked images convey the figure of a man facing the harsh blows of police violence and then returning home to his family—or of not returning.

Beyond the overt appearance of the photographic spread in *Témoignage Chrétien*, one way to make sense of Kagan's visit and photographic work in Nanterre on 21 October 1961 is that he was trying to develop further the photographic narrative he crafted four nights earlier, while working to establish a portrait of life among those affected by the police violence in the *métropole*. I would venture that Kagan was attempting, consciously or without clear conscious awareness, to round out the photographic portrait of the wounded man in Petit-Nanterre, and in an analogical way, with images of other men, and a woman with child, without a husband present, apparent in the newer photographic scenes.

While in Nanterre on 21 October, Kagan searched for resemblance within a backdrop of absence. A visual logic of substitution and alterity informed his photographic inquiries, which are patterned by associations and displacements. The personnages presented in these photographs emit visual echoes of the man Kagan had photographed in Petit-Nanterre, whose identity he did not know and was unable to discern, and of any possible family that this man might have had in a residence in a bidonville in Nanterre—or, more distantly, in Algeria. After the night of 17 October, this man was absent in Kagan's photojournalistic encounters, and then forever elsewhere in Kagan's documentary vision. The photographs taken in Nanterre on 21 October 1961 completed a scene and figuration of that absence. With the images printed as a set in *Temoignage Chrétien* on 27 October 1961, the portrait of the apparent mother with her child stands in for the possible wife and child of the wounded man photographed by Kagan. The woman's partner is absent from this scene. A man pictured as he stands in a dignified way in the street of the bidonville, holding a child in his arms, could have been wounded or killed that week, like others Kagan had observed. This man likely attended the collective demonstrations on 17 October and survived the police onslaughts. In the photograph, he stands as a visual substitute for the man Kagan photographed in Petit-Nanterre, while obliquely pointing to his absence. An unlocatable spectral figure haunts these photographs.

Kagan's photographs from October 1961 are suspended within a taut play of absence and presence, actuality and resemblance, recognition and an absence of recognition. With this, it's not enough to consider single photographs on their own, as if they are distinct and separate entities in the world. Rather, it's necessary to consider how images relate to and correspond with one another in direct or oblique ways. Kagan's photographs proceed in relation to one another, as well as to other images in the world more broadly, as though certain images recall or look toward other images. Bodies, standing or lying prone; persons wincing in pain; wounds and wounding apparent; despondent looks; the looks of photographed subjects toward the camera, toward the photographer or any viewers, distant, distanced looks—these image-motifs are in conversation with one another within unending fields of images. Visual echoes and ruptures and displacements mark scenes of intensive looking and representation, plagued by colonial neuralgia.

Perhaps it's also the case that Kagan was tracing out affinities within the tenuous strands of appearance, disappearance, and potential reappearance or nonreappearance within the family, friends, and neighbors he knew in the early 1940s, when more than a few persons—entire families, at times—were arrested and banished from life by agents of the German occupation in France during World War II. Members of families known to Kagan's family were in hiding or still around or gone forever. Kagan was retracing shadows and silhouettes, the afterlives of presences and absences.

We pursue that which haunts us.

While taking photographs in the bidonvilles of Nanterre on 21 October 1961, Kagan had no way of knowing that the man he had photographed in Petit-Nanterre four nights before was no longer alive. On the day that Kagan visited the bidonvilles in Nanterre, Bennahar's deceased body was being brought to a forensic morgue in Paris for postmortem examination.

The Digital Archive

It's late at night and I am looking at images. In the midnight shadows of a corner room I consider a set of images, one after another, through the luminous glow of a computer monitor. The LCD monitor and accompanying laptop are set on a desktop at my home in New York. I have seen these images before, but it's worth looking at them again, pensively, in a mood of return.

I keep looking at two images in particular. The first is from a digital library of Kagan's photographs, posted online. The image is a digital reproduction of one of Kagan's photographs from 17 October 1961—specifically, the photograph of Bennahar as he lies facing the ground, an oil-dark stain near his right arm. The photograph radiates its themes starkly in this hour. The second image is a visual echo of that photographic image, a work of art that builds on a doubling of the photograph's visual forms. But this second pictoral image is not strictly a photograph. Rather, it's a digital reproduction of a drawing of Kagan's photograph. The drawing, composed with graphite powder and pencil, is by Éric Manigaud, an artist who lives in France. In retracing the photographic image, the drawing revisualizes the pain resulting from police violence.

The night dreams on, and I move from one computer window to another, then back again. The more I look at these images, the more immersed I become in a scene of imaginal creation and recreation, resemblance and alterity, a differential doubling of bodies and visual forms.

And so we might consider the dispersive journeys and destinations of the photographs taken by Kagan in October 1961, the ways in which photons of light were grafted onto the surface of photosensitive films and then underwent stints of photochemical processing, with latent images transformed into negative images, which in turn became positive images. We can track the ways in which these images, moving far beyond the sources and subjects of their making, were transferred into marks on print paper, the pictures subsequently and variably marked, cropped, combined, and recombined, with some negatives never making the cut, never moving beyond the interiors of a darkroom; and then for months, years later, successive images came to be reproduced, disseminated, celebrated or condemned, altered, exhibited or forgotten. From these scatterings and machinations in image making, we might trace out the ways in which certain surviving images have been narrated, counternarrated, interpreted, and reinterpreted, as though those assessments have come to be grafted onto the images. Many of the photographs still circulate today, in their spore-like ways, latching onto the surfaces of books or glossy paper or the luminous glow of computer screens, while the persons shown in the photographs appear to linger, remote and forlorn, in virtual realms of time and space.

Two further developments of Kagan's photographs from October 1961 have emerged in recent years. One involves the creation of an online digital library of his photographic oeuvre, with several sets of photographs posted there coming from his work on the night of 17 October 1961. The second development relates to certain works of art that draw from the visual imagery of those photographs.

Since 2020, digital versions of most of Kagan's photographs, including those from October 1961, have been accessible at the Argonnaute, the digital library of La Contemporaine.[29] This digital library now offers a clear, precise, and user-friendly access to Kagan's photographs, with over fifty thousand digital reproductions of photographic images in all. Each set of photographs is clearly named and delineated, with the digital reproductions of individual photographs relatively easy to access, along with accompanying archival information.

The archivists at La Contemporaine have undertaken a great deal of work in identifying and coding the polymorphous compendium of Kagan's photographic prints and negatives, organizing them into specific sets (named and dated—following, whenever possible, Kagan's naming and dating of many sets of photographs). They then converted these many images into digital reproductions, which have now been posted in the digital library. The digital reproductions to be found in the library almost always involve digital scans of the negatives of Kagan's photographs. Only in rare cases, when the apparent original negative of a specific photograph could not be located, did the curators scan other negatives or existing prints of the same photographic image.

With the emergence of this digital library, the materialia, diffuse multiplicities, and labyrinthine complexities of Kagan's photographic oeuvre have been ordered, clarified, pared down, and streamlined. The digital library operates like a screen memory that represents in clarified, secondary form the more diffuse and disorderly compendium of Kagan's analog oeuvre.

There are now, in fact, two archives of Kagan's photographs, which implicitly stand in dialogic and unsettled relation to one another. One is the digital library, fully realized by 2023, which can be accessed online and is available to the public. The other, earlier archive is La Contemporaine's in-house collection of the negatives, photographic prints, and contact sheets resulting from Kagan's work. These were the materials that I was able to engage with in person, in July 2018. This second, analog archive is not immediately available for consultation by the general public. Access to view the materials can be achieved only after a formal request has been granted by the custodians of this archive. In fact, when I wrote to La Contemporaine in May 2023 to request access to the in-house collection again, I was advised to consult the digital library. I gather that the archivists of the Fonds Élie Kagan now deem it unnecessary for anyone in general to consult the in-house collection, given that high-quality reproductions of most of Kagan's photographs can be accessed online. The archivists would prefer it this way, apparently. For one, the original analog materials can be kept safely and securely in-house, without the risk of damage, theft, or loss.

The loss of the original photographic negatives is, in fact, one concern here. On the web page for the digital versions of the photographs that Kagan took at Rue des Pâquerettes, it's noted that "negative B06 has disappeared. We have another version of this negative (11×8 format), which may not be original."[30]

"Negative B06" refers to the code for the photograph of Bennahar standing, hunched over, by the wall and wire netting at Rue des Pâquerettes (figure 1.11 in this text). Its identifying code is KAG/00004/N/B06. *Le négatif B06 a disparu.* The negative has been lost.

Each photographic reproduction in the digital library of Kagan's photography carries a specific code along these lines. The codes for the photographs of Bennahar that Kagan took in Nanterre on 17 October 1961 number from KAG/00004/N/B01 to KAG/00004/N/B11.

I have come to know these codes well, for I have been consulting the digital library since the summer of 2023. This engagement marks another scene of photographic return. In particular, I have returned time and again to several sets of photographs that are featured in this book. I have been visiting the "reportages 'numerotés,'" the numbered reports, for these specific sets of photographs:

Le 17 Octobre 1961: Métro Concorde
Le 17 Octobre 1961: Métro Solférino
Le 17 Octobre 1961: Rue des Pâquerettes
Le 17 Octobre 1961: Vélo abandonné
Manifestation des femmes Algériennes devant la Santé
Bidonvilles de Nanterre: une famille Algérienne
Bidonvilles de Nanterre

Photographs central to this book's inquiry are to be found in these sets of high-quality digital reproductions of Kagan's photographs from October 1961. Each of these photographs carries a specific code (which are also noted in the captions accompanying the photographs shown in this work). For several of these sets, notes are included that detail any complications or irregularities in the nature of specific photographs or their reproductions.

I have been engaging with these images, further emanations of Kagan's photographs. When I am working with the photographs at home, the images appear on the digital screen of an LCD monitor. Several of the images carry the apparitional form of Bennahar's body as it moved precariously through that October night.

While countless numbers of digital reproductions of Kagan's photographs from October 1961 circulate in the world today, the Élie Kagan estate continues to own the intellectual rights to the photographs. In line with the laws of the French Republic, any formal reproductions of the photographs for public or commercial uses require specific payments to Kagan's beneficiaries. The formal rights to the photographs have survived through generations. A statement on the main page of the Fonds Élie Kagan at the website for La Contemporaine specifies the terms of use and reproduction of the images: "The reproduction, publication, or quotation of the documents are subject to the prior agreement of La Contemporaine, which manages the photographer's rights on behalf of his beneficiaries."[31]

Fair enough. All of the photographs taken directly by Kagan shown in this book come from high-quality digital reproductions (in TIFF format) prepared by La Contemporaine and sent to me by electronic transfer, upon my formal request to La Contemporaine for reproductions of the photographs. Along with paying a fee for each digital reproduction, I paid for the intellectual rights to reproduce each photograph in the book, with those funds going to the Kagan estate. The details for this transaction were quite specific: in requesting the rights to reproduce the photographs, I needed to note the expected print run for the first edition of the book and the size of each photographic image as it would appear in the printed book (full-page, half-page, etc.). These details factored into the fee for each photograph reproduced in the book. I then received an itemized bill for the sum total of my requests, which I duly paid in full. Each image comes at a cost, in one way or another.

The advent of the digital library of Kagan's photographs suggests a metamorphosis of the nature of the images, specifically from analog photographs to digital reproductions. Negatives and photographic prints have been used to create digital files that contain the numeric information necessary to reproduce the images. With this reconfiguration of the photographs, the form and substrates of the photographs have changed. This digital transformation of the photographic images reflects a shift in technological conditions in the world at large, which is largely moving from analog to digital photography. The digital library fixes Kagan's photographic images in certain ways. It establishes a clear and precise order to the photographs. In composing the digital library, the archivists at La Contemporaine have drawn from the kaleidoscopic array of images found in the analog archive and fashioned a clear and rationally organized display of discrete images. The photographic images are not the same once they have been converted into digital documents and set within the luminous glow of online viewing.

A great benefit comes with the digital library of Kagan's photographs, particularly in terms of the ordered presentation of hundreds of photographic images and the easy public access to them. Still, I find myself fortunate to have engaged with the many photographic prints and contact sheets in the analog archive of Kagan's work. In visiting this archive, I was able to hold the photographs in my gloved hands and sense their tactile materiality. I also saw firsthand the many different prints and contact sheets that Kagan worked with in his photographic life. The digital library's virtual array of images is not quite the same as the analog compendium. Something is gained, and something lost, in the transfer from photographic prints to digital reproductions presented online.

Redraw the Grain of an Image

Another significant development of Kagan's photographic images from 17 October 1961—a decidedly artistic one, this time around—comes from the work of Éric Manigaud, an artist born in 1971 who lives and works in Saint-Etienne, France. Manigaud's creative work is devoted to crafting series of drawings made by "redrawing" archival photographs of historical subjects, such as the judicial anthropometry at the beginning of the twentieth century, the bombarded cities of World War II, or the facially disfigured soldiers of the First World War. With each project, Manigaud retraces a wound, be it the wounds of sick or maimed persons or the collective wounding of violence and warfare.

Manigaud's creative process entails a scene of projection and drawing. In a dark room, with the use of a projector, he projects a photographic image on a large, white piece of paper. He then traces out all the marks apparent in the projected image, with the use of graphite powder and pencil. Gradually, through time, a drawing emerges on the paper that visually echoes the original photograph. It can take Manigaud two months to complete his large drawings, and fifteen days for his medium formats.[32] The completed drawing is not a direct copy of the projected photograph, however. Due to the materials that Manigaud uses for the drawing, and his artistic approach more generally, there are clear differences between the photograph and the subsequent drawing. Manigaud's drawings tend to appear as grainier, starker, more intensive renderings of the images apparent in the photographs he retraces. Through these image transfers, which produce something new, Manigaud's creative work attests to the iterable, alterable qualities of Kagan's photographs.

Vincent Sator, the founder of the Galerie Sator in Paris, which has shown Manigaud's work, spoke in knowing ways about Manigaud's drawings in an interview conducted in 2018. "Éric Manigaud is an artist I follow, whose work is based on the principle of 'revealing' (*révéler*) through drawing," said Sator. "His approach is to seize on photographs that are very often on the margins of history and society—old, historical or political photographs—and from these photographs that he redraws (*redessine*), his aim is to show again in a new light (*redonner à voir*). The question is to discern how drawing takes hold of the visual and creates a different relationship to the image" (Benaï 2018).

Through his drawings, Manigaud has established new perceptual and affective relationships to Kagan's photographs. For a series titled *October 61*, exhibited at the Galerie Sator in May–June 2018, Manigaud crafted twenty-three large drawings, composed in pencil and graphite powder, that re-presented the visual elements of photographs and film footage taken the night of 17 October 1961. Three of Manigaud's drawings in this series trace out the graphic features of three of Kagan's photographs, including a close-up image of Bennahar lying on the ground (figure 1.6). Kagan's other two images that Manigaud re-created are the photograph of the man seated on a city bus, which had been requisitioned by the Paris police to transport Algerian men they had detained, and the photograph of the abandoned bike, shoes, and other items strewn on the ground. Other drawings that Manigaud created for this series are from photographs by French photographers Georges Azenstarck and Georges Méanger, and stills from Jacques Panijel's 1962 film *Octobre à Paris*.[33]

The series *October 61* was on exhibit in 2017 at the Musée National de l'Histoire de l'Immigration in Paris. The museum's website included a brief text about Manigaud's work:

> Éric Manigaud's approach aims to reveal, "remember" (*remémorer*) through drawing events, individuals, who have remained on the margins of society or hidden by history. Starting from the photographs, which he projects onto a sheet of paper, the artist endeavors to reproduce line by line, shading after shading, using pencil and graphite powder, every detail of the photographic projection. The work of the artist, if it is based on archives, is far removed from these photographic documents, by a change of scale and by an absolute mastery of the surface by the drawing. From his drawings emanates a ghostly character, accentuated by enlargement, the play of light and shadow and the play of matter produced by graphite powder. Up close, the forms dissolve until they are no longer identifiable.
>
> The image loses a large part of its documentary status to become an art work [*oeuvre*], and is enriched with plastic qualities and plays on the ambiguity of statuses. The works of the *October 61* series creates unease: men penned in, bloody bodies on the sidewalks, others, more evocative, nevertheless recall the countless abuses that were committed during these demonstrations. . . . By their monumentality, their immediacy, the works of Éric Manigaud impose themselves on the gaze, preventing any possibility of hiding. The artist's work comes out of oblivion and highlights the abuses that took place during the demonstrations of 17 October 1961, while questioning the collective memory and the processes of writing history.[34]

"I had wanted to work on the Algerian war for a long time," the artist is quoted as saying in a May 2018 article in *Libération*. "This is a subject that is still hard to talk about. This intrigues me: why this repression (*refoulé*)? I was confirmed in my intuitions: today we still confuse 17 October 1961 with the police violence at the Charonne Métro station in February 1962. That says a lot about our hole-riddled memory (*memoire trouée*)" (Mercier 2018).

Linked to the French verb *trouer*, "to make a hole in," the phrase *memoire trouée* suggests a memory that has holes and tears in it—much as the phrase *un bas troué* can be translated into English as "a stocking with a hole/holes in it."

In France, the collective memory of 17 October 1961 is rife with holes, gaps. Memories of that event are porous and fragmentary.

Manigaud's reflections on the aphasic histories and fragmentary memories of the Algerian war of independence indicate that his artwork is a way for him to engage with and graphically recall (*remémorer*; re-member) the histories involved. Through this work, he tries to counter the repression of memory and discourse known in his life and the lives of other residents of France. By recrafting a few photographs and film stills from October 1961, which trace out the force and consequence of police violence against Algerian demonstrators, he is able to immerse himself in the histories involved and conceivably gain certain perspectives on them. His artwork entails a ground for reflection and potential transformation by painstakingly regrafting visual traces of violence.

Manigaud's creative work implies an art of anamnesis—a generative process of remembrance, counter to collective amnesia. In retracing scenes from the past, he strives to fill in the gaps evident in fractured memories of French colonialism and state violence. This creative effort relates to broader collective engagements in contemporary France, in which many are trying to come to terms with the forces and consequences of French colonialism and the Algerian war of independence while working through difficult histories of violence and wounding. With the completion of a drawing comes a visual and perceptual transformation of the photograph regraphed. A shift from historical document to artwork is evident. The artist's work moves from actual historical subjects to spectral figures rendered in pencil and graphite powder. He retraces elements of the past in ways both actual and metaphoric.

We might imagine the artist in the cold and dark of his studio, sketching out graphic traces of dirt and smudges, light occluded from appearance, as a photographic image is projected expansively onto a large white tableau on which fine rough marks are graphically inscribed. I gather that in these moments of drawing the projected photographic image takes on a spectral form, appearing in apparitional ways on the paper. With this arrangement comes an intricate play between actuality and spectrality.

In drawing what appears on the paper through the projection of a photographic image, Manigaud's creative process is the inverse of the technology of standard monochrome photography. Whereas analog photography is premised on the "writing of light," Manigaud's drawing technique is geared toward the tracing of dark. We might say that his drawing leads to a *skoto-graph*, rather than a photograph, to draw from the ancient Greek word for darkness, *skótos*. The draftsman marks wherever there is an absence of light. Through this process, dark tones tend to be accentuated in the drawings.

Manigaud adds further insight to his creative techniques in an interview published in *Artpress* in February 2021. "The studio needs to be described," Manigaud relates to his interlocutor:

It's a dark room, a room with no windows, which is a reconstruction of the camera obscura: in the center, a slide projector facing a white sheet unrolled on a wooden panel. I work on a projected image that serves as a screen: the drawing covers the projection. The projected image therefore disappears as the drawing progresses. Graphite, unlike paper, which is perfectly matte, shines and makes it impossible to evaluate the grey factor during the process. The drawing is almost invisible in these conditions: it's too dark. I draw blind and it's the tactile sense that takes over to make up for the visual deficit. It's more about modelling than drawing. . . . Hence the importance of the choice of paper, its *grammage* [weight], structure, composition, the support on which it's placed—not to mention the pencils, the importance of their oil content for adequate ductility and the way in which the lead is sharpened. It's only in a second stage that the drawing is taken up again in daylight to be able to combine near and far vision. . . . For me, drawing is always the occasion for an enlargement and above all a projection, very special conditions for the appearance in the photographic image, but very revealing: the motifs float like ghosts.[35]

The visual motifs "float like ghosts" in the dark room and on the screen/paper. Manigaud first "draws blind," working primarily through a tactile sense in a dark room. He then shifts to working on the drawing in daylight, to gain perspective on it. The drawing gradually emerges from this graphic process.

One of Manigaud's drawings for the series *October 61* is titled *Elie Kagan #2* (figure 3.10). Made with pencil and graphite powder on paper, it measures 163 × 163 centimeters and is a drawing of the Kagan photograph depicting Bennahar's body as he lay on the ground. The photograph and its double: the secondary image carries tones darker and more granular than those in the photographic prints Kagan crafted from that night. The grain of the image is highlighted, certain features accentuated—the lines embedded in the coat Bennahar wore, the strained lines of the sock on the foot of the deceased man leaning toward the wall. The strands of Bennahar's hair, the shadow about him. Toward the upper right, the body fades into darkness. Particles of dark have been regrafted, and this unsettles any renewed engagements with the photographic image.

What would it be like to redraw the grain of the photographs so faithfully, so intimately, so minutely and graphically, working for weeks on a single image, reproducing in graphite the living form of the wounded body onto a second surface, drawing each particle of this scene of death and wounding, the pencil and graphite powder blurring the paper and staining the drawer's hands, and then to have the grain of these images enter one's thoughts and consciousness and shadow a life? Would this graphic process be analogous to writing about the same photographic images in close and pensive ways?

I have not had the opportunity to view in person any of Manigaud's drawings. I have seen only reproductions as they appear in published texts and digitally online. Others, however, have written of the experience of encountering the actual drawings. All accounts suggest that viewing the drawings, many of which are of considerable size, is a distinctive one. As for the drawings in Manigaud's *October 61* series, the themes of the images are powerful and affecting, for they depict the force and impact of the colonial violence that night. Vincent Sator has spoken about the reception of Manigaud's drawings at the Galerie Sator in Paris: "What really moves me is that visitors have reacted so strongly.... When we previewed a few pieces from this series at *Drawing Now* last March, the project fascinated [viewers] and many visitors spoke about it. We heard deeply moving testimonies from French people of Algerian origin who had lived through the events during the 1961 demonstrations in which they had taken part, as well as from French people who had witnessed and recounted the horror of these events, and the lies perpetuated by the government of that time."[36]

Yet there is more to the experience of viewing the drawings than taking in the political and historical significance of the scenes depicted. Any close perceptual-sensorial engagements with the drawings can be disruptive and disorienting. One commentary on an exhibit of Manigaud's work relates:

> Manigaud's method is simple but effective: he projects the found images on paper, on a much bigger scale than the original. He traces the projected contours, shades and lights with pencil and graphite powder. It is a slow and labour-intensive process that lends weight to the volatile snapshots Manigaud started from. The enlargement of these often graphic and shocking images to a monumental scale turns them into a physical and disruptive experience for the viewer. Watched from a distance Manigaud's drawings seem photo-realistic, but coming closer, the countless dots and strokes start to blur and deconstruct the

FIGURE 3.10. Éric Manigaud, *Elie Kagan #2*, 2017. Pencils and graphite powder on paper, 163 × 164 cm. Photo: Cyrille Cauvet. Courtesy Éric Manigaud and Galerie Sator.

spectator's vision. This ghost-like and elusive quality offers the viewer a way of distancing himself from the hard reality of what is depicted. . . . By means of the often graphic nature of his drawings, Manigaud urges his audience to remember painful parts of history that some would rather forget.[37]

When asked about the possibility that his work "risks flattering the viewer's voyeurism," Manigaud himself said:

An injunction to see-off-screen, yes. Culture has its offscreen. Photography is on the side of the scopic impulse, but drawing by no means. It's by principle unfinished. It remains on the surface, the white of the paper serving as background, reserve. This is why the viewer's voyeurism may soon be disappointed. If they take the the trouble to get closer, they'll see that the transition to drawing involves a lack of detail rather than an excess of detail. There's emptiness, air. . . . It is first of all through shadows that the figures escape their outlines. Under these conditions the risk is indeed that the spectator be satisfied with a vision from afar, with the illusion of resemblance. But even at a certain distance, the viewer is invited to move, because all the shadows created with graphite reflect light, disturbing the capture by effects close to the negative or daguerreotype.[38]

What appears to be a hyperrealist drawing becomes, on closer inspection, hyporealist. Seen from a relative distance, the drawings tend to resemble the photographs they visually echo. Yet when a viewer comes close to the image, any of these assumed photorealistic qualities dissolve into a shadowy array of blurred marks on the surface. The graphite marked on the paper reflects light (much as a daguerreotype does), making it difficult to grasp the imagery traced in the drawing with a clear and steady act of looking. Vision becomes disturbed and disrupted, complicating any reflections on the histories of violence traced through the drawings.

Without having been able to view Manigaud's drawings in person, I have had to consider reproductions of them, which appear in forms smaller and flatter than the actual drawings. But still, as I view these reproductions, my perception of the photograph-like images has been altered. I first encountered Manigaud's drawing *Elie Kagan #2*—and his work in general—in reading Cyril Burté and Audrey Leblanc's 2022 book, *Élie Kagan: Photographe indépendant 1960–1990*. A high-resolution copy of the drawing, which I received courtesy of Éric Manigaud and Galerie Sator, appears in this book (Burté and Leblanc 2022, 119).

"I often feel, when facing an image, as though I am in front of some unknown flower at an unknown stage of its transformation," writes Georges Didi-Huberman in *The Eye of History* (2018b, xxvi). Manigaud's drawing of Kagan's photograph of Abdelkader Bennahar transpires at a certain stage in the transformational currents of Kagan's photographs. Considering the many stages involved with these images is akin to watching a time-lapse recording of Kagan's photographs and their subsequent incarnations as they have changed through time. For the record, the genealogy of the drawing shown in figure 3.10

goes something like: latent image, photograph taken by Kagan but not yet developed; negative image, as chemicalized on a film "negative"; a digital scan of that negative image, years later; a digital reproduction of the photograph projected onto a screen; a drawing made by Manigaud of that projected image; a digital photograph taken of that drawing; a digital copy made of that digital photograph, which is then printed in a book. There is a clear-cut, zigzagging "traceability" to the imagery of Éric Manigaud's *Elie Kagan #2*. Presumably, each successive incarnation of the earlier photographic image alters the image in some way. Each new image implies slight modifications in form and appearance.

In looking at the digital reproduction of *Elie Kagan #2*, I encounter differently the scene at hand and glean aspects I had not fully taken in before. I notice a flower in the upper right corner; punctum of life close to Bennahar's foot, this radiant plant reaches out as if in postapocalyptic survival. Near to his right arm and elbow, an oil-dark spillage has seeped into the ground. The ground itself is marked by dirt, grass, mud, and seemingly bleached-out turf. A small black object lies in soil. Two fingers are apparent in the drawing. Bennahar's left hand is touching the ground.

I had not really noticed these details before, in viewing the photograph on which the drawing is based. These perceived details in the photograph-like image bring to mind Walter Benjamin's reflection on the contingencies that might occur with photographs and that might be noticed by later viewers. "No matter how artful the photographer," Benjamin (1999b, 510) writes in his 1931 essay "A Little History of Photography," "no matter how carefully posed his subject, the beholder feels an irresistible urge to search such a picture for the tiny spark of contingency, of the here and now, with which reality has (so to speak) seared the subject, to find the inconspicuous spot where in the immediacy of that long-forgotten moment the future nests so eloquently that we, looking back, may rediscover it."

Tiny sparks of contingency mark Kagan's photograph of Bennahar lying on the ground, beyond the most apparent visual motifs of the image: the weedy flower, an object on the ground, fingers touching earth. Inconspicuous spots sear the subject with a sense of actuality and long-ago immediacy. Looking back at this recorded moment, we might rediscover these select contingencies. The odd thing is that only with Manigaud's drawing of Kagan's photograph did I notice these details in keen and vivid ways. The artist's rerendering of the image enlivened anew my perceptions of it. The intensive graphite tonalities of the drawing must have something to do with my altered perceptions of the photographic image.

Manigaud's drawings of Kagan's photographs thus bring further transformations to the images and the wounding engraphed. Through a painstaking process of drawing and regrafting, the draftsman-as-regrafter comes to know intimately the intricate features of the image retraced. Yet such acts of perception and absorption come about through processes of reworking, transferring, revisioning, and reimagining. At the same time, a photograph with historical significance is transformed into a work of art by way of the social circumstances and discursive conditions that shape the object as art within an age of digital reproducibility. A drawing with a graphic air to it carries traces of the complicated histories involved in the reproductions and circulations of the image. Manigaud's artwork suggests the palimpsestic nature of Kagan's photographs through time, with layers on layers of graphic inscription, erasure, and affectively charged perceptions marked within a prismatic series of images.

Wounding recurs through the process of drawing, in making graphic marks on paper. The wounding marked in Kagan's photograph comes to be re-marked in Manigaud's artwork. This has the effect of doubling the wound caught within the image. Imaginally and neuralgically at work is a transfer of pain and wounding from body to photograph to artwork to any perceivers of that image. The wound comes to be rescarred, respored into a new surface of appearances. The drawing is the scar of a scarred wound. The act of drawing involves processes similar to those found with scarification, a mark left on skin, derived from previous wounding or partial healing. The draftsman doubles the image in such a way that the subsequent image does not simply have an identical resemblance to the earlier image. Certain features are accentuated, others diminished. The body conveyed in Manigaud's drawing is not the same body portrayed through Kagan's photograph. The wounding is not the same wounding. The wound alters through time, through subsequent iterations and inscriptions.

The drawings have contributed to the afterlife of Kagan's photographic images, as well as the afterlives of the man portrayed through these images. With the afterlives of Kagan's photographs of Abdelkader Bennahar, multiple scenes and modalities of inscription proceed, spore-like, from 1961 to 2018 to 2024 and beyond, from darkroom to studio to gallery, from analog archive to digital library, from monochrome photographs to an image projected onto blank paper to drawing on that paper and then subsequent viewings of that graphite drawing.

Abdelkader Bennahar's name is nowhere to be found in the digital library that holds Kagan's photographs of his wounded form. Nor is that name directly associated with Manigaud's drawing of Bennahar's body. Kagan's name recurs, but not that of the person portrayed through the photographs. The digital and artistic reproductions are consistent with the fact that Kagan never linked Bennahar's name to the subject of the photographs. The subject of the image so often goes nameless, the person seen remains anonymous. This, in itself, is a lasting wound, which singes the history of these images.

THE AFTERLIFE OF A DEATH

Naming the Dead

He would not know of the many photographic and imagistic machinations that stemmed from his singular physical form, photonically transferred into a camera, with resulting photoimages reproduced time and again. He would have had no idea of the affective and phantasmal intensities that pictures of his wounded figure promoted years beyond his actual presence in the world, though perhaps he had an inkling, with the camera's flare still traced within his eyes, that the photographs might count for something, might show and say something in the days to come.

Élie Kagan never learned the identity of the man he photographed at Rue des Pâquerettes the night of 17 October 1961. In the pages of the coauthored book *17 Octobre 1961*, published in October 2001—twenty months after Kagan died, forty years after the violent wounding was photographed—Jean-Luc Einaudi wrote that "Élie would never know the history of the man that he photographed on rue des Pâquerettes and that he then accompanied with the American journalist to the hospital of Nanterre" (Einaudi and Kagan 2001, 54).

The photographer did not learn the man's name that night or in the days that followed. After that, he had only the photographic negatives and prints of the encounter to go by, as well as his memories of the event.

It was only in February 2000 that Einaudi learned the man's name and history. While he was in Oran, Algeria, at the invitation of an association, a man came to see him. His name was Mohamed Bennahar. Bennahar explained to Einaudi that for a long time he had wanted to inform him that the man shown in the photograph on the cover of his 1981 book *La bataille de Paris* was his uncle, Abdelkader Bennahar. Mohamed Bennahar explained that his father, also named Mohamed, had "formally identified" his brother through the cover image, as well as through one other photograph in the book.[1]

"The stranger in the rue des Pâquerettes found an identity," wrote Einaudi in *17 Octobre 1961*. "This name was not unknown to me" (Einaudi and Kagan 2001, 29).

Einaudi was already familiar with the name Abdelkader Bennahar. It was one of fourteen names of deceased persons recorded as being interred at the Parisian Cemetery of Thiais from 17 October to 31 December 1961. In composing a list of victims of the violence of October 1961, Kagan had noted Bennahar's name but had no other information about him. That name is noted on page 13 of the first edition of *La bataille de Paris* and again on page 314, in appendix 7, "Liste nominative de tués et de disparus" (Nominative list of killed and missing), under a list of those killed:

BENNAHAR Abdelkader
Tué par balles, date Indéterminée; inhumé le 7.11.61
(Bennehar, Abdelkader. Killed by bullets, undetermined date; buried
7 November 1961)

And yet Einaudi had never matched this name with the photographic image of the person depicted on the cover of his book until he spoke with Bennahar's nephew in Oran. Two graphic traces of a life death were in place—a name, inscribed, and photographic images—yet for some time those traces were not linked to the same life and death. For Einaudi and others, Bennahar's name subsequently came to be associated with the photographic prints.

I take it that, from the start, Kagan and Einaudi would have wanted to know the name of the man Kagan photographed, whose images were placed on the cover of Einaudi's books. Not knowing this man's identity would have been disconcerting. The images of an "unknown Algerian man" carried specters of anonymity and uncertainty. The absence of a name also risked being politically problematic, with representations of colonized persons often appearing in image and word without a proper name noted, or lacking any name at all, like the "Arabs" invoked but never given actual names in Albert Camus's novel *L'étranger* (*The Stranger*) ("I saw a group of Arabs leaning against the front of the tobacconist's shop. They were staring at us in silence, but in that way of theirs, as if we were nothing but stones or dead trees" [Camus (1942) 1989, 48]).

The absence of any knowledge of the name of the man shown in the photograph can be likened to the phenomenon of an unidentified dead person in a particular society, as with tombs of unknown soldiers—the names of the deceased are lost to others. Something remained missing, in a marked and disconcerting way.

To learn Bennahar's name was to give a more precise and tangible history to the afflicted. To a significant degree, the research into and writings about the events of October 1961 in Paris by Einaudi and others in France can be taken as efforts to name and identify the dead, unknown and known, and to trace out their histories, in gestures of personal and collective testimony and homage—to have these life deaths "count" and "be counted" in significant, lasting ways. The writings resulting from these acts of naming have also tried to name those responsible for the deaths. In effect, some of the writings, historical research, and recording of testimonies of the events of October 1961 have worked to symbolically "name" the event at hand. Such naming is conveyed in the subtitle of the 1991 book *Le silence du fleuve: Ce crime que nous n'avons toujours pas nommé* (The river's silence: The crime that we have not yet named) (Tristan 1991). To name the dead here is to bring the memories of their lives and the causes of their deaths into the language, discourses, and collective thought and memory of two nations. It's to name the criminal violence and the colonial regime that spawned it.

The identification of Abdelkader Bennahar gave renewed significance to the photographs of him that were included in Einaudi's books, including the image on the cover of the book he coauthored with Kagan, *17 Octobre 1961*, published in 2001 (figure 4.1). This image shows Bennahar as he is emerging from the automobile upon its arrival at the hospital of Nanterre. The frame of the Volkswagen door fits well within the frame of the image. The subject of the photograph looks at the viewer of the image, and implicitly at any readers of the book, in a seemingly direct visual exchange. At the same time, the book cover's image and inscriptions speak to the intersecting lives of Bennahar, Kagan, and Einaudi.

FIGURE 4.1. Cover, Jean-Luc Einaudi and Élie Kagan's *17 Octobre 1961* (Actes Sud, 2001), with image of Abdelkader Bennahar. Cover photo by Élie Kagan; see figure 1.13.

Did Einaudi keep in touch with Bennahar's family and let them know what he learned about his death through subsequent research in the archives of the forensic morgue and the records of the Paris Prefecture of the Police? I believe he would have wanted to do this. Perhaps, though, he simply moved on to other histories.

Jean-Luc Einaudi died in Paris on 22 March 2014, at the age of sixty-two, of a "cancer fulgurant," a searing cancer. His body was buried in the cemetery Père-Lachaise, on the eastern side of Paris. Einaudi's death marked one end point in a series of intersecting life deaths that entailed fractal forms of appearance, disappearance, and reappearance.

At least now we have the name of the man photographed by Kagan in Petit-Nanterre the night of 17 October 1961. Otherwise, he might have remained an unnamed figure coursing through Maghrebi and French imaginaries within the repeated flash of an image.

Rue des Pâquerettes

One day in July 2018 I set out to locate the area alongside Rue des Pâquerettes where Kagan photographed the two men assaulted the night of 17 October 1961. At midday I took a massive, bustling RER train from Les Halles in the center of Paris to the station just across from the Université Paris Ouest Nanterre. In no special hurry, I gained my bearings outside the station and threaded a path through the university campus, built on lands where the bidonville of La Folie once stood. Where homes patched together out of leftover wood and sheet metal once stood appeared concrete sidewalks, watered lawns, sleek buildings. I walked down a long, straight sidewalk, passed the metal and glass structure of Bâtiment Max Weber, and came, eventually, to a worn walkway running along the edge of route A86. Buses and automobiles were moving slowly through a tangled knot of on-ramps and off-ramps, crammed with vehicles on their way elsewhere. "La route n'est pas une poubelle!" (The road is not a garbage can!) shouted a billboard sign set between arteries. Stamped onto the cement walls of a concrete underpass were the words "NANTERRE AGIT POUR SON AVENIR!" (Nanterre takes action for its future!). I turned away from the delayed rush of the highway traffic and spotted a sign for Rue des Pâquerettes. Street of daisies. This small, short road ran between Avenue de la République and Rue du 11 Novembre—markers of warfare and victory in the realm of the Republic. A low wall stood along the right side of the street, about a meter high, with a green metal fence fixed above it (figure 4.2). Could this

FIGURE 4.2. Rue des Pâquerettes, Nanterre, July 2018. Photo by the author.

have been the area where Kagan took the photographs? The wall was not of the same materials as the one conveyed in the photographs from that night, but the previous structure could have fallen into disrepair and a new one built in its place, with similar dimensions and purposes to it.

Beyond the wall was a small park-like area, with a few trees and plots of grass, a bench or two. I could picture the two men somewhere by this wall, in an earlier epoch, trying to escape their attackers. Kagan came upon the scene and photographed the two men.

The land and roadways were different then. The course and scope of the street have been reworked, with some sections of its earlier route remaining much the same as before, and other parts effaced.

I walked along the sidewalk and came to a metal gate bearing two metal doors, painted green, closed. I could not see much beyond the gated entrance. Peering through a small partition in the gate I was able to make out a few men moving about in that area, shaded by trees. I could hear the sounds of pétanque balls being tossed and clanking against one another. I glanced through the frames of a fence and saw several men playing the game. Would the men there, who looked to be in their senior years, know of what had happened on this street some sixty years before? What would they want to recall, or forget? Affixed to the gate was a sign that read, "Club de Pétanque du Petit-Nanterre," and above that, another sign, of the same dimensions, bearing the statement "Vivre mieux au Petit-Nanterre" (Live better in Petit-Nanterre). A few steps further down the street stood a modest church that carried the name Église Ste Catherine on the archway above its entrance. Fixed to the wooden doors of the entrance was a small noticeboard, surfaced in glass. One of the notices posted was a piece of paper that held the words "Écoute des blessures" (Listen to the wounds). The announcement invited victims of sexual abuse on the part of members of the church to call a telephone number, provided by the Diocese of Nanterre, where trained professionals would listen to and support the victims.

So many histories of wounding searing through time; forces of bodily violence, assault, accusation and denial, silence, speech, erasure, naming and unnaming. Along the outer facade of the church, names and initials had been inscribed on the soft, pliant stones, as if the inscriptions scratched into its surfaces denoted a registry of souls trying to enter or leave that hallowed hall.

Just past the church, and the sidewalk that bordered it, the street came to an abrupt end. Here, I believe, Rue des Pâquerettes once continued further to the north. At some point, in tandem with a round of urban renovations in Petit-Nanterre—old structures torn down, new social housing and public conveniences erected in their place—the street was severed, and the surrounding lands reshaped. The city's architects drew lines and erased others in their maps and blueprints, and then the bulldozers chopped into the earth.

The rushed exhaust of cars could be heard as motorists cruised down the avenue and the highway just past it. I returned to the area by the park and took out the camera. I photographed the low wall running along this stretch of the street (figure 4.3). I thought again that this could have been where several men were wounded and killed the night of 17 October 1961. But I could not be sure of this. The wall was not the same wall. The death was elsewhere. Yet that low perimeter seemed to mark, intangibly, a site of death and wounding.

I cannot say I picked up on any great spectral presence along the side of this street. There were no ghostly shades, no haunting reverberations. What I perceived most was a sense of absence, void of past histories. Something less than spectral.

FIGURE 4.3. Rue des Pâquerettes, Nanterre, July 2018. Photo by the author.

Two Deaths in Colombes

Two deaths in Colombes, a commune adjacent to Nanterre, on the night of 18 October 1961 apparently evolved around the appearance of a gun that shot blanks. The deaths are multiple, and not grounded in any clear-cut actualities. Ambiguity and fragmented uncertainty lie in the strands of the events recalled. The meanings of the deaths are in flux. They change through time, forms of life death swirl about, depending on the currents at hand. There is no set historical record to this minor history. New possibilities and uncertainties reveal themselves through time, new intensities in life death, while others fade away or are altogether absent.

It's likely that more than two people died in the western suburbs that night. On Wednesday, 18 October 1961, the FF-FLN called for all Algerians who owned businesses to go on a twenty-four-hour strike, with workers compelled to defy evening curfews by demonstrating in Paris and its surrounding towns. The Prefecture of Police countered these plans by forcing businesses to remain open and arresting café owners who tried to close their establishments. By that day, the Paris police, led by Papon, had deployed a massive security force around the perimeter of the central city, blocking access for any demonstrators coming from the suburbs. As a result of these constraints, and lingering fatigue and fear from the violent clashes the previous night, only a small number of FLN activists demonstrated in the city. At the same time, two major demonstrations took form in the western suburbs. Some three hundred men tried to cross the Pont de Neuilly around 9:30 p.m. but were turned away at a barrier from which the police opened fire, wounding at least one person. After this, as House and MacMaster (2006, 126) report, in drawing from journalistic and historiographic sources, "The police managed to break up another column of some 1,500 men and one part of this, a body of about 300 to 400, was marching close to the station of Nanterre chanting, 'Down with the curfew,' 'Algeria for Algerians,' and 'Free Ben Bella,' when the police operated a pincer-movement during which two men died, Achour Belkacemi from gunfire, and Abdelkader Bennahar from a massive skull injury. Several other demonstrators were injured and at least one of these, Ahmed Abaidia, was hospitalized with shot wounds."[2] House and MacMaster write as well, "Throughout the industrial suburbs late into the night of 18 October, as on the previous evening, mobile police units engaged in further ratonnades, the pursuit and killing of individuals or small and isolated groups" (126).

"DEUX MORTS A COLOMBES" ran the headline of an article in the 20 October 1961 edition of *Le Monde*, which reported on the events of that night (figure 4.4). Two dead in Colombes. One of these deaths has been narrated through a complicated story told and contested. The other death has remained obscure. Several varied accounts of the violent clashes in Colombes speak of a violent skirmish between Algerian protestors proceeding down an avenue and a group of French police officers. A man from Algeria, named Achour Belkacemi, was brought down by a police officer. He was reported either to have shown a gun or to have fired at a police car or at a group of police officers. Other reports note that he had "a fake gun," a starter pistol that shot blanks only. Reportedly, a police officer saw the gun possessed by Achour Belkacemi and held by the belt of his trousers. Protecting his commanding officer, the officer fired three rapid shots with his own gun, killing Belkacemi.

The other reported death that night was of Abdelkader Bennahar. His death is noted, but the manner of his death has gone unnarrated. This lacuna in written narratives and police reports is disconcerting. The actuality of the death remains forever amiss and elsewhere.

A series of accounts, drawn from the archives and journalistic registers by Einaudi and others, speaks to what took place. Each account is positioned differently within the language used, the testimonial implications, and the legal and political forces at work—a dense weave of statements laden with political and ideological connotations, justifications moral or immoral, perturbations,

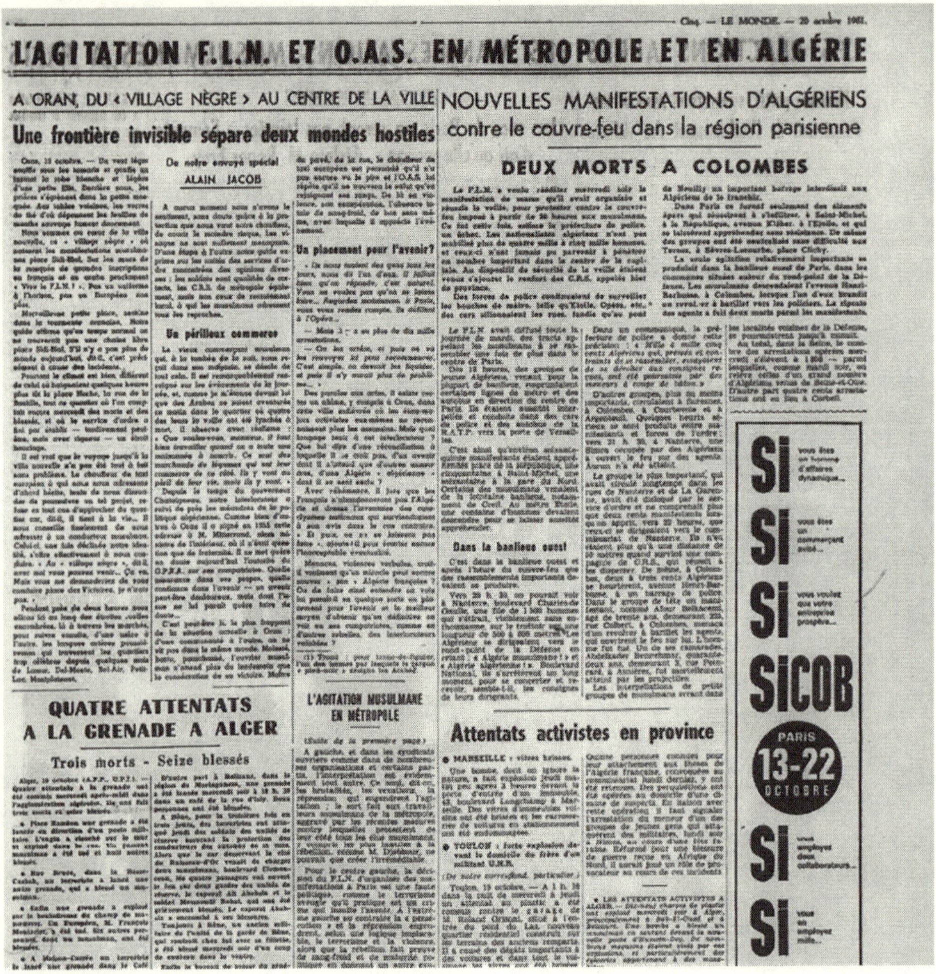

Cinq. — LE MONDE. — 20 octobre 1961.

L'AGITATION F.L.N. ET O.A.S. EN MÉTROPOLE ET EN ALGÉRIE

A ORAN, DU « VILLAGE NÈGRE » AU CENTRE DE LA VILLE

Une frontière invisible sépare deux mondes hostiles

De notre envoyé spécial
ALAIN JACOB

Un placement pour l'avenir?

Un périlleux commerce

NOUVELLES MANIFESTATIONS D'ALGÉRIENS contre le couvre-feu dans la région parisienne

DEUX MORTS A COLOMBES

Dans la banlieue ouest

QUATRE ATTENTATS A LA GRENADE A ALGER

Trois morts - Seize blessés

L'AGITATION MUSULMANE EN MÉTROPOLE

Attentats activistes en province

Si Si Si SICOB PARIS 13-22 OCTOBRE Si Si

FIGURE 4.4. *"Deux morts à Colombes," Le Monde*, 20 October 1961.

and possible distortions and omissions. Einaudi documents several of these accounts in his 2001 book *Octobre 1961: Un massacre à Paris*, while adding assessments of his own:

1 From Einaudi, restating findings noted at the Archives of Department of Justice: "Around 10 p.m., in Colombes, BELKACEMI Achour, born 27 August 1931 in Haussonvilliers (Tizi-Ouzou), is shot dead by a policeman. The autopsy will establish that he was hit by three shots in the thorax."[3]

2 Shortly after midnight on 19 October 1961, the Prefecture of Police gave the following information to Agence France-Presse: "The only

serious incident is in Nanterre: a police surveillance bus was shot at. During the ensuing retaliation, two Algerian Muslims were killed, one with a weapon in his hand."[4]

3 The next day, Chief Commissioner Raymond Lavasseur gave the following version: "I met a group of about twenty FMA [Français Musulman d'Algérie; French Muslims from Algeria] who went up in the same direction, but on the left sidewalk: I passed this group slightly and made my convoy stop. Quickly, the troops dismounted and invited these demonstrators to raise their arms; one of them, who was at the rear of the group, at the moment of his arrest by a brigadier, took out a barrel pistol from the inside pocket of his jacket; he was immediately shot by the guard L., who was protecting his officer. Another FML [member] who was nearby was wounded."[5]

4 The *synthèse quotidienne* (daily summary) of SCINA (Service de Coordination des Informations Nord-Africaines), from 20 October 1961, related the following:

> On 18 October at about 10:15 p.m., a group of five hundred Muslims who were walking along Avenue Henri-Barbusse, not far from the police station of Colombes, chanting the well-known slogans "Algérie Algérienne" and "Libérez Ben Bella," ran into the service of order. One of the demonstrators, Belkacemi Achour, born 27 August 1931 in Haussonvilliers (Tizi-Ouzou), residing in the bidonville located at 225, Rue Colbert in Colombes, took out a revolver and fired at the police. He was immediately shot dead and his death was noted. The peculiarity of this case lies in the fact that Belkacemi Achour used a weapon that could shoot only blanks. In fact, twenty blank cartridges were found in the pockets of his clothes. In this regard, several hypotheses can be advanced, among others:
> - or else Belkacemi thought he was carrying a real weapon;
> - or else he was a provocateur.

Archival information: known as a dangerous militant of the FLN (Fiche Z60/25504) (Einaudi 2011, 350–51).

5 Divisional commissioner of the IGS Christian Mignonneau wrote in a report dated 27 October 1962: "Patrols in the area led to new engagements with groups of demonstrators who used their weapons. An immediate riposte allowed the taking down of two [persons], who remained dead on the ground" (Einaudi (2011, 351).

After noting these distinct statements, Einaudi remarks: "Thus, to try to justify the death of the same man, we have here four successive and different police versions: according to the first version, Achour Belkacemi fired on a police bus; according to the second, he took a weapon out of his pocket without firing; according to the third, he fired a blank bullet. According to the fourth, finally, it is no longer a question of a single weapon but of several with which no longer a [single] demonstrator but groups of demonstrators shooting" (351).

Police logs and historiographic inscriptions like this imply disparate strands of writing, years ago, tracts of memory that trace and obscure what happened that night. A kind of Rashomon effect is at work in the police accounts, with different stories told of a violent clash on the streets of Colombes that night. Each narrative is charged with political force. There is a good chance that many of the versions sided with the interests of the police. The varying reports, by different police officers and supervisors, multiplied and obscured the possible reasons for the state violence that night in Colombes. That obscurity and blurred comprehension could be taken, in itself, as a condition and force of violence. Without a clear sense of what happened, individuals and family members could not seek justice or learn about the actions and names of those responsible for the deaths.

Several other accounts of the events of October 1961 mention Bennahar's name and life, each giving different, fragmentary perspectives on his death. In the 1991 collaborative book *Le silence du fleuve* (The silence of the river), Anne Tristan relates the words of a resident of Colombes who recounted what he saw the night of 18 October 1961 in a local communist newspaper several days later:

> Around 10 p.m. three hundred Algerians passed under my windows on Avenue Henri-Barbusse. Not one [vehicle] was on the road. They walked in silence. Not a word, not a shout. Only the sound of shoes on the cobblestones. Then a patrol arrived, five or six policemen, sub machinegun and revolver in hand. A few minutes later, I heard a series of gunshots. The police blocked off the avenue, and about thirty Algerians were brought there by armed guards. An officer in a cap shouted, "Search them, and no care [if you're too rough]." So, they started to tear off the clothes, to club them. Hysteria won over them, they finished by hitting on the head [of each person], one of them broke his matraque into three pieces. (Tristan 1991, 76–77)

Tristan goes on to write, "At the same time, farther on, somewhere on the avenue, two inhabitants of the neighboring town of Asnières lay there, shot dead [*abattus*]. Afour Belkacem [*sic*] and Abdelkader Bennehmar [*sic*] are the only dead of the 18th [of October 1961] of which we know the names" (Tristan 1991, 77).

Yet another version comes from Raoul Letard, who had told of his experiences as a member of a police *compagnie d'intervention*. During that 1993 interview, Letard related:

> We arrived at Colombes and what do we see before us? A demonstration of Algerians, several hundreds, and we went down very quickly. . . . So it must be said to you that, to the contrary, with these demonstrations we had a huge confidence in our chief, he was someone who was in good form and certainly according to the instructions he received also covered all that was to be covered. . . . There was no reason to hold back. . . . So we went down and I have a colleague who was the driver of the car. . . . He goes down and down, kills, an Algerian. . . . The chief is panicked: "You're crazy, don't start like that!" But he was not wrong, he had seen under the coat, moving, he had seen a weapon, and he had not waited for him to touch his weapon. He had lined him up, but then really clean, killed him outright. . . . Well, it turned out that indeed there was a weapon, but it was a dummy weapon.[6]

An odd and perplexing aspect of Letard's account is that, according to the transcript of the 1993 interview, Letard was apparently recalling the actions of his police company on the night of 17 October 1961—while Belkacemi and Bennahar reportedly died the night of 18 October, in circumstances similar to what Letard related. Perhaps Letard, speaking some thirty years after the events involved, had somehow melded together the actions of two nights, later recollecting them as the events of a single night.

There is a phenomenological tenor to Letard's account, with the narrative voice describing a descent into killing: He goes down and down, kills, an Algerian ("Il descend et descend, tue, un Algérien"). The narrator observed an alert officer who *killed outright*: He had lined him up, but really clean, killed him outright ("Il l'avait aligné, mais alors vraiment propre et net, tué net").

The language in its precision is disturbing. The violence is aestheticized in the narration of acts of police killing, neat and proper. Yet there was an excess to the death and the death that occurred alongside it, a murky obscurity to causes and pathways that has left unsettled remainders.

The history of the deaths in Colombes the night of 18 October 1961 hold layers of inscription, speech, testimony; years of sediment piled on, stored in the archives; histories and counterhistories. Other data figure into the complications of the multiple discourses that bear on what took place that night, with none of this adding up to a coherent, comprehensible whole.

- According to Jean-Paul Brunet (1999, 259), a note of the police preserved in the dossiers of the office of the prefect states that "20 cartridges of blanks had been discovered in the pockets of his [Belkacemi's] clothes."
- Brunet (1999, 259) notes that Belkacemi was declared on file as "dangerous" by the services of the Prefecture of Police and was "said to have been prosecuted in 1959 and 1960 for carrying weapons, death threats, and breach of a ministerial decree of expulsion."
- Brunet remarks that the autopsy conducted of Belkacemi's corpse indicated that he was in "un état alcoolique léger"(a mild alcoholic state) (260).
- Brunet considers the possibility that Belkacemi wielded the fake gun as a means to provoke the protestors and the police into a violent clash.
- Brunet also considers the possibility that police officers placed the fake gun at Belkacemi's side after he had been killed, to establish a "legitimate defense" (259).
- "The precision of the projectiles, fired from the front, also poses a problem: if B. really threatened the police sergeant, it was because he had to be placed more or less in front of him; now the peacekeeper seems not to have hesitated for a moment to shoot, risking the injury of his sergeant. . . . Would this amount to a murder pure and simple?" (260).

Complicating these disparate reports and contradictory observations further is the understanding that, at the time, the Paris police force was engaged in systematic attempts to hide, cover up, and dissimulate the actualities of many acts of violence, particularly when enacted by officers of the force. Police documents from the time therefore cannot be counted on to provide reliable accounts of what took place in encounters between the police and Algerian demonstrators in October 1961. They are patterned by the consequences of "bureaucratic deceit," "techniques of concealment," and "multi-layered corrupt or falsified police reports," to use the words of Jim House and Neil MacMaster (2008, 207, 208, 213). As House and MacMaster (2006, 107) write of the police accounts now preserved in the archives of Paris, "In this world of mirrors and obfuscation, of propaganda and counter-propaganda, the historian would seem to be faced with the impossible task of trying to uncover the truth through police archives that were falsified in their very constitution."[7] Alaine

Dewerpe (2006) writes of similar systems of dissimulation and falsehoods among the Paris police in his important study *Charonne 8 février 1962: Anthropologie historique d'un massacre d'état*, which explores in depth the Charonne massacre of 8 February 1962. House and MacMaster (2006, 208) summarize Dewerpe's findings on these events and the police responses to them:

> Dewerpe has been able to identify not only the same individuals and police units at work as on 17 October [1961], but an identical and well-practiced *modus operandi* of systemic cover-up, from ministerial rank down through Papon to the lower levels of the force. Dewerpe shows not only how brutal violence was built into police training and procedures, but also how the police and judicial archives reveal "a system of dissimulation," the fabrication of an official "truth" or "mensonge d'Etat," and how the complex battery of legal procedures was deployed to cover up the murders so that the cases could be eventually filed away as lacking in evidence (*sans suite*) without any police suspects (although clearly identifiable) ever being brought to justice.[8]

The police accounts of what happened in Colombes the night of 18 October 1961 cannot be trusted, in other words. Any inscribed recollections of that night bring with them a morass of uncertain possibilities and unclear implications. What is minimally clear, though not really clear, is that Achour Belkacemi was shot dead by a police officer. Was this because the officer saw that Belkacemi was holding a gun? Either Belkacemi fired a starting pistol at the officers, shooting blanks, or he was holding the gun and the officer feared he would use it against him and his colleagues. Or the gun was placed in his hands after he was killed. Or the police simply said that Belkacemi had a gun, to provide a reason he was killed. If the gun was Belkacemi's, then it's unclear whether he knew he was carrying a fake gun or what his intentions were in carrying it. Was the gun a show of potential force?

The police records briefly mention the second death reported that night: "An immediate response enabled them to take out [*abattre*] two of them, who remained dead on the ground."[9] Perhaps this is another trace fragment of Bennahar's death: "Another FMA who was nearby was wounded."[10]

Was Abdelkader Bennahar caught up in the violent clash between the police and Achour Belkacemi? Did he get violently ensnared in the "pincer movement" wielded by the police? There is mention of a police car. "So, we went down and I have a colleague who was the driver of the car. . . . He goes down and down, kills, an Algerian" ("On est donc descendus et j'ai un collègue qui était chauffer du car de commandement. . . . Il descend et descend, tue, un Algérien").

These words mark the descent trajectory of a police vehicle, resulting in a death—as though a man was run over by the onrushing vehicle. But the words that follow appear to indicate the violent clash with Achour Belkacemi: the sight of the gun, shots in riposte.

Did Bennahar die at some point in this violent clash? He was not shot, this seems clear. The article published in *Le Monde* on 20 October 1961 mentions the death by gunfire of Achour Belkacemi and then notes: "One of his comrades, Abdelkader Bennehmar [*sic*], forty-two years old, living at 3, rue Poincaré, in Asnières, was fatally hit by the bullets."[11] This hurried dispatch states the last name incorrectly. It's doubtful that Bennahar died from wounds sustained through gunfire.

His skull was crushed, according to the autopsy reports. There are no existing words for the specifics of this death. My guess is that the death was anything but precise and clean. Was there something in the death—a horrific killing, base descent, a messy distortive death—that could not easily be explained in police reports, that would try to present the death as being legally or morally justified?

Bennahar's death is there, on the ground of that night, but little or no mention is made of how he died, in either the police reports or the newspaper articles. Nothing was written accurately about the cause or manner of the death, only that he figured among the two deaths in Colombes that night. There is a blank spot in the actions and cause of death as noted in the historical record. A kind of exscription might have been at work—the causes of the death left out of a system of signification, be it the porous assemblage of texts generated by the police or later historical assessments of the events involved.

Only a few forensic traces remain. It's as if the words gravitate toward Belkacemi and the sudden appearance of a gun and steer clear of Bennahar's demise. The death lies outside the narration, outside the paradigm of a legally justifiable killing. The death has gone unsigned, unspoken, unwritten. Bennahar's demise is the other death that night, one that remains unexplained.

Presumably he left the hospital, hurting, exhausted, away from the danger, still sore from his wounds, possibly healing. Perhaps he sought shelter that next day, yet comfort and safety alone were apparently not sufficient for him. By the next night he had rejoined the collective effort. He and others walked toward Colombes, down Avenue Henri-Barbusse, where protesters risked their lives against police forces. Within these movements ran a multiplicity of forces in life death. Moments in this life were rife with striving vitality or impairment, with annihilation threatened.

He fell. What I see, without any ground for such a partial vision, in a phantasmal regard sixty years past the occurrence, is a police vehicle barreling down an avenue, approaching a group of protestors, other officers on foot stepping close to opposing bodies. A gun is seen; the driver of the car swerves or rushes away or plows straight on; in movements defensive or aggressive there is a turn of the wheel and the car knocks a man down, a body caught under the car's heavy frame just as a world comes to an end. That body-in-death remains opaque, unchronicled. In other ways, that body was powerfully inscribed, in death as in life, by the powers of the French governmental regime. Or so runs one biophantasmatics in life death.

I cannot know the cause or circumstances of the death with any clarity or certainty. It could be that no one alive now knows what happened in the turbulence of that night. Perhaps no one ever knew for sure how Abdelkader Bennahar died.

One reason that Bennahar's death was recorded along with his name was that he was evidently carrying identifying papers with him on the night that he died. Those papers, or any residence permit that he carried, were part of a powerful apparatus of colonial governance. Through such documents and accompanying technologies, persons were registered, identified, tracked, and surveilled by forces of the French state.[12]

In his 1999 book *Police contre FLN*, Jean-Paul Brunet provides further details on the death of a man he identifies as "Abdelkader B., age 42." Brunet reports that the autopsy for the deceased spoke of "multiple fractures of the skull realizing a crushing of the cranial box" and some contused lesions on the level of the hands. The summary of a judicial inquiry on the death indicated that "the expert doctor, resuming a hypothesis emitted by the investigating department, considered the possibility of the crushing of the head by a vehicle, B. having fallen to the ground as a result of blows received at the time of the intervention of the police." On this hypothesis Brunet remarks, "In its current state, our documentation does not allow us to go further. One can, however, wonder about the case of this man over whose body a vehicle would have passed— probably a police vehicle, because otherwise, the police would probably not have left him on the public road before leaving—and it's hard to believe that it was inadvertent" (Brunet 1999, 262).

And then the horrific thought arrives that the police might have placed the already deceased body on a road and then driven over it with a police vehicle, crushing the head so as to destroy the body further and obliterate traces of the causes of death.

Possible, then, was a tripartite series of wounds, culminating in death: the first blows were received at Rue des Pâquerettes the evening of 17 October 1961;

a second beating, later that night, at the hands of the police in an unknown place; and a third traumatic blow, in Colombes the night of 18 October, caused by the crushing weight of a police vehicle. Each possible history of wounding gives possible form to different pathways into death. The deaths of Abdelkader Bennahar are multiple, within the terms of what we can know and perceive of them. They are shape-shifting in intensity and refractive potentiality through obscurities of time.

After Jean-Luc Einaudi, while in Oran in 2000, learned the name of the man Kagan photographed, he undertook additional research to try to unearth additional traces of Bennahar's life death. Searching further into the police and court archives, Einaudi found records of a judicial inquiry into Bennahar's death, for the possible charge of manslaughter. Bennahar was reported wounded after the dispersal of a demonstration by North Africans in Colombes on 18 October 1961. His death was registered when the cadaver arrived at the Departmental House of Nanterre. The inquiry did not lead to anything conclusive. Einaudi wrote in 2011: "The *parquet* of the Seine requested the opening of a judicial inquiry on 31 October. The examining magistrate Boucly was in charge of it, under number 51.408.... A letter rogatory [letter of request] was sent to the Service Inspectorate on 8 November. On 1 January 1962, there was still no return of this letter rogatory. A dismissal [*non-lieu*] was rendered on 25 February 1963" (Einaudi 2011, 353).

The French legal term for a "dismissal" is *non-lieu*, literally a "non-place," in the sense of a declaration by a judge that states that there is no *lieu*, no grounds or reason, to follow a complaint or a course of justice, ending in a nonsuit.[13] Juridical inquiries into the death went nowhere.

Einaudi also found a brief record of Bennahar's death, noted in the register of the morgue at the Maison Départemental of Nanterre. This record states: "Dépôt de corps BENNAHAR Abdelkader 42 ans—amené par car PS Colombes le 18-10-1961 à 22 h 45—agent 13986." This record suggests that the body of "BENNAHAR Abdelkader" was brought to the morgue at the hospital of Nanterre by the police secours vehicle from Colombes on 18 October 1961, at 10:45 p.m., by agent 13986. His corpse was delivered there at the same time as that of Achour Belkacemi. According to the records lodged at the time, he died of multiple fractures of the skull.

"Death may be a domain where one expects to find stillness, yet medicine's traffic continues after life dissipates," writes Harris Solomon (2022a, 176) of the forensic work on corpses received in hospital morgues in urban India. Much the same could be said of a state's biopolitical management of life into death. Bennahar's deceased body was recovered from the place of his death in Colombes and then transported to the morgue at the hospital in Nanterre. And then, on 20 October 1961, agents of the state transferred the body, along with the cadaver of Achour Belkacemi, to the Institut Médico-Légal, the morgue at the Quai de la Rapée in Paris, close to the banks of the Seine. This forensic morgue, overseen by the Paris police, is where most corpses found in rivers, canals, or open spaces in the city of Paris and the Department of the Seine were brought for registration and forensic assessment, autopsies, and legal determination. Once the work of the morgue was completed, the bodies were then often transferred to Parisian cemeteries for burial.[14]

The register kept at the Institut Médico-Légal indicated, for Bennahar's death, "Coups-Homicide."[15] Blows-homicide.

Commenting on the police and medical-autopsy reports, Einaudi (2011, 354) writes: "What had happened between the time Élie Kagan and the American journalist brought this man to the Nanterre departmental hospital, wounded but alive, on 17 October 1961, and the moment a police car dropped him off at the morgue? We will probably never know. But what we do know is that police officers had come to pick up wounded Algerians even inside the Maison Départementale de Nanterre, which, it should be remembered, was a service of the Prefecture of the Police." The implication is that the police, having the power then to detain, arrest, beat, torture, and kill, could have found Bennahar in the hospital at the Maison Départementale de Nanterre and taken him into custody, and he died in their hands. Or he died in the hospital from wounds suffered at Rue des Pâquerettes. The stated reason for the death—multiple fractures to the skull—is not at odds with the apparent wounds to Bennahar on 17 October 1961, as suggested by the blood streaming down his head as seen in Kagan's photographs of him. The report on his being mortally wounded at the demonstration in Colombes on 18 October was, perhaps, a way to occlude the location and causes of the death and obscure the identities of those responsible for it. This is Einaudi's conjecture, which remains unsubstantiated.

Would Bennahar have been able even to attend a protest demonstration the day after he was seriously wounded in Petit-Nanterre? Would he have wanted to attend such a demonstration and risk further blows and traumatic violence to his body? Or was it the case that he recovered sufficiently from his injuries from the night of 17 October 1961 such that he left the hospital and then participated in the demonstration in Colombes the following night? Could it be that the wounds he carried from the previous night were serious enough that, with fracture on fracture, further blows to the head brought on his death?

Perhaps the beating he suffered the night before made him want to protest further, with even greater anger and defiant determination. Perhaps he met again the same tormentors and was further brutalized to death. The death is surrounded by unclear endings.

Several interested parties have sought to understand what happened to Bennahar. There was, for one, the juridical gaze of those persons who undertook the legal inquiry into the death, agents of the Paris court system who tried, however expediently and provisionally or thoroughly—or cynically, callously—to comprehend the causes of the death and determine any criminal actions involved through the forensics of an autopsy and police reports, ostensibly trying to determine the "truth" of the death. The case, ending in a *non-lieu*, was dismissed. The family, too, might have tried to trace out what happened to their relative in the final days and hours of his life by piecing together any words or hearsay or scant images that came their way. Jean-Luc Einaudi tried to search the archives of the Paris police, the Institut Médico-Légal, and the cemetery in Thiais; the few documents made available to him shed some light on the death. Other historians have come upon related materials, each presenting differing accounts of the death. A palimpsestic array of disjointed images, thought, speech, and tracts of writing has emerged in time over the wound and absence in the death.

An ellipsis marks the endspan of a life death. The best that one can fathom, years later, of the final hours of Bennahar's life and his passage into death is that there are different possibilities, different scenarios, different lives and endings in play within the same flux of time.

The vagueness with this death is unsettling. There are no precise words for the death, no clear image with the end of a life.

Mourning Elsewhere

The family of Abdelkader Bennahar apparently had no clear, precise knowledge of his death or where he had been buried. Einaudi wrote in 2001, after meeting Abdelkader Bennahar's nephew in Oran, the son of Mohamed Bennahar:

> In October 1961, Mohamed Bennahar was in Algeria. When he returned to Nanterre, he heard that his brother was dead, that he had been buried in a cemetery, that an American journalist had taken him to the hospital. But having never seen the corpse of his brother, doubt always lingered in his mind. This would last until 1992 [when family members saw the cover image of Einaudi's book *La bataille de Paris*]. As for their mother, she would never really believe it. The elderly woman would say only, "Perhaps he is dead" [*Peut-être qu'il est mort*]. (Einaudi 2001, 354)

The fragmentary nature of this man's death might have meant, for the family that survived him, fragmented processes of mourning. Apparently, the family never knew for certain where Abdelkader Bennahar was, or what became of him. They had just a few remote words to go by. To discover hearsay about a violent death is not the same as knowing for sure. It's not the same as seeing or holding the deceased body, which might permit the family to recognize and acknowledge the death. Without having seen firsthand the body of this son and brother, and apparently without having been notified by the French state about the death (the French police and administrators of the morgue probably would not have known whom to contact, and even if they did, they might not have taken the trouble to do so), his burial, or the location of the grave, family members could not know for sure that Bennahar had died. The family might have encountered forms of ambiguous loss, to invoke a concept recently developed in psychology and the social sciences, which speaks to the stress and anxiety, emotional suffering, embodied distress, and prolonged uncertain mourning that many families experience when loved ones go missing, with no clear indications of their lives or deaths in absence, often facing "loss that defies resolution, extending indefinitely in time" (Crocker et al. 2021, 599).[16]

Such forms of continued uncertainty and lingering grief were in effect for many Algerian families in Algeria and France during the war of liberation and years after, for family members often did not know for sure, or at all, what had happened to missing relatives and loved ones. Or they thought vaguely, half-knowingly, that a daughter or brother or father or son had died, though nothing was certain.

For families who lived in Algeria, it could be especially difficult to learn about any family members who might have died in France in conflicts with the police. It often proved difficult to receive direct news about a death or to determine its actuality or circumstances, for any number of reasons. House and MacMaster (2006, 166) write of such concerns, "One final reason for the failure of families or relatives to identify the dead or to initiate judicial investigation was that most were poor and illiterate peasants and workers located in Algeria who simply did not know when sons or husbands had 'disappeared.' . . . Even when families in Algeria did hear by letter or word-of-mouth, they were usually ill-equipped to find out from a distance what had happened or to penetrate the dense smokescreen thrown up by the authorities."

The grounds of Bennahar's death apparently remained unclear and uncertain for his family—a lingering, tentative death, and thus a provisional, still-possible life—until the brother was shown the photographic image on the cover of Einaudi's book, published in 1991. In identifying his brother in that image, it was as though Mohamed Bennahar was formally identifying his brother's corpse and confirming the death within a shock or calm of recognition. The virtual image of the brother's wounded body stood in for a stark image of his corpse. To encounter the image of his brother on the cover of the book was to see the face of his brother, before and after he died.

Einaudi (2001, 354) related that Mohamed Bennahar "formally identified" (*formellement identifié*) his brother through the photograph on the cover of the book. This detail is noteworthy, for such a process of postdeath recognition was common during the years of the war of liberation, particularly in Algeria. Family members, relatives, and neighbors were often called on—and often, forcibly, by the French police or military—to identify the bodies of those who had died through violent means. The French police or military then filed reports that hid the actual causes of the deaths through acts of dissimulation. They forced people to make the identifications, and they often blamed Algerian "rebels" for the killings. The formal recognition tied into the politics of life death and the interpretive assessment of dead bodies and violent actions during the years of the war.

Without the trace of certain images, the family would probably have never learned for sure about the death of Abdelkader Bennahar. While the family never received direct news or a formal notification of the death, at least the photographs that surfaced with Einaudi's book, viewed some thirty years after the death, charted a visual record from that night, the brother's wounding and his arrival at the hospital. The brother's absence after that night, with no subsequent news from him, tentatively implied his death.

Still, it's said that, without having seen her son's lifeless body, the mother never really believed that he was dead. Without a tangible trace of the corpse, without the remains of the son's body returning home and being reburied there, Bennahar's death and life continued to have something uncertain and open-ended about them. As Einaudi put it in an article published in 2002, paraphrasing what the nephew told him of Bennahar's mother, "Elle n'y crut jamais vraiment, n'ayant jamais pu voir le corps de son fils" (She never really believed in it, having never been able to see her son's body) (Einaudi 2002, 44).

This statement has been passed on, has lived on—a survivant trace in itself—through a sequence of texts and utterances. What reiteratively recurred was the mother's tentative statement "Peut-être qu'il est mort," which situates the *peut-être*, "can be," possibility of her son's death within the greater likelihood of continued life. Her hedge of a statement marked a tentative speech act that suspended knowledge of the death and held out hope for the possibility of life beyond a possible death.

With the phrase "peut-être"—or, conceivably, a parallel phrase voiced in Darja (Algerian Arabic) or with an Amazigh language—I hear oscillating possibilities within the life death of an absent son. Perhaps, can be, could be dead or alive, can be/cannot be; the potentialities inherent to a life death continued on in uncertain conditions of possibility.

I wonder if the mother still held out hope for her son's continued life, even after seeing the photographs of her wounded son. There is nothing immediately present in those images that directly indicates his death; there is only the nonsign of continued absence, of not hearing from him for years on end. What the mother imagined her son to be, what she wanted him to become or remain as, was perhaps more significant than other actualities in life and death.

"Nothing could be worse, for the work of mourning, than confusion or doubt," Derrida (1994, 9) writes in reflecting on loss, mourning, and the potential for the unsettled, haunting return of the dead. What kind of mourning can take place when one cannot identify the bodily remains or know for sure that a death has occurred? What kind of resolutions and transformations in grief can take place when the death remains uncertain, unknown—when the disaster of a death keeps on going, uncertainly? The death remained an unreality in suspension. There could be no closure, if closure was something needed or desired.

Was there ever a house in mourning (as in, for example, *Antigone*)? Or were there, instead, small fragments of uncertain grief, strewn here and there, displaced and deferred, in a work of impossible mourning?

It's said that the family had heard that their son and brother had been buried in a cemetery. But the surviving family might not have known precisely in which cemetery the body rested or in which place in that cemetery. There was not necessarily a distant graveyard to visit, no clear location or placement for the body of their blood relation.[17] Speculatively: the family was not able to render tangible the remains of this deceased family member, nor could they make present his absence, by identifying or localizing his remains. For the family, the death and the possible remains of the deceased existed in a kind of *non-lieu*, a nonplace of life death, an unplace of provisional, tentative mourning.

The obscurity around the death implied a slow, vague, corrosive violence. Not knowing about a possible death can entail a lingering wound.

The forms that mourning might take, the shifting forms of grief within a life, a family, a community, so often proceed in variable ways in relation to a body, a body absent, lost, found, burnt, buried, forgotten, abandoned, or recovered; or in relation to something like a body, a form or object, trace fragment, an image or intensive memory, that one might relate to within the reaches of absence and loss.

For the family, the visual image of the man as appearing with Einaudi's book could have been at once unsettling and comforting, provoking complex possibilities and processes of thought and life and identification within uncertain streams of time. This is what I imagine, without knowing if my speculative imaginings of another's history of violence and sorrow reflect anything that was actually going on with the family. I write from the outside, on the margins of a life death.

Each strand of thought and language, each effort in unresolved searching implies an elsewhere that the writing and knowing cannot reach, elsewheres in time, space, language, life, and death. No grasping awareness, no fragile constructs of words can reach beyond the limits of what can be known or not known. At times, there is not even an elsewhere to consider. Any elsewhere conceived is not there at all; there is no there in the elsewhere imagined.

And survivance, speculatively: that Bennahar's name would carry on, within the family and elsewhere. In complex survivance others would recall his living image, the breath and voice of him, spectral materialia living on: *You have your uncle's eyes.*

The family's identification of the man pictured on the cover of Einaudi's book could have been the first step in a formal, collective mourning for his loss. Would the family have performed funeral rites for the apparently perished son and brother, once they saw the image of him and surmised his death? Or did the family refrain from any such rites, for a time indefinite and open-ended, in holding out hope that this loved one would return, alive, one future day? To undertake funeral rites, however abstract and virtual, for someone who might still be alive could be unsettling and problematic, perhaps unthinkable. It's possible that the son and brother was never ritually mourned by a family that held out hope for continued survival.

For the family, the death might always have been elsewhere. It could not be fully present or perceived. The death was away in time and space, unclear, unmarked, nondetermined. Perceptually, affectively, the mourning might have been deferred, riddled with frayed strands of time and memory.

They could never know for sure. The disappearance of their son from their lives might have implied an indeterminate horizon in life, one that never gained greater relief as the years wore on; no matter how closely they approached this horizon, it remained unclear to them, beyond their reach. As the family moved forward in time, that vague, indeterminate horizon shifted further away.

So many persons have been compelled to engage in speculative thanatographies in trying to comprehend what has happened to absent others in their lives. A colleague from Scandinavia, who has conducted extensive anthropological research in Vietnam, with close ties with the people she works with, once read a draft version of these passages on the uncertain mourning possibly faced by the family of Abdelkader Bennahar. She spoke with me about the text and asked if I had considered noting other places in the world where people had lost track of family members who had disappeared from their lives, due to violence, warfare, clandestine killings, other disasters. "This happened a lot in Vietnam, during and after the war with the United States," she told me. "Families never learned what happened to sons and daughters, or their brothers and sisters, or parents, who had fought in the war and probably died then. Their bodies were never recovered and people never learned what happened to them. And with this, the mourning for lost family members has often been vague and uncertain."

Streaming through one's mind is the scope of disappearances throughout the world, with families at a loss as to how to account for such absences and mourn the absent absences of loved ones. There are the parents of daughters killed in Mexico, victims of random violence or misogynistic hatred, grief without a body to grieve; of young men gone missing, their lives or bodies never found. "It's a horrible uncertainty I don't wish on anyone," said one woman from the state of Chihuahua, who spent two years looking for her son, twenty years old when he vanished after finishing work one night at a local taqueria. "If I knew he was dead, then I would know that he's not suffering. But we don't know and it's like torture, that not knowing" (Lopez 2021). The not knowing can entail lingering anguish. There are the voices of the Madres de Plaza de Mayo, a collective of women who lost sons and daughters to the dictatorial military regimes of the 1970s, who came to protest the disappearances and turned images of the missing into political action. In Algeria, members of the Collectif des Familles des Disparus have gathered weekly since 1997 to demonstrate silently in town squares and at bus stops in Algiers, Oran, and other cities. "They stand in the streets against the law's injunction to forget, summoning ghosts of those who have disappeared—siblings, children, parents—by holding portraits of their faces and banners with their names. Posters appear on alley walls; anonymously authored graffiti record the proper names and disappearance dates of loved ones" (Jarvis 2021, 179). There are the families of desaparecidos in Guatemala, or Peru; persons shot by callous enemies, bodies dumped into hastily dug ditches covered with soil to hide traces of execution. Travelers and migrants have been lost at sea, refugees lost to desperate treks across arid deserts. Absented to kidnappings, state appropriations in life and death, military onslaughts; disappearances in Algeria during the war of liberation, bodies never found or fully recovered, deaths not clearly grasped or known about, many deceased going without proper burials or funerals, with all this set within the nearly genocidal "disappearance of the colonized people" (Fanon [1961] 2005, 85) in North Africa.

To configure the fabric of life death within the valence of disappearance is to conjure aspects of life that are porous, reedy, knotted with holes; patched-up traceworks frayed at the seams singed by ruptures, gaps, distortions, uncertain endings. It's to know disappearance as uneven force running through life death, and to recognize continued life. "A terrifying overflowing of life, after the failures and the distancings, life is still there, bumping against the potentials or forms of new lives. Life clings to life: this is the principle. In spite of every death" (Farès 2020, 335).

Life survives life.

Faces of the Dead and the Right to Opacity

What phantasms are required to make sense of a death or to live in its midst?[18] What images do we assign to death, or to a particular death, and in life death more generally? In giving thought to such questions, we cannot think of images as being altogether clear and steadfast in meaning or affective resonance. Images alter and deviate, they swirl about through time, and work and appear in different ways for various subjects and interpretive events and political force fields. An image is not a singular, unchanging phenomenon in a steady world but rather multiple and shape-shifting in fractal form and intensity as it scurries through time.

What forms does the face of a person take in life and in death? If we keep in mind certain complexities in perception and entangled temporalities within fields of life death, then we can work toward understanding the different frames and appearances of a face in death—the distinct and multiple ways a face can be perceived or remembered, imagined or harmed; beheld by loved ones in presence or absence; circulated, passed along, disturbed or effaced through time.

The photographs of Bennahar's face as shown on the covers of Einaudi's books are from the night when he was wounded. He is not visibly disfigured in the hour of those images, as he apparently was in death. In those photographs he was not "unrecognizable" (*méconnaissable*), as was often the case with the faces of men and women after they had been tortured by French soldiers or bludgeoned into death, or their bodies violently disturbed after death. With the actual death the body was probably disfigured and perhaps unrecognizable through its facial features. Bennahar was likely identified by police officers and at the forensic morgue through his identification papers.

Méconnaissable. *The "unrecognizable" became a recurrent, troubling motif in Algeria and in France during the years of the Algerian war of liberation. Lifeless bodies found, faces of the dead unrecognizable to those who encountered them or to family members introduced to unfamiliar corpses. Faces unrecognizable after rounds of torture; eyes, mouths, cheeks, and noses pummeled by French military personnel or police officers; distorted visages marking harsh acts of violence exacted. In histories of violence, hard to say, unrecognizability is a theme. Colonialism disfigures and dissolves, messes up lives and deaths.*

Consider the written statement signed by Ali Hadj, a journalist from Algeria, testifying to his confinement in December 1958 at the Direction de la Surveillance du Territoire in Paris, where he and other Algerian men were reportedly "questioned," interrogated and tortured by Paris security police:

> *I met Mr. Khebaili on the stairs of the D.S.T. headquarters on rue des Saussaies [in Paris] one morning during December, 1958, when I was being led to be questioned. I shall never forget the image I saw then, although it was before my eyes no longer than twenty or thirty seconds. There are memories which remain graven on the mind and it is possible to recall them at any moment. This is one of them. As I was climbing up the stairs, M. Khebaili was coming down, and he was moving so slowly that I had time enough to make out the form—or rather the formlessness—of his face. It was like a vast wound and only his eyes—protruding, haggard eyes—indicated that it was the face of a human being. . . . When I passed him, I could guess from his look of a man lost in space how terribly he had suffered. (Silvers 1960, 90)*

The family saw the face and look of the wounded son and brother while he was alive. They did not see his face in death, a face that, presumably, would be utterly still and have the appearance of stillness. "Death is the immobilization of the mobility of the face," writes Emmanuel Levinas (2000, 12, 14). "Someone who dies: a face becomes a masque." In death there is a lack of a living look or regard, the lack of a vital face engaged in life.

While members of the family later saw the photograph printed on the cover of Einaudi's book and glimpsed the small black-and-white pictures inside, those images were drawn from hours before the catastrophe of the death. These photographs do not show a face that is frozen and immobile but, rather, a face that is very much alive, searing possibly onto continued life. The photographs presented a displaced image and limited knowledge of his death. They were not from moments of the death or after the death. These wound-images did not line up well with the death to come. Something was off; the images were in a sense premature and then, after the fact, indeterminate.

The photographic image on the cover of Einaudi's book *La bataille de Paris*, published in 1991, has changed affective significances through time. Through the years of its circulation and perception, the circumstances surrounding this image have altered its sense and import, including how it has variably worked in time. In one stream of perception, the cover picture conveyed a biographic image, a snapshot within a moment of the (unidentified) wounded man's life, one that continued, uncertainly, conceivably, after the moments of photographic capture. The image was, for many, a sign of precarious life, of wounding and state violence within fragile streams of life death—but of life, nonetheless, even if the wounded life conveyed was potentially verging on death. That cover picture later became, for some, a thanatographic image, signifying this man's imminent and subsequent death. The image became a sign of death, of life into lifelessness—of a man who would soon die, with the possible causes of the death indicated in the photograph. The image also came to convey the deaths of others in and around Paris the night of 17 October 1961, and other nights that year; one man's wounding and imminent death metonymically signified the suffering and deaths of others. Death became the latent image in Kagan's photographs. A later, subsequent understanding—a later development of the photographic negatives—brought out that latent image and turned it into a directly apparent image.

For a time, the image was primarily one of wounding. The photograph was a wound-image, an image of a wound and image as wound. Could it be that, once the man seen in the photographs was identified as Bennahar and the history of his death was understood, the image lost some of its wounded, wounding qualities? Or, to put it differently, could there have been a transformation of wound and wounding involved in certain encounters with this man's image? For the family, news of the death might have altered the nature of the perceived wounds, much as the wounds that a corpse bears in unsensing flesh are distinct from the wounds in a living sentient body. In time, for some perceivers of the image, the wound of the photograph might have related less to the wounding of Bennahar, at the time when the photograph was taken, and more to the searing wound that came with comprehending his death.

These scenarios and possible engagements with the photographic image alter and refract through time, depending on how and when one person or another looks at the images, and what ideas, histories, and fantasies stream through a body or consciousness or a specific terrain of life death. With a single glance, in complexities of time and imagining, the photographs embody different temporal, phenomenal, and imaginal processes.

An imagined body alters in form, an actual spectral body, lost life; wounded body, corpse, wound-image, tender fantasies. Perceptions of death shift and waver. One looks at a death, looks elsewhere, moves away, comes close, closer still; look at the image, look away, try to forget, bury the dead, entomb memories or efface them.

I imagine Bennahar's family keeping a copy of Einaudi's book in their home near Oran. ("The family, your figure of the family," writes A., the family as phantasmally conceived.) The text with its wounded, wounding cover image is set on a mantel, alongside portraits of family members and honored ancestors, close to a simple, elegant vase holding freshly cut flowers. Or the book-image is kept safe and relatively sight unseen in a cabinet, valued and preserved like a sacred object or the relics of a saint. Now and then the book is taken out and held in the hands and the picture of the man found on the cover is considered with care and reverence. When special guests are welcomed into the home, they are shown the book and quiet, respectful words are shared about the lost son and the terrible wages of the war. Or perhaps the images of the family's lost relation are too wounding, too painful, and they do not keep the book around.

Can a book become a surrogate corpse? It's possible Einaudi's book and its surface image came to stand in for Bennahar's unrecovered body, and the family related to the presence of the book as they might to the preserved remains of the dead. The image of the book could have served as an effigy of sorts or a lasting relic that could be held in one's hands.

Other affinities come to mind. A book is a body assembled out of a corpus of remnant traces. The present pages cobble together a clump of whitened bones, exhumed, polished, and reordered years after a crushed life and its sullen burial in an unmarked grave.

I have come to imagine (imagine, only) other scenes at the end of Bennahar's life. All this is wounded imagining.

A series of images, vague, fleeting, dissolute, of images straggling through time, combines with the visual afterlives streaming from the photographs.

Other moments go unknown, unnoticed, without image.

No mention of a wife, or children of his own. No mention of a father.

If Bennahar was born in 1919, then he died at the age of forty-two or forty-one.

Of his death Bennahar keeps silent. The silence in death brings to mind a journal entry of Mouloud Feraoun, dated 6 October 1956, during years of murderous conflict, in which this Kabyle-Algerian writer and educator relates a dreamed encounter. It begins, "In a city of the Mitidja where I traveled in a dream, S. stuck to the facts when he told me his story":

They came for me at my home around midnight. The soldiers, the DST [Direction de la Surveillance du Territoire], who else? They had to break down three doors to get to me in my bed. They took me away. No, I did not say anything. I knew I was done for, and I did not say a word. So they started beating me up. I had a big advantage, I was thin. The first blows almost knocked me out, so the rest was of little interest to me. Afterward? Anything you can imagine. They ripped my poor rags to shreds: they sliced pieces of flesh from my body, pierced me with their bayonets, broke my ribs and my arms and legs, cut my throat according to the Muslim ritual as we perform it back home, riddled me with bullets, stamped their feet both with fear and joy, and I just let them do it. I let them do it after a certain point. After a relatively short point. That is the advantage of being thin. And as I looked at them from a distance, I felt both amused and triumphant, out of their reach, free, and happy.

It is a good thing they did not notice.

With contempt, they abandoned me under a bridge, several miles from town. The next day, in full daylight, they went back to my home to arrest me as a suspect. They had most likely forgotten that they had taken me away the day before. Nevertheless, I had to be found under the bridge, my father had to identify me, which, believe me, was not easy. Yet, in the end, when my father flatly declared that the feet on the cadaver could be only those of his son, they were able to complete the inquest with the conclusions that you know and that the press reported: It was a [*sic*] FLN leader killed by the rival MNA faction. My family was left alone. As for me, I continue to secretly chuckle about all this. Because, you see, I would not want them to hear me. (Feraoun 2000, 139)

Feraoun's dream vision is part of the afterlife of this man's death. It is remarkable how Feraoun narrates the facts of "S.'s" story of death and postlife body and speech and his quiet, uncanny (non)presence in recent death—as if the writer suddenly leaped into a fantastically empathic imagining of this man's death and its cryptic implications, the dream folds of a speculative thanatography. The soldier's arrest and seizure of this man, the brutal beating and mutilation of a "thin" body, the contemptuous treatment of the corpse, the father's formal identification of a son's lifeless body, the dissimulation of the causes of death: all of this speaks to recurrent nightmarish scenes of capture, arrest, torture, and murder in Algeria at the hands of the French police or military and the strange, unsettled remainders of such deaths in surviving families. (The dream and its narration foreshadow aspects of the novelist's own death, six years later.) The man relates the facts of his death through Feraoun's dream travel while secretly chuckling about it all. He does not want the soldiers to hear him, for fear of further damage. He keeps silent, while communicating obliquely through the sounds and sights of a dream-vision.[19]

All of these words have been written about Abdelkader Bennahar, dream-visions of his life and death, and he, too, keeps silent. Words and images congeal around a death. Language stands in place of the disappeared.

He is quiet in the matter of his death, an unending silence. It's not like he is looking on, aware of his death and my regard of him or any writing of his life death. Silent, unseen, nonspectral, nontactile, his blunt absence lies within the thought of this writing. Yet he is still there, in a way, ever so slightly.

If he were to appear to me in a dream, what story would he tell? Would he speak of contempt or the rough treatment of a thin body? What facts would he relate and what would he keep silent about? Would he secretly chuckle about it all?

I have yet to dream of him.

Permit him his privacy, keep to him his life. I wish to support his name and sustain a memory of him, yet to write about Bennahar is to cast him within a net of language and image.

Do the dead have a right to opacity? "We demand the right to opacity," Édouard Glissant (1997b, 189) proclaims in speaking of the proposed rights of colonized and disenfranchised peoples throughout the world for opaqueness, in avoiding interpretative systems of transparency, comprehension, appropriation, and surveillant knowing possibly placed on them by various powers. "Nous reclamons le droit à l'opacité" (Glissant 1990, 203). This is a right to not be understood, to not be held as an object of study and knowledge, to remain within domains of unknowability, and thus to not "reduce anyone to a truth he would not have generated on his own" (Glissant 1997b, 194).[20] With this proposed, politically important right there might lie a tentative, desired freedom from consequential systems of observation and analysis. The opacities achieved or imagined can imply strategies of protection and forms of postcolonial resistance against domination. More broadly, they can imply a philosophy of life among others. "Widespread consent to specific opacities is the most straightforward equivalent of nonbarbarism," writes Glissant (1997b, 194).

For the living, yes, agreed, there should be a right to opacity, and one should respect the opacity of others while also appreciating the opacities within oneself and in relation to others; "opacities can coexist and converge, weaving fabrics" (Glissant 1997b, 190). But what about the dead? Perhaps deceased persons deserve a similar right to opaqueness, a freedom from cutting analyses of the formations of their lives and deaths. Or some dead, at least, the colonial dead included. Perhaps the dead need the right to opacity even more, as they cannot directly contest any scrutiny of their life deaths; they need others to proclaim this right for them. Perhaps some dead might want to hold onto a right to be forgotten. Can one envision a right to not be part of the historical record—a right to not have one's joys and losses examined by others?

And yet isn't it worth knowing about the political forces that shaped the life and death of Abdelkader Bennahar and the circumstances and aftermath of his death and those of others within the complex folds of that colonial moment? Perhaps stories of the dead belong to some kind of public realm. To know well, or to hold off on such knowledge, displaces the knowing, respects the opacities of the dead and the living—there is an abiding tension here, which cannot easily be resolved. (There is also an aporia in the idea that the dead can hold certain rights usually reserved for the living.) Should I strive to know some of the features of Bennahar's life death, or hold off on such knowledge?

In his essay "The Black Beach," in *The Poetics of Relation*, Glissant writes of the beach at Le Diamant on the southern coast of Martinique, which holds a "subterranean, cyclical life" grained by black sands, secret winter winds, high waves, branches of manchineel and sea grape; "brown seaweed piled there by the invisible assault buries the line between sand and soil." For the author, the edge of the sea "represents the alternation (but one that is illegible) between order and chaos" (Glissant 1997b, 121). Along the shifting shores of this vol-canic coast Glissant notices an enigmatic figure, a young man, silent, who fre-quently passes by Glissant's vantage point on the beach. "This is where I first saw a ghostly young man go by; his tireless wandering traced a frontier between the land and water as invisible as floodtide at night. I'm not sure what he was called, because he no longer answered to any given name. One morning he started walking and began to pace up and down the shore. He refused to speak and no longer admitted the possibility of any language" (122).

Glissant describes the quiet, wayward occurrence of this young man but stops short of describing his appearance. "It doesn't feel right to have to repre-sent someone so rigorously adrift, so I won't try to describe him. What I would like to show is the nature of this speechlessness. All the languages of the world had come to die here in the quiet, tortured reflection of what was going on all around him in this country.... All this he rejected, casting us out to the edges of his silence" (Glissant 1997b, 122). The writer nonetheless makes an attempt "to communicate with this absence":

> I respected his stubborn silence, but (frustrated by my inability to make my-self "understood" or accepted) wanted nonetheless to establish some system of relation with this walker that was not based on words. Since he went back and forth with the regularity of a métronome in front of the little garden between our house and the beach, one day I called him silently. I didn't exactly know what sign to make—it had to be something neither affected or condescending but also not critical or distant. That time he didn't answer, but the second or third time around (since without being insistent I was insisting) he replied with a sign that was minute, at least to my eyes; for this gesture was perhaps the utmost he was capable of expressing: "I understand what you are attempting to undertake. You are trying to find out why I walk like this—not-here. I accept your try-ing. But look around and see if it's worth explaining. Are you, yourself, worth my explaining this to you? So, let's leave it at that. We have gone as far as we can together." I was inordinately proud to have gotten this answer. (122–23)

As those few days passed, the writer and the silent walker developed a quiet, modest sign language between them, through gestures of barely lifted hands, a sign of complicity between them. With this tempered communication, Glissant came to think "of the people struggling within this speck of the world against silence and obliteration," and of those throughout the rest of the world "who have not had the opportunity to take refuge, as this walker has, in absence—having been forced out by raw poverty, extortion, famines, or massacres" (Glissant 1997b, 123).

It could be said that the silent walker, in his solitary pacing along the beach at Le Diamont, was maintaining his right to opacity, and thus trying to hold onto a freedom of absence and silence, or so I read Glissant's semi-allegorical tale of Black Beach. I have kept in mind the poetics of this delicate relation in think-ing and writing of Bennhar's life and death, the thought of this "voiceless man" implying another silent figure (Glissant 1997b, 127). In the system of relation I have established with this opaque figure, I have been reaching out, trying to understand the grounds of his existence. I have been communicating with the absences involved, through various sign languages. I would like to think that my efforts would be accepted, possibly appreciated by some. But in moments it doesn't feel right to represent someone so rigorously absent. Perhaps the silent opacity of him would respond or not respond, "I understand what you are attempting to undertake. I accept your trying. But look around and see if it's worth explaining. Are you, yourself, worth my explaining this to you?"

With this admittedly conjectured, spectral exchange come moments of nonknowing, opacity, ambiguity, errance, relation, relay, detour, and multiplicity, to invoke Glissantian terms, within *la pensée archipélique* (archipelagic thinking) and a sustained ethics of relationality (Glissant 1997a, 31). ("We hate ethnography: whenever, executing itself elsewhere, it does not fertilize the dramatic vow of relation" [Glissant 2010, 122].) Still, I am unsettled by the fraught relations of power and knowing involved in my attempts to understand the life death of another, especially given that this man faced hard circumstances in his life up to and into the obscurities of death, and that I write from a position of relative power, of secure and stable knowing.

A concern here is that I am writing of the terrain of another's life death, digging archaeologically, speculating on death and mourning, searching for signs and traces that might indicate who this person was in life, and this delicate, archival searching proceeds in correlation with the reverberations of military campaigns and expeditions, surveillance apparatuses, scientific inquiries, the colonization of life and death, the anthropological grasping of other peoples and myriad related efforts toward comprehension and steadfast knowing engrained in colonial processes, imperialist encroachments, and violence of thought, knowledge, and language within the transparency of the Western world.

An altogether different approach to the subject of this book would be to undertake in-depth ethnographic research into forms of life, death, afterlife, memory, and history among Algerian peoples, to understand better the cultural sensibilities and social and political forces that might have shaped Bennahar's life death. I have refrained from working along these lines, however, in large part because I think this would eventually lead to an ethnography of a once-colonized people authored by one more scholar not from the sociocultural worlds portrayed. Such an enterprise would not sit well with me. I can't chase that particular ghost, or be haunted further by it. It would be far better to have someone from a Maghrebi social world or of Algerian cultural heritage undertake research along these lines. I would, in fact, welcome a future conversation with scholars from Maghrebi circles, in which the life deaths retraced through the present book are considered anew.

TRACEWORK

The Book of the Dead

The book was large and bulky. It needed support. I set the aged registry of the dead down on the soft, pillow-like cushion I had been given minutes before. The volume's dark cover stood in contrast to the beige-white fabric of its soft prop. The cushion lay on a section of a clear, smooth table in the consultation room in the Archives of the Prefecture of the Police, housed in a modernist-looking building on a quiet side street in Le Pré-Saint-Gervais, just north and east of Paris.

I had come to the police archives that day to look for any records that noted the arrival and registration of Abdelkader Bennahar's corpse at the Institut Médico-Légal (IML) in the days after his death in October 1961. The morgue had kept records of all bodies received there, for many years, and those records were available for viewing at the archive. I had been at the police archives before and so was somewhat familiar with how things worked, the procedures and etiquette of state archival inquiries. I entered the reception area of the archives, showed my *carte de lecteur*, and explained what materials I was interested in viewing that day. The woman working at the reception desk examined some documents on her computer console and then wrote out my name and "IML/Registre 1961" on a sheet of paper, *bulletin de demande*. She passed that consultation request to a colleague, who stepped into the inner sanctum of the archives.

Police records, affidavits, legal documents, court records, financial records, and policy statements and strategic plans; materials of the occupation and the internment camp in Drancy; "sensitive files" (*dossiers sensibles*) from the liberation of Paris in 1944; and communications from the Cold War and May 1968 were among the 4,500 "references" held at the archives, with *les trésors* arranged along nearly nine kilometers of shelving, in varied media of texts, letters, registers, photographs, microfilms, digital files, and cartons dating back hundreds of years. (The majority of documents collected before 1871 were lost in a fire during the fierce battles of the Commune that year, as noted on the website for the archives.)

In the *cadre de classement* categorical system of the police archives, Séries L denoted the records held by the IML. Sous-série LA, a categorical subsection, contained the yearly registers of the morgue, from "an VI" (Year 6 in the *calendrier républicain*; 1796–97) to 1973. I had requested the registry of the morgue for the year 1961, which logged records of the cadavers deposited and registered at the IML.[1]

At the gates of the archive: if Ann Laura Stoler (2009, 20) were to visit the police archives during one of her stays in Paris, she might want to look at these archives as "condensed sites of epistemological and political anxiety," as she has done with her research on Dutch colonial archives in Indonesia. She might also give thought to the challenges of "writing the disquiets of a colonial field," in trying to grasp the administrative anxieties, ambivalences, ambiguities, and moral and epistemic complications of any archival holdings or research (Stoler 2020, 274–78). Stoler might also encourage any interlocutors accompanying her to think about what she calls "the 'recursive' quality of colonial history marked by the uneven, unsettled, contingent quality of histories that fold back on themselves and in that refolding reveal new surfaces, unexposed fissures, undisclosed planes" (276).

If Jacques Derrida had considered the archive of the Paris police or happened to visit the structure that housed its documents, he probably would have identified the ways in which it was an institute of centralized state power; a "domiciliation" of precious records, kept under "house arrest"; and a "consignation," a "gathering together [of] signs," within the order of a single corpus.[2]

The archives, localized in a fixed space, were kept by guardians; the figure of the *archon*, in ancient Greece, held the power to access and interpret the documents held within the archives' corridors. That power coincides with the power of the state more generally. "There is no political power without control of the archive, if not memory" (Derrida 1996, 4).

If, meanwhile, Nancy Rose Hunt (2016, 9, 21) came to study the archives of Paris, she might advocate an approach privileging "nearness," "to isolate bits, detect repetition, parse import, and sense moods." In paying attention to myriad traces that "hover in the archive," one can "bring the state *near*, to make it perceptible through reading sounds, images, persons, and moods" (10, 9). Hunt advocates "listening" to traces of the past as much as acts of archival reading or the viewing of photographs of colonial horror alone. "Listening is a 'technique of nearness,' in the sense proposed by Benjamin," she remarks. "Such moving in close conveys the everyday and the spectacular. Minor moments and slight words bring near a human scale within the immediacy or remembering of violence. It means attending to dins and echoes, the unsayable and silenced, but also wondering about nonnarrativity and agitated, disturbed sounds of madness."[3]

If, in turn, Achille Mbembe (2002, 19) happened to pass the same way, he might remark that the police archive "held something of the nature of a temple and a cemetery." As Mbembe knows it, the archive is a religious space because a set of rituals is constantly taking place there, and it's a cemetery, "in the sense that fragments of lives and pieces of time are interred there, their shadows and footprints inscribed on paper and preserved like so many relics." The archive, Mbembe contends, constitutes "a type of sepulcher" where the remains of the dead are laid to rest.

> The act of dying, inasmuch as it entails the dislocation of the physical body, never attacks totally, nor equally successfully, all the properties of the deceased (in either the figurative or the literal sense). There will always remain traces of the deceased, elements that testify that a life did exist, that deeds were enacted, and struggles engaged in or evaded. Archives are born from a desire to reassemble these traces rather than destroy them. The function of the archive is to thwart the dispersion of these traces and the possibility, always there, that left to themselves, they might eventually acquire a life of their own. Fundamentally the dead should be formally prohibited from stirring up disorder in the present. (22)

Assigning the dead to the consecrated space of an archive, Mbembe (2002, 22) suggests, "makes it possible to establish an unquestioned authority over them and to tame the violence and cruelty of which the 'remains' are capable, especially when these are abandoned to their own devices." While the state lays to rest the dead in the form of an archive, these remains nevertheless constitute a constant threat to the state. The archives have the potential to "stir up disorder" in the present, for they can offer trace remnants of life and death that work counter to the aims and projects and cultivated memory and "instituting imaginary" of the state. In turn, the power of the state, writes Mbembe—perhaps with the archives of apartheid South Africa most in mind, and how that country's archives might be figured and refigured by archivists and historians in postapartheid times—rests on "its ability to consume time, that is, to abolish the archive and anesthethetize the past. The act that creates the state is an act of 'chronophagy'" (23). Mbembe might also caution that many historians and archivists bring the "ghost" of the dead back to life "precisely to kill it or to exorcise it by turning it into an object of knowledge."[4]

One might add to these concerns and ambivalences the observation that the archives of the Paris police carry trace histories of bureaucratic logics, criminology and forensic medicine, nosological categories, legal inquiries, and the obscure lives of many. This is an archive of the dead, one that kept those dead from complete and utter oblivion—an ossuary, of sorts, or a collective grave, and the phantasm of such a grave.

Such conceptual specters were with me as I placed my belongings into one of the storage lockers by the entrance and stepped into the reading room. I took my place at a table, just by a small sign on the surface of the table that bore the number I had been assigned, 07. Minutes later a man working at the desk there, officially *le président de la salle de lecture*, called out that number. I walked to the desk and gave him the piece of paper held in my hands. The man lifted up the book and the cushion and passed them to me. I carried these materials and carefully set them on the table. I wasn't sure how to use the support well, and I looked toward the man working toward the desk. He nodded, left his station, and came to where I stood near the materials. With a soft voice and kind gestures he explained how the cushion support was best placed on the table and the book placed on the cushion so that its two sides, when opened, rested well.

This will give it some support, he said. *C'est fragile.*

The man returned to his station at the desk. The room was quiet. At another table sat a man, his back toward me. He was sorting through a set of papers preserved in a prim carton. He paused every few moments to consider something closely. I had with me a few blank sheets of paper, a pencil, and my camera. I had permission to take photographs, *sans flash*. No bursts of light should damage the materials. No pens that could harm the documents. No folders in which one could steal away precious folios.

I gave felt thought to the shape and density of the book. The cover was composed of a coarse black surface, worn from years of use. The cover bore a single inscription, "1961," printed in fading pink-red ink on a sticker fixed to the center of the book's facade. Toward the right side of the cover, close to the year noted, was a tear-like gouge, possibly caused by the blade of a knife or the sharp edge of a metal bookshelf.

The first page held a preamble, an official statement in thin, capitalized letters:

LE PRÉSENT REGISTRE CONTENANT QUATRE CENT CINQUANTE
FEUILLETS DESTINÉS À L'INSCRIPTION DES CORPS DÉPOSÉS À
L'INSTITUT MÉDICO-LÉGAL A ÉTE COTÉ ET PARAPHÉ PAR NOUS
SECRETAIRE GÉNERAL DE LA PRÉFECTURE DE POLICE.

PARIS LE I JANVIER 1961
LE SÉCRÉTAIRE GÉNERAL

Which is to say, in translation:

This register containing four hundred and fifty sheets intended for the registration of the bodies deposited at the Institut Médico-Légal has been numerated and signed by our Secretary-General of the Police Prefecture.

Paris 1 January 1961
The Secretary General

Below these words was the signature of the secretary general at that time, and the official stamp of that office—the imprimatur of the authorizing agent. The exergue and signature carried the force of law.

The word *corps* could be read as either "body" or "corpse/cadaver."

The register was an official ledger of the morgue, a yearbook of the dead sanctified by the state that was prepared, signed, and formally established at the start of the new year. Its pages were destined for the "registration" of hundreds of corpses expected to pass through its forensic chambers. Deaths were anticipated each day. The register's purposes were largely practical and legal, to keep track of the dead and their trace histories: who, where, when, how, and, if possible, why the death occurred. Each new body brought a new round of clerical writing. Each death required registration, giving a surface scriptive order to marked deaths. At work was an intricate relation between uncertainty and writing. Names, events, acts, possessions, death histories, and assessments were "noted down," "included," "carried back, brought back," within "a list" of "matters recorded," to invoke etymological connotations of the French word *registre* and the English *register*. The writing then remained.

Taking my time, engaged with an observance formal and delicate—solemn rites for the dead—I opened the book and began to turn its four hundred and fifty pages, thick, heavy "leaves" (*feuillets*) bound together. How many unknown others had perused these same pages through the past years, family searching for lost brethren or historians sifting through fading parchments?

The first pages began with notations entered into the morgue's log during the first days of January 1961. There were eight entries for each two-page spread, with distinct categories to be completed. The tome was of a rational design, like an accountant's tables. Each entry noted, when possible, the identity of a corpse received at the morgue (name, age, place of residence); the possessions and valuables found with the body; the name, address, and relation of anyone who had come to claim the body; the nature and causes of the death; the time elapsed since the death; and the date and place of inhumation (*époque de l'inhumation*). Different kinds of deaths (*genre de mort*) were noted, within a system of classification: drowning, auto accidents, asphyxiation, strangulation, illness, fall, gunshot, stabbing, blow, natural. Another category designated the presumed causes of the death (*causes présumées de la mort*): homicide, suicide, accident, illness, unknown. The record book inscribed a transfer and transformation of signs, from the archive of death that is a corpse to the state's archive of the dead. Each corpse inscribed charted a passage from life to death, from a public space in Paris to the Institut Médico-Légal, from body to text, and then, after the proper examination, from the morgue to a place of burial. Such registers for the dead had a similar form in Paris for at least a hundred years or more; the *musée* of the Prefecture of the Police, housed on the third floor of a police precinct in the Latin Quarter, has on display, under glass, a register from 1855 that holds similar categories, in a format of similar size and inscriptions.

In the Institut Médico-Légal register of 1961, distinct handwriting suggested that the entries were essayed by different *greffiers*, "registrars" or "clerks" (*greffier* relates to the French verb *greffer*, "to graft," "to transplant"). The governmental function is one of writing, recording, registering; grafting marks into the logbooks; making official graphic marks, be they in court cases or in the tracking of persons alive or dead. All that took place at the forensic lab at the time: the delivery and registration of the corpses, the examination of bodies received, the inspection and recording of clothing and material possessions, the detailed autopsies, the sending off of cadavers—in time, all of this has become condensed into a few inscriptions.

Who were the readers of these logs at the time? Who were the scribes? Some now unknown clerk at the morgue jotted down the dead man's name in clear, precise black ink, the still-legible marks from the hand of an unsigned greffier, possibly now expired himself, or living at the age of ninety-five in the Normandy country-side, visited by grandchildren on Sundays, the mind webbed in defunct memories of the morgue, passing entries in a long life.

What did the morgue technicians and medical experts think of the damaged bodies that were being brought to them in those days and the lesions they carried? Were they aligned with the police in their drive to control the supposed "North African types" who resisted French rule, or were they troubled by the marks of vio-lence shown on the bodies that they worked to examine and prepared for transfer to cemeteries for burial in paupers' graves? What anxieties lay in the uneasy crevices of the work of forensic examination and colonial administration in Paris 1961, in which civil servants tended to the dead produced by state violence?

The entries, appearing on the page in distinct forms and flows of writing, noted the cadavers received at the forensic morgue on the day noted. These were bodies found in the public fairways of Paris, overseen by the Prefecture of the Police. Many of the deaths recorded were violent ones, or something marked or strangely errant in a deceased body had raised suspicions that vio-lence had caused the death, and this concern called for medical-legal exami-nation. Each corpse brought through the institute's doors required an evalu-ation—an autopsy, quite often—to determine, if possible, the cause of death. The morgue's technicians would try to interpret the signs of a death, recording the marks on a body. Once the cause of a death was known, the city's legal ap-paratus determined whether a legal inquest (*enquête*) should be undertaken into the reasons for the death. Within the gaze of a certain male science, a body was made to signify in order to develop a legal-forensic understanding of the causes of death and to establish the body's passageway and ultimate destination within French juridical determinations in life and death.[5]

Each of the book's sheets of paper turned stiffly as I sifted through the months of that year: February, August . . . September. I came to October and found the entries for the seventeenth. There were a number of entries for 20 October 1961, signifying a series of cadavers deposited at the morgue that day. I saw his name there, among others, the surname inscribed in block letters on one line, followed in the next with the first name, Abdelkader, the letters leaning slightly toward the right. Entry number 2174. Registered at 12:15 that day. Male, forty-two.

BENNAHAR,
Abdelkader

There you are, I thought. In partial permanency.

In the registry, the *lieu de naissance*, the place of birth, for Abdelkader Bennahar was noted as Marnia, Oran. Other information had been inscribed in the same black ink:

ADRESSE: 31 rue H. Poincaré, Asniere.
GENRE DE MORT, coups
TEMPS écoulé depuis la mort: 2
CAUSES PRÉSUMÉES de la mort: homicide.

Address: 31 Rue Henri Poincaré, Asnière-sur-Seine.
Nature of death: blows
Time elapsed since the death: two [days]
Presumed causes of the death: homicide.

Other notes in the entry recorded details of the delivery of the body to the morgue. An autopsy was performed on 21 October 1961.

The biographic information noted must have been taken from any identification cards that Bennahar carried at the time of his death. Asnière-sur-Seine is a commune just to the north of Colombes, close to a looping turn of the Seine west of Paris. And so Bennahar might have died close to where he had been living at the time. Then again, the address noted could simply have been one that he gave to the authorities when he was issued a *certificate d'identité*. The location could have been that of a hotel or boardinghouse or the home of an acquaintance.

Under the category for "vêtements et objets"—clothes and objects, apparently, that had accompanied the corpse into the morgue's holdings—an ink stamp had been placed for this particular deceased, as it had been for other corpses noted on that page and elsewhere in the logbook. The stamp was a sign of bureaucratic categorization, routine corpse accounting. The entry held further information:

DATE de naissance 1919
DATE de décès 18 Octobre 1961

After the words "pouvoir de M. [authority of Mr.] _____" nothing was written. With many other entries in the log, a name was jotted down of the person who had come to claim the body and its remaining valuables, along with the residence of this person and that person's relation to the deceased. I took the absence of such notations in Bennahar's case to mean that no one had come to claim the body. Instead, someone had written, in faint red ink, a slash mark and the word *abandonée*. Abandoned, forsaken.

Bennahar's clothes and possessions had probably been discarded or incinerated.

The room was quiet. I lifted my eyes away from the book and turned toward the desk overlooking the room. I saw that the man, in line with his official duties, was keeping an eye on me and the other researchers in the room. (Article 11. Manipulation of archives: "The reader is responsible for the documents communicated to him and must ensure that they do not suffer any damage, by his actions or those of others. . . . It is forbidden to press on or make notes on a document, to make marks or annotations.")

A strange ambivalence emerged when I thought about the fact that I was sitting in a bright and peaceful room lodged within an office of state power and governmental memory. The women and men working at the archives struck me as good and respectful persons—kind, even—and yet the agency of their work was linked to the Prefecture of the Paris Police and its long history of forceful oppression, marginalization, and violence. I felt I was stepping into the home of an enemy—an enemy for some, at least—and while there, seated in a reading room, I was perusing the documents of an archive that could be read as a palimpsest of state-authorized power, often forceful in actions and effects. The forensic care apparent in the preparation and preservation of the archives of the dead stood in contrast to the lack of care for the lives of certain persons whose deaths were recorded there.

I returned to examining the book. It rested on its bed like an infant nestled in a crib. The final entries for the year, found on page 351, were penned on 31 December 1961, New Year's Eve. Below the last entry, recorded at 7:20 p.m. that day—"suicide, immersion"—someone had written the word *fin*, "end," and then with a blue pen drawn wavering lines down toward the bottom of the page. The remaining prepared pages of the register were free of any handwritten inscriptions. The register had ended for that year. A new one began the day after, for the forensic year of 1962.

Pasted to the back inside cover of the morgue's register for 1961 was a sheet of paper, on which was inscribed an integrated set of tables noting sums and figures for the year as a whole, a *bilan* of sorts, a summary balance.

For the year as a whole, 2,766 corpses, *déposés*, were received by the morgue. Of those, 2,608 underwent autopsies.

2,539 *connu*, "identified," corpses.

93 *inconnu*, "unidentified," corpses.

From these tabulations, numbers could be drawn and statistics rendered from different yearly accounts and analyzed in terms of rates of homicide, suicide, deaths by drowning; variable rates of death for women, men, children.

The book lay inert, like a preserved corpse, and could be examined like one, its parchments like desiccated skin. Survivance was in play here, but any surviving traces were mixed in with rampant cessance. Aspects of life death had remained like fossil fragments, embedded in layers of petrified mud, pressed under a weight—exoskeleton of life death.

The morgue register had once been kept at the Institut Médico-Légal. I had gone to the IML one Sunday afternoon to gain a sense of its structure and history. I took a Métro to the Quai de la Rapée, walked to 2 Place Mazas, and approached one of the side entrances. The institute was closed that day. Inaugurated in 1923, after delays in its construction due to World War I, the building is made of red bricks. This gives the edifice a sense of solidity and permanence, like a science lab or a long-standing medical research center. A discreet dominion of the dead, it's a place off-limits to most of the living. Only those with formal permission from the Prefecture of the Police can enter the morgue, which prompts the question: Who is permitted to see the dead in modern bureaucratic states and who is not?

The building rests close to the Seine, on the far side of a motor roadway running alongside the river. The proximity to the water echoes earlier incarnations of the Paris morgue that were set along the Seine so that bodies could be brought by boat.

Standing outside the building, I imagined that its structure held forensic labs, toxicology kits, refrigerated storage units, computer systems, a break room, record books—an assemblage of technical devices and communication systems for the recording, observation, analysis, and passage of cadavers through the interiors of a legal-forensic morgue.

The corpse was an actant, still is. Inert, unresponsive yet oddly potent, strange like an image is strange, the cadaver brought to the morgue must have affected those who encountered, touched, or imagined its nonworldly status or gave thought to it years later.[6]

I came to a side entrance to the building and stood by a doorway framed by stone-marble columns. An inscription etched in stone above the doorway read nobly, "INSTITUT MEDICO-LEGAL." The doors were shut. I walked around the building, along the perimeter of a tall, spiked metal fence, and came to another entrance, near a sign affixed to the brick facade noting that this entrance led to the "Laboratoire de Toxicologie de la Préfecture de Police." This was where bodies were brought and where, once the forensic work of the morgue was completed, bodies were taken away, by families, funeral homes, or cemetery employees. A threshold for the transfer of cadavers, the main doorway was made of large and formidable-looking metal doors, bearing a sign that read,

ENTRÉE INTERDITE

A TOUTE PERSONNE

ETRANGERE AU SERVICE

Entry is forbidden to all persons foreign to the service.

The doors were closed here as well. Two benches were placed near the doors. No one was seated there.

Toward the side of the entrance, close to another door, "Départ de Convois" (Departure of Convoys), was another bench. On one beam of the bench, the back support, someone had painted in small white figures,

2017

1995

The tracks for the #5 Paris Métro line pass right by the IML, curving a few meters away from its gated fence, as if engineers had designed the tracks to wrap around the side of the institute with no direct disturbance to its structure or the solemn work undertaken within. I doubt that many riding on a passing Métro train know where the morgue is or even notice the building standing so close to the tracks. Those working in the institute must hear the trains pass as they toil expertly with the dead. With the southbound line, the train passes a meter or two from the metal fence that surrounds the building, continues over the Pont d'Austerlitz spanning the Seine, and then arrives at the Métro stop at Gare d'Austerlitz.

Now that I know where the Institut Médico-Légal is, whenever I take a Métro train in Paris along that stretch of the #5 line I try to look out from a window when the train curls along that winding steel-tracked curve and passes by the morgue. Mornings, I sometimes see people waiting by the entrance where corpses are brought to the morgue and subsequently recovered from its confines. Most often, these persons appear to be stunned and grief-stricken family members waiting to receive the body of a loved one who died hours before.

One morning, while I was taking the #5 Métro train as it passed on a bridge across the river, heading north, I turned toward the window of the rickety car to look at the area around the institute's entrance and exit. I saw another man, seated close to me and wearing a taqiyah, turn as well. He raised his head toward the window and looked toward the area outside the institute. We saw several people standing by the entrance. Once the train passed, he turned his glance back to thoughts in the Métro, as did I. He knows this place, I thought. He has been there, years or months before, maybe more than once. Perhaps he and others came one morning to recover the body of a friend, or a brother or cousin, an uncle, younger sister, and he stood outside the doorway like those standing there now, waiting for the doors to open, so that they could receive the dead.

Photos of the *Inconnus*

Inconnu. Unknown. Unrecognized, unidentified.

Some of the entries on the pages of the IML morgue register from 1961 did not have actual names noted. Instead, the word *inconnu* had been written in pencil, usually in capital letters, the word signifying "unknown" penciled in, as it were, in the event that the body was later identified and the lettering erased and an actual name added in ink to the entry.

With many of the "inconnus" there was the notation "type NA": "Type, nord-africain" or simply "N.A." Encoded in this appellation was the idea that North Africans had, in general, a particular physical phenotype, distinct from other "types" in the world, and the peoples of North Africa could commonly be identified and classified by this purported racial-ethnic phenotype. This designation was a vestige of racial science and hegemonic colonial thought and empire. The concept of physical "type" and the specific appellation "N.A., nord-africain" (North African) are still in currency in police discourses and everyday speech in France, an active trace and force of neocolonial racism.[7]

Other entries did not carry any supplemental inscriptions of the race or "phenotype" of the body received at the morgue. Presumed whiteness was a neutral category, unmarked. The cadavers of persons apparently from North Africa were classed in a marked category, perhaps indicative of the "incorporative exclusion" (Moten 2016, 12) of such persons in French society—incorporated within the expanse and political reach of the Republic, yet excluded from a certain kind of inherent belonging to the "space" of the Republic and its legal frameworks, including its incorporative spaces of death. The bodies were characterized in crucial ways in death, much as they were in life.

Also noted were the approximate ages of the unidentified bodies: 30, 40, and so on.

The entries for the *inconnus* were tentative. The inscriptions were anticipatory, for a future possibility. The officers of the morgue apparently hoped that at a later time—that day or the next, or weeks or months later—someone would come to the morgue and identify the body. The provisional trace-entries maintained that possibility, supported it.

With those noted as "inconnu," given that this word remained penciled into the record book, with no revisions, no actual names later inscribed, and no photographs removed from the morgue register, it appears that no one had ever come to the morgue and identified or claimed the respective bodies of these unidentified dead.

With those listed as being "inconnu," causes of death were noted—submersion, in one case; drowning—and the places of the death. Further information on the delivery of the corpse to the morgue and remnant "observations" were also noted. And then, in the final column of each page of entries, in a category designated as "PHOTOGRAPHIE," there were photographs of the faces of the unidentified deceased. This was in contrast to those identified by a proper name—with those corpse-persons, no photograph was included. There was no need for a picture in the register, as the body had already been identified. In most cases, a corpse was designated with either a name or a photographic image.

I was not expecting to encounter such vivid images of the dead when I came to the archives that day. I thought the morgue's register would contain words and dates only, the fine print on corpses received. Yet here in the shadowlands of the archive, glued to the sides of some entries, were small square icons of the dead. Black-and-white photographs, cut precisely into small blocks, these pictures served as a means of possible identification of the unknown. The photographs were a way to retain a visual trace of the deceased. They were like so many identification pictures for the unidentified dead.

The photographs set up a spectral future. They anticipated the possibility of visitors to the morgue, possible witnesses, acquaintances, family members, police officers; they anticipated a connection made, the recognition of certain facial features that spoke of a friend, a family member; and then the penciled word *inconnu* might be erased and replaced in ink, in legible letters, with a proper name. And so here, within a looping circuit of time, we are looking back onto the past, at a once-spectral future, which led to an absence of response. The visualized dead are enmeshed in multiple temporalities of obscurity, looking, and possible recognition. Given the absence of any changes in the nature of the entries, it appears that many of these bodies had never been identified, never claimed, at least within the police-medical-legal system of the French state.

It's possible that, for some bodies at least, family members and friends and neighbors knew that certain persons had died and their bodies taken up by the French police and medical-forensic apparatus. Apparently, no one ever came to the morgue to identify the bodies or provide for a burial. Some might have been afraid to approach this office of the French state, for fear of repercussions, wounding, or further deaths at the hands of the Paris police. The work of the Institut Médico-Légal proceeded within the realm of state governance and its operations of control and surveillance, and many Algerians probably perceived it as a site of potential violence and death.

It was also the case that many men who had traveled from North Africa to France in those years lived on their own, in small flats shared with other migrant men or in boardinghouses or cheap hotels. There might not have been many around them to notice their absence or to take a serious enough interest in finding out if they had died or if their bodies were to be found in hospitals or morgues.

It wasn't necessarily by chance that certain cadavars arrived at the IML morgue without accompanying identification and with no direct way of being identified. In the late 1950s and early 1960s, police officers in and around Paris were known to remove any identification cards found with many of the Algerians that they killed, before or after the death, such that the resulting deceased bodies could not readily be traced back to specific identities or circumstances in life.[8] The name was thus severed from the person who bore it. The police reportedly also placed bodies in the Seine in part because any identifying features and direct and identifiable signs of violence would, through time, dissolve in the river's waters.[9] Such actions severely diminished the possibility of later identifying the bodies and lives involved.

The river's waters dissolve, erode, submerge, and obscure, the currents carry along and away. The Seine as it flows through Paris is known as a site of great beauty, yet its waters can also erode and annihilate within streams of life death.

Entrenched in the Institut Médico-Légal morgue in those days was a somber relation between acts of dissolution and anonymization and processes of registration and attempted identification. Acts of denaming and defacing were followed by efforts to inscribe, analyze, and identify the unknown dead. Strip a body of a name, and then leave it to others to try to give a name to the body

—that body denied a name. This has led to a strange discrepancy with each photograph of the unidentified Algerians in the morgue register. The corpse was *right there*, as glimpsed in the photograph, the face bearing the precision of a singular life, yet that appearance came with no distinct name or precise identity.

The faces apparent in the register appeared to be at once inanimate and animated. Their features invoked themes of the visible and the unseen, looking and nonlooking, coherence and dispersion, emergence and disappearance, living nonliving. It's as if the corpses were suspended within a liminal transitional process between life and death. The bodies pictured were at once lifelike and deathlike, in effect living dead. This intricate mix within the same photographic image, of a semblance of life and a semblance of death—the look of death after a life's end, death with the vitality and quick of life still in it—made for appearances unusual, unsettling.

These were *death life images*—images, that is, that suggest the close imbrication of processes of death and life in a biological system, moment of time, field of thought and representation or political order. The concept of "life death" is geared toward avoiding the static reproduction of a life/death oppositional logic, while emphasizing the intricate interweaves of life and death. With the photographs of the *inconnus*, the emphasis is on *death life*—inverting the customary sequence—for the primary terrain of the photographs is that of death, while deeply intertwined with processes, temporalities, and imaginings of life.[10]

Death life. The ways in which a death lives on in life, seeds further in life and in death and in fields of life death. The ways in which life lives on after a death. The survivance of a death, elements dispersing, generating further or lying dormant among the tracework of other lives and deaths. The life and afterlife of a death. Death in life, the living dead of colonial subjection; barely alive, moribund existence. Slow death life, living within a deadening atmosphere of living death.

Many photographs of the living tend to carry a sense of death within them, including the arrest and surcease of the moment photographed, and intimations of the future death of the subjects photographed.[11] In contrast, the photos of the unidentified dead carried an ambit of life within them, including the expired yet still apparent living form of the body and person pictured. Traces of life were apparent in the vitality of the faces, the disarranged matted hair; in the marks of a complex range of life snuffed out days or hours before; in the political forces that figured in those deaths; in the life-into-death work of morgue technicians and doctors and the minimal, nearly forgotten survivance of a record kept within the pages of a morgue register. Life shadowed images of the dead.

The records for the first months of the year 1961 held just a few photographic images of the unknown dead. Then, toward late August, into September, October, and early November, more *inconnu* corpses were registered at the morgue, with photographs of the unidentified dead fixed more often onto the pages of the register. Most of these unknown dead appeared to be persons from the Maghreb. The timing of the deaths matched the timing of the violence in Paris through those months, which had intensified in the early fall. And then, in late November and through December, such images were not so common, their frequency lessening by the end of the year. Images of the dead appeared through the pages of the morgue book like shades passing into a netherworld.

Most of the photographs showed the faces only of the cadavers, presumably while the bodies were laid out on an autopsy table in the morgue. A white cloth had been placed over other parts of the body, such as the neck and chest, which could have also appeared in the photograph. When the body was no longer being recorded, examined, assessed, the white sheet was probably draped over the face again. Respect the dead; show only what was necessary for the purposes of identification and examination. In the photographs, the white blankness surrounding a face appeared to bring out, through contrast, the features of the face. The whiteness in the cloth recalled, for me, the oblivion of death and forgetfulness.

The two photographs I saw that showed more than the faces of the deceased were of a man whose body was recovered from the Seine and who appeared to have been beaten badly before then, and a man who had died from strangulation, apparently by a wire sliced into the neck. With both of these images, the torso and head of each person were photographed—perhaps because the wounds inflicted merited visual documentation. The bodies lay flat, chests exposed. With one photograph, a set of numbers was printed onto the photograph. The numbers looked like ink tattooed into the flesh of the dead—a numbered corpse.

For many of the photographs, a small placard sign had been set on the white cloth, close to the face. One of the signs included the inscription "X. FMA," along with an identifying number and the date of death. FMA was the abbreviation for *Français musulmans d'Algérie*, which was once the formal, legal—and politically charged—designation in France for those identified as "French Muslims from Algeria." The "X" likely meant "unknown" or "unidentified," *inconnu*.

What was the process involved in preparing such photographs? Getting the light right. Loading the film stock into a sturdy camera. Positioning the body, the face, in good light. Adjusting the camera's aperture and shutter speed. Patiently getting tones and the framing right. Clicking the shutter, producing a negative image clear and focused. Developing the film in a darkroom. Printing a copy or two; neatly gluing a picture to the page of the registry. Preserving rolls of the dead in light-proof film canisters.

There was an immediacy in the images, a concrete tactility; an intimacy in the regard of those photographs. The photographs were clear and precise, with the visual qualities relating to an implicit aesthetic of social and physiognomic realism—mortuary realism, let's say.

Trace specters of different technologies of visual documentation and display shadowed the photographs affixed to pages of the morgue's register, along with correlated histories of the body and the dead. Different genealogies of visual observation, surveillance and forensic identification, formations of the body, and visualities of the dead were at work, with these genealogies tied to particular histories of the body. Each perception, each act of sensing or looking, carries myriad genealogies.

There is, first, the tradition of postmortem photography, from the nineteenth century on, with photographs of the recently deceased serving as a font of memory—keepsakes to remember the dead within families and or communities.[12]

Second, there is also the genre of criminal identification photographs, known to many police practices throughout the world, be they simple "mug shots" or more complex and sophisticated systems of identification. In France from the nineteenth century on, serious effort was invested in the criminological practice and science of taking and preserving photographs of arrested subjects, in the event that these persons could later be identified if suspected of further criminal acts. The focus was on the head and face of subjects, partly in line with the spirit of physiognomy and phrenology, two purported sciences of that time. If studied and documented properly, the face and head were thought to reveal the personal and moral characteristics of its bearer. In nineteenth-century France, this criminology ranged from police technologies of the 1840s that combined a "physiognomic code of visual interpretation of the body's signs—specifically the signs of the head—and a technique of mechanized visual representation" (Sekula 1986, 16) to the late-century methods of Alphonse Bertillon, director of the Identification Bureau of the Paris Prefecture of Police, which relied on a system known variably known as "Bertillonage" or the "signaletic notice." As Bertillon wrote of his system in 1893:

In prison practice the signaletic notice accompanies every reception and every delivery of a human individuality; this register guards the trace of the real, actual presence of the person sought by the administrative or judicial document. . . . [The] task is always the same: to preserve a sufficient record of a personality to be able to identify the present description with one which may be presented at some future time. From this point of view signalment is the best instrument for the proof of recidivation, which necessarily implies the proof of identity.[13]

The police took photographs of distinct parts of prisoners' bodies—chiefly, features of their faces and heads: ears, eyes, foreheads, noses, mouths, and so on—and then stored these photographs in file-cabinet archives of photographic information and categorization, in anticipation of future use in the identification of possible repeat offenders. The police's photographic technologies fed into the idea of a generalized, inclusive archive, a machine for the recording, observation, and identification of repeat criminal offenders. More generally at stake was the idea of a generalized, inclusive criminal archive, "a shadow archive that encompasses an entire social terrain while positioning individuals within that terrain" (Sekula 1986, 10).

In the case of photographs of the *inconnus*, the unknown dead chronicled at the Institut Médico-Légal, the register similarly guarded a trace of the actual presence of the person, in the event that the body could later be identified. The identification of suspected criminals, the identification of the unknown dead—uses of photographs were similar in each of these legal-forensic efforts. The archives of the Paris police have preserved both images of perceived criminals and images of the dead—abject figures meriting documentation and archivization.

A third context is the display of dead bodies in the Paris morgue in the nineteenth century. For years the morgue contained an exhibit room that presented some ten or twelve bodies neatly arranged on black marble slabs and, for a time, kept fresh with trickling flows of water. These were the corpses of recently dead *inconnus*, unidentified, found in the Seine or at other places in the city. Visitors could enter the morgue, built in 1864 near Notre-Dame on the Quai de l'Archevêché (presently the site of the Mémorial à la Déportation), and freely come in to the exhibit room to see these bodies, with the idea that some might be able identify one or two of the corpses and so give names to the unnamed cadavers. Often a crowd was at hand, with visitors eager to get a look at the persons displayed through glass windows. Commentators at the time, and historians and cultural theorists years later, observed that the exhibit could be characterized as a spectacle. "It is nothing but a *spectacle à sensation*, permanent and free, where the playbill changes every day," remarked one writer in 1891.[14] A poet named Clovis Pierre wrote of the morgue that "each visitor comes to exercise his retina at the window."[15] "The morgue, in short, was a spectacle of the real," observes Vanessa Schwartz (1999, 48) in her book *Spectacular Realities*.

The morgue's exhibit gallery provided the setting for scenes in several novels of the time, including Émile Zola's *Thérèse Raquin*, published in 1867. One passage tells of a man named Laurent, who repeatedly visits the morgue on the way to his office in search of the body of a man named Camille, whom Laurent and his paramour had tried to kill by drowning days before. Zola writes:

> Although it made him feel sick with repugnance and occasionally sent shivers down his spine, he went there regularly for over a week to examine the faces of all the people who had drowned, laid out on the slabs. . . .
>
> He went straight over to the glass screen which separated the onlookers from the corpses, pressed his pale face up against the glass, and looked in. Rows of grey slabs stretched out in front of him. Here and there naked bodies stood out in patches of colour, green and yellow, white and red, against the slabs; some of them had kept their flesh intact in the rigidity of death, while others looked like heaps of bloody, rotting meat. At the back, hanging against the wall, were pathetic rags of trousers and skirts grimly contorted against the bare plaster. At first Laurent saw only the greyish background of stones and walls and the blotches of red and black made by the clothes and the corpses. There was a tinkling of running water.
>
> Gradually he began to make out individual bodies; then he went along from one to another. He was only interested in those who had drowned; if there were several corpses swollen and blue from the water, he would examine them avidly in the hope of recognizing Camille. Often, the flesh of their faces would be peeling off in strips, with bones poking through the softened skin, so that the whole thing looked mushy and formless. . . .
>
> Sometimes he reached the last row of slabs and there were no drowning cases, so he breathed more easily and his repugnance diminished somewhat. Then he became simply a curious visitor, taking a strange pleasure in looking violent death in the face and seeing the lugubriously bizarre and grotesque attitudes in which it takes people. (Zola 1992, 74–75)

The morgue in late nineteenth-century Paris was a site of looking. It was a civil space for displaying and viewing the dead, of cadavers shown and seen. The dead bodies were often exhibited, studied, registered, and recorded. At times, the displays reached the level of a public spectacle, in which crowds would pass through the display rooms to view the recent dead, in acts of seeing and being seen.

With the medical-forensic practices that came to take form in the modern era, the body was also seen firsthand: the word *autopsy*, *autopsie* in French, etymologically suggests "seeing with one's own eyes, eye-witnessing; personal observation or inspection." The word, which comes from modern Latin *autopsia*, from Greek *autopsia*, "seeing (or seen) for oneself," took its modern form around 1650. By the mid-nineteenth century, the word had taken on the sense of "dissection of a dead body, so as to ascertain by actual inspection its internal structure, and *esp.* to find out the cause or seat of disease; postmortem examination."[16] Medical experts "opened up a few corpses" in efforts to determine the signs of deaths within them.[17] As with the modern sense of postmortem examination, an autopsy implies seeing the body for oneself, gauging and decoding signs of death. One sees the body, expertly or spectacularly. The dead body itself, like the morgue, became a site of looking.

From 1877 on, photographs assisted in the display and possible identification of the dead. Photographs prolonged the period a corpse might be seen by the public, for they tended to last longer than the corpses themselves. Schwartz (1999, 58) relates that "in 1877 the morgue staff began photographing all its inhabitants and posted the photos of corpses that had been buried but remained unidentified on the wooden barrier at the entrance, thus prolonging the display of any unidentified corpse long after the usual three days of display." Photographs also began to be included in the morgue's register—fixed to the far right of an entry, as with the register of 1961.[18]

In March 1907, the prefect of the police ordered the morgue to be closed to the general public. From then on, only those who might be able to provide useful information about the identity of the deceased were given access to the exhibit room. The site of the morgue was transferred in 1921 to its current site by the Quai de la Rapée. It ceased being formally called the "morgue" and became instead the Institut Médico-Légal. These changes in purpose and conceptualization were in line with shifts in the nature of the institution during the twentieth century, when the morgue went, as Schwartz (1999, 49) observes, "from an institution that relied heavily on public visits to one run by medical experts." The showing and visual regard of corpses brought to the Paris morgue thus became, in time, less a public spectacle and more a forensic process within the medical-legal apparatuses of the state. The visual regard of the dead came to imply a more private, expert field of relations and perceptions.

Finally, by the late nineteenth century, the concept of the *inconnu*, of the unknown and unidentified dead, had become an important phenomenon in Parisian culture and European societies more generally, from soldiers deceased on battlefields without precise identification in death to bodies recovered from the Seine, many of them apparent suicides without clear identities, forlorn and mysterious in their postdeath conditions. These histories of the unknown dead include "L'inconnue de la Seine," the physical trace of a woman whose body was reportedly found in the river in the 1880s and remained without postmortem identification. The putative "death mask" of this young woman, said to be designed by a pathologist working at the Paris morgue, became a fixture in artists' homes in Paris and elsewhere, her enigmatic smile traced through the features of the mask.

The unknown dead in the nineteenth and twentieth centuries became a marked category in France and elsewhere. The lack of clear identities in death troubled and intrigued the living. The broader cultural and ethical sensibility in effect here is that the dead should retain or receive names whenever possible. "Ours is the age of necronominalism: the precise counting and marking of the dead," remarks Thomas Laqueur (2015, 414) in his magisterial *The Work of the Dead*. In reflecting from a long anthropological perspective on the "deep time" of the dead in Western Europe and North America, Laqueur contends that "We live in an age of necronominalism; we record and gather the names of the dead in the ways, and in places, and in numbers as never before. We demand to know who the dead are. We find unnamed bodies and bodyless names—those of the disappeared—unbearable" (10–11, 366). For many, an unrecorded, unnamed body in death is a marked category, a disturbance at once psychological and political in form. "In our age, names are filled with human life; each one demands a denouement" (414). In France, any deceased persons marked as *inconnu* presumably lacked a clear-cut denouement.

Such histories and genealogies of looking, corpses, autopsies, and forensic technologies of observation and surveillance of the living and the dead alike contributed to the composition of the 1961 morgue register book that I examined while at the archive that day, as well as my own means of perceiving the photographs of the unidentified dead.

There was a tenderness to the photographs. The preparations of the body, setting up the pose. Likewise, the tenderness of the photograph itself; the image cut carefully and placed on the surface of a page, precise gentle details in the fragility of the image. Care was an element in the photographs of the *inconnus*—care for the appearances and destinies of the dead; getting the photos right, and perhaps the identities as well. Care against anonymity, oblivion. Care against sheer absence, the erosion of a life. The register inscriptions were acts of care as well—watchful, institutional care; keeping track of bodies; writing, tracing, retracing. All of this ran in cutting tension with the brutality of the deaths and the political and violent regimes that made such brutality possible as well as the recurrent dissimulations of police powers and violent actions, including the anonymization of the recent dead.

And then, later on, there is the idea of archival care: keeping the records, preserving and maintaining them, for the sake of collective memory, for posterity's sake; care for the possibility of reading, analyzing, and interpreting the archives, at some future date. *An archive is for the future.*[19]

The photographs embody brief visual moments in complex folds of time. With these intricately entangled temporalities of life and death, that which is called life and that which is called death are not easily separable as such. Shifting instances of perception brought flickering glimmers of life death, life fused with death, death in life, survivant traces in death life. Each photograph carried the vestige of a body. Each photograph implied a disappearance—the sudden or delayed absence of a vital presence within a family.

I found it remarkable to regard these images some sixty years after the imprint of photographic impression. There was a clear trace of the deaths at hand; of the wounding, and the severity and harshness of what took place. There were marks of the violence that caused the death and trace effects of such violence after the death. The cruel aura of the blow. Knife cut. The finality of hands around a neck. The dead, inert fact of a death, irrevocable. The lives in the deaths were not fully effaced.

The photographs and their accompanying inscriptions were some of the final and lasting traces of these persons, who apparently were never identified and subsequently were buried as *inconnus*. With this comes the sense of a limit, of what I or anyone else can possibly know about these life deaths at the present time. They are lost to an opaque oblivion. There is no direct sense of who these people were, what their lives were like, nor how and why they died. Just a few words, an image. Nothing else. What lies behind these enigmatic images is forever at a remove. Here there is not simply the aura of the image but rather the obscurity surrounding the image, which gives the image an intensified energy.

There was a rough physicality to many of the persons imaged (the faces shown so unlike the beatific face-in-death apparent with the cast of L'inconnue de la Seine). Features of a body remained contorted, displaced, thick with violence in an entropic necrophysiology. Frantz Fanon ([1961] 2005, 15) wrote of the "muscular dreams" of colonized subjects: "the colonial subject is a man penned in; apartheid is but one method of compartmentalizing the colonial world. . . . Hence the dreams of the colonial subject are muscular dreams, dreams of action, dreams of aggressive vitality." The faces of the *inconnus* marked muscular deaths. The strain sensed in the faces conveyed tense struggles of those who had fought against the colonial regime. There were signs of violence, after the onslaught; morphologies of cruelty. The faces of some appeared battered, others bloated due to immersion, drowning. Some cadavers appeared to be sleeping or mired in drunken sleep. The figment of this unconscious state occasions a quiet regard of them, lest they be woken. Others looked as if they had been injured, or insulted—slapped, moments before—and they had turned their faces away from the agent of violence.

As I looked and thought about the faces, a dark visual poetry came voiced into scant words—

> *The semblance of a mug shot.*
> *Film star glossy portrait.*
> *War victim. Hospital convalescent.*
> *Secret stolen photo of a café-goer.*
> *Seine immersion.*
> *Friends joined in death.*
> *Bad dream of a night. Ghoul.*
> *Frankenstein's monster.*
> *A body life force patched from once-inert parts.*
> *Epidermal skin darkened by water. Skin darkened in death.*
> *Torture victim, cruel lacerations.*
> *Death blow. Squashed face.*
> *Beaten to death, beaten past death.*
> *Blood mouth.*
> *Puffy faced bird whistle.*
> *Migrant's death in a foreign land.*
> *Past dreaming.*
> *Dead writer.*
> *Older brother sleeping on a sofa. Stalin's tomb.*
> *Wounded son.*
> *Water distortion. Immersion takes a toll. Water bloats a body.*
> *Sleeping grandfather, knife wound on skulled head.*
> *Sculpture of a human form.*

—as well as phantasmagoric lines from Baudelaire's poem "Une charogne" ("A Carcass").

> *And it rose and it fell, and pulsed like a wave,*
> *Rushing and bubbling with health.*
> *One could say that this carcass, blown with vague breath,*
> *Lived in increasing itself.* (Baudelaire 1993, 60–61)

The dark poiesis of death multiplied into forms and images. A corpse is fecund with imagery, generative of phantasmal imaginings. With death as in life, perceived actualities and phantasmal imaginings are caught up in one another. Looking at a corpse can engender myriad scenes and imaginings that go far beyond what is perceived directly at the sight of a lifeless body. Images proliferate around a dead body.

And here, now, as I write, there is the unsettling phantasmal image of my lingering presence at the archive that day. I was contemplating corpse images in ways not all that different from Zola's (1992, 74–75) character Laurent, in his own visit to the morgue, *looking violent death in the face and seeing the lugubriously bizarre and grotesque attitudes it takes in people.*

> The murderer walked slowly over to the glass screen as though drawn by a strange attraction, unable to take his eyes off his victim. He felt no pain, only a sensation of deep cold inside and a slight pricking of the skin. He would have expected to be shaking more than he was. He stayed stock still for five long minutes, lost in unconscious contemplation, engraving in his memory, in spite of himself, each horrible line and each foul colour of the picture which he had before his eyes. (Zola 1992, 77)

How much are the current reflections on these photographic images caught up with the spectacle of looking at the dead? I undertook my own archival autopsy of the dead, staring closely at a corpse or corpus or two, decoding signs of death life, while myriad genealogies of perception patterned each look hazarded.

The photographs brought sundry phantasmal associations to a febrile mind. Ghosts were at work. They still are.

Alongside such verdant imaginaries was the point-blank factum of the dead. Matted hair. Teeth. Swollen jowls. Bruised eyelids. Fractures, abrasions. The photographed bodies emitted a blunt sense of the reality of death.

Eyes were as if closed by death, in violent rest. The faces held the blankness of deceased life. Yet there was still a person there, to be seen and sensed, within most of the likenesses, well preserved. I could readily envision the man pictured as someone's father or brother. Spectral relations swept into the frame each time I gazed at an image. Strange like a corpse is strange, the images carried vague specters of lives lived and then snuffed out.

The photographs held an unusual tension between effacement and what might be called "facement." With no name assigned to these corpses, the identities of the persons were unknown, absent, effaced. And yet the photographs gave to these faces distinct identities, or at least the semblance of singular identities. The vivid countenances of the faces were distinctive, singular, alone in an obscure death existence. These were singular persons who had died, each life an ipseity. Each death as well, singular, alone, unrepeatable. Effaceable.

As trace vestiges of the absent dead, the photographic images imply a combination of disappearance and survival. "Traces, does not that mean precisely that there was *disappearance*, but also that in this disappearance a *survival*, however lacunar it is, remains within reach of our sensation? Is there not a potential life even in the most devastated things?" writes Georges Didi-Huberman (2018a, 25). The photographs suggest a minimal survival, a living-on survivance of traces of a life. Yet so much of these life deaths is gone.

The men I saw were as though looking out from the page and not looking out. They appeared incognizant of what had happened to them and what occurred after their lives ended. They would not know of the subsequent independence of Algeria, the fulfillment of the collective dream longed for. (Some might say, later on, that these men had sacrificed their lives for the cause of independence—that they were "martyrs." Through such discourses and actions, life deaths were transformed, converted into new vital forms.) These men had no awareness of being photographed or of their faces being posted in the morgue's logbook. Nor was there any apparent alertness to my reading that volume decades later and regarding their remote countenances. Just inert regard.

The faces were immobile. Inert, stuck there. The bodies, unmoving, had to be positioned for the photograph, untensed head supported by a metal brace. Yet what wild energies seared through the images. Contorted forms. Desperate life. Unformed and forming death. There was a wandering, errant quality to these photos of the dead. The looks moved about the page, ghosting disturbed sounds. Images emerged from the photographs like phantoms hovering about a site of death. Not pictured but disconcertingly imagined were violent encounters, blows to a skull, hands breaking a larynx, bodies immersed in water, slow necrosis, unnamed corpses buried in unmarked graves. These death lives circuit my consciousness—a legion of the dead, interspersed with other deaths, caught up in violent tides of history.

"I think that the photographs are violent," said someone in an audience of scholars when I showed one or two—not many, at all—of the photographic images from the IML morgue during a presentation at a symposium on "emptiness" held on a cold, damp fog of a day at Oxford University in England. At first, I thought this person was criticizing my showing of the images during the presentation. But she went on to say that she thought the photographs taken by those working in the morgue in 1961 were violent.

Are the morgue photographs violent? Do they violate the bodies and names in death of the deceased as well as wound and offend any living survivors or viewers? Or were the photos taken in moments of forensic care, out of concern to trace and locate the identities of the dead? Could the intentions and consequences of these photographic acts be altogether multiple, complex, and ambiguous?

No such photographs are reposted here. It would be too much to show the photos of the inconnus as they appear in the morgue record book.

In turning the thick, leafy pages of the book I touched the grain of the paper with the tips of my fingers. I would never have wanted to touch the surface of the photographs. It would be disrespectful to do so. I did not want to smudge the images with any soiled fingerprints or staining thoughts. For years, I imagine, the photos have gone untouched.

And yet looking can entail a kind of touch. There is a tactile, haptic quality to many forms of looking, watching.[20] But who has really *seen* or *touched* these photographs since they were fixed to the pages of the registry?

For a few of the *inconnus* inscribed there were no photographs. To the far right of the open book, where a photograph could have been placed, there was, instead, a single word written, *nonphotographiable*. Nonphotographable, unphotograpable. In these cases, the remains of the dead were apparently too eroded, decayed, obliterated, or diminished to merit a photograph. There was no clear, distinct face to be photographed, to be possibly identified later on, and so it was pointless to photograph the remains in that unpicturable state. No identifying visual features could be significantly represented through a photograph and logged in the register. This prompts the question: What are the limits of representing a human form? When is it that a person's identity can no longer be detected through the photograph of a deceased face or body? When does a human form cease to be figurable? What in death life is nonphotographable?

And what here, in my own writing, cannot be represented through writing?

A few entries on the unknown dead noted "examen toxicologique," toxicological tests of biochemical remains, trace elements of a once-there life.

Other images showed bodies torn asunder, close to dissolution, close to the limits of the photographable.

Death itself is kind of nonfigurable. And yet all representation stands in relationship to the negations of death.

In a quiet hour I stood up, took the camera out of its case, and held the lens above the open text. I set the aperture to f/5.6 and began to photograph the photos fixed to a page. I waited until each image was in focus, lines and features of a face coming into precise clarity, and then pressed the shutter button. I turned the pages until I came upon another image and photographed anew. I duplicated the realisms involved, metaphotographically. I took around forty photographs that day at the archives, collecting details for my own research archive, an ill-sorted compendium of unfamiliar faces. Some might find this act of photographic doubling weird and uncaring of the dead pictured, but I think I photographed the morgue photographs out of care and respect for the unnamed dead. I also wanted a tangible record of the images I came upon in the morgue register, so that I could later engage with these images through rounds of pensive writing.

I have since been considering these images, which are stored as JPEG and TIFF files on a cloud server—a select, partial collection, photos from the morgue. I hesitate to print out many of these images. I do not want them lying around, tossed among notes and folders, capable of turning up at any moment, unsettling specters spewing forth, *looking at me*, not looking. It's as if the persons shown are quietly reading the situation at hand, while being read. I am wary of studying the images while working at cafés or libraries in Paris or in New York, out of concern that their sudden appearance might disturb someone else's eyes and peace of mind. And so I gaze at the images within the solitude of an apartment I temporarily take as home.

When I am not looking at the photographs, I tend to picture the eyes of the unnamed dead to be open, looking back. When I return my gaze, I find that the eyes are closed. My regard of these images is blunted, as though I cannot see them for what they actually are. It's as if my look bounces off the surface of the image and I cannot see the features of a face clearly.

There are times when I look at and then do not look at the photographic images, even when I am far away from the photos. I turn my eyes away, then return my sight to the images, then look away, look anew, away. It's not easy to keep looking at the photograph of a corpse. And yet not looking can also entail a certain kind of regard.[21]

Staring pensively at these images and contemplating the obscure histories brings a sense of vertigo. I fear falling into an unresolved obscurity of time. Still, there is a net of sorts with the images, for the weave of writing in the surrounding inscriptions and forensic categories, the support of the paper, and the fabric of the writing here keep me from falling too deeply into nameless absence.

I wonder if the writing that the *greffier* clerks undertook at the morgue worked in similar ways, with the lines of writing marked in the book serving as a protective net that kept the dark terrors of death a few scripts away. Their entries placed the dead within a scriptive economy of writing, image making, and legal-medical reasoning. In chronicling the nature and aftermaths of each violent death received and autopsied, the register tells a minimal story of life death, of death analyzed and thus transformed. Perhaps such processes and re-figurings helped to make the intolerable tolerable.

Marked in the morgue register was an intricate play of image and textuality. On some pages was what looked to be a flurry of writing around the images, for both entries of the *inconnus* and entries of the identified deceased, noting details on the death. In some places, the writing surrounds the image in a seeming frenzy of annotation, circling about the lucid image of a dead man, that image surrounded by opaque circumstances in life and death—as if the writing spawned from anxiety and nervousness was fueled by the unsettling image, though the proximity of words to the photographs could have been circumstantial and my sense of anxious writing circling about a fecund space of death could come from my own phantasmatics of death images in correlation with anxious writing. The writing is like that of a *greffier* clerk of the dead, keeping tabs on life death while staring into an inaccessible depth.[22]

In my memory, in this life, it's as if I have encountered these images in a strange dream, fevered fragments. The faces linger as fleeting apparitions, rough features gleaned out of the corner of an eye along the margins of a page, restless look of another. With these shades of the dead a brief side glance lodges in my skull.

No photograph was attached to the entry for Bennahar in the morgue register. His body in death was elsewhere to such photographic arrangements. Apparently, this was because an identification card had been found with his deceased body and clerks at the morgue were able to inscribe his name and other biographic features in the annual register. If not for the identification card that he carried, Bennahar likely would have had the same forensic fate as those categorized as *inconnu*, with a photograph of a deceased face glued to the far-right side of the book. And then, morbidly, a somber thought: If the skull and face had been crushed too badly, would the morgue technicians have deemed the cadaver to be nonphotographable?

It is in small, quiet moments like this that the brutal force and overwhelming reach of the French colonial regime impress most on a body.

Yet might there also be a way in which these photographic images of the unknown dead *press back* against the powers of the French state, years later, quietly sounding the trace-mark of their lives and the harm brought to them?[23] The Prefecture of the Paris Police has built an archive of its actions and documents, from years of police work in Paris. Others might then come along and use these materials to build a counterarchive that works against the interests of the police and the state. In the shadow of one such possible counterarchive, it's as though these fragile faces have been waiting to be seen and recognized for what they were and can be still. An uncommon agency limns the faces of the dead, inert and lifeless yet dormantly active in their physical and affective afterlives. Perhaps it's true that the archived dead can acquire a life of their own and stir up disorder within the instituting imaginary of the state.

Perhaps it's also the case that the present book strives to give a proper name and vital image to Abdelkader Bennahar. Through this act of recognition, his life might be given a specific place in time and history. The worrisome concern with this writerly gesture is that it might appear to some that a vulnerable, remnant body has been put on display, for the viewing pleasure of others.

Each photograph of the inconnu *is like a corpse, at once inert and potent. Each image doubles the corpse perceived. The photographs of the unknown dead are of postwounding, of a dead time after the wounding that brought a death. The images linger after the in-between phenomenon of the wound itself. Each photograph stands like a scar on the mortal wound of a life death. And yet these scar-images continue to wound. The images wound back. The photographic images perceived involve multiple temporalities before, during, and after intensities of death life. Each photograph carries a wounded, wounding temporality, as though time itself was wounded.*

Division 97

He passed different thresholds in life death, between a vital, legal sense of personhood and then something unlike living personhood, between the composed actuality of a physical body and its gradual dissolution, from vital connections in life to an isolated death. The timing of this liminal dissolve was manifold, with different temporalities at work, surcease of body, end of direct action and personhood, fading flesh and materiality, end traces of a life. Life death in its shape-shifting ways holds different registers, calculuses and potentialities, figures and figurations through diverse passages in time. Certain intensities of life death can emerge in any given moment and then fade away, depending on the circumstances. Blooming vitality, frailty, sheer absence, vibrant marks of a life, and echoic voice move on.

On more than one occasion I have followed in Jean-Luc Einaudi's textual footprints, retracing the histories of violence that he himself was trying to record and understand. This happened to be the case as I was tracing out the fate of Abdelkader Bennahar's body. In reading Einaudi's account of the events of October 1961, I came across a passage that noted that Bennahar's deceased body had been buried on 7 November 1961—twenty days after the death—in the Parisian cemetery of Thiais (Einaudi and Kagan 2001, 30). This is one of three extra muros cemeteries managed by the city of Paris, in the commune of Thiais, a few kilometers south of the city's borders. Eight other inhumations of cadavers identified as being from North Africa took place that same day in Division 97 of the cemetery.[24]

Early one spring morning I set out for the cemetery, in the hopes of finding the burial site for the remains of Abdelkader Bennahar. This was in early March, once I had returned to France after being away for several long winter months. The day before, I had logged onto the website for the Archives of Paris. I scrolled through the numerous headings and, within a few minutes, located the databases that held the listings of those buried in the cemeteries of Paris.[25] Twenty cemeteries were noted in all: fourteen intra muros, within the city of Paris itself, including those of Père-Lachaise, Montmartre, and Montparnasse; and six extra muros cemeteries, situated outside the limits of Paris but managed by the city, including the one in Thiais, a suburban town about seven kilometers southeast of the city of Paris. Working with a database titled "Répertoires annuels d'inhumation" (Annual directories of burial), I searched the records of the cemetery of Thiais for the name and year of inhumation. The result of that search brought up thirty-one images, each a scanned page of the cemetery's directory of deaths for the year 1961.

Scrolling virtually through the alphabetic listings I came to a page starting with names beginning with the letters "Ben-." His name was listed there, in clear blue ink, the eighth entry down, amid a score of other names. The surname, "Bennehar," was spelled differently from that found in Einaudi's histories, where it was written "Bennahar," the choice of spelling a matter of transliteration. Before the name was a number designating the registry record of the inhumation, along with the date of inhumation, *7.11.61*. I saw how the cursive spelling of the last name, the second *e* in particular, could have made it possible for someone to read the surname as "Bennchar." The *situation de la sépulture* was noted as Division 97, Ligne 1, Numéro 20. There was this place for him in death.

Setting out the next day, I took the #7 Métro from Paris to Villejuif and then caught a tram to a suburban stop in Thiais, near the entrance to the cemetery, the perimeter walls of which brought an expansive quiet. Opened in October 1929, it eventually became one of the largest of the Parisian cemeteries. Some ninety years later it held an estimated 150,000 graves, placed in 123 numbered divisions, including one for stillbirths, a division for ashes of the dead donated to science, sections for deceased military personnel, and eight divisions for the burials of those who could not afford interment or who could not be identified, which gave the place a reputation as a "cemetery of the poor and penniless" (Landru 2009).

Past the entrance was a building that held the conservation office. I walked through a set of sliding glass doors and came to the main office, where several women and men were working—some answering phones, others busy at their desks, within the vast bureaucracy of the dead.

I spoke with a woman who met me at the registration desk. I told E. that I was looking for the burial site of a man named Abdelkader Bennahar, who was buried in the cemetery in November 1961. E. stepped away, reached for a bulky registry book, and returned to the desk. This looked to be the same text that had been scanned and digitally archived at the archives of Paris. She opened the book, searched for the correct page, and soon found the record of Bennahar's name.

E. walked to a bookshelf near her desk and returned with another bulky register book.

There was no record of any family having visited him, she said.

One moment, she added. She took the book and walked toward another section of the room, to a smaller room, bordered on two sides by glass partitions.

She returned a few minutes later. I spoke with my boss, to check on something, she said. I wanted to see if his remains were still in the place noted.

She went on to explain that Bennahar was buried as an *indigent*, "a poor man." Usually in such cases, she explained, the remains (*les restes*) are exhumed after five years and then placed in a separate holding spot at the cemetery, where the remains of the individual dead are kept in small metal boxes. Not even the family can see them after that. But with Bennahar this had not happened.

FIGURE 5.1. Map of the Parisian Cemetery of Thiais.

His remains had not yet been transferred to the depository, but it could happen at any point, said E. If his family comes to visit, later on, or you return at a later date, his remains might not be there anymore.

So, at this time his remains are still there?

Yes, it appears so.

E. gave me a map of the cemetery, an elegant diagram printed on a sheet of paper (figure 5.1). She explained how I could find the division and the location of the grave in the cemetery. 97.1.20. Division 97, a fifteen-minute walk northeast of the conservation office. Row 1, the first row of that division, and then count to twenty, starting from the left.

The rational design of the Cimetière Parisien de Thiais was reminiscent of the landscape architecture of certain gardens in France, such as the Jardin des Tuileries or the Gardens of Versailles, organized and patterned with grid-like arrangements of lines and quadrants, a style known as *jardin à la francaise*, founded on symmetry, order, and long perspectives. The geometric layout and administrative order of the cemetery appeared to reflect the rational order of the French state in its ideal, crystalline form—mapping, classifying, and burying like a state.[26] As with other terrains of interest, the French state created a territory, staked it out, and oversaw its procedures and policies. Yet beneath the grid-like order lay obscurities of death and violence.

FIGURE 5.2. Entrance to Division 97, Parisian Cemetery of Thiais, March 2019.
Photo by the author.

Not all the graves will be clearly marked, E. advised me.

The map told obliquely of histories of colonialism, empire, and diasporic peoples seeded into the grounds of the cemetery, with peoples from different societies and religious faiths buried in distinct areas, and memorials for soldiers who died for France in different wars and violent conflicts.

The cemetery grounds were quiet, with early spring sunlight streaming through the air. I heard a few birds chirping and singing and the cawing of crows above cultivated fields. From a near distance came the soft rush of cars, trucks, and motorcycles cruising along an expressway. A cemetery caretaker, seated in a small, motorized cart, passed along the paved walkway. Few other visitors appeared to be there that morning. I held the map in my hand and took note of the "avenues" I was passing, Avenues C, D, E. Minding the grid-like structure I walked farther along and then turned up Avenue H. I walked past several distinct quadrants of land and gravesites, each its own division, one of them visited in that hour by a young couple carrying flowers and walking slowly toward a gravesite. Eventually I came to Division 97, near the far northeast perimeter of the cemetery, as though it marked the banlieue of Paris's extra muros dead (figure 5.2).

The area near the entrance to this division looked rather vacant, empty. There was a grassy area toward the front of the division. I took this to be where the graves were, set along row 1. A few indistinct burial plots could be seen here and there, but there were few markers, no lines or borders signaling separate grave sites. Keeping in mind what E. had told me, that each *tombe*, each grave site, was assigned a number, even if there was no actual tombstone set above the buried remains at that time, I tried to calculate where the twentieth burial plot might lie. Without many distinct and consistent markers and no clear *points de repère*, it was difficult to locate where Bennahar's bodily remains would have been placed beneath the earth. I tried to determine the twentieth grave site, marking my steps along what seemed to be the trajectory of the first line, starting in the near corner, counting one, two . . . eleven . . . twelve . . . but I soon got lost in vagueness.

I walked toward the far side of the first row and stood quietly in an errant field of fertile, unkempt grass, overlaid with scattered twigs and fallen branches. I looked toward the ground. He had been buried here, somewhere under this earth. His remains were still there, somewhere in this damp stretch of soil. I could not be sure where this was, precisely. But I had found him, in a way. The end of a journey, perhaps. What remains of a body, of a life death long after? I looked toward the grass. The field struck me as being as silent and as opaque as he himself was to those alive today. What had he been buried in? A pauper's coffin, perhaps, made of thin and simple oak.

I could write that there were ghosts haunting the place, wayward specters troubled by unsettled deaths and meager burials, but I sensed little of that. It was quiet there, calm, peaceful. A bird called out. I glanced about the division, at the tall, leafy trees that bordered each side and looked beyond that stretch of land. To the northeast, past the final perimeter of the cemetery, I noticed a big, blue box-like structure with letters inscribed in yellow, IKEA. To the west, in another division, the sounds of workers could be heard as they toiled on an unseen project.

All of the graves in this division were designated for deceased Muslims, much as other sections in the cemetery were designated for Jews, Christians, Hindus, and Buddhists. The earliest graves in Division 97 dated from the early 1960s. At least that appeared to be the case for those that carried an inscription of some sort, a year engraved into a tombstone. Further north, away from the remnants at the foot of the division, were apparently newer, better-kept graves and tombstones, a community of the recent dead, apart from the terrain of the older, vaguer deaths. These grave sites were well cared for, with flowers and photographs placed at the bases of the tombstones, suggesting continued relations with the living. Families apparently still visited these sites, vital survivors of the deceased. Away from that area—farther "below," it seemed, and further back in time, somehow—lay a sector of decay, ruin, and remote anonymity, as if the division as a whole embodied a history of death among Muslims who had lived and died in Paris. To walk about the soggy grounds of the division was to chart the archaeology of a burial ground.

The remnants of violent deaths, misfortunate casualties of the war of liberation and France's colonial regime, were seeded along the first two rows, and perhaps the second and third as well. A few markers stood in this expanse of grass and soil, not much more. A patch of land, forlorn, half-kept, the field of grass loomed like a wild of random, errant growth spored with twigs, fallen leaves, branches—a terrain seemingly abandoned to the elements, nearly forgotten. But the land must also have been tailored and cultivated, at least once in a while, by the cemetery's caretakers, within the state's care for the dead.

Division 97, like the cemetery as a whole, carried a sense of rational order, a geometric plane of grid-like arrangements, in which each deceased life was assigned a particular place within the systematic register of Parisian deaths. Alongside this governance of the dead came forces of decay, erosion, forgetting. Within the grid of burials was the slow erasure of individual personas.

Much remains uncertain, including the care and treatment of the corpse. Bennahar's body was buried some nineteen days after it was brought to the morgue. According to Muslim traditions, a corpse should be buried as soon as possible after death. Would the forensic morgue or the offices of the cemetery in Thiais have prepared Bennahar's body for inhumation in accord with Muslim tenets for proper preparation and burial of the dead? If the body was embalmed, that would have gone against Muslim teachings. Did a Muslim man perform the washing of the body (ghusl), according to Islamic principles? Was the body shrouded and covered in an appropriate way? Did a Muslim imam perform the funeral prayers (salat al-janaza)?[27] Or was it the case that the burial of the cadaver was treated as a legal-medical-mortuary matter, an expedient, functional process with little spiritual significance and with little or no concern given to a religiously proper way to conduct last rites and bury the corpse? Hauntingly recurrent is this sentence by House and MacMaster (2006, 164): "Algerians were keen to wrest control of the bodies of loved ones from the much feared and detested French authorities, and ensure burial with full nationalist honours and following Islamic ritual."

A few days after I visited the cemetery in Thiais, I returned to the website for the archives of Paris and looked again at the virtual records of the deceased.

This time, I explored a second database, known by the name "Registres journaliers d'inhumation" (Daily burial registers). These yearly registers chronicled the burials that took place at each of the cemeteries of Paris, day by day. I located the register for the Parisian cemetery of Thiais for the year 1961. I turned through the pages virtually, clicking on an arrow to move through the dates in the fall months. Names of the dead flashed past. The record for each of the burials was written in an ornate script, a flourish of cursive lettering that gave each entry a dignified, stately appearance.

I came to the pages for 7 November 1961. Twenty persons were buried that Tuesday, in various divisions of the cemetery: 3, 50, 89. Nine bodies were buried in Division 97 that day. Each set of remains was presumably that of a Muslim man who had lived in or near the city of Paris and who had died days or weeks earlier. One was that of Abdelkader Bennahar. Each entry noted the body had come from the IML. My guess is that the nine were brought together—a delivery of autopsied bodies, transported in a van or a set of hearses and buried in Division 97 through a collective work of interment. Shovels, graves, displaced earth. Workers calling out to one another, taking breaks between each body buried. Autumnal light. Leaves on the ground, losing the integrity of their physical form.

Each entry in the register for 7 November 1961 listed the last and first name of these deceased persons. No ages were noted. Each was said to be from the 12th arrondissement of Paris (a curious geographic intensity). The site of each burial was noted, according to the classificatory system. My reading of the names and places of burial of these nine persons is recorded in table 5.1.

The buried remains of the eight other persons were Bennahar's companions in death. Their bodies rested close to his own.

Achour Belkacemi, the man who died the same night as Bennahar (18 October 1961), in Colombes, was buried in row 1, plot 23—three grave sites down from Bennahar's burial ground. From the site of their deaths to the morgue to the cemetery, these paired bodies moved in parallel into the aftermath of death.

I spent the next several hours reading through the rest of the cemetery's register for 1961, looking for any other burials recorded for Division 97, particularly in the first two rows. In time I was able to come up with a select register of "North Africans" who died during those days of conflict and were subsequently buried in the cemetery (table 5.2).

The corpses, registered and analyzed, were brought to the same cemetery and buried close to one another in a grassy field. Each inhumation was neatly inscribed in the cemetery's record books, the names a scroll of the dead strung out like a deranged sentence.

TABLE 5.1. Persons Buried in Division 97 of the Parisian
Cemetery of Thiais, 7 November 1961

Name	Row	Plot
Zebir, Mohamed	2	4
Bouaris, Mouloud	1	27
Bennahar, Abdelkader	1	20
Belkacemi, Achour	1	23
Mehani, Ramdane	2	8
Yassa, Mohammed	1	29
Guesri, Ameur	2	2
Meklouche, Amar	2	6
Djahmouni, Saïd	1	25

Source: Daily burial register, "Cimetières," Paris Archives, http://archives.paris.fr/r/216
/cimetieres/.

A few of the listings carried the inscription "transp. to Algeria," with a specific date noted. I took it that each of these inscriptions designated the exhumation of remains on the date noted and then their transport to Algeria where they were buried again, possibly at a cemetery close to the homes of the deceased's family.

It's not entirely clear to me why I sought to retrace the names of those buried in the first rows of Division 97. Looking back on it now, I think I inferred a certain kind of "ethical loneliness" (Stauffer) with these deceased persons, of those having been abandoned by humanity, of not being heard or recognized. Perhaps I wanted to make them less lonely, less unacknowledged in their deaths.[28] Can the dead, like the living, be ascribed a status of ethical loneliness at times, in that they can remain alone in death, unrecognized and unacknowledged, even if such an ascription is entirely speculative and imaginary in design?

Writing out the names of those buried in the first rows of the division could also involve an effort toward "being with the dead" (Ruin), with this effort consisting of an ongoing responsiveness toward the dead, a recovered care for them, sustaining an active, vital memory of them long after they were buried and near oblivion.[29] With such thoughts, we are touching on a deep chord of life death, namely, the ways that human beings relate to others in life and in death.

A reflection by Theodor Adorno, on memory and the dead, comes to mind. "Our memory is the only help that is left to them," Adorno wrote in 1936. "They pass away into it, and if every deceased person is like a man who was murdered by

TABLE 5.2 Persons Buried in Division 97 of the Parisian
Cemetery of Thiais, 28 October–13 November 1961

Name and Age (where noted)	Burial Site (Division, Row, Plot)	Observations
28 October		
Benali-Youcef, Djillali (age 37)	97, 1, 1	
Meziane, Akli (32)	97, 1, 3	transp. to Algeria, 12 March 1970
31 October		
Kara, Brahim (30)	97, 1, 21	
Ligli, Aouad (45)	97, 1, 2	
Bareck, Ben Brahim (72)	97, 1, 4	
Benmeddour, *presumé*	97, 1, 9	
Inconnu, FMA	97, 1, 7	
Inconnu, FMA	97, 1, 11	
Inconnu, FMA	97, 1, 15	
Inconnu, FMA	97, 1, 19	
Inconnu, FMA	97, 1, 13	
Derous, Abdelkader	97, 1, 5	transp. to Algeria, 12 March 1970
Nekakra, Abdelgkram	97, 1, 17	
Djemal, Hocine (19)	97, 1, 6	
3 November		
Zemouri, Ahmed (65)	97, 1, 12	
Mokaden, Mohamed (26)	97, 1, 8	
Azzout, Mohamed (59)	97, 1, 10	
4 November		
Issaadi, Mohamed (50)	97, 1, 16	transp. to Algeria, 13 June 1969
Tlemsani, Guendouz (23)	97, 1, 14	
7 November		
Zebir, Mohamed	97, 2, 4	
Bouaris, Mouloud	97, 1, 27	
Bennahar, Abdelkader	97, 1, 20	
Belkacemi, Achour	97, 1, 23	
Mehani, Ramdane	97, 2, 8	
Yassa, Mohammed	97, 1, 29	
Guesri, Ameur	97, 2, 2	
Meklouche, Amar	97, 2, 6	
Djahmouni, Saïd	97, 1, 25	
9 November		
Kassouri, Arezki (46)	97, 2, 1	
Bouharat, Tahar (28)	97, 2, 3	

(Continued)

TABLE 5.2 (*Continued*)

Name and Age (where noted)	Burial Site (Division, Row, Plot)	Observations
10 November		
Inconnu, Musulman	97, 1, 22	
Inconnu, Musulman	97, 2, 5	
Inconnu, Musulman	97, 1, 26	
Inconnu, Musulman	97, 2, 7	
Inconnu, Musulman	97, 2, 10	
Inconnu, Musulman	97, 1, 24	
Lasmi, Smail	97, 1, 30	transp. to Algeria, 13 June 1969
Laidani, Brahim	97, 1, 28	
Gargouri, Abdelkader	97, 2, 14 (?)	
13 November		
Bendada, Saïd Ben Ahmed (65)	97, 2, 9	
Laïla, Abdalhal (7)	97, 3, 1	

Source: Daily burial register, "Cimetières," Paris Archives, http://archives.paris.fr/r/216/cimetieres/.

the living, so he is also like someone whose life they must save, without knowing
whether the effort will succeed" (Adorno [1936] 2002, 79).

In my imagining, I found these men lonely in death. I wished them company,
gave them company.

The first body inhumed in Division 97 was that of a thirty-seven-year-old
man whose name was written as Djillali Benali-Youcef. He was buried on 28
October 1961, in the first designated plot, number 1, of ligne 1 (line 1). That
same day the remains of a man named Akli Meziane, age thirty-two, were buried in the third grave site of row 1. Other burials took place in the days that
followed, in a checkerboard-like way. No burials occurred in adjacent plots on
the same day. Rather, they were spaced apart, most likely because it was easier
to dig in separate places rather than work simultaneously on graves set alongside one another. Once most of the places in line 1 were taken, the gravediggers
began to work in line 2. By 13 November 1961, most of the grave sites in line 1
had been filled, and a number of bodies had been buried in sites along line 2.
On the thirteenth of November the first burial in line 3 took place, at number 1, for the body of a seven-year-old child named Abdalhal Laïla.

Each body was buried separately, in a lone grave. The grave sites marked the
legacy of bodies that had been recovered, recorded, and buried by the French

state. The fate of other deceased Algerian men, presumably killed by French police officers, had largely gone unknown and unrecorded.

Ten of those buried in rows 1 and 2 of Division 89 were recorded as *inconnus*, "unknown," with their identities while alive noted as being either "FMA" (*Français Musulman d'Algérie*) or "Musulman" (Muslim). These bodies had also been brought from the Institut Médico-Légal.

Some formal writing had to occur to register all inhumations at the cemetery. For clerical purposes, the name of an unidentified body interred in the cemetery was marked with an X in the registry of inhumations. This designation was followed by a general sociopolitical and ethnic designation: FMA, then a formal, government-subscribed appellation for Algerians living in France, which is usually translated into English as "Muslim French people from Algeria."[30] It's unlikely that anyone associated with the French state would have tried to identify the once-living persons assoociated with any of the obscure remains. What remained was a minimal record, with no clear naming, tracemarks in the record books of the cemetery.

The archival records of the Parisian cemetery of Thiais encode a cryptic history of power and political force and domination. In France, the police and the administrative state largely controlled the means of inscription and erasure in chronicles of life and death, though there were points of resistance against that strong-arm control. And yet if it were not for the bureaucratic record, it would have remained unclear, years later, what had happened to Abdelkader Bennahar with his death and in death. A scant trail of traces in life death remains. This trail shows, among other things, that Bennahar's death and his posthumous fate were ensnared in complex circuits of power and instituted, "set up," in particular ways, within "the grid of the state" (Stepputat 2014, 8). In moving from the police to the morgue to the cemetery, through a passage in which the body was seized, identified, autopsied, transferred, and disposed of, the cadaver was buoyed along interlocking mechanisms of the state, outside the sphere of possible care or knowledge of his family. This was a bare, colonial death, under unclear circumstances, finalized by an inhospitable burial in an unmarked grave in a foreign land.

Verdant Growth

Why this need to locate the dead and fix them in a time and place and secure their afterlives in stable forms of meaning and language? A yearning drive to know the names and places of the deceased brought me back to the Parisian cemetery of Thiais on a sultry summer afternoon, several months after I first visited.

This time I had with me the names of those buried in the first two rows of Division 97. I wanted to see if I could chart and graph more precisely where some of those named might have been buried, the remnant body of Abdelkader Bennahar included. The cemetery had changed since early spring. There was more verdant growth, with trees having taken on rich coats of leaves and grasses flourishing in grounds unmarked by structures or paved roads. Moving away from the entrance, past the office of conservation, I heard the shearing buzz of what appeared to be an electronic weed cutter slicing through thickets of grass. I walked along the grid of divisions and pathways, past tombs large and small, and found my way to Division 97. A large vehicle was parked on the road before it, with a crane suspended in the air. Three men were working to trim and sever branches from trees that swayed precariously over the roadway.

The division bore thriving growth where there had been only desolate traces before. Thick, sweeping beds of wild grass had grown in the southern part of the division, where the first rows had once been furrowed. Insects abounded in that thicket of growth. Butterflies fluttered low to the ground. Tiny black beetles scavenged in damp, clumpy soil. When I walked along my shoes fell within the soft sod plushness of grasses, stalky weeds, small leaf-thick plants and thriving flowers seeded with small white and yellow buds. That vegetative surge encroached along the bases of tombstones and old stone structures apparently once more fully there. The grounds of the cemetery were shifting, taking on new formations, novel folds and fissures with each returning season.

The roar of a chainsaw blasted in the trees above the road, and branches cracked and came crashing to the ground. I took out my camera and photographed the field's green-brown thickets in the cooling heat of late afternoon (figure 5.3).

Set along the first row, close to the footpath entrance to the division, was a tombstone with a flat base, placed on the ground, and a stone slab set upright. On that stele a name had been carved into stone: *Ahmed Zemouri*. This name was on the list of those buried in the cemetery on 3 November 1961—a man who died at the age of sixty-five, perhaps in a nonviolent manner. The family apparently had enough money to pay for a tombstone at some point. The burial site was number 12, along row 1.

If that stone marked the twelfth burial site dug out and completed in the fall of 1961, then the twentieth burial site was not far from there, eight grave sites further down the line. I walked a bit farther on, stepping through stems of grass

FIGURE 5.3. The first rows of burial sites, Division 97, Parisian Cemetery of Thiais, June 2019. Photo by the author.

and leafy plants, and stood in a field of rampant greens and whites. Somewhere around here, I thought. Nothing clearly distinct or marked precisely, yet still the sense of a location, a small field of flowering grass. A placement in death, remote domicile in earth and sod, far from home.

I had located him in a bounded space of death. Still, I cannot reach him. Unfathomable grave.

This was not him.

In the realm of a possible actual: I had the list of names with me that day, printed on a single sheet of off-white paper. While at the cemetery I held the paper in my hands. Out of some sense of sacred burial and remembrance, or like an act of sympathetic magic within a fulcrum of death and regeneration, I folded the piece of paper once and then twice, until I held a compact corpus of writing in my hands. I reached down, knelt, and placed the paper cemetery beneath a tuft of grass close to the soil. I set it there, the names left to the elements; the feuille de papier *now lay among the leaves of plants and weeds, paper to earth. In that spore bed the names inscribed will turn with the seasons, through erosive rains, light, and wind, and darkness, too, until the names fade into damp, sodden growth. Or some grounds-keeper with a weed cutter will slice the paper into shreds while trimming the grasses of Division 97 and its pulpy patches will splice and merge with severed verdant leaves and silken sepals, coronas, and petals of white flowers. Trace molecules of ink sink into the ground and mix with earth, wood, bone, and fragments of cloth and leather, the names sutured into the ground.*

It has become clear to me that I am engaged in an act of mourning for the loss of this man. This is a recovered mourning, at once actual and simulated; a surrogate work of mourning, standing in place of the elsewhere-mourning that the colonial death enforced. There is a ritual quality to this mourning: inscribed in these pages are syncopated images of the corpse and lost life, vital images that move from the harsh wounds of a violent death to the possibility of a final resting place. The span of the writing parallels a ritual process; tex-tualization here is ritualization. There is a final "viewing of the body" of the deceased; a transformation in the form and name of the dead man; burial, exhumation, and the phantasm of reburial. Images shift in time, until a final placement in a land of ancestors. I have been writing a coda for the death and the absent, unresolved mourning that ensued. Ambiguous losses haunt these pages.

(The hubris in this work of textual mourning is that Bennahar's family might have mourned his death in ways altogether different from and unknown to this writing.)

Or, the current text implies a metonymic mourning, part for whole, at once singular and collective. In mourning the death of a single man and his family's loss, this writing—beyond the confines or agency of any singular subject— might also mourn the loss, disappearance, and wounds of countless other lives in Algeria and France during the war of liberation and during centuries of colonialism.

In leaving Division 97, I walked out onto the road, past the men trimming the trees, and stepped into a neighboring section of the cemetery. In Division 89, some of the unidentified dead had been buried in the fall of 1961. I had the recorded numbers with me, of the rows and burial sites of some of the *inconnus* buried here, but that proved of little help. Amid tombstones and monuments, a few inscribed with the names of the deceased, were stretches of ground where no discernible signs of burial could be found, outside of a few unkempt markers.

I thought I had taken photographs that day of the barren burial ground for the unidentified dead and had kept at least two or three images from when I passed

FIGURE 5.4. Burial sites for deceased French soldiers and auxiliary police officers, Division 17, Parisian Cemetery of Thiais, June 2019. Photo by the author.

through. I have since tried to locate any such recorded images in a digital database of photographs. Indications of movement are there but no images. I recall finding the area desolate, dirt-strewn, neglected with unmarked space, no distinct grave sites perceived—a site not of memory but of oblivion. It could be that I thought the desolate scene would not lend itself to effective photographs. I regret the nonimages, the unlife.

Stepping again into the paved roadway, I walked toward the north, in search of Division 17, which in a way stood in parallel relation to Divisions 89 and 97, on the far northwestern side of the cemetery. The map for the cemetery noted that this division held a monument "aux policiers auxiliaires," in honor of men from Algeria who served as auxiliary officers in police commands in Paris. Walking through a quiet expanse, far from the gates and conservation office of the cemetery, and keeping track of the numbered divisions that I passed, I soon came to Division 17, which, by geopolitical design, was dedicated to deceased members of the French military. Here, in reverential quiet, neat rows of uniform steles had been bolted into the ground, with most noting the individual buried remains of fallen soldiers. Toward the front right of the division, set apart from the other lines of steles and grave sites, was a row of twenty steles, each fastened into a narrow column of cement (figure 5.4). Upright and silent, the steles stood like soldiers at attention, waiting for a general's inspection or an official honor. The grave markers stood on the front lines, a phantom army guarding the borders of a ghost colony.

On each of these stone markers was a sign that noted the name of the deceased, followed by the words *Victime Civile*, and then another line that noted the year of death with the words *Mort pour la France en* ___. Several of the persons laid to rest here had died in 1961, possibly in relation to violent conflicts with other persons from Algeria, who were seeking to gain independence from France. It's possible some of those dead might have been assassinated by members of the FLN, in retaliation for the recurrent violence enacted by French police officers.

The inscriptions included the names of these persons who had died in 1961—counterparts to the names of others I had been writing about. The steles jutted up from the earth, seemingly tall and proud, while the representations were a far cry from any actualities in the life deaths memorialized.

Midway along this row of burial steles stood a stone monument, larger and more substantial than the individual steles. On the front surface an inscription had been carved into the stone, followed by the names of twenty persons:

1959 A LA MEMOIRE 1962
DES AGENTS DE LA FORCE DE POLICE AUXILIAIRE
MORTS EN SERVICE COMMANDE
POUR LA FRANCE

The base of the monument was inscribed with the words,

LA FRANCE RECONNAISSANTE
LA VILLE DE PARIS RECONNAISSANTE

Members of the auxiliary police—likely known to others as "Harkis"—these men had died in their service to France, and they were being recognized and honored for their service to the grateful Republic and the city of Paris.[31] State monuments and sacrificial creeds, *France recognizes, the City of Paris recognizes . . .*

A sense of formal order reigned in this division, within the cemeterial remembrance of those who had served their country, in either the police force or the armed forces, and who had died in the course of that service. Many other military cemeteries chart a similar formal order, with rows upon rows of fallen soldiers. The remembrance here was clear and distinct, neatly ordered, in ways at odds with the dissolute traces of those buried in Division 97, where most graves went unmarked. At least some of those who had been aligned with the French state, military, and police received posthumous recognition of their service to the Republic in a lasting, commemorative way, while the burial sites of others, opposed to the forceful powers of French rule, were left to erode in a quasi-ruin of time.

The auxiliary police officers interred there had "died for France." In leaving Division 17, I noticed a sign at the entrance, with the phrase "LE SOUVENIR FRANÇAIS." French remembrance. The placard urged any visitors to the site to not "modify the harmony of this military square [*carré*] by adding personal ornaments (plants, steles, plaques)."

I left the cemetery soon after.

Do not disturb the harmony of the militarized deaths.

THE SPECTRALITY OF REMNANTS

Phantasms of a Life

And if this life has ended? And if this life never ends? A life that has ended is over, done with. A life that has ended lives on. It moves, budges, recalls and reminds, nags, haunts. The life changes forms, takes on new pathways, acquires new possibilities in life death. A life can become rather spectral, continuing on in oblique, apparitional ways.[1]

Archives both offer and constrain. To date, my attempts to retrace the life death of Abdelkader Bennahar have engaged primarily with the French language and, at times, with the *dispositifs* of French colonial thought. The archival and historiographical materials I have been working with imply certain ways of knowing and orders of thought and language, systems of classification and signification, the formal arts of bureaucratic records. These epistemologies and semiologies tend to entail themes of clarity and obscurity, trace and absence, with dissimulation always possible, potential histories possibly hidden, obscured. It's as if

I am perceiving faint aspects of a life through a prism of some kind, and this prism refracts in certain ways; there are particles and convex lines in the optics involved, shaping what I can sense and know. Elided are forms of life and thought to be found conceivably in forms of Darja (Algerian Arabic), Kabyle, or any linguistic-semiotic and political formations or spiritual-religious sensibilities by means of which Bennahar's life death might have proceeded.

There is another exergue to this work, inscribed on the margins or between the lines, in invisible ink or no ink at all. These faint interlinear notes cross out what I have written. They rewrite the terms of a biography, replace them with other names, trace-marks, language in thought. Composed of a series of erasures and inscriptions, voiced in different languages, this exergue writing chronicles other histories, temporalities, life deaths. This writing on the margins is a kind of counterexergue, an "other thought" (pensée-autre [Khatibi 2019]) to my thought and language. A writing unknown, uninscribed, unread by me, this writing comes from elsewhere; I cannot anticipate or trace out its textures. An unseen writing carries the tracings of Maghrebi lives, ways of living and dying, history and memory, forms of signification, knowing and ethics that might pattern those lives. Much of this goes unknown by the most apparent author of this text. There's just a glimmer of nonapparent marks and traces.

With this unknown writing the wounds are different. A tracework other than the one marked here is possible. I sense the textures of this tracework, though I have no real sense of it. It's like there are underground river currents that I have not been able to access.

I imagine another writer of this text, a historian, let's say, broadly Maghrebi in writerly poetics and narrative modes and richly knowledgeable of Algerian lives and Maghrebi-Franco histories. She supplants me in the writing of the biography, they take the pen from my hand and write otherwise. Within the open horizon of this writing emerges a philosophy of life death and wounding distinct from the one I have been graphing.

What forms of knowing and perceiving were specific or recurrent in Bennahar's life, and in what ways might they be at odds with how I make sense of him? What phantasms and aspirations enlivened his life, guided him forward? What kinds of personhood did he carry with him, what forms of becoming and relationality were with him, and how might my own takes on personhood and political agency entail possible misreadings of his own ways of being in the world?

Perhaps I am ascribing too much individuality to him, grafting onto him a singular form of personhood and subjectivity, whereas he might have thought of himself in more collective, politically engaged terms in those years of conflict, with his life death an integral part of a revolution. Were the existence and perseverance of a singular life of less importance to him and others around him than the communal cause?

What was his voice like? How might he have voiced his name in introducing himself to others or repeating it under duress to the French police while being searched and patted down, his identification card examined, or interpellated at gunpoint by French paramilitary in Algeria, or in reporting his status to immigration officials at ports in France, the sounds not carrying directly over into French pronunciation? The name perhaps was poorly heard, yet it could be the name was said proudly, defiantly. Did the sonorous timbre of that voice slowly fade away, back home, among family and friends? Could it be that, in time, loved ones could no longer recall well the voice of the deceased son, brother, father? Would the voice be different from what I take or imagine it to be? (How I imagine his voice remains unclear.) An absent voice becomes an afterimage, aftersensation, "this phantom being of the voice . . . that sonorous grain which disintegrates and disappears. I never know the loved being's voice except when it is dead, remembered, recalled inside my head, way past the ear" (Barthes 1978, 114). This phantom being of a life.

The phantasm of subjectivity: one infers certain forms of thought and feeling with another life, yet all this is half-traced conjecture, daydreamed interiority, with nothing really to latch onto—imaginal drifting in an intersubjective space.

What are the ethics and politics of knowing about a life so remotely yet so intensively, spectrally? Or, more precisely, knowing scantly about a life primarily through that life's endings?

There's a plan for this, at least. The idea is to travel to Algiers, stay there for a week or two, and then make my way to Oran. From there I would take a bus to Maghnia, in Tlemcen Province, and then quietly try to find anyone who might recall a man named Abdelkader Bennahar. I would ask around and attempt to locate someone from the Bennahar family, if a family by that name still resides in that region. I might need to travel to a small town or farm-settled hamlet outside of Maghnia. I would do that, if possible. I would probably go with a guide, someone who could help me with the languages spoken and carry a sense of safety, protocol, the right things to say and to do. If I were able to meet someone from the family, and that person met me at a café, or members of a family welcomed me into their home, I would tell of my research into the life and death of their uncle, great-grand uncle, brother, father, or grandfather, of my efforts in care and respect to trace the features of his life death. I would carry with me a copy of the book manuscript, to show the words inscribed to anyone interested in knowing something of that. Anyone who looks through its pages would see the photographic images printed there, the semblance of his wounded form (although the photographs might wound again). I would try to learn more about Bennahar's life, what the family knew of his death, the burial and resting place of his remains, how he has been remembered since then, in fractured mourning, fondness, absent presence. With the family's permission, I would include these histories and reflections in a final section of the book, a postscript of sorts, which might bring the writing to a close.

Or, any such engagements with the family might break everything open. Perhaps any such visitor would dust up troubling memories and wreck any peace of mind found among descendants of the man buried outside Paris. Perhaps any surviving members of Bennahar's family would prefer not to have any personal details and fissures of their lives and deaths pressed into the pages of a book that, admittedly, goes far beyond the interests of the family. And yet without any communication with members of the family, they might remain silent on the matter.

Would my going to Algeria for this purpose be the right thing to do?

No Ghost to Him

Ghost images, these photographs.[2] *The body photographed is no longer around, but there is still a body nonetheless. A body-image, or image-body, recurs through the imaginaries of the photographs. This photographic body is at once motionless and active, virtual and actual. Adrift. Long gone yet still remaining, this body is rather spectral in form, faintly translucent. Shimmering reflections of a life live on, haunting past, present, and future. Here, as elsewhere, we move from vital graphs of a life to spectrality.*

The spectral trace of this other life is with me now. It's in these pages, the words I write, images perceived, the lands and archives visited. He is (not) there. It's as if I have summoned a non-ghost through the conjuring rites of writing and recalling. Write about a life death and revive the spirit of a life, just barely.

There is no ghost to him. No ghostly revenant haunting the living, as far as I can tell. No vital ghost recurs for me, faint scribe of his life death. A spectral visitant might appear for others, any surviving sons or daughters, grandchildren, heirs to a trace who might recall his voice in life. Or for a killer who saw his face as he lay dying, and the look in those dimming eyes remains still in an annihilator's aging dreams or the dusk before sleep.

That is not my haunting. The haunting is another. For me he is unghosted. Any apparitions of him are vague, distant, endlessly spectral. He is not a well-formed revenant. No haunting, haunted phantomness to him. No weight or density at all to this apparition. He is scarcely there, in an altogether scarce way. Think of a ghost that never appears in a mirror, never slams a door or rattles a painting, and then take away the slight palpable sense of that ghost and you're left with the idea of a ghostless specter. What kind of appearance is this, if any? Can it even be called an appearance? What kind of phenomenology is required in tending to such faint, scarcely there, scarcely perceived emergences in thought, script, or phantasmal imagining? A spectral phenomenology is called for, perhaps, one attentive to shifting apparitions in life death, cast and perceived in a spectral light.[3]

If there is a need and necessity to live among specters, within a politics of haunting, memory, and justice—as Derrida has called for in *Specters of Marx*, "this being with specters would be also, not only but also a politics of memory, of heritage and generations," to "live otherwise" and "more justly"—then I, like others, have been trying to learn to live with ghosts, "in the upkeep, the conversation, the company, the companionship, in the commerce without commerce of ghosts."[4] Yet what enigmatic commerce and companionship this is. With the being with specters apparent here, there is not much being to the specters. His is a weightless specter, hovering about the chambers of these pages. Less ghost than specter, opaque. There is something spectral in this nonappearance and nonpresence of him in my life as I ruminate over trace fragments. When I write of him, think on him, there is an ever-so-faint haunt and apparitional appearance of his postlife presence, which is not there. A few absent features, remnant qualities adhere to the specter of him now, the after-shadow of a faint trace. Just the words I write and their afterlife echoes.

In anthropological circles of late, there has been a burgeoning interest in ghosts and hauntings within an emergent framework of "hauntology," the study of haunting.[5] There are no direct ghostly hauntings to be traced in the pages of the present writing, as far as I know. There are no restless ghosts about, spooking others. Everything is rather spectral, however—spectral in the sense of absent presences, of lingering unseen traces of past lives and situations, of unspoken, faintly sensed knowledge, of the spectral force of certain moments and figures past, present, and future.

Negative hauntology, trace effect, unghosted nonbeing marks the wavering appearance of something never quite there. Once there, long ago. Oblique, obscure, diffuse. No direct sense impression of him. No voice, direct or mute. He never speaks. Silence, only. There is no clear language, signature, no signing or countersigning of any words I write of him. Traces of his life death emit signs, within a vague, spectral semiology, but he himself does not sign directly. There are no messages from the dead. No look of him. There is a regard, faint and spectral, if imputed, conjured only.

No sentience but the specter of sentience.

With the spectrality of the dead there is often the sense of a remnant spirit or trace afterlife wandering about, restless, far from any fixed dwelling. Here, there is a faint and remote sense of a wandering trace-presence of a life and the blunt absence of such wandering.

If there is any restlessness attributed to the dead here, perhaps I have been the one conjuring this restlessness, while rendering restless.

The spectral force of him is watching, a force recalled, summoned, not quite there. He is observant, looking on. He demands something of me—to get the story right, get him right, more justly. Carve the graft of his life death. I have a responsibility toward him. Care and duty toward the dead. This is one way to be with the dead.

He is (not) watching me. He is watched by me. I do not speak to him, directly. I write about him. Revive the conjured specter of him.

If anything, I am haunted by the nonhaunting.

Survivance can entail a certain kind of ghostliness. Or nonghostliness.

How might one relate to a dead man? Can we align ourselves too closely with traces from the past? Can such an affinity bring a life closer to sheer spectrality and absence?

He is scarcely not there.

Still, in writing about him, it feels like I am writing to him and for him. With such a distant, silent correspondence, it's as though I am waiting to receive words or a gesture in response, which will never come.

With each mark of tracing, grafting, I am reviving the conjured specter of him, absence too. His name impresses on my thought within a fog of phantasmal possibilities. As I come closer to him, his shade comes closer to me. It's just a shade, shadow of what remains.

I am immersed in the life death, within its forms and effacements. He has marked me, as I mark him. There is a steadfast distance and an unsettling intimacy in such markings and re-markings.[6]

Spectral Responsivity

This is not simply a biography anymore, pure and simple, if it ever could be just that. It's not just a set of words framing a life, clear and distinct, separate from that life, detached bios, the biothanatographer a healthy step away from the life death portrayed. I have gotten entangled in words, linkages, a density of connections, histories, life death intergraftings, the tissue that connects different lives.

This writing inevitably deals with spectral possibilities (as perhaps any writing does). To me he is at once dead and alive, in a complex, indeterminate weave of life and death. He watches over me. A hallucinated reader lightly shadows this text.

Writing brings the emergence of specters. This includes the specter of possible readers of a text. Acts of writing can anticipate the possibility of a response to any words inscribed, with any such responses being either quite direct or indirect and oblique in form, including what might be considered spectral forms of response. Philosophers and anthropologists have argued that "responsivity" is a fundamental aspect of being alive in the world.[7] Human beings, for one, are responsive to the presence of others in their lives and are deeply affected by the ways that others respond to their own presence. Themes of alterity and relationality inform the ground and nature of such acts and situations of responsivity. Most philosophical reflection and anthropological research on responsivity tend to focus on the relations that human beings have with other persons and other sentient life forms through the course of their lives. Yet other kinds of responsivity should also be taken into account.

A certain kind of *spectral responsivity* has emerged with the writing of this book. In working on this text, I have come to acknowledge the potential responsiveness of the spectral as well as the specter of potential responses. The specter of a singular life death stands in a responsive relation to this text and its primary author. That author in turn finds himself responding to the possible occurrence and recurrence of this spectral responsivity. I write, and there is no response. Yet still there is the faint specter of a possible response. There is the specter of a future spectral readership, a revenant reader, yet to arrive.

There is also the spectral possibility of any number of readers of this work, including surviving members of Bennahar's family, and potential readers more generally. I write with care for all of these possible readers. At the same time, a certain anxiety and wariness lurk in these pages, in relation to the possibility that any actual readers will find fault with my writing about Abdelkader Bennahar.

When it comes to tracing absence, a lot depends on the kinds of language used. This includes the use of certain pronouns, such as *he, she, you, I, we, they.*

These pronominal deictics are rather spectral in nature from the get-go. In his seminal essay "The Nature of Pronouns," Émile Benveniste (1971, 220) reflects on the ways pronouns, like other forms of deixis, are "'empty' signs that are nonreferential with respect to 'reality.'" They are empty of content until they become "full" in particular instances of discourse. "What then is the reality to which *I* or *you* refers?" Benveniste asks, and answers: "It is solely a reality of discourse, and this is a very strange thing" (218). The strange and empty quality of pronouns speaks to their spectral nature, in which an intricate play of absence and presence, here and not quite there, "empty" forms until momentarily filled, shapes instances of their use. Pronouns like *he, you*, and *I* can easily ghost up the house of language, especially when absence joins the mix.

I have been writing in reference to a third-person subject, the *he* that designates the person of Abdelkader Bennahar. The subject that I have been writing about refers to a distant figure, remote in time and place and potential connection. I do not know Bennahar directly, I refer to him only. The communication is never immediately dialogic, as can be the case with instances of discourse between an *I* and a *you*. This touches on something that Benveniste (1971, 225) also writes about, namely, that the third-person pronoun is "completely different" from *I* and *you*, which imply a "polarity of persons" that is foundational to the phenomena of language and subjectivity. References to a *he* or *she* in discourse do not necessarily indicate the same qualities of personhood and subjectivity that uses of *I* and *you* do. Benveniste argues that the use of a third-person pronoun carries a sense of reference to an "objective situation"; "forms like *he, him, that*, etc. only serve as abbreviated substitutes (Pierre is sick; he has a 'fever'); they replace or relay one or another of their material elements of the utterance" (221). As Maria Giulia Dondero (2020, 24) writes of this, "According to Benveniste, the *he/she/it* of the third person is associated with another time and place whereas the pronominal pair *I-you* is associated with a here and now."[8] The *she* or *he* is elsewhere to an immediate dialogical moment.

Benveniste's reflection on the nature of pronouns helps to explain the remote and substitutional qualities that infuse my writings of Bennahar's life death (as they surely infuse any kind of biographical writing). The elsewhere tonalities of the writing are compounded by distances in time, memory, and the circumstances that inform writing about someone who died before I was born, who lived in a sociocultural world different from my own, and whose life was deeply shaped by colonial forces and state violence. Doubly elsewhere and elsewhen, the subject and subjectivity of Abdelkader Bennahar are forever steps removed from my writings about him. There is no immediate rapport, no direct dialogue or intersubjective knowing to speak of.

And yet, faintly, there is the specter of a *you*, a phantasmal, imagined possibility, if only that, of my writing to Bennahar with the use of the second-person singular. Gradually, through time, within the emergence of writing, the glint of a faint and spectral *you* roams the grounds of this writing, like a phantom appearing near the threshold of a home, an apparition fleetingly absent in its presence, barely there yet sensed nonetheless. The possibility of such a second-person address admits a faint specter only, yet this faint address is intensively, endlessly spectral. In phantasmal play is the uncanny possibility of my writing to this *you*, traces of whom I have been writing about, and all the potential dialogue and intimacy that a *you* relating to an *I* might bring. The second-person possibility traced and conjured here is just as remote and spectrally elsewhere as the third person I have been grafting on, perhaps even more so. It's as if the remote and fragile elsewhereness of the *he* inscribed in this biographical work carries over to an apparitional *you*, faintly imagined. In wavering, nearly unperceived moments of spectral apparition, the *he* implied in the writing comes close to shifting into a *you*, leading to the sense of a second-person presence in an obscure and barely sensed plane of signification. This *you* appears apparitionally from elsewhere and stays forever qualified by elsewhereness, even if inhabiting the here and now in certain moments.

There is a faint trace of an *elsewhere you*, listening to, reading any words I might write. This unvoiced dialogue resounds in unsettling ways. Also recurrent is the spectral possibility of a response from this *you*, however unrealistic, conjured, and conjectured that possibility might be. Within the imaginary of this writing, I can anticipate a second-person address to me, of a *you* writing in response to what I have written, of a *you* speaking spectrally to me as a *you*, and of my listening to what this spectral voice is trying to tell me, especially about my writing about and to him, *to you*.

All this is to say that a spectral grammar haunts these pages. The theoretical considerations that guide my thinking here are altogether spectral in nature, in that I am drawing from fleeting traces and obscure potentialities in trying to grasp the distant life of another. This spectral theory—faint, fragile, obscure, and intangible, sensed through hesitant words and images—might make possible an alliance between the living and the dead, in which a relation is sustained. Then again, aren't all theories spectral in form and haunting effect? Theories are like ghostly apparitions; they haunt the living and the dead, in moments even of nonhaunting.

The specter of his reading weighs on my mind and on any sentences written here. A spectral density presses on these pages. It's as if he is quietly looking over my shoulder, reading the scant tracewords I write, erase, alter. I sense his potential judgment, his regard of any words inscribed.

What would you make of someone writing about you so intensively, doggedly, years past the severed arc of your life, tracing out vestiges of your life and death, a stranger unknown to you and your family carving out inscriptions, interpreting life death, finding records of your death, approaching your grave site and looking for traces of what remained of your life? Would you have found such biographic trackings problematic; reminiscent of police interviews, body searches, identity card checks, police surveillance files and photographs; darkly echoic of the military ethnographies that surveilled peoples through decades of governmental rule and a callous mission engineered for the purpose of conquest and exploitation? Would you find this work to be an oppressive document or a fitting skein of memory during and after a time of struggle?

Unrepresentable

And so writing wounds and writing sutures. Words incised in these pages dig into the wounds shown in the photographs, the visceral wound of photography, the wounding blows of colonialism and state violence. At times, it feels like I am picking at a barely settled scab or scratching at the rough mark of a scar, irritating the skin of a body. At other times, it feels like I am trying to suture wounds, threading a row of stiches at the edges of a laceration. Perhaps the wounds need to be treated first, before applying any sutures. I doubt that any lasting repair can come of these phantom sutures.

If a life can be likened to a river, which flows from a source along a winding course toward its ultimate destination, then it can be said I know little about the flow and currents of Bennahar's life, its rapids, shoals, and hidden depths. In place of such an understanding—lost in time to me and most others—I have been trying to chart the geological terrain, the mountains, plains, and valleys that inform the riverine run of that life and the delta of its end. This terrain is rife with intensive forms of power and resistance, circuits of language and potent imagery, trace elements of finite existence. Coursing through this land, like a mistral wind, is a sense of life, loss, spirit, remainder. The writing that wanders this landscape, traversing it in crisscrossing ways, chronicles as much the terrain of forces that embed a life as the life itself.

The image of a turbulent river winding through a rugged terrain brings to mind a brief poem of Bertolt Brecht (2003, 55) titled "On Violence":

The headlong stream is termed violent
But the river bed hemming it in is
termed violent by no one.[9]

Here, the political geography of French colonialism is termed violent. That violence has shaped the lives and deaths of many.

The pages of this book have traced the myriad developments of a set of black-and-white photographs taken in Paris and Nanterre on 17 October 1961. From the darkroom to numerous prints and circulations of the images, from the 1960s to the current digital age, there has been an unending development of Kagan's photographs. A spore-like growth and spread have propelled the photographic images through time, from analog prints and journalistic articles to digital reproductions and archives to artworks fashioned from the graphic tones of the photographs. This polymorphous development has been beyond the agency or consideration of any single actor or subject in the world. The constant reappearance of the photographic images speaks to their iterable, alterable qualities. The images have been made and copied, cropped, refashioned, and circulated, returning time and again, like revenant ghosts.

Other developments have coincided with these photographic emergences. Kagan's recollections of the events of his photographic encounters in Paris and Nanterre in October 1961 have developed through time, both through his own narrations while he was alive and with later iterations of his first-person accounts. Kagan built a story around the photographs he took on 17 October 1961 and then furthered that story through other images. Also emergent through the years have been the different perceptions, significances, and affective intensities at work in engagements with Kagan's photographs by any number of activists, artists, historians, and other scholars. With this recurs the specular optics of a wounded man glimpsed in the photographs and the many imaginal renderings of the life and death of the person snared within these pictures.

Beyond this lie the ways in which the photographs of Bennahar in Einaudi's *La bataille de Paris* might have tied into tentative understandings for Bennahar's family that he had died on the outskirts of Paris in October 1961. The photographic image printed on the cover of Einaudi's book, along with other images set within its pages, apparently led members of the family to recognize the event of the death, while possibly furthering any uncertain mourning for the lost life. Emergent through time are imaginaries of a body, an actual, wounded, and then dead body, then buried remains, as these imaginal forms move from life to death, from wounding to photographic image to textual inscriptions.

In correlation with these lines of emergence is the development of my own writing on the photographic images. Combined, the words engraft an understanding of what's at stake with these images. They add up to a crystalline growth on the surfaces of the images. This pensive writing has brought rounds of interpretative assessments and phantasmal conjectures as well as fleeting spectral resonances, which tie into forever partial understandings of the life death of Abdelkader Bennahar.

A slew of images, understandings, and phantasms have thus radiated spore-like out of photographs taken one rainy night in France. They have come to germinate here, there, and elsewhere. The development of the photographs is far from finished. Any resulting picture is still not clear.

The imaginal absent presence of the person that gradually takes form in the pages of this book is not unlike the image that appears in a darkroom with the making of a photographic print. As with the printing of analog photographs, an image appears slowly on the surface of receptive paper, with this image then fixed in appearance with certain technical processes. Yet here, within the darkroom of this writing, the features of a face never appear so clearly or vividly. In the photographic plate of this work, there's just the faint impression of a life passing through moments in time. Dim light and low contrast bring the silhouette of a form.

In certain respects, this book marks a failure in representation. Readers do not come to know much about Bennahar's life. We are left with a few surface images only, a few postlife impressions. Maybe this is all right. Perhaps more important than obtaining a complete biographical portrait of a life is the awkward, striving effort to acknowledge the actuality of a life and to appreciate the fact of its onetime existence and its connections to other lives. I would like to think that there is value in giving a tangible sense of a life and its afterlife echoes, no matter how robust or limited that sense might be.

A few words from Judith Butler's *Precarious Life* come to mind. In this 1994 work, Butler considers the implications of Emmanuel Levinas's (1996, 167) reflections on the phenomenon of "the face," which, for Levinas, conveys "the extreme precariousness of the other." The face of the other makes an ethical demand on us, and yet we do not quite know what demand it makes.[10] That demand calls for a response. In Butler's reading of Levinas, one viable response to the face of the other is to recognize the precariousness of another's life and the precariousness of life itself. "To respond to the face, to understand its meaning," writes Butler (2004, 134), "means to be awake to what is precarious in another life, or, rather the precariousness of life itself."

Yet the face of the other tends not to appear or be represented in direct or fully apparent forms. This is perhaps necessarily so. Butler points out that, for Levinas, the face of the other can never be clearly or fully represented—there is a kind of unrepresentability in the ways that the face appears in life, be it in human expressions or the cries of another. Representations of the face, including in Levinas's own writings on the subject, are characterized by displacements, substitutions, and indirect expressions.[11] The face, understood as human suffering, as the cry of human suffering, "can take no representation," Butler (2004, 144) finds in her reading of the Levinasian philosophy of the face. "Here the 'face' is always a figure for something that is not literally a face," writes Butler. "In this sense, the figure underscores the incommensurability of the face with whatever it represents. Strictly speaking, then, the face does not represent anything, in the sense that it fails to capture and deliver that to which it refers" (144). There is always something unrepresentable, something left out and unachievable in representations of the face of another. Butler continues, "For Levinas, then, the human is not *represented* by the face. Rather, the human is indirectly affirmed in that very disjunction that makes representation impossible, and this disjunction is conveyed in the impossible representation. For representation to convey the human, then, representation must not only fail, but it must show its failure. There is something unrepresentable that we nevertheless seek to represent, and that paradox must be retained in the representation we give" (144).

Something similar is involved with the impossible representations that limn my attempts to convey an absent presence, the vital cries and expressions of Abdelkader Bennahar. This book shows the failure in trying to represent the unpresentable in life, namely, the face of another. That paradox is retained in its pages. To quote Butler (2004, 144) again, "The face is not 'effaced' in this failure of representation, but is constituted in that very possibility."

Any failure in representation marks the ground of being alive, and relating to others. The face of Abdelkader Bennahar makes a demand on us. We are called to respond. In this work, the face is constituted through a failure of representation. We do not really perceive or know Bennahar except through a series of trace fragments and indirect impression of the only partially known life of this person. This limit reflects, in perhaps intensified form, the impossibility of representing the face of another. Perhaps it needs to be this way. In any case, it's better to stay within the frame of this fragile (non)representation than strive to "capture" Bennahar's image in a fixed appearance and narrow personification.[12] It's also better to have a well-intentioned failed representation than no representation at all. Otherwise, the life might go unrecognized and the person reflected in the photographs could remain relatively nameless.

Imaginal Affinities

A few flint remnants and hazy images, then, found and lost past the span of a life and death—such are the indications of a life death, the tracks left in its wake, along with other potential remainders. And sheer remains, unnamed, unperceived, immaterial nonpresence, anything but substantial.

It's those remains I have been grafting toward. In underscoring the trace histories of a single life, the writing might further that life death within a series of graphs that move on toward the future and any potential further marks of writing and recollection, such that the mark of that life might possibly live on, *sur-vive*, through an open-ended series of words and figures. This possible survivance of a life death disturbs any clear-cut binary logic of life and death that says these two categories are completely opposed. Aspects of a life, its survivant inheritance, can live on after the actuality of a life has ended. They can also cease, or err on.

The many potentials in life recur, variants of life death continuously twisting, turning, shape-shifting into new forms and possibilities within domains of actuality, matter, thought, imagination. Isn't life itself composed of such changing forms and possibilities, actual and virtual? Life death is like a crystalline structure, multiform and polyvalent, unfinished and open-ended, through which elements of light and dark appear, combine, refract, intensify or diminish, vanish and sometimes reappear in unstable, ever-shifting ways.

Bennahar and I share a certain existence. There is no way for me to identify directly with him. The circumstances of our lives are too different for that. For one, Bennahar's life was cut short by state violence. And yet the onetime presence of his life and its inevitable end are akin to my own as well as to the lives of others. As time skips on, the graph-writing on another's life death has become a refraction of the arc of my own passing life, its minor significance cast within a span of potential wounding, fading into increased oblivion.

The photographs play a significant role in this sense of affinity. The fact that Kagan's photographs of Bennahar tangibly convey a vital, wounded person, his life at risk, promotes the recognition of that life and its threatened circumstances. These stark images have drawn me to relate to the subject of the photographs and the lifeworld implied. While the subject of the life perceived might be ultimately unrepresentable in direct words or images, the impression of that life has reached me in powerful ways. Any affinities discerned are not necessarily tied to any similar political positionings or historical circumstances but rather to the sheer fact of being alive, once. The perceiver of the photographic images is, like the subject of them, and like any other possible viewers, capable of being harmed, faced with the possibility of dying, entrenched within terrains of life death.

Of direct relevance here is "the miracle of analogy" that Kaja Silverman (2015) writes about in reflecting on the analogical principles inherent in photography. Silverman argues that, before and beyond any potential for photographs to refer indexically to aspects of the world, a powerful principle of analogy has been rooted in the very enterprise of photography since its inception in the nineteenth century. The technologies and visual principles of photography underscore principles of similitude, affinity, and mutual resemblance among different forms of life, pointing to the "authorless and untranslatable similarities that structure Being" (11). A photograph is, in itself, an analogy, which opens up to other analogies in the world. As Silverman puts it, "Photography is also an ontological calling card: it helps us to see that each of us is a node in a vast constellation of analogies" (11).[13]

The analogical correspondences that Kagan's photographs of Bennahar present, which suggest similarities between different forms of vulnerable life, contribute to a felt sense of existential affinity. I doubt that a few handwritten inscriptions found in an archival record alone would generate the same sense of recognition and sympathetic relation. The pictures of a man standing in pain along the side of a banlieue road sear into the lives of others and make the shared condition of wounding and finitude tangible and real. Others who spend time with the photographic images, tracing out their contours, might arrive at similar arrangements of recognition and sympathy.

The writing follows an unfinished line. It anticipates an end point in this line and asks how the life in question might be graphed, remembered, once it is gone, until any trace memories fade into oblivion. How might my own life, once past, with no vital speech or body remaining, how might this life live on, *sur-vive*? Will the pulse of a life jolt on? Will a name carry on? The writing traces any number of open-ended scripts, graph marks, and woundings within a horizon of possible lives and ends. The words pretrace figures in life. Obliquely, spectrally, I write my own life death.

I have been trying to mark the actuality of a life by grafting its remnant images and textures, many of which are known to me only faintly, speculatively, through fragments. The curious equation—remarkable, to me—is that, while there might be only a few paltry traces at hand, the vitality and singularity of a life come through. This has not been effaced. The life death of Abdelkader Bennahar is unmistakable. The absent presence of another being, the trace of a life, does not easily fade.

What might you make of your own life death in this dense skein of words? What scant traces, what vital wounds and phantasms will trail your own passage in time? What will be lost or recovered? And what powers will make this so?

He is not of earth any longer, nor buried in the earth. He is not of water, caught in the river's depths. He is not of paper, fount of an inscription. He is not image. He is more like light, luminescent light flashing intermittently, fleeting apparitions appearing here and there, like the light that glances off the cresting waves of the Mediterranean in late summer.

Acknowledgments

This book has emerged out of numerous engagements, each of which has contributed in important ways to the research and writing of the work. Many colleagues and friends have contributed in generative ways to the inquiries involved. My heartfelt thanks go to Maria Elena Garcia, Aurora Donzelli, Michael D. Jackson, Howard Eiland, Alexa Hagerty, Anne Lovell, Tyler Zoanni, Lisa Stevenson, Eduardo Kohn, Anand Pandian, Joshua O. Reno, Sabina M. Perrino, Anthony Stavrianakis, Tyler Zoanni, Aidan Seale-Feldman, Margaux Fitoussi, Maria Speyer, Melody Howes, Andrés Romero, Serena Bindi, Yasmine Harrison, Adriana Molina, Caroline Hoepffner, Jean Hoepffner, and Mary Kairidi. Todd Meyers has encouraged the development of this book in sustained ways and, along with Nancy Rose Hunt and Achille Mbembe, helped to arrange for its inclusion in the series Theory in Forms. The mentorship and sustained collegiality of John G. Kennedy, Arthur Kleinman, and Byron Good have been a guiding light in my research and writing efforts for years now. Claudia Lang generously offered an insightful reading of the penultimate version of the text, at just the right time. Khalil Habrih deserves special thanks for their friendship, scholarly acumen, and encouraging support of this project, along with coauthoring with me *Traces of Violence: Writings on the Disaster in Paris, France* (University of California Press, 2022)—a work that set the grounds for the present endeavor.

Colleagues and students at Sarah Lawrence College have enriched the work in many ways. I would especially like to thank Bella Brodzki, Barbara Schecter, Una Chung, Kristin Sands, Robin Starbuck, David Hollander, and Eduardo Lago for our conversations through the years. Along with discussions of the materials at hand in this work, several students in particular worked closely with me on the development of the research and writing that have gone into the book. Special thanks go to Anna Drzewiecki, Sophie-Beatrice Nyiri, Sophia Lynch, Hania Al Muayyad Al Azm, and Amelia Katherine Kuhara Patrick for their inspired contributions. Research funding from the Faith Whitney Ziesing Fund for Social Science Research helped me to conduct research in France.

The Department of Anthropology at the University of Copenhagen provided a scholarly home for me in 2020 and generously provided the resources that helped me to continue with the writing of this book during the height of the COVID-19 pandemic. Tine Gammeltoft, Hanne Overgaard Mogensen, Quentin Gausset, Lina Dalsgaard, Helle Bundgaard, Henrik Vigh, Ayo Wahlberg, Susan Reynolds Whyte, Michael Whyte, Bjarke Oxlund, Aja Smith, and Susanne Bregnbæk kindly offered their friendship and intellectual companionship during this time and during several subsequent visits to Denmark.

A fellowship at the Institut d'Études Avancées de Paris in 2020–21 enabled me to develop key aspects of the research and writing of this work. Special thanks to the staff of the IEA-Paris at that time, most notably Saadi Lahlou, Simon Luck, Solène de Bonis, and Claire Jeandel, as well as to the other fellows in residence that year, for making my residence in Paris a stimulating and fruitful one. Colin Jones, in particular, offered incisive thoughts on this project.

A Humboldt Research Award from the Alexander von Humboldt Foundation enabled me to further develop the book while residing in Berlin and in Halle, Germany, in 2023–24. Affiliations with the Institute for Social Anthropology at Freie Universität Berlin and Martin Luther University in Halle-Wittenberg have enabled me to engage with colleagues and students at both of these renowned academic institutions. Special thanks go to Anita von Poser, Hansjörg Dilger, and Sandra Calkins for making all of this possible, and for their vital friendships and scholarly collegiality. Ursula Rao sponsored a fruitful residency for me at the Max Planck Institute in Halle in the summer of 2022. I would like to thank Professor Rao and her colleagues and students in Halle for welcoming me so kindly to the MPI in Halle and for their rich engagements with my work. Conversations in Halle with Julia Vorhölter and Jovan Maud have been especially enriching. In July 2023, the Max Planck Institute was the site for a workshop of the "Spectrality Meeting Group," with which several colleagues and I have recently been engaged. Thanks go to Amy McLachlan, who has wisely led this group, as well as other participants in it, including William Mazzarella, Khalil Habrih, Claudia Lang, Damien Bright, Cameron Hu, Gretchen Bakke, and Anne Dippel, for joining in on our collaborative inquiries into processes of spectrality in contemporary life.

Several aspects of the book were presented to audiences at the Institute of Social and Cultural Anthropology, and the Affective Societies research center, at Freie Universität Berlin; at Aarhus University; at Duke University and Binghamton University; at the Institute for Ethnography and African Studies, University of Mainz; at the Center for the History of Emotions at the Max Planck Institute for Human Development, Berlin; at the 2023 conference of the German Anthropological Association, in Munich; and at the Annual Meetings of the American Anthropological Association. The feedback I received during each of these engagements has been highly beneficial.

The archivists and librarians of La Contemporaine: Bibliothèque, Archives, Musée des Monds Contemporains, in Paris and Nanterre, have assisted in commendable ways in my engagements with Élie Kagan's photographs from October 1961. La Contemporaine also made possible the inclusion of a number of digital reproductions of these photographs in the current work. Éric Manigaud and Galerie Sator have graciously permitted me to reproduce the drawing *Elie Kagan #2* in the book. The kind assistance of staff members at the Archives de la Préfecture de Police and the Cimetière Parisien de Thiais is greatly appreciated.

I would also like to thank Elizabeth Ault, senior editor at Duke University Press, for her encouragement of this project and her insightful reflections on it. Thank you as well to Benjamin Kossak, assistant editor at the Press, for helping me to complete the final version of the manuscript. The reports by two anonymous readers offered highly perceptive readings of an earlier version of this work, which enabled me to clarify and take further many aspects of the text.

This book is dedicated to my parents, Robert Charles Desjarlais and Helen Lajoie Desjarlais. From love and care emerges infinite inheritance.

To all involved, thank you for the generous, creative spirit of your lives and work.

INTRODUCTION

1. See also Mbembe 2008.

2. It's entirely unclear how many persons from Algeria died the night of 17 October 1961 at the hands of the Paris police or in the days that preceded or followed that night of violence. In fact, several scholars have been engaged in what has been called a "numbers battle" in terms of accounts of the deaths resulting from the state violence in France in October 1961, with different researchers proposing significantly different tallies. Starting in the 1980s, Jean-Luc Einaudi conducted research into the events, drawing from documents provided to him from the FF-FLN, interviews he conducted with witnesses to the events, and evidence from the archives of the Paris morgue and the cemeteries of Paris. In his book *La bataille de Paris: 17 Octobre 1961*, Einaudi (1991) estimated that approximately two hundred people had died. This number largely confirmed the FLN's original estimate (Cole 2006, 120). In later publications Einaudi stood by this estimate of hundreds of deaths. Partly in response to Einaudi's findings and the sensational trial and court proceedings of Maurice Papon in the 1990s, the Ministry of Interior released a report in 1998 that proposed that no more than thirty-two people were killed by the police on 17 October. In turn, Jean-Paul Brunet, a historian at the École Normale Supérieure and the University of Paris, undertook research of his own; he worked largely with police reports to which he was given access by the Paris Prefecture of Police. In his book *Police contre FLN: Le drame d'octobre 1961*, published in 1999, Brunet determined that thirty-two persons had died. Several other historians have pointed out, however, that the police reports could not be trusted to give accurate, truthful, and comprehensive accounts of the events of October 1961 and any violence inflicted on Algerians by the Paris police (see, for instance, House and MacMaster 2006, 2008). To date, there is no clear consensus as to how many persons were killed by the Paris police. As House and MacMaster (2006, 166) note, "If there is one thing that we can be certain of in relation to the Paris massacre, it is that a conclusive or definitive figure as to the number of Algerian deaths will never be arrived at." A reflection offered by Joshua Cole in 2006 is still relevant today: "Ever mindful of France's libel laws, journalists have now resorted to the unwieldy formulation

of 'between thirty-two and two hundred' or simply 'dozens' to speak of the number of dead. It is not difficult to see how painful such approximations are to the families of victims, nor how much comfort they give to those whose political interests still require a degree of damage control" (Cole 2006, 121). For more on the estimates and accounts of the number of deaths resulting from the violence of 17 October 1961, see Thibaud (2001); House and MacMaster (2006, 161–68; 2008); Cole (2003); and Einaudi (2001, 2011).

3. For writings on the events of October 1961 in Paris, see, among others, Péju (2000), Einaudi (1991, 2001, 2009, 2011), Haroun (1986), Cole (2003, 2006), Tristan (1991), and House and MacMaster's comprehensive account, *Paris 1961* (2006). Documentary films on 17 October 1961 include Panijel (1962), Denis and Lallaoui (1991), Brooks and Hayling (1992), and Adi (2011). See also Leïla Sebbar's novel *La Seine était rouge* (1999) and William Gardner Smith's novel *The Stone Face* ([1963] 2021).

4. Testimonial account of Ahmed Djoughlal, recorded on 22 October 1961 (Einaudi 1991, 111–12, 168–69). This account is found, along with the testimonies of other Algerians, in a set of historical archives collected by the FLN. As Joshua Cole (2003, 33) notes, "Ali Haroun gave the historical archives of the Federation in 1986 to Georges Mattei, who had been an important clandestine supporter of the FLN during the war years in France. Georges Mattei passed the archives to his friend Jean-Luc Einaudi, who used the documents to write *La Bataille de Paris*." (On this, see in particular Einaudi 1991, 14–15.)

5. Djoughlal, quoted in Einaudi (1991, 111–12, 168–69). All translations are mine, unless otherwise noted.

6. As noted, for one, in House and MacMaster (2006, 271), in citing an interview that Jim House conducted with the journalist Farid Aïchoune: "Farid Aïchoune argues that Kabyle cultural codes forbid dwelling on the past, hence the expression 'the past is dead' (*li fat met*)."

7. To quote Algerian-French writer Leïla Sebbar on the matter (Mortimer 2008, xvii).

8. Ann Stoler (2016) aptly speaks of a "colonial aphasia" limiting speech and thought around the unruly histories of colonialism in France and elsewhere.

9. In her comprehensive study of the "anarchive" of cultural traces of the violence in Paris on 17 October 1961, Lia Brozgal (2020, 31–64) identifies several distinct waves of anarchival texts: the "first wave texts" that emerged in the months after October 1961 (including Jacques Panijel's 1962 documentary film *Octobre à Paris*); a second wave of novels, *beur* literature, and documentary works, from 1983 to 1989; and a third wave, from 1999 and beyond, which Brozgal glosses as "the post-Papon anarchive," involving the historiographic, cultural, and artistic representations that emerged in the wake of the trial of Maurice Papon in 1999 (including Leïla Sebbar's 1999 novel *La Seine était rouge*). The time frames noted in Brozgal's archaeology and excavation of "the anarchive" of cultural works on and representations of 17 October 1961 is consistent with the temporalities inscribed in the present work.

10. See Desjarlais and Habrih (2022) and Desjarlais (2020).

11. See, for instance, House and MacMaster (2006), Blanchard (2011), and Brozgal (2020).

12. See, for instance, Stora (1991), Shepard (2006), Silverstein (2014, 2018), and Stoler (2016).

13. In her 2016 book *A Nervous State: Violence, Remedies, and Reverie in Colonial Congo*, Nancy Rose Hunt draws from Walter Benjamin's (1999a, 545) invocation of a "technique of nearness" (*Technik der Nähe*) in historical analysis in considering closely the nervousness, reveries, and afterlives of violence and harm in King Leopold's Congo Free States. I employ a similar technique of nearness in this work, with this orientation possibly leading at times to a "pathos of nearness," as alluded to by Benjamin (1999a, 545).

14. See Hartman (2007, 2008), for instance. In the opening pages of her book *In the Wake: On Blackness and Being* (2016), Christina Sharpe writes in compelling ways about the challenges faced by members of her family through several generations.

15. As quoted in Saunders (2008, 7).

16. See George Marcus (1998) on the idea of "multi-sited ethnography," the methods of which Marcus advocates include "follow the plot, story, the allegory" and "follow the life or biography" (93, 94).

17. To invoke the title, in English translation, of Derrida's *Mal d'archive*, "Archive Fever" (1996); and to cite the words of Ariella Aïsha Azoulay (2017), who, in her essay "Archive," remarks that "'archive fever' is not simply a problematic translation of a book title, Derrida's *Mal d'archive*. It is a real phenomenon that Derrida ignores. It is the result of numerous individual initiatives of creating new archives and depositories, and of claiming the right to re-arrange and use existing ones. . . . Archive fever is also the claim to revolutionize the archive; the claim to a different understanding of the documents it holds, of its supposed purpose, of the right to see them and to act accordingly; the claim to the forms and ways of categorizing presenting, and using these documents."

18. To note two well-known studies in social history and cultural history, which have since been identified as being exemplars in the field of "microhistory": Carlo Ginzburg's *The Cheese and the Worms: The Cosmos of a Sixteenth-Century Miller* (1980) and Alain Corbin's *The Life of an Unknown: The Rediscovered World of a Clog Maker in Nineteenth-Century France* (2001). The latter has particular relevance for the current work, as Corbin examines the circumstances of life and society in nineteenth-century rural France, building his interpretive work on the historical records of a single man, "a forester and clog maker," chosen at random from historical records. See also Davis (1983, 1988).

19. The relevant works that come to mind within the field of historiographic writing known as "microhistory" include Jonathan Spence's *The Death of Woman Wang* (1978) and Colin Jones's *The Fall of Robespierre: 24 Hours in Revolutionary Paris* (2021). For the theory and practice of microhistory, see Magnússon and Szijártó (2013) and Ginzburg (1989, 2012). Saidiya Hartman's *Lose Your Mother: A Journey Along the Atlantic Slave Route* (2007), Ivan Jablonka's *A History of the Grandparents I Never Had* (2016), Javier Cercas's *Lord of All the Dead* (2020), and Guillaume Lachenal's *The Doctor Who Would Be King* (2022) have been important resources for me, along with more conceptual overviews of the textual strategies of contemporary historiographic writing with a literary sensibility, such as Jablonka (2018), Carrard (2017), and Traverso (2020).

As Catherine Gallagher and Stephen Greenblatt (2000, 52) note, "Counterhistory opposes itself not only to dominant narratives, but also to prevailing modes of historical thought and methods of research"; such counterhistories "make apparent the slippages, cracks, fault lines, and surprising absences in the monumental structures that dominated a more traditional historicism" (17). On the idea of anthropological inquiry and interpretation as a mode of "thick description," see Geertz (1973). The current inquiry also bears some affinities with the "histoire des mentalités" approach that emerged in historiography in the late twentieth century.

20. Anna Lowenhaupt Tsing (2015, 227–28) writes of spores in her polyphonic ethnography, *The Mushroom at the End of the World*: "Both in forests and in sciences, spores open our imaginations to another cosmopolitan topology. Spores take off toward unknown destinations, mate across types, and, at least occasionally, give rise to new organisms—a beginning for new kinds. Spores are hard to pin down; that is their grace. In thinking out landscapes, spores guide us to in-population heterogeneity. In thinking about science, spores model open-ended communication and excess: the pleasure of speculation."

21. See also Lynes (2018), McCance (2019), Wills (2016), Vitale (2018), and Trumbull (2022).

22. As Derrida (2008, 31) puts it in *The Animal That Therefore I Am*, "Beyond the edge of the so-called human, beyond it but by no means on a single opposing side, rather than 'the Animal' or 'Animal life' there is already a heterogeneous multiplicity of the living, or more precisely (since to say 'the living' is already to say too much or not enough), a multiplicity of organizations of relations between living and dead, relations of organization or lack of organization among realms that are more and more difficult to dissociate by means of the figures of the organic and the abyssal, and they can never be totally objectified."

23. On the concept of social death, see Patterson (1982). On bare life, see Agamben (1998).

24. In his later writings, Derrida tended to switch from exploring the implications of the French verb *survivre*, "to survive," to philosophical reflections on the word *survivance*. (For specifics on Derrida's use of the terms *survivre* and *survivance*, see Naas [2012] and Saghafi [2020].) Derrida (2011, 131) remarked that he preferred "the middle voice 'survivance' to the active voice of the active infinitive 'to survive' or the substantualizing substantive *survival*." This usage is similar in linguistic spirit to Derrida's creative use of words such as *différance* and *revenance*, for the *-ance* ending in each of these terms "marks a suspended status between the active and passive voice" (Saghafi 2015, 21). *Survivance* could be translated into English as "survival," but I keep the spelling of the French word *survivance* here, as that phrasing works well in its nonactive middle voice.

25. And *cessance*, here, rather than the more active gerund "ceasing" or more substantive noun "cessation," to match in counterpart the suspended, not quite active or passive grammatical phrasing of *survivance*.

26. See Desjarlais (2018) for an exploration of the concepts of phantasms and "phantasmography" as they apply to perception and anthropological inquiry in the contemporary world.

27. To invoke a phrase from Adorno (2000, 27).

28. As Derrida (2011, 117) notes, "But the logic of this banality of survival that begins even before our death is that of a survival of the remainder, the remains, that does not

even wait for death to make life and death indissociable, and thus the *unheimlich* and fantasmatic experience of the spectrality of the living dead. Life and death as such are not separable as such."

29. *Oxford English Dictionary* (1989), s.v. "exergue."

30. Such as with *The Blind Man: A Phantasmography* (Desjarlais 2018) and *Traces of Violence: Writings on the Disaster in Paris, France*, coauthored with Khalil Habrih (2012).

31. As quoted in Hartman and Nelson (2022).

32. See Anna Lowenhaupt Tsing (2012) on the "unruly edges" of interspecies relations and assemblages in the world.

33. Notable earlier works of reflexive anthropology include Paul Rabinow's *Reflections on Fieldwork in Morocco* (1977), Jeanne Favret-Saada's *Deadly Words* (2010), and Vincent Crapanzano's *Tuhami* (1980).

34. For an earlier focus on an anthropological approach to the phantasmal in life, see Desjarlais (2018) and Desjarlais and Habrih (2022).

CHAPTER 1. WOUND IMAGES

1. On the idea of "the right to look" and forms of "countervisuality" that can work to contest political forms of visuality and silence among state and colonial arrangements of power, see Mirzoeff (2011).

2. Thanks go to Todd Meyers for prompting me to consider the "time signature" of the subject matters of this inquiry.

3. To quote the subtitle of Crapanzano's book, *The Harkis: The Wound That Never Heals* (2011).

4. To draw from Lisa Stevenson (2014, 14), who writes of the affective and imaginal force of images from dreams, in uncertain moments in life and death, "life beside itself."

5. The digital archive of Kagan's photographs can be found at the Argonnaute, the digital library of La Contemporaine, https://argonnaute.parisnanterre.fr/ark:/14707 /tpwf7vjs31m8?cbs=b25ab502-4dd6-4b28-8d36-8011fd7ea9da.

6. See Pinney (2012, 2023) for incisive reflections on "world-system photography."

7. See, for instance, Poole (1997), Pinney (1997, 2023), Edwards (2001), Strassler (2010, 2020), Wright (2013), Didi-Huberman (2008), and Silverman (2009, 2015).

8. On the "social life of things," see Appadurai (1988). On "the social life of Indian photographs," see Pinney (1997). Other works that trace out the many uses and significances of specific photographic images through *longues durées* of cultural history include Shamoon Zamir's *The Gift of the Face* (2020); Georges Didi-Huberman's *Invention of Hysteria* (2004) and *Images in Spite of All* (2008); Krista Thompson's essay "'I was here but I disappear': Ivanhoe 'Rhygin' Martin and Photographic Disappearance in Jamaica" (2018); Sampada Aranke's *Death's Futurity* (2023); and the 2020 volume edited by Ilisa Barbash, Molly Rogers, and Deborah Willis, *To Make Their Own Way in the World*.

9. On this, see Silverman (2015, 39–66).

10. As Silverman remarks (2015, 52–53).

11. Talbot (1841), as quoted by Silverman (2015, 52–53).

12. In her book *Humane Insight: Looking at Images of African American Suffering and Death*, Courtney R. Baker defines human insight as a "kind of looking" in which "the onlooker's ethics are addressed by the spectacle of others' embodied suffering. . . . Whereas the gaze ignores or denies the humanity of the person being looked at, humane insight seeks knowledge about the humanity of that person. It is an ethics-based look that imagines the body that is seen to merit the protections due to all human bodies" (2015, 5). The ethics of looking that Baker advocates can in fact go beyond the human, in considering the wounding and suffering of other forms of life in the world.

The question posed in the main text is directly informed by discussant comments that Karen Strassler offered on the papers presented at a session titled "Imposing Images: Figures of Interruption, Interlocution, and Exposition," at the Annual Meeting of the American Anthropological Association, held in Seattle in November 2022. At this session, organized by Jenny Chio and Daniel Fisher, I presented a paper titled "Wound Images."

13. Similar questions have arisen in efforts to research and write about histories of violence and suffering among Black persons residing in the Americas from the time of slavery to the present day. In the opening pages of her 1997 book *Scenes of Subjection: Terror, Slavery, and Nineteenth-Century America*, Saidiya Hartman reflects on existing narratives of spectacular violence inflicted on enslaved people by their owners and other subjugators in nineteenth-century America—such as Frederick Douglass's account of the beating of his Aunt Hester, a "horrible exhibition" related in the first chapter of his 1845 text *Narrative of the Life of Frederick Douglass*. Hartman then explains her decision not to reproduce that account in her writing, for it would risk reinforcing "the spectacular character of black suffering," among other things. She then poses a series of incisive questions:

> What interests me are the ways we are called upon to participate in such scenes. Are we witnesses who confront the truth of what happened in the face of the world-destroying capacities of pain, the distortions of torture, the sheer unrepresentability of terror, and the repression of the dominant accounts? Or are we voyeurs fascinated with and repelled by exhibitions of terror and suffering? What does the exposure of the violated body yield? Proof of black sentience or the inhumanity of the "peculiar institution"? Or does the pain of the other merely provide us with the opportunity for self-reflection? At issue here is the precariousness of empathy and the uncertain line between witness and spectator. Only more obscene than the brutality unleashed at the whipping post is the demand that this suffering be materialized and evidenced by the display of the tortured body or endless recitations of the ghastly and the terrible. In light of this, how does one give expression to these outrages without exacerbating the indifference to suffering that is the consequence of the benumbing spectacle, or contend with the narcissistic identification that obliterates the other, or the prurience that too often is the response to such displays? This was the challenge faced by Douglass and the other foes of slavery, and this is the task I take up here. (Hartman 1997, 2)

Hartman goes on to write, "There, rather than try to convey the routinized violence of slavery and its aftermath through invocations of the shocking and the terrible, I have chosen to look elsewhere and consider those scenes in which terror can hardly be discerned. . . . By defamiliarizing the familiar, I hope to illuminate the terror of the mundane and quotidian rather than exploit the shocking spectacle" (Hartman 1997, 2).

In the opening pages of his book *In the Break*, Fred Moten reflects on Hartman's explanation of her decision not to reproduce Douglass's narrative of Aunt Hester's beating. Here Moten (2003, 4) argues that "the decision not to reproduce the account of Aunt Hester's beating is, in some sense, illusory. First, it is reproduced in her references to and refusal to it; second, the beating is reproduced in every scene of subjection the book goes on to read. . . . The question here concerns the inevitability of such reproduction even in the denial of it." Although Hartman does not include Douglass's narrative of the beating, in other words, the narrative still exists in Hartman's text in an unstated but still present way, one that is foundational to histories of anti-Black violence. The performance of the narrative continues on, in powerfully spectral, haunting ways, even when it is not overtly recounted. It's worth noting that Moten (2003, 19–22) includes Douglass's narrative in *In the Break*, and this in relation to Douglass's reflections on the vital role that music plays in the lives of slaves.

More recently, Sampada Aranke (2023) engages with the debate that Moten stages with Hartman in considering the politics of visual reproduction of anti-Black violence, specifically photographs and visual representations of the deaths of Black Panther Party members in the 1960s and 1970s.

The current work is informed by the vexed questioning and lines of thought voiced by Hartman, Moten, and Aranke, as well as other writings on the politics and ethics of representations of violence. This includes the disturbing but necessary book, *Without Sanctuary: Lynching Photography in America* (Allen 2000).

14. *Online Etymology Dictionary*, "scrutiny (n.)," https://www.etymonline.com/word /scrutiny.

15. The idea of taking one's time with images comes from a passage by Raymond Bellour (2012, 14): "Its point of anchorage, as well as its flip side in the quite sensible activity, really, of taking your time before the image, stealing its time from it, time that is then sold off for knowledge, research, thirst for ideas."

16. Susan Sontag (1997) wrote, for instance, that "all photographs are *memento mori*" (15) and likened a photograph to a "death mask" (154); while Roland Barthes (1981, 15) posited that "death is the *eidos* of [the] Photograph." Eduardo Cadava (2021, 60) writes, in turn, that "the photograph always has been associated with death." He continues, "There can be no image, then, that is not also an image of death, an image of the death of the distinction between life and death" (61).

17. In his essay "Fire and Ice," Peter Wollen (1984, 118) observes that "photographs appear as devices for stopping time and preserving fragments of the past, like flies in amber."

18. The thought here carries the trace of a reflection voiced by the narrator of Chris Marker's 1983 film *Sans Soleil*: "Who said that time heals all wounds? It would be better to say that time heals everything—except wounds. With time, the hurt of separation loses its real limits. With time, the desired body will soon disappear, and if the desiring body has already ceased to exist for the other, then what remains is a wound . . . disembodied."

19. The complete sentence here is, "As *Spectator* I was interested in Photography only for 'sentimental' reasons: I wanted to explore it not as a question (a theme) but as a wound: I see, I feel, hence I notice, I observe, and I think."

20. For a comprehensive review of "wound culture" in anthropological thought and research, as well as in the contemporary world more generally, see Solomon (2022b). For ethnographic writings that engage with the idea of personal and collective wounding in relation to histories of political violence, see Nelson (1999) and Mookherjee (2015).

21. See Dewachi (2015, 61) on the ways in which "social wounds" travel "across different social worlds and local histories of violence."

22. Kagan's *témoignage*, his "testimony," also appears in several sections of Einaudi's (1991) *La bataille de Paris: 17 Octobre 1961*, as drawn from an interview Einaudi conducted with Kagan on 16 September 1986.

23. These and the following series of quoted passages are taken directly from Einaudi and Kagan (2001, 1–17) and translated into English here. Unless noted otherwise, all translations from French into English in this book are my own.

24. As H. Feldman (2014, 193) notes, for instance. In an interview from 2021, journalist and writer Georges Chatain noted of Kagan's photographic engagements on 17 October 1961, "The French Federation of the FLN had contacted him to follow the demonstration. He hadn't stumbled upon it by accident" (as quoted in Burté and Leblanc 2022, 88).

25. Kateb Yacine, "Dans la guele du loup" (Yacine 1962, 22–23):

> Peuple français, tu as tout vu
> Oui, tout vu de tes propres yeux.
> Tu as vu notre sang couler
> Tu as vu la police
> Assommer les manifestants
> Et les jeter dans la Seine.
> La Seine rougissante
> N'a pas cessé les jours suivants
> De vomir à la face
> Du peuple de la Commune
> Ces corps martyrisés
> Qui rappelaient aux Parisiens
> Leurs propres révolutions
> Leur propre résistance.
> Peuple français, tu as tout vu,
> Oui, tout vu de tes propres yeux,
> Et maintenant vas-tu parler?
> Et maintenant vas-tu te taire?

26. See also Brozgal (2020, 172–75) for an incisive reading of Kateb Yacine's poem.

27. My narrative account of Kagan's arrival and encounters in Nanterre the night of 17 October 1961 is drawn from Kagan's own narrative accounts, as found in Kagan and Rotman (1989), Einaudi (1991), and Einaudi and Kagan (2001).

28. As of this writing, digital versions of Kagan's photographs from the night of 17 October 1961 can be viewed at the digital archive of La Contemporaine, with the Répertoire numérique du Fonds Elie Kagan (digital index of the Elie Kagan collection): https://argonnaute.parisnanterre.fr/ark:/14707/l6mh2xzb9g5d. The photographs Kagan took

at Rue des Pâquerettes can be accessed here: https://argonnaute.parisnanterre.fr/ark:
/14707/pozr7txv52qg.

29. See Didi-Huberman (2008, 89) for an "interpretative montage" in a phenomenologically attuned analysis of four photographs taken in Auschwitz in August 1944 that
indicate the killing of Jewish prisoners in the concentration camp. Didi-Huberman's
attentive focus on "intersecting memories," topographical knowledge, contemporary
testimonies, and retrospective testimonies by members of the *Sonderkommando*—"a sort
of interpretative montage which, even if woven as tightly as possible, will always have that
inherent fragility of the 'critical moment'" (89)—informs the interpretive reading in the
current work. Didi-Huberman's *Bark* (2017a) is also relevant, as are his writings *Phalènes*
(2013) and *Survival of the Fireflies* (2018c).

In considering the visual, semiotic, and phenomenological aspects of an image or a series of images, we might come to regard the complexities of images—or their "implexities"
(*implexités*)—so as to understand "life in the folds" of an image. On the phenomenological
"implexity" of images and the effort to understand "life in the folds" of an image, see Didi-
Huberman (2020, 22–23; 2013; 2018c). Through such an interpretative endeavor, one might
"put into motion" the images, as Didi-Huberman envisions this process (see De Cauwer
and Smith 2020). If we are able to "stand before an image as we do *before a complex
time*" (Didi-Huberman 2017b, 19), then a focused consideration of Kagan's photographs
implies tracing out the complex strands of time coursing through them.

30. In presenting and commenting on the photographs that Kagan took at Rue des
Pâquerettes the night of 17 October 1961, I am following the sequence established by La
Contemporaine for the digital collection of Kagan's photographs, with the individual
photographs numbered from KAG/00004/N/B01 to KAG/00004/N/B11 (https://
argonnaute.parisnanterre.fr/ark:/14707/pozr7txv52qg).

The web page for this set of photographic images notes that "les vues ne se suivent
pas nécessairement, les négatifs n'étant pas numérotés à l'origine" (the views are not
necessarily sequential, as the negatives were not originally numbered). The sequence
established in the digital archive, which I follow here, is a plausible one, with the photographs showing Bennahar first lying on the ground, then trying to stand, and then being
brought to the hospital of Nanterre. It's unclear, however, which photographs Kagan
took initially: those of Bennahar alone (as shown in figure 1.5) or those of Bennahar
and the dead man lying across the stone wall (as shown in figures 1.6 and 1.7). Hence the
phrasing "one of the first photographs that Kagan took."

31. In her 2014 book *From a Nation Torn: Decolonizing Art and Representation in
France, 1945–1962*, Hannah Feldman (2014, 193) argues that, in a more general way, "the
Kagan photographs stand as proof of a subaltern appropriation of the reins of representation through the mechanical prosthesis of the camera. This, I propose, is true of all of the
photographs of the demonstration of 17 October 1961, and part of why we must attend to
the emphasis that the French term *manifestation* places on the aspects of producing and
making manifest, real, and concrete, even when such realities can only be witnessed in the
temporal duration provided by the image they produce."

32. The photographic flash can be a violence of light that produces shocks among
photographed subjects, as with Charcot's subjects of hysteria when photographed

(see Didi-Huberman 2004). As Ulrich Baer (2005, 34) notes in his book *Spectral Evidence*:

> The flash takes you by surprise, no matter how long in advance you have been warned. It cuts into a scene with the violence of the lightning bolt and yet instantly displaces attention from itself to the darkness of its surroundings. Presumably you recover, only momentarily blinded by an excess of artificial light, and try to regain your composure. The flash creates a physical disorientation.... An excess of light that promises total (as we will see, illusory) visibility, and that goes out at the same moment that it goes on, the flash cannot be integrated into sensory experience but only registered, belatedly, incompletely, possibly as shock; too much light produces a loss of sight.

33. The passages quoted are drawn from archival materials cited by House and MacMaster.

34. As noted by House and MacMaster (2006, 172), citing an interview with Raoul Letard consulted at Archives IHESI (Institut des Hautes Études de la Sécurité Intérieure), Paris: Raoul Letard interview, 11 May 1993, oral archives of the police, transcript, pp. 8–10.

35. Raoul Letard, as recounted to Jean-Marc Berlière and reported in Laurent Chabrun, "La confession d'un policier," *L'Express*, 16 October 1997, 38, 40. The translation draws from the text found in Cole (2003, 22) and Einaudi (2011, 351–52); ellipses in the original.

36. See House and MacMaster (2006, 126).

37. It's worth noting here that the timing does not quite match up, according to Letard's and Kagan's accounts: Kagan said he arrived at Rue des Pâquerettes around 10 p.m. the night of 17 October 1961, while Letard recalled that his company arrived in Colombes after 11 p.m. that same night.

38. Cixous (2005, xii) writes of scars in this way so as to contrast them with stigmata: "Unlike scar, *stigmata takes away*, removes substance, carves out a place for itself."

39. Compare to "all literature is scarry. It celebrates the wound and repeats the lesion" (Cixous 2005, xii).

40. Camille Gilles, *Paris Press*, 20 October 1961, as quoted in House and MacMaster (2006, 164–65). House and MacMaster also note, in citing an interview with Monique Hervo, that "it is possible that some clandestine burials took place within the bidonvilles" (265).

41. On the physiological processes of pain, see Osterweis, Kleinman, and Mechanic (1987, 124–42). See also Michael Taussig's 1992 book *The Nervous System* for reflections on the "nervous system" at hand in situations of life, violence, and nervous states of emergency in Latin America and elsewhere.

42. In my estimation, pain in photography relates most to the "liquid intelligence" evident in certain aspects of natural forms and photographic conveyance, in contrast to the dry character of photography's glass lens and shutter mechanics. On photography and "liquid intelligence," see Jeff Wall's 2007 essay by that title, as well as Silverman (2015, 67–69, 83–85).

43. On cultural and political processes of anesthetics and desensitization to perceptual shocks and forms of violence and pain, see Buck-Morss (1992) and A. Feldman (1994).

44. See Michel Foucault's *Discipline and Punish* (1995), for instance.

45. On the night of 17 October 1961, the residents from the bidonvilles in and around Nanterre who joined the collective demonstrations in Paris and its margins returned to their homes, deeply affected by the police violence they had encountered that day. Many men were injured. Monique Hervo, a member of a team of the Service Civil International, lived and worked for several years in the bidonville in Nanterre known as La Folie, forming close ties with residents there; she had joined in on the procession of people walking from that bidonville to Pont de Neuilly that day. In a journal she kept at the time, later published, Hervo wrote of the atmosphere at La Folie that night, on into the next day: "The condition of most of the men would require hospitalization. Some, with serious fractures, are condemned to be handicapped for the rest of their lives, for lack of adequate care. But their refusal to be transported to a hospital is categorical. Too afraid to be taken back by the police when they leave the hospital, as it happens every day. Too afraid to be beaten again [18 October 1961]" (Hervo 2012, 181–82).

House and MacMaster (2006, 164) note, along similar lines, "Algerians, even when severely wounded, desperately attempted to avoid going to hospital and with good reason: the Prefecture of Police instructed hospital administrators after 17 October to inform the police of any wounded Algerians and to prevent their discharge and injured men were even transferred by the police directly from hospitals to detention centers."

46. See also Campt's *Image Matters* (2012) for a similarly inspired reflection on the affective, haptic, and multitemporal qualities of photographic images.

47. To riff on a passage in Fred Moten's *In the Break*, which considers "the sound before a photograph" (2003, 200).

48. In responding to a presentation that I gave at a symposium titled "Death Drives, or Thinking with the Corpse" at the Humanities Center at Duke University in October 2018, a person in the audience invoked the phrase "overphotographed subject" in speaking of the way that Kagan took a number of rapid photographs of Bennahar.

On the concept of "hypervisibility," particularly in terms of Black visibility and representations of the Black body, see Fleetwood (2011). Nicole Fleetwood (2011, 16) defines "hypervisibility" as "an interventionist term to describe processes that produce the overrepresentation of certain images of blacks and the visual currency of these images in public culture. It simultaneously announces the continual invisibility of black as ethical and enfleshed subjects in various realms of polity, economies, and discourse, so that blackness remains aligned with negation and decay."

CHAPTER 2. A SPORADIC HISTORY OF IMAGES

1. For more on the "afterlife" of images of political violence, see Sampada Aranke's (2023) inquiry into the afterlife of images that speak to the murders of Black Panther Party members Lil' Bobby Hutton, Fred Hampton, and George Jackson in the 1960s and 1970s and the political uses made of these images by Black radicals.

2. As Joshua Cole (2003, 32) remarks in assessing the significance and recurrent circulation of Kagan's photographs from that October night, "These photos have now become icons of the event and are reproduced whenever journalists write about the demonstrations."

Hannah Feldman (2014, 265n68) writes of Kagan's photographs, "Individual images have been reprinted in conjunction with the literally hundreds of newspaper articles that have issued since the mid-1980s in regard to the events of 17 October 1961, where they are often singled out for providing unique visual testimony."

3. In her 2020 book, *Demanding Images*, Karen Strassler advances a compelling conceptual analysis of what she calls the "evidentiary" mode of image making and reception in Indonesia, of "documentary photographs as authoritative, indexical records," in terms similar to how I write the "evidential mode" here. As Strassler observes, "Evidentiary images promise to ground public truth claims in a technological guarantee of transparency" (Strassler 2020, 24).

4. As noted in Burté and Leblanc (2022, 32).

5. The photo of Abdelkader Bennahar was printed in a page inside the newspaper; a photo of a man wounded at Métro Solférino appeared on the cover. In 2001, Einaudi recalled the title of the *France Observateur* article as reading, "Vous ne pouvez plus ignorer ça" (You can no longer ignore that), though perhaps he was drawing from his, or Kagan's, memory of the publication (Einaudi and Kagan 2001, 20).

6. On this publication and statement, see Welch and McGonagle (2013, 67).

7. For insightful readings of the film *Octobre à Paris*, see M. Sharpe (2017) and Brozgal (2020).

8. This perception echoes a theme in Laura Mulvey's writings on film. As she writes in her 2019 book *Afterimages*, "In *Death 24× a Second* I discussed the ghostliness that has often been associated with the filmic and photographic medium and I return occasionally in *Afterimages* to the way the medium preserves the living presence of human figures, often long dead, through the film machine" (10).

9. See Riceputi (2015) for a comprehensive account of Einaudi's research inquiries into the events and police violence of 17 October, 1961, including his engagements with archival institutions in Paris.

10. This is the statement as Einaudi recalls it in *17 Octobre 1961* (Einaudi and Kagan 2001, 29). Another version, perhaps rendered in translation: "I don't doubt at all that they were doctored" (Golsan 2000, 239).

11. See the 2001 edition of Einaudi's book, *Octobre 1961: Un massacre à Paris*, in which the author summarizes the erroneous claim: "The FLN had organized the demonstrations with the project that they cause many deaths and it had foreseen the complicity of the photographer Élie Kagan" (Einaudi 2001, 26).

12. See Didi-Huberman (2008, 80–81).

13. On the term "veil-image," see Didi-Huberman (2008, 79–81).

14. Welch and McGonagle (2013, 68) note that they understand the "visual career" of 17 October 1961 as involving "the changing ways and contexts in which it has been expressed visually through time."

15. The title of the article can be translated into English as "In the course of our memories: 17 October 1961, emblem of police violence."

16. The 23 February 2005 "French law on colonialism" was passed by the National Assembly, which imposed on high-school (*lycée*) teachers a requirement to teach the "positive values" of colonialism to their students (Article 4, Paragraph 2). See *Loi n° 2005–158*

du 23 Février 2005 portant reconnaissance de la Nation et contribution nationale en faveur des Français rapatriés (Law No. 2005–158 of 23 February 2005 regarding recognition of the Nation and national contribution in favor of the French repatriates), Légifrance, https://www.legifrance.gouv.fr/loda/id/JORFTEXT000000444898/.

17. In using the term *actant* here, I am drawing from the "actor-network theory" approach advanced by Bruno Latour. In an essay, Latour (1996, 7) characterizes an actant as "something that acts or to which activity is granted by others."

18. On this see Azoulay (2016, 157). See also Azoulay (2019, 239–40) on the "untaken photographs of rape" that can be traced indirectly from other photographs and records of life in post–World War II Berlin.

19. Karen Strassler's 2020 book *Demanding Images: Democracy, Mediation, and the Image-Event in Indonesia* explores a number of image-events that have occurred in the messy, "complexly mediated" (11) public spheres in Indonesia, through photographs, posters, contemporary art, graffiti, selfies, memes, and other visual media. "By image-event," writes Strassler, "I mean a political process set in motion when a specific image or set of images erupts onto and intervenes in a social field, becoming a focal point of discursive and affective engagement across diverse publics. Image-events are political happenings in which images become the material ground of generative struggles to bring a collectivity into view and give shape to its future" (9–10). Strassler's important research on such image-events has informed my inquiry here.

20. As noted in Lebas (2007).

21. See Levinas (1991), for instance.

22. See Altez-Albela (2011) and Wentzer (2022, 214).

23. As Saidiya Hartman (1997, 129) observes, "Breach triggers memory, and the enormity of the breach perhaps suggests that it can be neither reconciled nor repaired." See Desjarlais and Habrih (2022, 148–225) on the lingering aftermaths of histories of violence and wounding in Paris and its surrounding communities, including colonial forms of domination and subjection.

24. On the cultural and political dynamics of Black visuality and representation, including spectacularized images of Black bodies in North America and elsewhere, see, for instance, Fleetwood (2010), Hartman and Nelson (2022), Young (2010), and Allen (2000).

25. "In-Depth Guide to How Google Search Works," https://developers.google.com/search/docs/fundamentals/how-search-works.

26. "Spectrality effect" is a term sometimes used by Derrida. See Derrida (1994, 48), for instance.

27. On the idea that images can "burn," see Didi-Huberman (2006).

CHAPTER 3. INTERSECTING LIVES

1. As cited in Gerrin (1999).

2. See Desjarlais (2003) for the idea and practice of a "sensory biography."

3. A scanned copy of the handwritten journal is printed in Burté and Leblanc (2022, 110). The extract of the poem can be found on page 2 of a four-page PDF document

titled "'Ratonnades du 17 Octobre 1961': Déroulé du parcours d'Élie Kagan de Paris à Nanterre," located on the website for La Contemporaine: https://www.lacontemporaine .fr/pdf/de_paris_a_Nanterre.pdf.

4. The competing ideas and historiographic assessments involved in the attempt to understand what has been involved here are conveyed well by Joshua Cole and Michael Rothberg. In his 2003 essay "Remembering the Battle of Paris" Cole writes,

> The sixteen-year Papon affair and the sensational trial in 1997–98 were extraordi-nary media events, and Papon's dual role—loyal servant of Vichy and Gaullist police enforcer—created an indelible connection between the memory of the Shoah and the memory of the French-Algerian war in the mainstream press. For twenty years, from 1981 until the 40th anniversary of the events in October 2001, this conjunction [of Vichy and Algeria] was the engine that drove widespread public discussion of 17 October 1961 in France.
>
> In order to understand how the repression of 17 October came to widespread public attention in France, one cannot avoid an examination of the scandal's connection to the Papon affair and subsequent trial. The two controversies seem to be linked in so many ways by their common themes: repressed memory, official complicity with atrocity, and the impression—however mistaken—of a public taboo being broken. Nevertheless, the connection and the presumed parallels between the two affairs mis-leads as much as it illuminates. In the first place, nobody in France seriously questions any longer that Vichy's activities during the German occupation were criminal. (Cole 2003, 32–33)

Writing in 2009, Rothberg comments specifically on this reflection of Cole's: "Cole and other commentators are correct that the events and contexts of Vichy and de-colonization, as well as their memory, do not fully correspond to each other, although House and MacMaster have now shown significant continuities in tactics and personnel between these different contexts (see House and Macmaster 2006, 34–35). Despite Cole's objections, however, the fact remains that such parallels have been asserted continuously *since the very moment of the events*—and it is this fact, a fact about the multidirectional-ity of memory, that must be taken into account" (Rothberg 2009, 235; emphasis in the original).

5. House's essay appeared in a special collection on the topic of "*Noeuds de mémoire*" (knots of memory) in the journal *Yale French Studies*.

6. House (2010) also considers the life histories of Monique Hervo, Jacques Panijel, and Adolfo Kaminsky, each of whose experiences during World War II influenced their understandings of French colonial rule and the Algerian war of liberation.

7. As Barthes (1976, 9) writes in *Sade, Fourier, Loyola*:

> For if, through a twisted dialectic, the Text, destroyer of all subject, contains a subject to live, that subject is dispersed, somewhat like the ashes we strew into the wind after death. . . . Were I a writer, and dead, how I would love it if my life, through the pains of some friendly and detached biographer, were to reduce itself to a few details, a few preferences, a few inflections, let us say: to "biographemes" whose distinction and mo-

bility might go beyond any fate and come to touch, like Epicurean atoms, some future body, destined to the same dispersion.

See also Österle (2017).

8. See also Rothberg (2009, 301–2) on this passage of Sebbar's novel. It's worth noting that Kagan is one of the four persons to whom Sebbar's book is dedicated.

9. See Fletcher (2013) on Freud's conceptualization of trauma as often involving specific "scenes of trauma," which often spurred latter manifestations of traumatic effects through a process of *Nachträglichkeit*, or "deferred action/afterwardness."

10. As quoted in Laplanche and Pontalis (1988, 112).

11. These passages are drawn from the interview with Marguerite Langiert, as found in Burté and Leblanc (2022, 26–29).

12. Thérèse Blondet-Bisch, "The Élie Kagan Collection at the Museum of Contemporary History. BDIC. Paris," https://www.visapourlimage.com/en/festival /exhibitions/la-collection-elie-kagan-au-musee-d-histoire-contemporaine-bdic-paris.

13. On this see Einaudi and Kagan (2001, 28).

14. Blondet-Bisch, "Élie Kagan Collection."

15. In late 2021, a new building to house all of the holdings of La Contemporaine— including the Fonds Élie Kagan—was completed on the campus of the University of Paris–Nanterre.

16. On the interfaces between warfare and technologies of writing, inscription, photographing, and filmmaking, see, for instance, Virilio (2009) and Kittler (1999).

17. See *Merriam-Webster*, "fractal," https://www.merriam-webster.com/dictionary/fractal. See Gausset (2010) for the related idea and analytic method of a "fractal anthropology."

18. To the archivists of Kagan's oeuvre, it remains unclear where precisely this photograph was taken. It is included in La Contemporaine's digital library of Kagan's photographs (https://argonnaute.parisnanterre.fr/ark:/14707/w69xh5vm10qg) and titled *Le 17 Octobre 1961: Vélo abandonné* (Abandoned bike). The listing for the photograph includes this note: "This negative was found in Kagan's [photography] sleeve for the report [*reportage*] on 'October 17, 1961: Rue des Pâquerettes.' However, the photo also appears on several contact sheets in the report KAG 00003 N." The code noted refers to the photographs that Kagan took at the Pont de Neuilly in Paris that night, before making his way to Rue des Pâquerettes in Nanterre.

19. As described in Einaudi and Kagan (2001, 31).

20. For a reproduction of the contact sheet of Kagan's fifteen photos taken at Métro Concorde, see Burté and Leblanc (2022, 104).

21. Hannah Feldman (2014, 197) writes of one of these blurred photographs—distinct from the more well-known Kagan photograph of the men in the Concorde Métro station: "Almost never reproduced because of its technical inferiority, the photo that Kagan shot less than a split second afterward gives the sense that the crowd of Algerians on the platform with their hands above their heads might stretch into an infinite distance. Those in the foreground face the wall, their heads bowed beneath the weight of their clasped hands. Deeper in this image, other men stare out, catching the eye of the photographer and offering their faces to anyone on the train who may (or may not) see them."

Of this photographic print Feldman remarks, "Permission to reproduce this image, or any of the other blurred shots from the same sequence, was denied by the Kagan estate and the BDIC, a refusal that is best understood in light of the estate's will to recast Kagan as an *auteur*" (H. Feldman 2014, 266n76). In other words, the Kagan estate and the BDIC/La Contemporaine control which images of the deceased photographer circulate in print and which do not.

For Kagan's Métro Concorde contact sheet, see Burté and Leblanc (2022, 104). Many of these photographs show blurred and blurry images. No digital copies of these blur photographs are posted on La Contemporaine's digital library of Kagan's photographs.

22. "Poor images," Hito Steyerl (2009, 32) contends, are those in which the "quality is bad, its resolution substandard. As it accelerates, it deteriorates. It is a ghost of an image, a preview, a thumbnail, an errant idea, an itinerant image distributed for free, squeezed through slow digital connections, compressed, reproduced, ripped, remixed, as well as copied and pasted into other channels of distribution."

23. The phrase "looked-at looking" echoes Kaja Silverman's phrase "looked-at look" (1996, 172).

24. House and MacMaster (2006, 165) consider the argument that a number of "disappearances" of Algerian men resulted from the "massive refoulement of some 1,781 FLN militants and others to Algeria in the weeks following 17 October."

According to the police and government these men were returned to "their home village," but in reality many were placed in military camps where they could have been subjected to interrogation, torture, and summary execution (*corvée de bois*). In some instances, particularly dangerous FLN militants were flown from Paris to Algiers, where they were interrogated by a special army unit, the 123rd Brigade, which then provided secret intelligence reports to the Prefecture of the Police. At present it is not possible to say how many of these men may have been liquidated (House and MacMaster 2006, 163–64).

25. A reproduction of this contact sheet can be found in *17 Octobre 1961* (Einaudi and Kagan 2001, 58).

26. Digital versions of the photographs that Kagan took in the bidonvilles of Nanterre on 21 October 1961 can be found at the website of La Contemporaine, in the Fonds Elie Kagan, under several sections titled "Bidonvilles de Nanterre," each with its own web page. For the Kagan collection as a whole, see https://argonnaute.parisnanterre.fr/ark:/14707/l6mh2xzb9g5d.

27. Digital versions of these photographs can be found at the website of La Contemporaine, in the Fonds Elie Kagan, under the section "Bidonvilles de Nanterre: Une famille Algérienne," https://argonnaute.parisnanterre.fr/ark:/14707/3vc9ozmgqk42.

28. A print of this two-page spread can be found in Burté and Leblanc (2022, 32).

29. The public "digital repertoire" of the Élie Kagan Collection can be accessed at https://argonnaute.parisnanterre.fr/ark:/14707/l6mh2xzb9g5d.

30. "Le 17 Octobre 1961: Rue des Pâquerettes," Élie Kagan, La Contemporaine, https://argonnaute.parisnanterre.fr/ark:/14707/pozr7txv52qg.

31. Élie Kagan, La Contemporaine, https://argonnaute.parisnanterre.fr/ark:/14707/l6mh2xzb9g5d.

32. As noted in Mercier (2018).

33. Other drawings in the series *October 61* can be seen at the website of Galerie Sator, which represents Éric Manigaud (https://galeriesator.com/octobre-61-manigaud).

34. Emilie Gandon, "Série Octobre 1961: Elie Kagan #1 et Elie Kagan #3," https://www.histoire-immigration.fr/collections/serie-octobre-1961-elie-kagan-1-et-elie-kagan-3.

35. As quoted in Manigaud (2021).

36. As quoted in Benaï (2018). Drawing Now is an art fair held annually in Paris.

37. "Artist: Eric Manigaud," November 9, 2018, https://www.artrabbit.com/people/eric-manigaud/artist.

38. As quoted in Manigaud (2021), with my translation from French into English.

CHAPTER 4. THE AFTERLIFE OF A DEATH

1. The photograph that shows Bennahar's face, in Einaudi's *La bataille de Paris* (2001, 354), appears as figure 1.14 in the present work. The photo in Einaudi's book is a slightly cropped version of the photograph shown here, with the cropping serving to omit the eyes of the hospital attendant standing behind Bennahar, who is being seated in the wheelchair—thereby rendering anonymous the personal identity of this attendant.

2. My summary of the events of 18 October 1961 in and around Paris is drawn directly from the account found in House and MacMaster (2006, 125–26).

3. Einaudi (2001, 215), quoting from the Archives du Ministère de la Justice: "Vers 22 heures, à Colombes, BELKACEMI Achour, né le 27 aout 1931 à Haussonvilliers (Tizi-Ouzou), est tué par balles par un policier. L'autopsie établira qu'il a été atteint par trois coups de feu dans le thorax."

4. Einaudi (2001, 216), quoting from the Archives of the Prefecture of the Police of Paris.

5. Einaudi (2001, 216), quoting from the archives of the Paris police. My account here includes the added last sentence that appears in Brunet (1999, 259); up to "qui etait en protection de son gradé" (who was protecting his officer) is in Einaudi (2011, 350).

6. Einaudi (2011, 351–52), drawing from a text he cites as "Témoignage de Raoul Letard recueilli dans le cadre de l'Institut des hautes études de la sécurité intérieure" (Testimony of Raoul Letard, interviewed for the Institut des Hautes Études de la Sécurité Intérieure). Einaudi notes: "Ce témoignage—encore inédit—a été recueilli dans le cadre d'une enquête de l'Ihesi (Institut des hautes études de la sécurité intérieure) (This testimony, as yet unpublished, was gathered as part of an investigation by the IHESI [Institut des Hautes Études de la Sécurité Intérieure])" (352). See also House and MacMaster (2008); Dewerpe (2006).

7. See also House and MacMaster (2008).

8. See also Dewerpe (2006).

9. As quoted in Einaudi (2011, 351).

10. As quoted in Brunet (1999, 259).

11. "Deux morts à Colombes," *Le Monde*, 20 October 1961.

12. See Blanchard (2011) on the use of national identity cards in France from 1944 to 1962, and the ways in which the police tried to "know, count, identify" Algerians residing

in France, in what was sometimes perceived as "milieu impenetrable," an impenetrable environment (217).

13. The term *non-lieu*, "nonplace," has also emerged as a concept that refers to empty, vacant spaces in modern urban existence, such as the terrain beneath a highway overpass, or an abandoned lot, that can then lie fallow and unused, or be used for various purposes not assigned by the state or urban planners—such as encampments created by homeless persons or squatters, or spaces of free art, or illicit activities (see Augé 2009, for instance).

14. As noted as well by House and MacMaster (2006, 162).

15. Einaudi (2011, 353), drawing from the "Registre de l'I.M.L." See also Boss (1999, 2022).

16. See also Boss (1999, 2022).

17. Mourning, Derrida (1994, 9) contends, "consists always in attempting to ontologize remains, to make them present, in the first place by *identifying* the bodily remains and by *localizing* the dead."

18. To echo Ranjana Khanna's (2020, 411) reflection on writings by Sigmund Freud and Jacques Derrida on modern forms of death: "Together, the essays ask about what phantasm it is necessary to grasp in order to tolerate death, or indeed the projected image of one's own death." And elsewhere: "Figuration is, in fact, what makes the corpse tolerable" (410).

19. See also Desjarlais (2019) for a reflection on this passage and on themes of life, death, and writing in Feraoun's wartime journal more generally.

20. See also Britton (1999).

CHAPTER 5. TRACEWORK

1. See Richard Cobb's *Death in Paris* (1978) for a compelling historical account of Parisian life and death in the late nineteenth century, as drawn from the records of the Basse-Geôle de la Seine, in which morgue records and inscriptions and descriptions of articles found on the bodies of deceased persons, such as buttons, reflected the circumstances of the living and the dead at that time.

2. See Derrida (1996, 2–3), for instance.

3. Hunt (2016, 31), citing Benjamin (1999a, 545).

4. As Sarah Nuttall (2002, 299) paraphrases Mbembe's argument.

5. The phrases "the gaze of a certain male science" and "a body was made to signify" are drawn from Francis Barker's (1995, 65) compelling analysis of Rembrandt's *The Anatomy Lesson of Dr. Nicolaes Tulp* (1632), an analysis that argues that the aesthetic and implicit political arrangements of this painting, in which several men are shown observing a doctor's dissection of the corpse of a petty thief who had hours before been condemned to death, articulates a "regime of subjectification" evident in modern forms of subjectivity and corporeality.

6. The idea that a corpse is "strange like an image is strange" corresponds to Maurice Blanchot's thought, in *The Space of Literature*, that "the image does not, at first glance, resemble the corpse, but the cadaver's strangeness is perhaps also that of the image. What

we call mortal remains escapes common categories. Something is there before us which is not really the living person, nor is it any reality at all. It is neither the same as the person who was alive, nor is it another person, nor is it anything else. What is there, with the absolute calm of something that has found its place, does not, however, succeed in being convincingly here" (Blanchot 1982, 256).

7. As Khalil Habrih has made clear to me (personal communication).

8. As Jim House (2001, 358) notes, "There was a well-established security force policy of 'anonymising' those Algerians it had killed, removing all distinguishing papers and belongings." See also Einaudi (1991, 230–32). House (2001, 358) contends that this "anonymization" of many of the Algerians killed by Paris police was one reason that it was difficult to establish collectively the state violence as a clearly remembered event. House cites a point made by anthropologist David Le Breton: "It is socially absurd to conceive of faceless men who can be remembered" (*il est socialement absurde de concevoir des hommes sans visage dont on puisse se souvenir*) (Le Breton 1992, 201). In this respect, the *inconnus* noted in the IML register for 1961 can be said to metonymically stand in for the many unidentified and untraced bodies of those killed by the Paris police that year and other years.

9. House and MacMaster (2008, 212) note, "Police death squads stripped many dozens of Algerians of identification, tipped them into rivers and canals so that by the time of eventual recovery of corpses individuals were no longer recognizable. These deaths were then falsely reported as being the result of internecine violence."

10. One might also say that these were images of ruin. As Eduardo Cadava (1997, 35) writes of such images, "There can be no image that is not about destruction and survival, and this is especially the case in the image of ruin. We might even say that the image of ruin tells us what is true of every image: that it bears witness to the enigmatic relation between death and survival, loss and life, destruction and preservation, mourning and memory." See also Cadava (2021).

11. Roland Barthes (1981), for one, has written on the ways in which death is an integral part of the phenomenology and ontology of photographs. See also Sontag (1977).

12. On this, see Ruby (1999).

13. Bertillon (1893, xiii); translation by Sekula (1986, 25).

14. The writer was Ernest Cherbuliez. See Schwartz (1999, 59).

15. Clovis Pierre, *Les gaietés de la morgue* (1895), as cited in Schwartz (1999, 61).

16. On the etymology and evolving definitions of the word *autopsy*, see the *Oxford English Dictionary* (1989, 1:808).

17. To cite a theme and the title of chapter 8 in Michel Foucault's *The Birth of the Clinic* (1973).

18. On this, see Schwartz (1999, 58).

19. As Derrida observes in his book *Archive Fever* (1996).

20. On photography and touch: Elizabeth Edwards and Janice Hart's (2004, 1) anthropological study of photography considers photographs as material physical objects "enmeshed with subjective, embodied and sensuous interactions," in which photography is not simply a medium of visuality but also one of touch; Laura Marks (2000, 2002) focuses on "haptic visuality" as an alternative mode of viewing in the analysis of film

and video; and Tina M. Campt (2012, 34) undertakes a reading of archival photographs of the African diaspora in Europe "through the sensory register of the haptic," as well as "haptic temporalities." Here, Campt seeks "to connect the visuality of images to the multiple ways that we touch photos and they in turn touch us to highlight important dimensions of racial formation and the deeply affective imbrications between race and gender, nation and family, domesticity and diaspora." See also Campt (2017).

21. On the anxious complications of looking and not-looking when faced with the presence of a corpse, see the perceptive analyses by Sarah Kofman (2007) and Francis Barker (1995) of forms of looking and not looking implicit in Rembrandt's painting *The Anatomy Lesson of Dr. Nicolaes Tulp*, in which none of the six esteemed doctors shown observing the anatomical dissection conducted by Professor Tulp are actually looking at the cadaver. Their gazes are trained instead on a book, presumably an anatomy textbook, set below the foot of the prone body.

22. The phrase "inaccessible depth" comes from a passage in Sarah Kofman's (2007, 237) essay "Conjuring Death."

23. A similar kind of question has been raised among scholars working with archives that reflect conditions of slavery and terror and the subjugation of Black persons in the United States and elsewhere. In *Scenes of Subjection*, Saidiya Hartman explores archives of slavery and terror in the United States to document the pain and hardship of slavery as well as strategies of survival and fugitivity among persons cast as slaves. In the preface to the 25th-anniversary edition of this book, Hartman (2022, xxxvii) reflects on her work with the archives by noting, "In *Scenes*, I first wrestled with questions of the archive— what it enabled and what it prevented us from knowing or discerning. Could I use its statements, yet destroy the master's tools?" In *Listening to Images*, Tina M. Campt (2017, 5) shows the ways in which the "quiet" photographic artifacts of governmental practices—such as mug shots, prison photographs, and passport photos—reflect both "the sovereign gaze of the regimes" that created the images and acts of refusal, fugitivity, and the affective registers of life, dignity, and creative vitality among those portrayed in the photographs. Or, as Fred Moten (2003, 1) puts it at the start of *In the Break*, "The history of blackness is testament to the fact that objects can and do resist."

24. Einaudi notes the cemetery division on page 488 of the 2011 edition of *17 Octobre 1961: Un massacre à Paris*, along with the names of the other eight men buried there that day.

25. "Cimetières," Paris Archives, http://archives.paris.fr/r/216/cimetieres/.

26. Cf. Scott (1998).

27. On Islamic customs and practices of death, funeral rites, and burial, see Cornell (2007).

28. As Jill Stauffer (2015, 1) conveys it in her book *Ethical Loneliness*, "Ethical loneliness is the experience of having been abandoned by humanity compounded by the experience of not being heard." I was not aware of this distinct concept when I was at the cemetery that day, or while working on the list of names, though it is an idea to which I can intuitively relate.

29. See Ruin (2018) on the idea of "being with the dead" as a fundamental aspect of human existence and society, as well as being integral to historical consciousness and human history and historiography.

30. See Shepard (2006) on the history and complicated implications of the term and political status of *Français Musulman d'Algérie* and *citoyens français musulmans d'Algérie* in the years leading up to Algeria's independence from French rule.

31. On the Harkis in Algeria and in France, see Crapanzano (2011), as well as Zahia Rahmani's (2016) powerful novel *Moze*.

CHAPTER 6. THE SPECTRALITY OF REMNANTS

1. The language of this passage stems from some writing I undertook during an online meeting of a "spectrality working group" that I have been participating in since 2021. Amy McLachlan, the lead organizer of this group, proposed a prompt for the writing session, in which each person in the group wrote on their own for several minutes. The prompt was, *"And if it is already ended? And if it never ends? Summon an object of mourning in your work (yours, others, absent)."*

2. Here it's worth noting the title of a book by Hervé Guibert, *Ghost Image* (1996).

3. On the idea of "spectral phenomenology," see Desjarlais and Habrih (2022).

4. To draw from Derrida's writing in the "exordium" of *Specters of Marx* (1994, xvii–xviii). As I have commented on these words elsewhere, in a coauthored work,

> I take this to mean there is political value in cultivating a sense of the spectral, haunting qualities of life and recognizing in careful, attentive ways, histories of violence and terror. In learning to live with ghosts one can engage with the complexities of the past, present, and future, maintain a sense of multiply haunted, haunting histories, and be aware of the complex intertwinements of the actual and the phantasmal of life-death. This being with specters, in thought and in writing, and in life more generally, can thus also be an ethics, for it offers a way to live in the world, to relate to others, recognize the histories of the dead and the wounded, remember the past and make sense of the present. This spectral awareness, this being with ghosts, can be a daunting, nearly overwhelming one. (Desjarlais and Habrih 2022, 184)

5. "Hauntology" is Derrida's word for the study of ghosts and hauntings, which riffs on the fact that, in French, the word *hauntologie* would be pronounced the same way as the word *ontologie* (1994, 10). On recent anthropological approaches to ghosts, haunting, hauntology, and spectrality, see, for instance, Kilroy-Marac (2019); Klima (2019); Good and Rahimi (2019); Rahimi (2021); Good, Chiovenda, and Rahimi (2022); and Desjarlais and Habrih (2022). See also Gordon (2008) and Tuck and Ree (2013).

6. An earlier version of the text found in this section of chapter 6 ("No Ghost to Him") appears as a brief text with the same title in an online publication with *Allegra Lab* (Desjarlais 2023). Thanks go to Aja Smith and Anne Line Dalsgård for making this collection on "Building Bodies of Thought" possible, and for their insightful reflections on my contribution.

7. See, for instance, Levinas (1991), Waldenfels (2011), Hollan and Throop (2011), and Leistle (2016, 2017).

8. I greatly appreciate conversations with Aurora Donzelli in helping me to think through the intricate linguistic and semiotic ideas conveyed in these pages.

9. Thanks go to Khalil Habrih for bringing this poem to my attention.

10. To paraphrase Butler (2004, 131).

11. As noted by Butler (2004, 133–34).

12. The idea of "capturing" a human being through representations comes from Levinas and Butler. To quote Butler (2004, 144–45) on this subject, "Something altogether different happens, however, when the face operates in the service of personification that claims to 'capture' the human being in question. For Levinas, the human cannot be captured through the representation, and we can see that some loss of the human takes place when it is 'captured' by the image."

13. See also Silverman (2009).

References

FILMS

Adi, Yasmina, dir. 2011. *Ici on noie les Algériens*. Agat Films and Cie.

Brooks, Philip, and Alan Hayling, dirs. 1991. *Drowning by Bullets*. Icarus Films.

Brooks, Philip, and Alan Hayling, dirs. 1992. *Une journée portée disparue*. Point du Jour.

Denis, Agnês, and Mehdi Lallaoui, dirs. 1991. *Le silence du fleuve*. Au Nom de la Mémoire.

Krief, Jean-Pierre, dir. 1989. *Les années Kagan*. KS Visions.

Marker, Chris, dir. 1983. *Sans Soleil*. Argos Films.

Panijel, Jacques, dir. 1962. *Octobre à Paris*. Les Filmes de l'Atlantle.

LITERATURE AND SCHOLARSHIP

Abdallah, Mogniss H. 2000. "Le 17 Octobre 1961 et les médias: De la couverture immédiate au 'travail de memoire.'" *Hommes et Migrations* 1228: 125–33.

Adorno, Theodor. (1936) 2002. "Marginalia on Mahler." In *Essays on Music*, edited by Richard Leppert, 612–18. Berkeley: University of California Press.

Adorno, Theodor. 2000. "The Actuality of Philosophy." In *The Adorno Reader*, edited by Brian O'Connor. Oxford: Blackwell.

Agamben, Giorgio. 1998. *Homo Sacer: Sovereign Power and Bare Life*. Stanford, CA: Stanford University Press.

Allen, James, ed. 2000. *Without Sanctuary: Lynching Photography in America*. Santa Fe, NM: Twin Palms.

Altez-Albela, Fleurdeliz R. 2011. "The Body and Transcendence in Emmanuel Levinas' Phenomenological Ethics." *Kritike* 5 (1): 36–50.

Appadurai, Arjun, ed. 1988. *The Social Life of Things: Commodities in Cultural Perspective*. Cambridge: Cambridge University Press.

Aranke, Sampada. 2023. *Death's Futurity: The Visual Life of Black Power*. Durham, NC: Duke University Press.

Arendt, Hannah. 1966. Introduction to *Auschwitz: A Report on the Proceedings Against Robert Karl Ludwig Mulka and Others Before the Court at Frankfurt*, by Bernd Naumann, ix–xxx. London: Pall Mall Press.

Augé, Marc. 2009. *Non-Places: An Introduction to Supermodernity*. New York: Verso.

Azoulay, Ariella. 2008. *The Civil Contract of Photography*. New York: Zone Books.

Azoulay, Ariella. 2015. *Civil Imagination: A Political Ontology of Photography*. London: Verso.

Azoulay, Ariella. 2016. "Photographic Archives and Archival Entities." In *Image Operations: Visual Media and Political Conflict*, edited by Jens Eder and Charlotte Klonk. Manchester: Manchester University Press.

Azoulay, Ariella. 2017. "Archive." *Political Concepts: A Critical Lexicon* 1. https://www.politicalconcepts.org/archive-ariella-azoulay.

Azoulay, Ariella Aïsha. 2019. *Potential History: Unlearning Imperialism*. London: Verso.

Baer, Ulrich. 2005. *Spectral Evidence: The Photography of Trauma*. Cambridge, MA: MIT Press.

Bailly, Jean-Christophe. 2020. *The Instant and Its Shadow: A Story of Photography*. New York: Fordham University Press.

Baker, Courtney. 2015. *Humane Insight: Looking at Images of African American Suffering and Death*. Urbana: University of Illinois Press.

Barbash, Ilisa, Molly Rogers, and Deborah Willis, eds. 2020. *To Make Their Own Way in the World: The Enduring Legacy of the Zealy Daguerreotypes*. Cambridge, MA: Peabody Museum Press.

Barker, Francis. 1995. *The Tremulous Private Body: Essays on Subjection*. Ann Arbor: University of Michigan Press.

Barthes, Roland. 1976. *Sade, Fourier, Loyola*. New York: Hill and Wang.

Barthes, Roland. 1978. *A Lover's Discourse: Fragments*. New York: Hill and Wang.

Barthes, Roland. 1981. *Camera Lucida: Reflections on Photography*. New York: Hill and Wang.

Barthes, Roland. 1989. "The Reality Effect." In *The Rustle of Language*. Berkeley: University of California Press.

Baudelaire, Charles. 1993. *The Flowers of Evil*. Oxford: Oxford University Press.

Bazin, André. 1960. "The Ontology of the Photographic Image." *Film Quarterly* 13 (4): 4–9.

Bellour, Raymond. 2012. *Between-the-Images*. Zurich: JRP Ringier.

Benaï, Yamina. 2018. "Vincent Sator: 'Révéler un pan meconnu du l'Histoire.'" *L'Officiel*, May.

Benayoun, Catherine. 1999. "Photopsie d'un Massacre," *Hommes et Migrations* 1219: 65–67.

Benjamin, Walter. 1999a. *The Arcades Project*. Cambridge, MA: Harvard University Press.

Benjamin, Walter. 1999b. *Selected Writings, Volume 2, Part 2, 1931–1934*, edited by Michael W. Jennings, Howard Eiland, and Gary Smith. Cambridge, MA: Belknap Press of Harvard University Press.

Benveniste, Émile. 1971. *Problems in General Linguistics*. Coral Gables, FL: University of Miami Press.

Bertillon, Alphonse. 1893. *Identification anthropometric: Instructions signalétiques*. Paris: Melun.

Blanchard, Emmanuel. 2011. *La police parisienne et les Algériens (1944–1962)*. Paris: Nouveau Monde.

Blanchot, Maurice. 1982. *The Space of Literature*. Lincoln: University of Nebraska Press.

Blanchot, Maurice. 1995. *The Work of Fire*. Stanford, CA: Stanford University Press.

Blanchot, Maurice, and Jacques Derrida. 2000. *The Instant of My Death/Demeure: Fiction and Testimony*. Stanford, CA: Stanford University Press.

Boss, Pauline. 1999. *Ambiguous Loss: Living with Frozen Grief*. Cambridge, MA: Harvard University Press.

Boss, Pauline. 2022. *The Myth of Closure: Ambiguous Loss in a Time of Pandemic and Change*. New York: Norton.

Brecht, Bertolt. 2003. *Poetry and Prose*. The German Library 75. New York: Continuum.

Britton, Celia. 1999. *Edouard Glissant and Postcolonial Theory: Strategies of Language and Resistance*. Charlottesville: University Press of Virginia.

Brozgal, Lia. 2020. *Absent the Archive: Cultural Traces of a Massacre in Paris, 17 October 1961*. Liverpool: Liverpool University Press.

Brunet, Jean-Paul. 1999. *Police contre FLN: Le drame d'Octobre 1961*. Paris: Flammarion.

Buck-Morss, Susan. 1992. "Aesthetics and Anaesthetics: Walter Benjamin's Artwork Essay Reconsidered." *October* 62: 3–41.

Burté, Cyril, and Audrey Leblanc. 2022. *Élie Kagan: Photographe indépendant 1960–1990*. Paris: Lienart Éditions.

Butler, Judith. 2004. *Precarious Life: The Powers of Mourning and Violence*. London: Verso.

Cadava, Eduardo. 1997. *Words of Light: Theses on the Photography of History*. Princeton, NJ: Princeton University Press.

Cadava, Eduardo. 2021. *Paper Graveyards*. Cambridge, MA: MIT Press.

Campt, Tina M. 2012. *Image Matters: Archive, Photography, and the African Diaspora in Europe*. Durham, NC: Duke University Press.

Campt, Tina M. 2017. *Listening to Images*. Durham, NC: Duke University Press.

Camus, Albert. (1942) 1989. *The Stranger*. New York: Vintage International.

Carrard, Philippe. 2017. *History as a Kind of Writing: Textual Strategies in Contemporary French Historiography*. Chicago: University of Chicago Press.

Caruth, Cathy. 1996. *Trauma: Explorations in Memory*. Baltimore: Johns Hopkins University Press.

Cercas, Javier. 2020. *Lord of All the Dead*. New York: Knopf.

Chakrabarty, Dipesh. 2007. "History and the Politics of Recognition." In *Manifestos for History*, edited by Keith Jenkins, Sue Morgan, and Alun Munsow. New York: Routledge.

Cixous, Hélène. 2005. *Stigmata*. London: Routledge.

Cobb, Richard. 1978. *Death in Paris: The Records of the Basse-Geôle de la Seine, October 1795–September 1801*. Oxford: Oxford University Press.

Cole, Joshua. 2003. "Remembering the Battle of Paris: 17 October 1961 in French and Algerian Memory." *French Politics, Culture and Society* 21 (3): 21–50.

Cole, Joshua. 2006. "Entering History: The Memory of Police Violence in Paris, October 1961." In *Algeria and France 1800–2000: Identity, Memory, Nostalgia*, edited by Patricia M. E. Lorcin, 117–34. Syracuse, NY: Syracuse University Press.

Corbin, Alain. 2001. *The Life of an Unknown: The Rediscovered World of a Clog Maker in Nineteenth-Century France*. New York: Columbia University Press.

Cornell, Rkia Elaroui. 2007. "Death and Burial in Islam." In *Voices of Islam*, vol. 3, *Voices of Life: Family, Home, and Society*, edited by Vincent Cornell and Virginia Gray Henry-Blakemore. Westport, CT: Praeger.

Crapanzano, Vincent. 1980. *Tuhami: Portrait of a Moroccan*. Chicago: University of Chicago Press.

Crapanzano, Vincent. 2011. *The Harkis: The Wound That Never Heals*. Chicago: University of Chicago Press.

Crocker, Rebecca, Robin Reineke, and María Elena Ramos Tovar. 2021. "Ambiguous Loss and Embodied Grief Related to Mexican Migrant Disappearances." *Medical Anthropology* 40 (7): 598–611.

Daeninckx, Didier. 1984. *Meurtres pour mémoire*. Paris: Gallimard.

Daeninckx, Didier. 2012. *Murder in Memoriam*. New York: Melville International Crime.

Darnton, Robert. 1985. *The Great Cat Massacre and Other Episodes in French Cultural History*. New York: Vintage Books.

Davis, Natalie Zemon. 1983. *The Return of Martin Guerre*. Cambridge, MA: Harvard University Press.

Davis, Natalie Zemon. 1988. "On the Lame." *American Historical Review* 93 (3): 572–603.

De Cauwer, Stijn, and Laura Katherine Smith. 2020. Foreword to *Critical Image Configurations: The Work of Georges Didi-Huberman*, edited by Stijn De Cauwer and Laura Katherine Smith, 1–2. London: Routledge.

Deleuze, Gilles. 1989. *Cinema 2: The Time Image*. Minneapolis: University of Minnesota Press.

Deleuze, Gilles, and Félix Guattari. 1994. *What Is Philosophy?* New York: Columbia University Press.

Derrida, Jacques. 1981. *Dissemination*. Chicago: University of Chicago Press.

Derrida, Jacques. 1984. "No Apocalypse, Not Now (Full Speed Ahead, Seven Missiles, Seven Missives)." *Diacritics* 14 (2): 20–31.

Derrida, Jacques. 1985. *The Ear of the Other: Otobiography, Transference, Translation*. New York: Schocken.

Derrida, Jacques. 1987. *The Postcard: From Socrates to Freud and Beyond*. Chicago: University of Chicago Press.

Derrida, Jacques. 1988. *Limited Inc*. Evanston, IL: Northwestern University Press.

Derrida, Jacques. 1993. "Circumfession." In *Jacques Derrida*, by Geoffrey Bennington and Jacques Derrida. Chicago: University of Chicago Press.

Derrida, Jacques. 1994. *Specters of Marx: The State of the Debt, the Work of Mourning, and the New International*. New York: Routledge.

Derrida, Jacques. 1995. "The Time Is Out of Joint." In *Deconstruction Is/In America: A New Sense of the Political*, edited by Anselm Haverkamp. New York: New York University Press.

Derrida, Jacques. 1996. *Archive Fever: A Freudian Impression*. Chicago: University of Chicago Press.

Derrida, Jacques. 2001. *The Work of Mourning*. Chicago: University of Chicago Press.

Derrida, Jacques. 2008. *The Animal That Therefore I Am*. New York: Fordham University Press.

Derrida, Jacques. 2011. *The Beast and the Sovereign*. Vol. 2. Chicago: University of Chicago Press.

Derrida, Jacques. 2020. *Life Death*. Chicago: University of Chicago Press.

Desjarlais, Robert. 2003. *Sensory Biographies: Lives and Deaths among Nepal's Yolmo Buddhists*. Berkeley: University of California Press.

Desjarlais, Robert. 2018. *The Blind Man: A Phantasmography*. New York: Fordham University Press.

Desjarlais, Robert. 2019. "And Other Deaths Have Followed . . . (with Mouloud Feraoun)." *Comparative and Continental Philosophy* 11 (2): 198–213.

Desjarlais, Robert. 2020. *Sur les traces de violence: Un essai anthropologique après les attentats de Paris*. Paris: Presses Universitaires de Paris Nanterre.

Desjarlais, Robert. 2023. "No Ghost to Him." In "Building Bodies for Thought," edited by Aja Smith and Anne Line Dalsgård. *Allegra Lab*. https://allegralaboratory.net /section-four-whose-thinking/.

Desjarlais, Robert, and Khalil Habrih. 2022. *Traces of Violence: Writings on the Disaster in Paris, France*. Berkeley: University of California Press.

Dewachi, Omar. 2015. "When Wounds Travel." *Medicine Anthropology Theory* 2 (3): 61–82.

Dewerpe, Alain. 2006. *Charonne 8 février 1962: Anthropologie historique d'un massacre d'état*. Paris: Gallimard.

Didi-Huberman, Georges. 2004. *Invention of Hysteria: Charcot and the Photographic Iconography of the Salpêtrière*. Cambridge, MA: MIT Press.

Didi-Huberman, Georges. 2006. "L'image brûle." In *Penser par les images: Autour des travaux de Georges Didi-Huberman*, edited by Laurent Zimmermann, 11–52. Nantes: Cécile Defaut.

Didi-Huberman, Georges. 2008. *Images in Spite of All: Four Photographs from Auschwitz*. Chicago: University of Chicago Press.

Didi-Huberman, Georges. 2013. *Phalènes*. Paris: Les Éditions de Minuit.

Didi-Huberman, Georges. 2015. "Knowing When to Cut." In *Foucault Against Himself*, edited by François Caillat. Vancouver: Arsenal Pulp Press.

Didi-Huberman, Georges. 2017a. *Bark*. Cambridge, MA: MIT Press.

Didi-Huberman, Georges. 2017b. *The Surviving Image: Phantoms of Time and Time of Phantoms: Aby Warburg's History of Art*. University Park: Pennsylvania State University Press.

Didi-Huberman, Georges. 2018a. *Aperçues*. Paris: Les Éditions de Minuit.

Didi-Huberman, Georges. 2018b. *The Eye of History: When Images Take Positions*. Cambridge, MA: MIT Press.

Didi-Huberman, Georges. 2018c. *Survival of the Fireflies*. Minneapolis: University of Minnesota Press.

Didi-Huberman, Georges. 2020. "Image, Language: The Other Dialectic." In *Critical Image Configurations: The Work of Georges Didi-Huberman*, edited by Stijn De Cauwer and Laura Katherine Smith. London: Routledge.

Dondero, Maria Giulia. 2020. *The Language of Images: The Forms and the Forces*. Cham, Switzerland: Springer.

Douglass, Frederick. 1845. *Narrative of the Life of Frederick Douglass, an American Slave. Written by Himself*. Boston: Anti-Slavery Office. Reprint, New York: New American Library, 1968.

Edwards, Elizabeth. 2001. *Raw Histories: Photographs, Anthropology and Museums*. Oxford: Berg.

Edwards, Elizabeth, and Janice Hart, eds. 2004. *Photographies Objects Histories: On the Materiality of Images*. New York: Routledge.

Einaudi, Jean-Luc. 1991. *La bataille de Paris: 17 Octobre 1961*. Paris: Éditions du Seuil.

Einaudi, Jean-Luc. 2001. *Octobre 1961: Un massacre à Paris*. Paris: Fayard.

Einaudi, Jean-Luc. 2002. "Octobre 1961 ou la solitude des Algériens." In *Des Français contre la terreur d'état: Algérie 1954–1962*, edited by Sidi Mohammed Barkat. Paris: Éditions Reflex.

Einaudi, Jean-Luc. 2009. *Scènes de la guerre d'Algérie en France: Automne 1961*. Paris: Le Cherche Midi.

Einaudi, Jean-Luc. 2011. *Octobre 1961: Un massacre à Paris*. Paris: Fayard.

Einaudi, Jean-Luc, and Élie Kagan. 2001. *17 Octobre 1961*. Arles: Actes Sud.

Fanon, Frantz. (1961) 2005. *The Wretched of the Earth*. New York: Grove.

Farès, Nabile. 2020. *Exile and Helplessness*. New Orleans: Diálogos Books.

Farge, Arlette. 1989. *Le gout des archives*. Paris: Éditions du Seuil.

Farge, Arlette. 2013. *The Allure of the Archives*. New Haven, CT: Yale University Press.

Favret-Saada, Jeanne. 1980. *Deadly Words: Witchcraft in the Bocage*. New York: Cambridge University Press.

Feldman, Allen. 1994. "On Cultural Anesthesia: From Desert Storm to Rodney King." *American Ethnologist* 21 (2): 404–18.

Feldman, Hannah. 2014. *From a Nation Torn: Decolonizing Art and Representation in France, 1945–1962*. Durham, NC: Duke University Press.

Feraoun, Mouloud. 2000. *Journal 1955–1962*. Lincoln: University of Nebraska Press.

Fleetwood, Nicole. 2011. *Troubling Vision: Performance, Visuality, and Blackness*. Chicago: University of Chicago Press.

Fletcher, John. 2013. *Freud and the Scene of Trauma*. New York: Fordham University Press.

Foucault, Michel. 1973. *The Birth of the Clinic*. New York: Routledge.

Foucault, Michel. 1995. *Discipline and Punish: The Birth of the Prison*. New York: Vintage Books.

Gallagher, Catherine, and Stephen Greenblatt. 2000. *Practicing New Historicism*. Chicago: University of Chicago Press.

Gausset, Quentin. 2010. *Constructing the Kwanja of Adamawa (Cameroon): Essay in Fractal Anthropology*. Ethnologie 18. Berlin: Lit.

Geertz, Clifford. 1973. *The Interpretation of Cultures*. New York: Basic Books.

Gerrin, Michel. 1999. "Kagan, un photographe engagé et libre." *Le Monde*, January 27, 1999.

Ginzburg, Carlo. 1980. *The Cheese and the Worms: The Cosmos of a Sixteenth-Century Miller*. London: Routledge and Kegal Paul.

Ginzburg, Carlo. 1989. *Clues, Myths, and the Historical Method*. Baltimore: Johns Hopkins University Press.

Ginzburg, Carlo. 2012. *Threads and Traces: True, False, Fictive*. Berkeley: University of California Press.

Glissant, Édouard. 1990. *Poétique de la Relation*. Paris: Gallimard.

Glissant, Édouard. 1997a. *Poetics of Relation*. Minneapolis: University of Minnesota Press.

Glissant, Édouard. 1997b. *Traité du tout-monde*. Paris: Gallimard.

Glissant, Édouard. 2010. *Poetic Intention*. Callicoon, NY: Nightboat Books.

Golsan, Richard, ed. 2000. *The Papon Affair: Memory and Justice on Trial*. London: Routledge.

Good, Byron, Andrea Chiovenda, and Sadeq Rahimi. 2022. "The Anthropology of Being Haunted: On the Emergence of an Anthropological Hauntology." *Annual Review of Anthropology* 51: 437–53.

Good, Byron, and Sadeq Rahimi, eds. 2019. "Special Thematic Collection: Hauntology in Psychological Anthropology." *Ethos* 47 (4): 407–529.

Gordon, Avery. 2008. *Ghostly Matters: Haunting and the Sociological Imagination*. Minneapolis: University of Minnesota Press.

Guibert, Hervé. 1996. *Ghost Image*. Los Angeles: Sun and Moon Press.

Gürsel, Zeynep Devrim. 2016. *Image Brokers: Visualizing World News in the Age of Digital Circulation*. Berkeley: University of California Press.

Hagerty, Alexa. 2023. *Still Life with Bones: Genocide, Forensics, and What Remains*. New York: Crown.

Haroun, Ali. 1986. *La 7e Wilaya: La Guerre du FLN en France 1954–1962*. Paris: Seuil.

Hartman, Saidiya. 1997. *Scenes of Subjection: Terror, Slavery, and Nineteenth-Century America*. New York: Norton.

Hartman, Saidiya. 2007. *Lose Your Mother: A Journey Along the Atlantic Slave Route*. New York: Farrar, Straus and Giroux.

Hartman, Saidiya. 2008. "Venus in Two Acts." *Small Axe* 12 (2): 1–14.

Hartman, Saidiya. 2019. *Wayward Lives, Beautiful Experiments: Intimate Histories of Social Upheaval*. New York: Norton.

Hartman, Saidiya. 2022. *Scenes of Subjection: Terror, Slavery, and Nineteenth-Century America*. Rev. ed. New York: Norton.

Hartman, Saidiya, and Max Nelson. 2022. "The Tragic Mode: Saidiya Hartman, Interviewed by Max Nelson." *New York Review*, November 19, 2022.

Hervo, Monique. 2012. *Nanterre en Guerre d'Algérie: Chroniques du bidonville, 1959–1962*. Paris: Actes Sud.

Hollan, Douglas W., and C. Jason Throop, eds. 2011. *The Anthropology of Empathy: Experiencing the Lives of Others in Pacific Societies*. New York: Berghahn.

Hopkinson, Amanda. 1999. "Camera Campaign" (Élie Kagan obituary). *Guardian*, April 13, 1999.

House, Jim. 2001. "Antiracist Memories: The Case of 17 October 1961 in Historical Perspective." *Modern and Contemporary France* 9 (3): 355–68.

House, Jim. 2010. "Memory and the Creation of Solidarity During the Decolonization of Algeria." *Yale French Studies* 118–19: 15–38.

House, Jim, and Neil MacMaster. 2006. *Paris 1961: Algerians, State Terror, and Memory*. Oxford: Oxford University Press.

House, Jim, and Neil MacMaster. 2008. "Time to Move On: A Reply to Jean-Paul Brunet." *Historical Journal* 51 (1): 205–14.

Hunt, Nancy Rose. 2016. *A Nervous State: Violence, Remedies, and Reverie in Colonial Congo*. Durham, NC: Duke University Press.

Jablonka, Ivan. 2016. *A History of the Grandparents I Never Had*. Stanford, CA: Stanford University Press.

Jablonka, Ivan. 2018. *History Is a Contemporary Literature: Manifesto for the Social Sciences*. Ithaca, NY: Cornell University Press.

Jamison, Leslie. 2014. "Grand Unified Theory of Female Pain." *Virginia Quarterly Review* 90 (2): 114–28.

Jarvis, Jill. 2021. *Decolonizing Memory: Algeria and the Politics of Testimony*. Durham, NC: Duke University Press.

Johnson, Douglas. 1999. "Obituary: Elie Kagan." *The Independent*, February 15, 1999. https://www.the-independent.com/arts-entertainment/obituary-elie-kagan-1071155.html.

Jones, Colin. 2021. *The Fall of Robespierre: 24 Hours in Revolutionary Paris*. Oxford: Oxford University Press.

Kagan, Élie, and Patrick Rotman. 1989. *Le reporter engagé: Trente ans d'instantanés*. Paris: Métailié.

Khanna, Ranjana. 2020. "Touching the Corpse: Reading Sinan Antoon." *New Literary History* 51 (2): 401–18.

Khatibi, Abdelkébir. 2019. *Plural Maghreb: Writings on Postcolonialism*. London: Bloomsbury Academic.

Kilroy-Marac, Katie. 2019. *An Impossible Inheritance: Postcolonial Psychiatry and the Work of Memory in a West African Clinic*. Berkeley: University of California Press.

Kittler, Friedrich. 1999. *Gramophone, Film, Typewriter*. Stanford, CA: Stanford University Press.

Klima, Alan. 2019. *Ethnography #9*. Durham, NC: Duke University Press.

Kofman, Sarah. 2007. "Conjuring Death: Remarks on *The Anatomy Lesson of Doctor Nicolas Tulp* (1632)." In *Selected Writings*, edited by Thomas Albrecht, 237–41. Stanford, CA: Stanford University Press.

Lachenal, Guillaume. 2022. *The Doctor Who Would Be King*. Durham, NC: Duke University Press.

Landru, Philippe. 2009. "THIAS (94): Cimetière parisien." Cimetières de France et d'ailleurs. https://www.landrucimetieres.fr/spip/spip.php?article1858.

Laplanche, Jean, and Jean-Bertrand Pontalis. 1988. *The Language of Psychoanalysis*. New York: Norton.

Laqueur, Thomas W. 2015. *The Work of the Dead: A Cultural History of Mortal Remains*. Princeton, NJ: Princeton University Press.

Latour, Bruno. 1996. "On Actor-Network Theory: A Few Clarifications." *Soziale Welt* 4 (4): 369–81.

Lebas, Clotilde. 2007. "Au fil de nos souvenirs: Le 17 Octobre 1961, emblème des violences policières." *Revue des mondes musulmans et de la Méditerranée* 119–20: 233–48. https://doi.org/10.4000/remmm.4293.

Leblanc, Audrey. 2022. "Élie Kagan: Photographe de presse indépendant." In *Élie Kagan: Photographe indépendant 1960–1990*, edited by Cyril Burté and Audrey Leblanc. Paris: Lienart Éditions.

Le Breton, David. 1992. *Des visages: Essai d'anthropologie*. Paris: Éditions Métailié.

Leistle, Bernhard. 2016. "Responsivity and (Some) Other Approaches to Alterity." *Anthropological Theory* 16 (1): 48–74.

Leistle, Bernhard, ed. 2017. *Anthropology and Alterity: Responding to the Other*. New York: Routledge.

Le Monde. 1961. "Deux morts à Colombes." October 20.

Le Monde. 2023. "Macron Says Teenager's Shooting by Police 'Inexplicable' and 'Unforgivable.'" June 28. https://www.lemonde.fr/en/france/article/2023/06/28/macron-says-teenager-s-shooting-by-police-inexplicable-and-unforgivable_6038766_7.html.

Levinas, Emmanuel. 1990. *Difficult Freedom*. London: Athlone.

Levinas, Emmanuel. 1991. *Totality and Infinity: An Essay on Exteriority*. Dordrecht, the Netherlands: Kluwer Academic Publishing.

Levinas, Emmanuel. 1996. *Basic Philosophical Writings*, edited by Adriaan T. Peperzak, Simon Critchley, and Robert Bernasconi. Bloomington: Indiana University Press.

Levinas, Emmanuel. 2000. *God, Death, and Time*. Stanford, CA: Stanford University Press.

Lippit, Akira Mizuta. 2012. *Ex-Cinema: From a Theory of Experimental Film and Video*. Berkeley: University of California Press.

Lopez, Oscar. 2021. "Gone." *New York Times*, October 3.

Lynes, Philippe. 2018. *Futures of Life Death on Earth: Derrida's General Ecology*. London: Rowman and Littlefield International.

Magnússon, Sigurður Gylfi, and István M. Szijártó. 2013. *What Is Microhistory? Theory and Practice*. New York: Routledge.

Manigaud, Éric. 2021. "Afterimages." *Artpress*, January 21. https://www.pressreader.com/france/artpress/20210121/282613150436109.

Marcus, George. 1998. *Ethnography Through Thick and Thin*. Princeton, NJ: Princeton University Press.

Marks, Laura. 2000. *The Skin of the Film: Intercultural Cinema, Embodiment, and the Senses*. Durham, NC: Duke University Press.

Marks, Laura. 2002. *Touch: Sensuous Theory and Multisensory Media*. Minneapolis: University of Minnesota Press.

Maspero, François. (1999) 2000. "Postface: Les mensonges grossiers de M. Papon." In Paulette Péju, *Ratonnades à Paris, précédé de les harkis à Paris*. Paris: Éditions la Découverte.

Mbembe, Achille. 2001. *On the Postcolony*. Berkeley: University of California Press.

Mbembe, Achille. 2002. "The Power of the Archive and Its Limits." In *Refiguring the Archive*, edited by Carolyn Hamilton, Verne Harris, Jane Taylor, Michele Pickover, Graeme Reid, and Razia Saleh. Dordrecht, the Netherlands: Kluwer Academic Publishing.

Mbembe, Achille. 2003. "Necropolitics." *Public Culture* 15 (1): 11–40.

Mbembe, Achille. 2006. "Qu'est-ce que la pensée postcoloniale? Entretien avec Achille Mbembe." *Esprit* 330 (12): 117–33.

Mbembe, Achille. 2008. "What Is Postcolonial Thinking? An Interview with Achille Mbembe." *Eurozine*, January 9. https://www.eurozine.com/what-is-postcolonial-thinking/.

Mbembe, Achille. 2019. *Necropolitics*. Durham, NC: Duke University Press.

McCance, Dawne. 2019. *The Reproduction of Life Death: Derrida's "La vie la mort."* New York: Fordham University Press.

Mercier, Clémentine. 2018. "Plein Cadre: Desseins aux plombs." *Libération*, May 25.

Metz, Christian. 1985. "Photography and Fetish." *October* 34: 81–90.

Meyers, Todd. 2022. *All That Was Not Her*. Durham, NC: Duke University Press.

Ministère de l'Information, FLN. 1961. *Les manifestations Algériennes d'Octobre 1961 et la répression colonialiste en France*. Algiers: Ministère de l'Information, FLN.

Mirzoeff, Nicholas. 2011. *The Right to Look: A Counterhistory of Visuality*. Durham, NC: Duke University Press.

Mookherjee, Nayanika. 2015. *The Spectral Wound: Sexual Violence, Public Memories, and the Bangladesh War of 1971*. Durham, NC: Duke University Press.

Mortimer, Mildred. 2008. Introduction to *The Seine Was Red: Paris, October 1961*, by Leïla Sebbar. Bloomington: Indiana University Press.

Moten, Fred. 2003. *In the Break: The Aesthetics of the Black Radical Tradition*. Minneapolis: University of Minnesota Press.

Moten, Fred. 2016. *A Poetics of the Undercommons*. Butte, MT: Sputnik & Fizzle.

Mulvey, Laura. 2006. *Death 24× a Second: Stillness and the Moving Image*. London: Reaktion.

Mulvey, Laura. 2019. *Afterimages: On Cinema, Women and Changing Times*. London: Reaktion.

Naas, Michael. 2012. *Miracle and Machine: Jacques Derrida and the Two Sources of Religion, Science, and the Media*. New York: Fordham University Press.

Nancy, Jean-Luc. 2005. *The Ground of the Image*. New York: Fordham University Press.

Nelson, Diane M. 1999. *A Finger in the Wound: Body Politics in Quincentennial Guatemala*. Berkeley: University of California Press.

Nuttall, Sarah. 2002. "Literature and the Archive: The Biography of Texts." In *Refiguring the Archive*, edited by Carolyn Hamilton, Verne Harris, Jane Taylor, Michele Pickover, Graeme Reid, and Razia Saleh. Dordrecht, the Netherlands: Kluwer Academic Publishing.

Österle, David. 2017. "A Life in Memory Fragments: Roland Barthes's 'Biographemes.'" In *Biography in Theory: Key Texts with Commentaries*, edited by Wilhelm Hemecker and Edward Saunders. Berlin: De Gruyter.

Osterweis, Marian, Arthur Kleinman, and David Mechanic, eds. 1987. *Pain and Disability: Clinical, Behavioral, and Public Policy Perspectives*. Washington, DC: National Academies Press.

Oxford English Dictionary. 1989. 2nd ed. Oxford: Oxford University Press.

Patterson, Orlando. 1982. *Slavery and Social Death: A Comparative Study*. Cambridge, MA: Harvard University Press.

Péju, Paulette. 2000. *Ratonnades à Paris, précédé de "Les harkis à Paris."* Paris: Éditions la Découverte.

Pierre, Clovis. 1895. *Les gaietés de la morgue*. Paris: E. Flammarion.

Pinney, Christopher. 1997. *Camera Indica: The Social Life of Indian Photographs*. London: Reaktion.

Pinney, Christopher. 2012. "Seven Theses on Photography." *Thesis Eleven* 113 (1): 141–56.

Pinney, Christopher, ed., with the PhotoDemos Collective. 2023. *Citizens of Photography: The Camera and the Political Imagination*. Durham, NC: Duke University Press.

Poole, Deborah. 1997. *Vision, Race, and Modernity: A Visual Economy of the Andean Image World*. Princeton, NJ: Princeton University Press.

Rabinow, Paul. 1977. *Reflections on Fieldwork in Morocco*. Berkeley: University of California Press.

Radford, Antoinette. 2023. "Anger in Paris After Police Kill Teen in Traffic Stop." BBC News, June 28.

Rahimi, Sadeq. 2021. *The Hauntology of Everyday Life*. New York: Palgrave.

Rahmani, Zahia. 2016. *Moze*. Paris: Sabine Wespieser Éditeur.

Rancière, Jacques. 1998. "The Cause of the Other." *Parallax* 4 (2): 25–33.

Riceputi, Fabrice. 2015. *La bataille d'Einaudi: Comment la mémoire du 17 Octobre 1961 revint à la République*. Neuvy-en-Champagne: Le Passager Clandestin.

Rothberg, Michael. 2009. *Multidirectional Memory: Remembering the Holocaust in the Age of Decolonization*. Stanford, CA: Stanford University Press.

Rubinstein, Daniel, and Katrina Sluis. 2013. "The Digital Image in Photographic Culture: Algorithmic Photography and the Crisis of Representation." In *The Photographic Image in Digital Culture*, edited by Martin Lister. London: Taylor & Francis.

Ruby, Jay. 1999. *Secure the Shadow: Death and Photography in America*. Cambridge, MA: MIT Press.

Ruin, Hans. 2018. *Being with the Dead: Burial, Ancestral Politics, and the Roots of Historical Consciousness*. Stanford, CA: Stanford University Press.

Saghafi, Kas. 2015. "Dying Alive." *Mosaic* 48 (3): 15–26.

Saghafi, Kas. 2020. *The World After the End of the World: A Spectro-Poetics*. Albany: SUNY Press.

Saunders, Patricia J. 2008. "Fugitive Dreams of Diaspora: Conversations with Saidiya Hartman." *Anthurium* 6 (1): article 7.

Schwartz, Vanessa. 1999. *Spectacular Realities: Early Mass Culture in Fin-de-Siècle Paris*. Berkeley: University of California Press.

Scott, James. 1998. *Seeing like a State: How Certain Schemes to Improve the Human Condition Have Failed*. New Haven, CT: Yale University Press.

Sebbar, Leïla. 1999. *La Seine était rouge*. Paris: Magnier.

Sebbar, Leïla. 2008. *The Seine Was Red: Paris, October 1961*. Bloomington: Indiana University Press.

Sekula, Allan. 1986. "The Body and the Archive." *October* 39: 3–64.

Sharpe, Christina. 2016. *In the Wake: On Blackness and Being*. Durham, NC: Duke University Press.

Sharpe, Mani. 2017. "Visibility, Speech and Disembodiment in Jacques Panijel's *Octobre à Paris*." *French Cultural Studies* 28 (4): 360–70.

Shepard, Todd. 2006. *The Invention of Decolonization: The Algerian War and the Remaking of France*. Ithaca, NY: Cornell University Press.

Silverman, Kaja. 1996. *The Threshold of the Visible World*. New York: Routledge.

Silverman, Kaja. 2009. *Flesh of My Flesh*. Stanford, CA: Stanford University Press.

Silverman, Kaja. 2015. *The Miracle of Analogy, or, The History of Photography, Part 1*. Stanford, CA: Stanford University Press.

Silverman, Kaja, and George Baker. 2010. "Primal Siblings: Kaja Silverman in Conversation with George Baker." *Artforum International* 48 (6). https://www.artforum.com/features/kaja-silverman-in-conversation-with-george-baker-193466/.

Silvers, Robert, trans. 1960. *The Gangrene*. New York: Lyle Stuart.

Silverstein, Paul. 2014. *Algeria in France*. Bloomington: Indiana University Press.

Silverstein, Paul. 2018. *Postcolonial France*. London: Pluto Press.

Smith, William Gardner. (1963) 2021. *The Stone Face*. New York: NYRB Classics.

Solomon, Harris. 2022a. *Lifelines: The Traffic of Trauma*. Durham, NC: Duke University Press.

Solomon, Harris. 2022b. "Wound Culture." *Annual Review of Anthropology* 51 (1): 121–35.

Sontag, Susan. 1977. *On Photography*. New York: Farrar, Straus and Giroux.

Sontag, Susan. 2003. *Regarding the Pain of Others*. New York: Farrar, Straus and Giroux.

Spence, J. D. 1978. *The Death of Woman Wang*. New York: Viking Penguin.

Stauffer, Jill. 2015. *Ethical Loneliness: The Injustice of Not Being Heard*. New York: Columbia University Press.

Stavrianakis, Anthony. 2019. *Leaving: A Narrative of Assisted Suicide*. Berkeley: University of California Press.

Stepputat, Finn. 2014. *Governing the Dead: Sovereignty and the Politics of Dead Bodies*. Manchester: Manchester University Press.

Stevenson, Lisa. 2014. *Life Beside Itself: Imagining Care in the Canadian Arctic*. Berkeley: University of California Press.

Steyerl, Hito. 2009. "In Defense of the Poor Image." *E-flux Journal* 10 (November). https://www.e-flux.com/journal/10/61362/in-defense-of-the-poor-image/.

Stock, Barry. 2006. *Derrida on Deconstruction*. London: Routledge.

Stoler, Ann Laura. 2009. *Along the Archival Grain: Epistemic Anxieties and Colonial Common Sense*. Princeton, NJ: Princeton University Press.

Stoler, Ann Laura. 2016. *Duress: Imperial Durabilities in Our Times*. Durham, NC: Duke University Press.

Stoler, Ann Laura. 2020. "Writing the Disquiets of a Colonial Field." In *Writing Anthropology*, edited by Carole McGranahan. Durham, NC: Duke University Press.

Stora, Benjamin. 1991. *La gangrène et l'oubli: La mémoire de la guerre d'Algérie*. Paris: Éditions la Découverte.

Stora, Benjamin. 2004. "France: Images vues, perdues, retrouvées." In *Photographier la guerre d'Algérie*, by Laurent Gervereau and Benjamin Stora. Paris: Marval.

Strassler, Karen. 2010. *Refracted Visions: Popular Photography and National Modernity in Java*. Durham, NC: Duke University Press.

Strassler, Karen. 2020. *Demanding Images: Democracy, Mediation, and the Image-Event in Indonesia*. Durham, NC: Duke University Press.

Talbot, William Henry Fox. 1841. "Letter to the Editor." *Literary Gazette*, February 19, 139–40.

Taussig, Michael. 1992. *The Nervous System*. New York: Routledge.

Thibaud, Paul. 2001. "Le 16 Octobre 1961: 'Un moment de notre histoire.'" *Esprit* 279 (11): 6–19.

Thompson, Krista. 2018. "'I was here but I disappear': Ivanhoe 'Rhygin' Martin and Photographic Disappearance in Jamaica." *Art Journal* 77 (2): 80–99.

Traverso, Enzo. 2020. *Passés singuliers: Le "je" dans l'écriture de l'histoire*. Montreal: Lux Éditeur.

Tristan, Anne. 1991. *Le silence du fleuve*. Paris: Au Nom de la Mémoire.

Trumbull, Robert. 2022. *From Life to Survival: Derrida, Freud, and the Future of Deconstruction*. New York: Fordham University Press.

Tsing, Anna Lowenhaupt. 2012. "Unruly Edges: Mushrooms as Companion Species; For Donna Haraway." *Environmental Humanities* 1 (1): 141–54.

Tsing, Anna Lowenhaupt. 2015. *The Mushroom at the End of the World: On the Possibility of Life in Capitalist Ruins*. Princeton, NJ: Princeton University Press.

Tuck, Eve, and C. Ree. 2013. "A Glossary of Haunting." In *Handbook of Autoethnography*, edited by Stacey Holman Jones, Tony E. Adams, and Carolyn Ellis. New York: Routledge.

Virilio, Paul. 2009. *War and Cinema: The Logistics of Perception*. London: Verso.

Vitale, Francesco. 2018. *Biodeconstruction: Jacques Derrida and the Life Sciences*. Buffalo: SUNY Press.

Waldenfels, Bernhard. 2011. *Phenomenology of the Alien*. Evanston, IL: Northwestern University Press.

Wall, Jeff. 2007. "Photography and Liquid Intelligence." In *Jeff Wall: Selected Essays and Interviews*, edited by Peter Galassi. New York: Museum of Modern Art.

Welch, Edward, and Joseph McGonagle. 2013. *Contesting Views: The Visual Economy of France and Algeria*. Liverpool: Liverpool University Press.

Wentzer, Helle Sofia. 2022. "The Staircase: The Ethics of 'Transcendence and Height' in Welfare Care." In *Imagistic Care: Growing Old in a Precarious World*, edited by Cheryl Mattingly and Lone Grøn. New York: Fordham University Press.

Wieviorka, Annette. 2006. *The Era of the Witness*. Ithaca, NY: Cornell University Press.

Wills, David. 2016. *Inanimation: Theories of Organic Life*. Minneapolis: University of Minnesota Press.

Wollen, Peter. 1984. "Fire and Ice." *Photographies* 4: 118–20.

Wright, Christopher. 2013. *The Echo of Things: The Lives of Photographs in the Solomon Islands*. Durham, NC: Duke University Press.

Yacine, Kateb. 1959. *Le cercle des représailles: Théâtre*. Paris: Éditions du Seuil.

Yacine, Kateb. 1962. "Dans la guele du loup." *Jeune Afrique*, June 25, 22–23.

Yacine, Kateb. 1990. "Dans la guele du loup." *Actualité de l'émigration* 207: 16–17.

Young, Harvey. 2010. *Embodying Black Experience: Stillness, Critical Memory, and the Black Body*. Ann Arbor: University of Michigan Press.

Zamir, Shamoon. 2020. *The Gift of the Face: Portraiture and Time in Edward S. Curtis's "The North American Indian."* Chapel Hill: University of North Carolina Press.

Zola, Émile. 1992. *Thérèse Raquin*. Translated by Andrew Rothwell. Oxford: Oxford University Press.

Meyers, Todd, 19
microhistory, 11, 281nn18–19
Monde, Le. See Le Monde
Moten, Fred, 224, 284n13, 289n47, 298n23
mourning: 24, 202, 255, 296n17; uncertain, 2,
    20, 199, 203, 269; work of, 201
Mulvey, Laura, 31–32, 290n8
Musée de l'Histoire de L'Immigration
    (Paris), 169

Nachträglichkeit ("deferred action"), 138,
    293n9
names: proper, 65, 181, 203, 225, 241
Nancy, Jean-Luc, 36, 63–64, 118
Nanterre (France), 2, 9, 20–21, 26, 39, 47,
    49–62, 66, 68–69, 73–74, 77, 85, 107, 137,
    143–44, 161, 165–66, 183–86, 189, 196–98,
    269, 289n45; bidonvilles of, 85, 157–63,
    166, 180–81; hospital of, 72–74, 78,
    196, 197
necronominalism, age of, 233
necropolitics, 16
North Africa, 8, 115–16, 204; French colo-
    nial control of, 2; and racist stereotypes,
    224

opacity, right to, 209–11
Oran (Algeria), 180, 196, 198, 220
Orly Airport (Paris), 3, 132
Ophüls, Max, 31
overphotographed subject, 75, 289n48

pain, 2, 71, 114, 118, 123, 146, 150–51, 162–63,
    176, 236, 273, 284; 284n13; and images, 26,
    176; and memory, 7, 8–9, 25, 116, 128, 134,
    143, 156, 163, 173, 207, 279n3; and photog-
    raphy, 28, 30, 34–38, 45, 50, 64, 67–68,
    70–72, 74, 82, 85, 94, 101, 104, 108, 118,
    123, 146, 150–51, 273, 288n42; physiology
    of, 71. *See also* wounding
Panijel, Jacques, 85, 94, 169, 280n9; *Octobre à
    Paris*, 85–94, 169, 280n9
Papon, Maurice, 3, 97–98, 134, 136, 143, 186,
    193, 279n2, 280n9, 292n4
Paris (France), 2–4, 279n2; in 1961, 8, 10,
    25–26, 79–80, 101, 132–35, 156–57; in
    1942, 128, 132–35; cemeteries of, 242, 257;
    morgues in, 222–23; 230–33; palimpsestic

histories of, 9; police violence in, 21–22,
    129. *See also* police of Paris
Péju, Paulette, 82; *Ratonnades à Paris*, 82,
    84–85
Penino, Jean-Louis, 96
pensive looking, 31; and writing, 32–33
pensive spectator, 31–32
Petit-Nanterre (Nanterre), 26, 51, 56, 66, 70,
    100, 104, 110, 138, 154, 160, 162–63, 183,
    185, 197
phantasmatics, 16, 51, 67, 80, 240; of wounds,
    67. *See also* biophantasmatics
phantasms, 16–17, 19, 21, 79, 125, 150, 204, 216,
    255, 259–61, 270, 274, 282n26, 296n18
photography: analog, 29, 81, 122, 165, 167,
    170, 176, 270; development of, 24, 29–30,
    67, 121–22, 164, 206, 269; digital, 122–23,
    167, 175; and the nonphotographable, 238,
    241; and wounding, 23, 33–38, 71
Pinney, Christopher, 28, 80, 283n6
Place de La Concorde (Paris), 4, 44
Place de la Republique (Paris), 140
Place Nelson Mandela (Nanterre), 21–22
police: 114–15; brutality, 62, 95, 102; of Paris,
    2–10, 25–26, 46–47, 49–50, 73–74, 95,
    97, 140–41, 147, 157, 168, 186–98, 200,
    213–14, 221, 226, 241, 279–80n2, 294n24,
    297n8; regimes, 12, 24; violence in France,
    21–22, 41–45, 65–67, 79, 81–82, 85, 94,
    101–2, 105–9, 113, 118, 128–29, 133, 135, 154,
    161–62, 169, 289n45. *See also compagnies
    d'intervention* (police units); Prefecture
    of the Paris Police
Pontalis, Jean-Bertrand, 138
Pont de Neuilly (Paris), 39, 46, 49, 137,
    154–55, 187, 289n45
Pontecorvo, Gillo, 113
Pont Saint-Michel (Paris), 106
poor image, 154, 294n22
Porte de la Chapelle (Paris), 4
postcoloniality, 2, 10, 19, 44, 99, 156, 209
Prefecture of the Paris Police, 42, 49, 73, 183,
    186, 188, 192, 197, 221–23, 229; archives of,
    214–22, 225, 230, 236, 241

Rancière, Jacques, 95, 114–15
ratonnades ("rat hunts"), 66, 72, 105, 130, 187.
    See also Péju, Paulette: *Ratonnades à Paris*

Wall, Jeff, 288

Welch, Edward, 99–103, 290

witness, 6, 10, 37–40, 44, 70, 98, 110, 134, 137, 141, 143, 284n13. *See also* testimony

Wollen, Peter, 285n17

World War I, 145, 156, 222

World War II, 45, 128–29, 132–34, 163, 168

wound culture, 36, 286n20

wound image, 35, 37, 64, 82, 113, 136, 205–7

wounding, 8–9, 284n12; collective, 168, 273; concepts of, 25, 67; and drawing, 176; histories of, 24–25, 104, 117, 125, 170, 185, 196, 241, 291n23; marks of, 17, 36; and memory, 139, 143; and photography, 23–24, 30, 33–38, 50, 64, 67, 98, 113–14, 116, 121, 135–36, 206–7, 241

wounds: colonial, 154, 168; social, 25, 286n21. *See also* wounding

Yacine, Kateb: *Le cadavre encerclé*, 51; "Dans la guele du loup," 49–50, 107, 286n25

Zola, Émile, 231, 236; *Thérèse Raquin*, 231